SCOTLAND The Team

SCOTLAND The Team

Andrew Ward

Breedon Books Sport

First published in Great Britain by
The Breedon Books Publishing Company Limited
45 Friar Gate, Derby DE1 1DA
1987

© Andrew Ward 1987

Photographs supplied by Colorsport, John Grainger, Steve Hale, Illustrated London News Picture Library, Popperfoto, Sportapics (Glasgow).

All Rights Reserved. No part of this publication may be reproduced, stored in a retrieval system, or transmitted in any form, or by any means, electronic, mechanical, photocopying, recording or otherwise without the prior permission of the Copyright holders.

ISBN 0 907969 34 8

Printed by Butler and Tanner Limited, Frome
Jacket designed by Graham Hales Artwork and Design, Derby and printed by The Echo Press, Loughborough.

Contents

INTRODUCTION

BY 20 MINUTES past nine on a November evening in 1984, a 33-year-old man had run himself into the Hampden turf. For over an hour he had chased, twisted and turned as the target for his colleagues in navy-blue shirts.

There was still a spring in his step, and yet his tireless efforts were beginning to drain the energy from his legs and he was certainly a candidate for substitution when he summoned up more reserves to dart towards the right-wing corner flag.

As Steve Nicol's throw-in sent the ball past his left side, he turned sharply and sprinted towards goal, fair hair bouncing, arms held low as he received the square pass which Davie Cooper had measured out.

Kenny Dalglish, Scotland's most capped player, controlled the ball sweetly, beat one Spanish defender and drifted into the penalty area, feinting moves until he found the precise angle he wanted. Then he clipped the ball with the inside of his left foot, sending it curling perfectly inside the left-hand post. Suddenly Dalglish looked 18 all over again — and the crowd roared their approval.

It is, of course, unfair to single out a magic moment from Scotland's 115-year international history when there are legions more stretching every decade — Joe Jordan's powerful header that finished off the Czechs; John Greig's last-gasp winner against Italy; Lawrie Reilly's rescue acts of the 1950s.....and so on, and so on.

This book is concerned mainly with the playing progress of the Scotland international team, but implicit in its pages are the administrative problems that have been the lot of successive SFA officials.

There has been continuing informal litigation to obtain the release of players from their clubs; travel has not always been easy, whether it be sea-sickness on 1890s journeys to Belfast, or cabin-pressure problems flying across Europe in the 1980s; diplomacy is essential, especially given the fiery tradition of clashes with some nations, like the Austrians and the Uruguayans; and there has been an increasingly commercial outlook.

There has never been a shortage of controversy. In Ireland, in 1892, a goal was awarded when Scotland's Ellis dropped a shot through a hole in the net, and a baying Irish crowd impolitely suggested an uncertain future for goal-nets — and the referee.

After the world's first international soccer match — Scotland-England in 1872 — the early years belonged to Scotland, who lost only one of 31 internationals between March 1873 and March 1888.

The world's first football league might have been the English League — but it was a Scot, William McGregor, who gave birth to the idea and organised it.

McGregor came from Braco, Perthshire, and had been introduced to football in the early 1850s by stone-masons working the house of Earl Cairns at Duneira. The workmen played in their leisure time and left the ball to lads like McGregor when they took up their tools.

In the 1850s, the lad who could punt the ball highest was the greatest hero, but soon Scottish football had its own lasting, distinctive qualities.

"We Scots endure a harsh, changeable climate," says Andy Roxburgh, Scotland's new manager. "We display toughness and adaptability in everyday life, and in the way we play soccer. Due to historical influences, Scottish football is often passionate, adventurous, creative and open, yet tempered to a degree with functional rigidity and discipline."

The Scottish 'system' is a framework for freedom — if you can't pass the man, pass the ball — and the result has been generations of exciting players. In the late 1920s, as the Scots dominated the era, there were Alan Morton, Hughie Gallacher and Alec Jackson, three members of the Wembley Wizards. A second major exodus to England, followed by curbs on the release of Anglo-Scots, ended that era.

Scottish emigrants took their talents further afield still. Scotsmen were responsible for developing the game in countries like Czechoslovakia, Uruguay and Hungary, particularly through renowned coaches like Johnny Madden and Jacky Robertson. John Dick (ex-Airdrie) coached in Prague and John Cameron (ex-Queen's Park and Scotland) in Dresden. Cameron was interned by the Germans in the First World War.

However, it came as a shock when the Austrians won at Hampden in 1950, and the gap beween British countries and foreigners was officially declared 'very narrow'. Slowly, the parochial outlook changed. The focus on the home championship, and the Scotland-England series, was replaced by talk of the World Cup, and later the European Championship. In 1984, the British tournament was killed off as largely irrelevant.

There have been substantial changes since World War Two. In the early 1950s, there was still no Scotland manager, and no substitutes. A touring party of players and trainer could have piled into an Armstrong Siddeley and most of them would have discussed the Celtic or Rangers game of the previous week — mostly the latter.

Come the 1980s and Scottish support is more widespread. Players are chosen from a greater variety of clubs, and the Scottish identity is just as much at its pinnacle for the World Cup as against the English.

When Scotland drew 1-1 with Iran in the 1978 World Cup Finals, there were claims that school absenteeism rose by 25 per cent in Glasgow, while economists studied the result's effect on industrial output.

If we measure achievement by the number of games played in World Cup Finals — a disadvantageous criterion to Scotland, considering recent near misses on goal-difference and the refusal to compete in Rio in 1950 — then Scotland lies sixth in the world ratings of success relative to population size. The list reads: Uruguay, Northern Ireland, Sweden, Austria, Hungary, Scotland...

For a relatively small nation, Scotland carry enormous football prowess, and her people eagerly await the spectacle of international matches.

"It's all about pride and passion," Kenny Dalglish has said of playing for Scotland, "It's an experience which never fails to make you feel proud to be a Scot."

Dalglish knows more about that than anyone. Yet he is just one of almost a thousand people who have won caps for Scotland in official internationals.

The international label still means a great deal to a player. His value to his club often increases once he is capped, while his importance also registers with journalists and paying spectators alike.

Former Rangers and Scotland centre-forward Willie Thornton has observed the Scottish football scene for over 50 years as player, manager, supporter and journalist. He says, "Before European games, the first question the Press boys usually ask is: 'How many internationals have they got?' And it's the same with spectators. You might go to a game counting up the internationals. You might think that it will be a good game because there are four internationals playing."

Willie Thornton is right. And it is even better when there are eleven Scottish internationals on the same side. Wearing navy-blue shirts, each with an emblazoned red lion over their hearts, when they are playing with fire in their bellies and the noise of the Hampden Park crowd in their ears. This book is a summary of their achievements.

Acknowledgements

Ian Alister, Bobby Brown, Dally Duncan, Alex Ferguson, Coosje Hoogendoorn, Annie and Mike Lean, Kevin McCarra, Ian McColl, Bob McPhail, Hamish Mackie, Tommy Malcolm, Colin May, Andy Roxburgh, Willie Thornton, Pat Woods, and the staff of the Scottish Football Association, in particular Marjory Nimmo and David Findlay. Also, special thanks to Anton Rippon for his editorial assistance and advice.

Special Acknowledgement

This book was compiled with the help of John Blair, Press Relations Officer of the Scottish Football Association.

A Note on Research and Statistics

Most of what follows has been taken from books and newspapers, particularly, *Scottish Sport*, *The Scotsman* and the *Daily Record*. Where possible I have consulted newspapers from other countries but my lack of languages (like Icelandic, Farsi and Serbo-Croatian) was a considerable drawback.

Yet, other perspectives are important, and the impression created is often vastly different. Take Scotland's 2-0 victory over Australia in 1985. Scottish newspapers wrote of how the rugged Australian defence was broken down by moments of genius from Davie Cooper, Kenny Dalglish and Frank McAvennie. Australian newspapers saw it differently. After a 'heroic first-half performance', the Socceroos were victims of two bad refereeing decisions: if anything it was a free-kick the other way when McAvennie ran into Yankos and won the free-kick from which Davie Cooper scored; and then came 'the controversial second' when McAvennie was 'dubiously-placed' in an allegedly offside position.

Not at the same game, eh? And I dare say my selection of material for this book will give rise to discussion. So be it. That is the essence of football culture.

As the first book on the Scottish international team, this book may be necessarily skeletal at times. There are many more stories than space and it is worth stressing that **all** the players mentioned in this book reached the top of their profession (or in some cases their hobby). A brief unflattering reference in the text — such as the own-goals by Jim Lundie (against Wales in 1886) and Jock Thomson (against Wales in 1933) on their only appearance — should not be allowed to conceal the players' achievements in the remainder of their careers.

Statistics in this book also come from a number of sources. Official records are not always complete so newspapers have been consulted to help compile teams, captains, goalscorers, attendances and referees. The spelling of referees' names may not always be reliable. Attendances ending in three zeros should be treated suspiciously, and there are usually discrepancies between 'tickets sold' and 'attendances on the day'.

In two cases newspapers differed in who they gave as the Scotland captain and judgement had to be exercised. Sometimes a captain was appointed when the team was selected but he later withdrew through injury. For example Davie Meiklejohn (v Ireland in 1931), Andy Cunningham (v Ireland in 1924) and Jimmy Simpson (v Czechoslovakia in 1937).

This confusion can spread to the teams themselves. One baffling example is the question of who kept goal for Scotland against Wales in 1933. Official records give Kennaway but most newspapers (not all) plumped for Harkness, which I think is correct.

Confusion abounds still further when trying to fathom early Scottish goalscorers. I looked at seven newspapers to see who scored the second goal against Wales in 1909. Three said Somers and four went for Paul. It was simply a question of making a decision, based on the quality of the newspaper and quantity of 'votes' for a particular goalscorer. Most of the problems were earlier than 1909 — the England game in 1887 was especially troublesome — so don't be surprised if statistics on goalscorers differ from those given elsewhere.

All statistics are up to 31 May 1987.

UNOFFICIAL ORIGINS

ON 5 FEBRUARY 1870, *The Sportsman* newspaper published a letter from Charles W. Alcock, honorary secretary of the English Football Association, announcing that a football match 'between the leading representatives of the Scotch and English sections' was to be played in London.

As a result of that letter, the first game between what can loosely be called England and Scotland took place at Kennington Oval on 5 March. The result was a 1-1 draw and interest was such that, the following November, Alcock wrote another letter, this time to the *Glasgow Herald* asking for the co-operation of Scotsmen in staging a second match, also at The Oval, on 19 November.

Altogether five games were played in a two-year period, but they have since been classified as unofficial on the basis that the rules were ill-defined and, more importantly, that selection was unrepresentative.

The first game was played when rugby and association rules overlapped. Most people are aware of Queen's Park's famous beginnings — seven and a half years without conceding a goal — but the scoring system in those days relied on goals *and* touchdowns.

For instance, on 29 May 1869, Queen's Park beat Hamilton Gymnasium by four goals and nine touchdowns. Playing for them at that time were two brothers, James and Robert Smith, who were major influences in the evolution of international football.

James Smith's enthusiasm and daring is indicated by one of his touchdowns against Hamilton Gymnasium when he tore through a hedge into the next field to reach the ball first, ripping his clothing and bruising and scratching his body.

> The 'Scotland' team which met 'England' at The Oval in November 1870 was: J.Kirkpatrick (Civil Service, captain), A.F.Kinnaird (Old Etonians), R.E.Crawford (Harrow), H.W.Primrose (Civil Service), C.E.Nepean (Oxford University), Quintin Hogg (Wanderers), G.G.Kennedy (Wanderers), W.Lindsay (Old Wyke-hamists), W.A.Hamilton (Old Harrovians), G.F.Congreve (Old Rugbeians), R.Smith (Queen's Park).

Robert Smith proved his daring in a different way. He moved to England. And when Alcock raised his second challenge, in November 1870, Smith was nominated by Queen's Park to arrange the 'Scotland' team because he was living in South Norwood.

All his players were London-based and among the other 'Scots' were W.H. Gladstone, son of the then Prime Minister and himself an MP; Quintin Hogg, philanthropist and grandfather of Mrs Thatcher's Lord Chancellor; and two players, A.K. Smith and Will Lindsay, who later played *against* Scotland for England in official internationals. Gladstone had withdrawn from the first

game 'owing to the exigencies of his political duties'.

The Scots lost 1-0 and there followed three more such games before the first official international.

MOVES AFOOT
In 1872, Queen's Park were anxious to test their strength against England's top team, Wanderers. They proposed a semi-international whereby Queen's Park would field all Scots, and Wanderers all Englishmen.

Negotiations were halted when Queen's Park were drawn against Wanderers in the English Cup semi-final. Both teams fielded their strongest teams and drew 0-0 in London. Queen's Park could not afford to return south for the replay and scratched from the competition.

C.W. Alcock then proposed that the London-Scots against London-English should be replaced with a true Scotland-England fixture, played alternately in Glasgow and London, back-to-back with the rugby international fixture that had just started.

FIRST OFFICIAL INTERNATIONAL
On a rainy November day in 1872, a crowd of around 4,000 converged on the West of Scotland Cricket Ground to see Scotland kick 'up the brae' at the birth of international football.

Although there was no score, a disjointed England team were lucky to escape. One report stated: 'Individual skill was generally on England's side, but the Southrons did not play to each other as well as their opponents who seem to be adept in passing the ball. Perfect order was observed.'

The game's biggest cheer came when Leckie appeared to have scored, but it was decided that the ball had passed above the England tape.

Glasgow Academicals had offered use of their ground, but Partick was chosen for a fee of £10 to the cricket club. A further £10 was payable if the gate receipts exceeded £50 and in fact they were almost £103.

From the outset, Scottish players wore a lion on their blue jerseys. All were members of Queen's Park, although five played with other clubs as well. The pre-match weather spoiled the Scots' chances of practising together, and the game itself was almost postponed.

A photographer was arranged but he left without taking any pictures because the players would not guarantee to buy any. A year later, the composite team picture was never printed because several of the England players were pulling funny faces.

SEQUELS
The following March, Scotland lost the match in London 4-2, but there were mitigating circumstances. The 'international fund' allowed only eight return tickets to London, so three of the team — A.F. Kinnaird, H.W. Renny-Tailyour and J.E. Blackburn — were London residents.

London-born Kinnaird, later an important English FA figure, qualified by being a Perthshire landowner. Renny-Tailyour also represented Scotland at rugby union.

The gate receipts were such that neither the English FA, nor the Scottish FA (formed in 1873) would ever again have financial problems in getting eleven players to a match.

The 1874 international was the first of Scotland's famous hours. They won 2-1 and Harry McNeil was carried shoulder-high from the field.

The Scots won by using passing methods, rather than relying on dribbling bursts from individuals. The influence of the Scots' 'scientific football' would eventually be felt throughout the game, and it worked well in 1874. McNeil schemed the Scots back into the game after England had scored first. The crowd went 'mad with delight' after the winner.

A draw in England was followed by a 3-0 victory at Partick

England against Scotland at Kennington Oval 1875.

BILLY McKINNON

1872 to 1879: Forward, 9 caps, 5 goals.
Born circa 1852.
Career: Queen's Park.
Billy McKinnon, who played in Scotland's first seven officia! internationals, was the country's first exciting forward. He was an excellent close dribbler, had great staying power, and was a reliable and deadly finisher.
He was the first captain of Queen's Park Strollers (October 1871) and in 1874, when serving on the Queen's Park committee, he further distinguished himself by scoring the first goal in the Scottish Cup Final, against Clydesdale.

CHARLES CAMPBELL

1874 to 1886: Wing-half, 13 caps, 1 goal.
Born: Perthshire.
Career: Queen's Park.
Charles Campbell, later president of the SFA, was a ferocious tackling half-back who was not surpassed for brilliant heading ability. There is one story of how an Irish spectator, enthralled by famous Campbell headers in an exciting match, exclaimed: 'To be sure, that man kicks well with his head'. Campbell was educated in Edinburgh but had ties with Ireland. Known as 'The Evergreen', he played ten times against England – only once on the losing side – before becoming one of Scotland's most renowned early administrators. He later owned a farm 35 miles from Dublin.

HENRY McNEIL

1874 to 1881: Inside-forward, 10 caps, 6 goals.
Born Rhu, Dunbartonshire.
Career: Third Lanark, Queen's Park.
Harry McNeil, elder brother of Moses McNeil, was one of the heroes of Scotland's early years, scorer and schemer as the Scots chalked up some notable successes against England. He played against them six times and was on the losing side only once. These games included Scotland's two biggest wins against England – 7-2 in 1878 and 6-1 in 1881. As a player, McNeil was lightweight and very fast. Later in life, he ran the Royal Hotel, Bangor, North Wales.

when all the Scotland goals came in the first half. In 1876, when Wales entered the international arena, Scotland were their more difficult opponents, a state that would remain for a number of years.

ENTER WALES

The Scotland-Wales series started in 1876, when around 20,000 people saw the Scots win 4-0 in Glasgow. But two years later, the Welsh FA wanted to cancel the game at a few days notice because they said they could not raise a team.

This presented the SFA with expenses to meet — like pre-match advertising — so enterprising secretary William Dick took a train to Wrexham. Dick toured a 40-mile radius of what was then the capital of Welsh soccer to find a team for the opposition.

The first set of brothers to appear in an international team were Harold and Moses McNeil, who played for Scotland against Wales on 25 March 1876.

Dick raised a side, though it was a scratch eleven suitable only for a 9-0 mauling from the Scots. Six goals came in the first half and Wales, accrding to one newspaper, 'played a plucky game but were deficient in the passing and dodging tactics observed by some Scotsmen'.

It was not until the fifth game between the two nations that Wales scored a goal, and England were also on the receiving end as Scotland dominated the era.

Three weeks before their 9-0 win over Wales, the Scots hammered England 7-2 at a windy Old Hampden following two days of heavy rain. Early in the second half, Scotland led 6-0, the

goals being shared between four 'Macs'.

In 1879, England had recovered sufficiently to beat Scotland 5-4 in a thrilling match in London. It was Scotland's only defeat in 31 internationals between 8 March 1873 and 17 March 1888.

Originally scheduled for 1 March, but postponed because of snow until Boat Race Day, the 5-4 defeat saw the Scots meet an England side adopting the 'Scotch passing game' for the first time. English FA secretary C.W. Alcock called it "the finest international ever seen".

Scotland led 4-1 at half-time, but Bambridge's fine run and shot turned the game. At 4-4, Scotland had an attempt ruled offside by the English referee. Five minutes later came Bambridge's winning goal.

SFA secretary William Dick was not too impressed with England's recovery. They had, he said, "a decided advantage over the Scotch, in playing their rules, in particular, using the throw-in in any direction".

Scotland were accustomed to a throw-in being made in the direction of their own goal. Some contemporary games with Wales pursued the English-Welsh rule in the first half and the 'straight-throw' in the second. In Scotland-England games this rule was an issue until 1882, when a compromise was reached.

In 1880, Scotland provided their own referee and won 5-4. Three Scottish goals were disputed, but the Scots had a commanding 5-2 lead when they lost Campbell, who broke his jaw in a heading duel with England's Sam Widdowson.

This began a run of victories over England which included a 6-1 win at Kennington Oval — still England's heaviest home defeat. The closest game was at Sheffield, where England claimed Dr John Smith's winning goal had been saved on the line by goalkeeper Swepstone.

SCOTLAND — SEASON BY SEASON

FIRST CHAMPIONS

1883-4 Ireland were welcomed to international competition and with three victories, Scotland were the first champions of what was to become known as the Home International Championship.

The Scotland-Ireland series began with the Scots scoring two goals before half-time and victory was then a formality.

A seventh-minute goal by Dr Smith beat England on the clay of Cathkin Park before Scotland suffered a scare against the Welsh.

A weakened Scottish team — Queen's Park were playing in the English Cup Final — went behind to a goal from Roberts before pulling level by half-time. The final outcome was a comfortable victory.

TRAVELLING PROBLEMS

1884-5 Like the Welsh, the Irish still had much to learn on the international field. 'Their goalkeeper was a source of much amusement,' commented the *Athletic News* after Scotland won the second game between the two countries by 8-2.

This resounding victory was achieved without players from Queen's Park, who were again involved in the English Cup, this time a replay against Nottingham Forest. And yet the Scots still managed to hammer Ireland, whose two consolation goals did not come until the closing minutes. Sandy Higgins scored four goals on his Scottish debut, but it was to be his only cap.

> *In early internationals, different coloured stockings were worn to identify the players who, of course, wore no numbers.*

Since 1877, away matches with England and Wales had been scheduled to form a tour — England on a Saturday and the Welsh two days later — but the expedition of 1885 illustrated the availability problems caused by taking players away from Friday until Tuesday. Some Scottish players declared themselves available only for the England game. The SFA threatened to omit entirely those who could not play in both games, but the dispute ended amicably.

At Kennington Oval, Scotland dominated the first half and Joe Lindsay gave them the lead. England equalised in the second half which left Scotland to beat Wales for the title because the Welsh had earlier succeeded in holding England to a draw. Scotland had their victory — scoring eight goals for the second time in nine days — and the championship was theirs.

EXODUS SOUTH

1885-6 In 1885, professionalism was legalised in England. Scottish players went south in large numbers and their skills and passing-

DR JOHN SMITH

1877 to 1884: Forward, 10 caps, 12 goals.
Born Mauchline, Ayrshire, 1855.
Career: Mauchline, Edinburgh University, Queen's Park.
John Smith was educated at Mauchline Parish School and Ayr Academy before Edinburgh University where he made a reputation as a scholar and all-round sportsman.
His early football was under the rugby code. Between 1874 and 1877 he played for the university and was almost selected for Scotland at full-back in 1876 when his selection was turned down by the casting vote of the chairman.
He turned to soccer and founded his university association club in January 1879, by which time he was an established international. Meanwhile his medical qualifications were attained and his sporting career fitted in with his work. For many years he practised at Brycehall, Kirkcaldy.
He played 18 games (7 goals) for the Corinthians and was in their team in December 1884 when they won 8-1 against the English Cup holders, Blackburn Rovers. A year later, the SFA ruled that Smith could play neither for nor against any Scottish club because he had helped Corinthians against a professional club, Bolton Wanderers.
He toured Australia with the 1888 Scotland rugby team, and he refereed the 1892 Scotland-England soccer game. Smith stood 6ft 3in and weighed around 15st – a significant figure in the history of sport.

game strategy helped to raise the standard of English football — although the full effects of this were not felt immediately on the international stage.

Scotland used 33 players in the season's three internationals, fielding second-rate teams against Ireland and Wales. Charles Heggie's four goals against Ireland equalled Higgins' feat of the previous season, and these two men probably share the best international strike-rate ever. (Some reports gave Heggie five goals).

One indication of the Scots' tactical progress was their persistent use of the offside trap, a ploy which upset the Irish.

A draw against England was a creditable performance because Lindsay was injured early in the game and missed the second half. A long lob from Lindley gave England a 35th-minute lead but Scotland's ten men fought hard and with ten minutes remaining, George Somerville equalised.

The draw enabled England to share the championship, while the Scots completed the formality of another victory over Wales. Although the Welsh managed their fifth goal in eleven games against Scotland, it was a gift from Jim Lundie who put through his own goal in his only international.

PRINCE OF GOALKEEPERS

1886-7 Three victories extended Scotland's unbeaten run to 17 games, but all three internationals produced their frights. Scotland were especially grateful to James McAulay, the so-called 'Prince of Goalkeepers', who played exceptionally well in his last season before sailing for Rangoon where he was to work as an engineer.

A much-improved Irish team had the impudence to equalise Frank Watt's early goal. Scotland regained the lead just before half-time and were relieved to score twice more in the second half.

The Scottish party stayed at Preston before the England game at Blackburn's Ewood Park. Again, McAulay was in brilliant form, in direct contrast to Roberts, his opposite number in the England goal. According to some reports, Roberts should have saved two goals and Scotland were fortunate to win.

Scotland took the lead three times, twice within four minutes in the second half. The winner came in the 53rd minute when John Marshall centered and England full-back P.M. Walters miskicked. With Roberts too far off his line, Jimmy Allan was left with a simple chance.

Allan's goal in the next match, against Wales, was also vitally important. It came in the 80th minute and gave the Scots a 2-0 margin. For this game at Wrexham, Scotland fielded an unchanged team for the first time.

Three consecutive victories was all the more creditable when one considers that the SFA had outlawed professionalism and stars like Nick Ross of Preston and Archie Hunter of Aston Villa were not considered for Scotland, while William

WALTER ARNOTT

**1883 to 1893: Full-back, 14 caps.
Born Pollokshields, Glasgow, 1863.
Career: Maltilda FC (Pollokshields),
Queen's Park, Pollokshields, Athletic,
Queen's Park, with guest appearances
for Corinthians and Linfield Athletic.**
As a seven-year-old child, Arnott saw
Scotland's first-ever international.
Sitting on top of a taxi cab, he watched
the game and was motivated to learn
the skills which took him to the top as
a full-back. He was admired for his
artistry and kicking.
Arnott prepared for a game with a
midday meal of 'milk and switched
eggs'. He always played in bare legs,
believing that shin-guards and stockings
spoiled the 'springiness of the limbs'.
He was especially adept at a pivot-
and-kick technique known as the
'screw-kick'. At full speed he could
turn on the run and kick the ball
straight back. The 1884-5 SFA Annual
said that Arnott 'has never been equalled
for screwing'.
When he replaced Smellie at a late
hour against England in 1892, it meant
that Arnott had played nine successive
times against the auld enemy. He was
not on the losing side until 1888 when
his below-par performance had a big
impact on the team, such was his
standing. He also excelled at bowls,
tennis and yachting.

Robertson, who was capped twice in 1887,
was playing rugby for Glasgow University
at the start of the season.

FIRST HOME DEFEAT

1887-8 England's 5-0 win in Glasgow was
Scotland's first-ever home defeat. It also
ended a remarkable sequence of 19 games
(and nine years) without an international
defeat.

The experiment of playing Wales at
Easter Road was deemed a success and
only the skill and bravery of the Welsh
goalkeeper restricted the Scots to five
goals. He was Jimmy Trainer of Preston
North End, so often a thorn to the Scottish
thistle.

The English disaster occurred on St
Patrick's Day. England led 4-0 at half-
time and one of their major influences was
John Goodall, born in London but raised
in Kilmarnock in the traditional Scottish
school of football.

> *Scotland's defenders decided on a
> man-for-man marking system for the
> 1887 England match. Bob Kelso took
> care of William Cobbold, England's
> so-called 'Prince of the Dribblers', so
> well that one English newspaper dubbed
> him 'the Renton Ruffian'.*

Gillespie and Hughes were unable to get
to Belfast for the Ireland match, but they
were hardly missed. At one stage, with the
score at 4-2, the Irish had slight hopes of a
recovery, but Scotland rattled home three
more before the interval.

Poor goalkeeping was blamed for the
Scots reaching double figures. Unusually
for this era, the Irish goalkeeper wore a
jersey of a different colour to those of his
team mates and some writers claimed that
this showed the Irish to be 'untogether'.
Alternatively, the goalkeeper might just
have been 20 years ahead of his time.

REMARKABLE GAME

1888-9 'The game of 1888-9 will pass into
history as one of the most remarkable of
the series,' said *Scottish Sport* after Scotland
had fought back to beat England 3-2.

The writer continued: 'It was won under
most depressing conditions, quite
unexpectedly, and against long odds. It
must do Scotch football a world of good.
It has proved that the professional in
football is not all powerful on the field of
play, and that amateurism is still possible
with a continuance of that supremacy
which Scotland had so long enjoyed over
other nations.'

> *In the 1880s, English teams recruited
> heavily north of the border, but perhaps
> the biggest piece of 'poaching' was
> Stuart Macrae, who was capped five
> times for England, playing twice against
> Scotland. Macrae was born at Port
> Bannatyne, Bute.*

In fact, the optimism of *Scottish Sport*
was not borne out, as Scotland's success
was destined to wane temporarily. But it
was well worth rejoicing at the time, as the
Scots produced a sterling display to come
back from 2-0 down.

After criticism of the committee's choice
of players for the previous England game,
team selection was now made by a smaller
group of SFA members — the 'Selecting
Seven'. A strong team was chosen to meet a
Canadian touring side when the international season opened early with an 80-
minute game.

Ireland opposed a Scotland team selected
primarily on the principle of encouraging
provincial talent and scattering represen-
tation. It was still good enough to score
seven times and leave goalkeeper Ned
Doig a spectator.

Then came a classic victory over England
at The Oval, while a separate, second-rate

Scottish eleven was sent to Wales. Five
players from Third Lanark were in the
team at Wrexham.

At half-time in London, England led
2-0. The two home full-backs, the Walters
brothers, were in splendid form, and Scotland
smarted from having what they thought
were two legitimate goals disallowed. The
second of these was when Jimmy Oswald
put the ball over the line as the referee blew
for half-time. As the teams left the field,
Oswald was heard to mutter, 'Aye, it was a
goal alright — but they won't allow it'.

In the second half, with Kelly and
Dewar having switched positions, Scotland
beat a trail to the English goal. Roared on
by a thousand Scots — who drowned the
noise of 9,000 English fans — the visitors
finally broke through on the hour. First
Munro, then Oswald, beat England goalkeeper Moon in a spell described by the
Scottish Sport correspondent thus: 'Down
came the Scots like a wolf on the fold, and
Moon was made to see stars.' Then Jimmy
McLaren, 'The Ould Giniral' struck home
a third goal with his famous left foot. It

> *More than 15 years elapsed before
> Scotland failed to score in an inter-
> national. The Scottish team for that
> game, against England in 1888, was
> chosen by a selection committee of 38
> people.*

WILLIAM SELLAR

**1885 to 1893: Forward, 9 caps, 4 goals.
Born Peterhead, Aberdeenshire, 1866.
Career: Battlefield FC, Queen's Park.**
A writer by profession, William Sellar
graced the football field either at
centre-forward or on the wing. He
played with 'dash, daring and deadliness'
according to one commentator, while
another said he was 'possessed of great
dodging and dribbling powers'. He
sprang to fame playing for Battlefield
when the young club won a surprise
3-2 victory over Queen's Park in the
1884-5 Scottish Cup. He was president
of the Scottish AAA (1899-1900).

The two umpires in the 1889 Scotland-Ireland game were both Scots called John Campbell, though they were not related. In those days, umpires generally made the decisions and only appealed to the referee where there was a difference of opinion.

was the last kick of the match and McLaren and Wattie Arnott were carried shoulder-high to the pavilion.

After this rousing victory, there was disappointment against Wales — the first drawn game between the two countries. A five-hour train delay at Warrington did not help the Scottish preparation, and yet the Welsh also had their problems. Goalkeeper Trainer missed his train and the game, despite a late kick-off. Wales began with a deputy goalkeeper and then introduced a substitute when the game was in progress. John Auld appeared to have put Scotland ahead, but the umpire ruled that the ball had passed on the wrong side of the tape.

JOHN 'KITEY' McPHERSON

1888 to 1897: Inside-left, 9 caps, 5 goals.
Born Kilmarnock 1868.
Career, Kilmarnock, Cowlairs, Rangers.
Born at Riccarton, near Kilmarnock, 'Kitey' McPherson played for Victoria and Brittania as a youth. During his teenage days he won innumerable summer prizes in football 'fours' and 'fives' in athletic sports competitions. He made his debut for Kilmarnock at inside-right in the 1885 Ayr Charity Cup Final. Later he moved to outside-left, partnering McGuinness before the latter moved to Great Lever. After being capped regularly at both Kilmarnock and Cowlairs, McPherson moved to Rangers where he spent 12 years as a player and nearly 20 as a director. His younger brother, David, was also a Scottish international, but the two never played in the same international team.
McPherson became an inside-left by chance when the Improbables found themselves with two outside-lefts before the 1888 Ibrox trial match against the Probables.

TROUBLE AT HAMPDEN

1889-90 'The Principality Peppered at Paisley,' ran one headline when Scotland hammered Wales on Abercorn's new pitch. It was Trainer against the Scots, whose own goalkeeper, Gillespie, handled the ball just once — after 75 minutes.

Ireland, on their own ground, were a tougher proposition. As the Scottish players disembarked in Belfast, a stranger confirmed that they would have a battle on their hands and that Peden was a grand player who had already broken five legs that season — presumably none of them his own.

It was Peden who equalised Gilbert Rankin's early goal, and for a time during a rough game, the Irish were on top. But the Scots hung on, fought back, and scored three times after the interval.

A huge crowd turned up for the England match. Thirty thousand paid to get in, but it was estimated that up to 10,000 more stole their way into the Hampden stadium where they left their marks. Hoardings were torn down, railings smashed, the track ruined, and litter was everywhere. The gates were shut about half an hour before kick-off, but the crowd spilled on to the pitch and at one time, a postponement seemed likely.

The game was dominated by the Scots, who forced 12 corners to England's two, but McPherson's equaliser was a scrambled affair and it was Scotland's sole reward for their superiority. The game had just five free-kicks — little wonder that most of the England players wore no shin-guards.

When Scotland played Ireland in 1890, the Scots wore their familiar dark-blue shirts, but half the team wore dark-blue shorts, and the rest played in white shorts. Ireland wore light-blue shirts — their normal colours then — and on dark days it was sometimes difficult to distinguish between opposing players.

DOMINANCE CHALLENGED

1890-91 By 1891, when Scotland lost to England at Blackburn, almost 300 Scottish players had gone south of the border to earn their living legitimately as professionals. The SFA blacklisted these players, so the first great era of Scottish dominance on the international stage was challenged by England and even, on occasions, Wales and Ireland.

Events surrounding the game with Wales indicated the problems of the day. Richardson dropped out of the team — he joined the exodus to England — and on the train journey back to Scotland after the game, Scottish stars were cornered by officials of English clubs who offered them the chance to play football for a living.

Against Wales, Scotland trailed 2-1 at half-time, but Wales lost the injured Parry — not the best ending to his honeymoon week — and Trainer conceded two more

JACK BELL

1890 to 1900: Winger, 10 caps, 5 goals.
Born Dumbarton 1869.
Career: Dumbarton Union, Dumbarton FC, Everton, Celtic, New Brighton Tower, Everton, Preston (later as manager coach).
'Bell has plenty of weight, runs fast and is a rattling good shot,' it was written of Jack Bell, who stood nearly six feet. Tracking down the wing, right or left, he was an exciting figure, but there was also a tough and rough side to the man's character. One story alleges that he was run over by a cab the day before an international, but still proved a thorn in England's side. Eight months after scoring in the 1897 FA Cup Final, Bell, then with Everton, was appointed chairman of the first attempt at a players' union. Anyone examining the relationship between amateurs and professionals might also look closely at Bell's tackle on C.B.Fry in a 1903 Cup tie between Everton and Portsmouth. Fry, a famous amateur, never played again.

goals. Then it was 3-3 but, facing ten men, Scotland surged forward and Boyd scored their winner.

At full-time, Scottish captain Tom Robertson challenged referee Crump's decision to disallow what had seemed a perfectly good goal. 'Mr Robertson, you have won the match,' replied Crump. 'Be content.'

This story indicates the tension creeping into games with the so-called 'minor countries'. For years, these fixtures had raised only two questions — who would be capped and how many goals would Scotland score? — but the 1891 games against Wales and Ireland were in doubt until the

JOCK DRUMMOND

1892 to 1903: Full-back, 14 caps, 1 goal.
Born Alva, Clackmannanshire 1870.
Career: Falkirk, Rangers, Falkirk.
As left-back for Rangers, Jock Drummond's partner on the right was Nicol Smith, but the two men linked up for Scotland on only three occasions. The first time was the 4-1 win over England in 1900.
Drummond was known for his sure-footed defending. His last appearance against Ireland was not so happy as Scotland suffered their first defeat at the hands of the Irish. On that day in 1903, Drummond equalled Walter Arnott's record of 14 caps.
Drummond believed football was a man's game. He rolled up his sleeves to his elbows, and wore a cap which he drew down over his eyes. He captained Scotland against England in 1896, and this was probably his best international.

final whistle. The Scots took a 2-0 lead after an hour of the Ireland game, but Gaffikin's late goal shook them.

The attendance for the Ireland game was more than that for the game at Blackburn, where locals boycotted the England-Scotland fixture because local players had been ignored by English selectors — and the Scottish for that matter.

A third of the 8,000 spectators were Scots, and they saw two debatable English goals. The first, after 23 minutes, came when Goodall received the ball opposite the Press bench and the journalists were of the unanimous opinion that he was offside. The referee allowed play to continue and the London-born 'Scot' scored.

The second goal, in the 35th minute, was a peculiar affair and focused attention on the goalnets which were being used for the first time in an international. Chadwick

---

In March 1891, a Scotland eleven beat the Corinthians 9-2 in front of 10,000 at Hampden. Corinthians took a 2-0 lead before being hit by goals from Watt (4), Sellar (2), Bond (2) and Rankin.

---

shot and Scotland goalkeeper Wilson dropped the ball which finished up behind the goal, but outside the net. Most people thought that it had, however, gone between the posts and after conducting a straw-poll, the referee allowed the goal. Some contemporary commentators suggested that goalnets might be a bad thing if referees relied totally on them, instead of concentrating on where the ball went.

IRISH TROUBLES

1891-2 Two decisions by a Welsh referee in Belfast galvanised the Irish crowd into mobbing and threatening the official, while there was more ammunition for the anti-goalnet lobby.

Trouble began when Ireland were 2-1 down, but pressing strongly in a close-fought second half. First Ireland's McKeown was sent off. Then Gulliland broke away for Scotland and sent in a shot which was cleared from around the goal-line. The referee, Mr Taylor, discussed the incident with the Scottish forwards and then decided against a goal.

There was a bigger commotion to follow. A shot from Scotland's Ellis appeared to go outside the post but burst the net and entered the goal. Mr Taylor pointed to the centre-spot and the home crowd were in uproar. After that, whenever a shot went harmlessly past a post, the Irish fans shouted ironically, 'Goal!'

Reporters watching the 1891 game against Ireland found Scotland's McQueen made their profession a hazardous one. A McQueen clearance skidded across the Press table, sending notepads and pencils flying. Another McQueen effort removed a reporter's hat.

Gaffikin made the score 3-2, but when the final whistle sounded, the crowd poured on to the pitch and referee Taylor had to be protected by the players. One spectator was arrested.

The first international at Tynecastle, against Wales, was heralded by a heavy snowfall. Conditions were so bad that the Welsh captain and goalkeeper, Jimmy Trainer, requested two 30-minute halves, but the Scots objected. In fact, Trainer was probably the warmest man on the pitch as he faced a rampant Scotland team for whom Kilmarnock centre-half 'Bummer' Campbell was in particularly fine form.

When they met England, it was Scotland's turn to be on the wrong end of a pounding. England scored after 35 seconds, led 4-0 after 21 minutes despite playing against the wind and into the sun, and it was the

---

30th minute before their goalkeeper touched the ball.

A final tally of corners (four apiece) showed that Scotland had come back into the game, and there was the excuse of players crying off at the last minute. But the message was getting clearer: amateurs (and in some cases even 'shamateurs') could no longer be expected to beat professionals.

BIG VICTORIES

1892-3 'Wales walloped' ran one newspaper headline after the Scots had struck eight past Sam Jones, Trainer's deputy, at Wrexham.

Then came another big victory, against Ireland. The Irish fixture was assuming greater importance in Glasgow and after

---

The McCall brothers were among four Renton players who withdrew from the team to play Ireland in 1892. The elder brother, James McCall, had been chosen as captain, but the two were never to play in the same international team.

JOHN CAMPBELL

1893 to 1903: Forward, 12 caps, 5 goals.
Born Glasgow 1871.
Career: Glasgow Benburb, Celtic, Aston Villa, Celtic, Third Lanark.
A versatile forward, he played in every position in the forward line for Scotland, but perhaps his greatest display was in the 1900 game against England when, together with Bobby Walker and Bob McColl, he starred in one of Scotland's finest wins.
Campbell might have won more caps had he not spent three years at Aston Villa, for whom he scored in the 1897 FA Cup Final. Campbell also won three Scottish Cup-winners' medals as a Celtic player.

the closeness of the previous season's international, Scotland selected a strong team.

Their reward was four goals in the first 28 minutes, one of them an own-goal when Irish goalkeeper Clugston's clearance cannoned off his full-back, Torrans. The players were affected by the heat, but Gaffikin still managed his customary goal for Ireland, just before half-time.

After two comprehensive victories, Scotland looked forward to the game against England at Richmond Athletic Ground, a late replacement for the original venue at The Oval. With Celtic and Queen's Park between them contributing nine of the team, Scotland looked likely winners when William Sellar put them 2-1 ahead early in the second half. But after Cotterill of Old Brightonians had equalised, three goals in six minutes sealed England's victory.

> In 1892, Baird (Hearts) was selected to play against Wales, and Keillor (Montrose) against Ireland. The players agreed to exchange places because they had already played against those countries and wanted a variety of caps.

PROFESSIONALS SELECTED

1893-4 For the first time, Scotland willingly included professionals, although only those from Scottish clubs were considered when the SFA voted 20-4 against selecting so-called Anglo-Scots. The result was dramatic. After three seasons of finishing runners-up, Scotland took the international championship.

Kilmarnock staged its first international match and the teams stripped at the Royal Hotel — Wales wore white — before driving to a packed Rugby Park where goalnets had been brought in specially for the occasion, although the linesmen had no flags.

With 40 minutes gone, the Welsh led 2-0 and a major upset looked possible. But Scotland fought back to draw level and in the 70th minute, came the goal that gave Scotland the lead, from the head of Chambers.

Belfast proved to be no place for faint hearts when the Scots took on Ireland, who had previously drawn with England. By the end of a perilous match, five Scots were carrying injuries. They included David Alexander, who was thrown on to the cinders after only ten minutes and who finished with a black eye and some shattered teeth.

'Kitey' McPherson, restored to the team for the England game, was the senior Scot when a 2-2 draw clinched the title. The match was notable for a record attendance which caused considerable disruption. People were injured and thick smoke from a nearby brickyard added to the already hazy, somewhat seedy atmosphere.

> ## NEIL GIBSON
>
> **1895 to 1905: Wing-half, 14 caps, 1 goal.**
> **Born Larkhall, Lanarkshire, 1873.**
> **Career: Larkhall Thistle, Larkhall Juniors, Royal Albert Rangers, Partick Thistle.**
> One of the stars of his generation, Neil Gibson equalled the existing record for Scottish caps and played 12 times for the Scottish League. Altogether he was with Rangers for ten years before moving to Partick Thistle, where he won his last cap. His six appearances against England included brilliant exhibitions in 1896 and 1900.
> Gibson came from the same town that produced Alex Raisbeck. The slim, fair-haired Gibson played for Scotland less than four months after joining Rangers. His speciality was the way he dealt with some high balls. After the ball had gone over his head, he would volley it clear with his heel, even in front of his own goal. His three sons were all professional half-backs. Willie won an FA Cup-winners' medal with Newcastle in 1924; Neil junior played 11 seasons with Clyde (1923-34); and Jimmy, capped eight times, was the first to be valued as high as £7,500 when Aston Villa signed him from Partick Thistle in 1927.

WORST SEASON

1894-5 In their worst season to date, Scotland conceded more goals than they scored and finished level with Wales in the international championship.

The trip to Wales was enjoyable enough — plenty of singing was reported on the train — but the result was far from satisfactory. The only highlight was the display of newcomer Neil Gibson. The Scots fell behind to a soft goal before John Murray's equaliser five minutes later.

Murray's shot went through a hole in the net, the usual debate ensued and one Scottish player bet the referee a shilling that it was a goal. Divers put Scotland in front soon afterwards, but skipper Donald Sillars twisted his knee and remained by the goalpost for most of the second half, during which Wales equalised.

The game with Ireland in Glasgow was also a close affair and Irish FA official Jack Reid said of his team: 'The whole eleven played like cats.' John Walker's goal was the best of Scotland's three and ended a plucky fight by the Irish.

The Press were allowed to witness the voting for team selection before the England game. One by one, the positions were dealt with. We know, for instance, that Gulliland got his place at outside-left by 19 votes to Taylor's six. Selection was back to full committee now. The 'Selecting Seven' had had their day.

Yet Scotland's display at Goodison Park raised a major policy issue: should Anglo-Scots be included? England scored three first-half goals and were now unbeaten in their last six matches against the Scots.

> On the morning of the 1895 England game, there was no sign of Scotland captain Dan Doyle. By lunchtime, the selectors had called up Bob Foyers (St Bernard's) for the game at Goodison Park. But Doyle, who had spent the night with an old Everton team mate, arrived in time to reclaim his place.

ANGLO-SCOTS

1895-6 Early in 1896, the Scots finally decided to include Scottish players from English clubs. Five Anglo-Scots were in the team that beat England 2-1 to register the first win against the 'auld enemy' since 1889.

Professionalism was now accepted in Scotland, but Scottish clubs were not always willing to release their players for international matches. Oswald and McCreadie were withdrawn by Rangers before the game against Wales, an act deemed 'unpatriotic' by the *Athletic News* 'for sake of a paltry club contest'. Celtic had earlier refused to release Martin.

RS McColl (Queen's Park) and Danny Paton (St Bernard's) were late replacements in the team which beat Wales 4-0.

Then the 'Home-Scots' drew with Ireland. The Irish came close to winning the fixture for the first time. Scotland trailed 3-2 for much of the second half and were missing the injured Peter Meechan. Playing the 'one-back game', they caught the Irish

> On 25 March 1896, a trial match took place between the Scotsmen in Scotland and the Scotsmen in England. The ex-patriots won 2-1 in front of 20,000 at Ibrox. After this, trial matches between Home Scots and Anglo Scots were played regularly.

Scotland team which met England in 1895. Back row (left to right): R.F.Harrison (vice president SFA), J.Drummond, W.A.Lampie, Archdeacon Sliman (president SFA), D.Russell, N.Gibson, R.Dixon (treasurer SFA). Middle row: W.Gulliland, J.Simpson, T.S.Waddell, J.Oswald (captain), J.McPherson, D.Doyle, D.McArthur. Front row: R.Foyers, J.K.McDowell (secretary SFA), J.Taylor (trainer).

Hugh Wilson won caps with Newmilns, Sunderland and Third Lanark.

Queen's Park's W.Gulliland, capped four times.

Don Doyle of Celtic who captained Scotland.

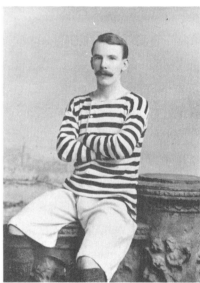

T.S.Waddell of Queen's Park won six caps.

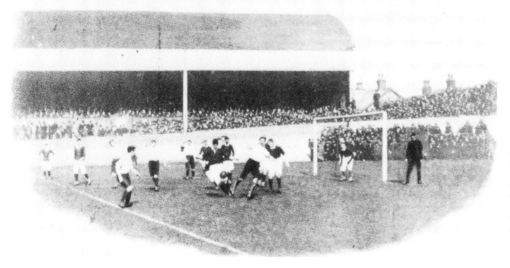

Action around the Scotland goal during the match against England at Villa Park in 1899. The Scots refused to include the Villa star James Cowan, after he had upset the selectors. Scotland appeared to miss Cowan as England held on for a rather fortunate 2-1 victory.

R S McCOLL

1896 to 1908: Centre-forward, 13 caps, 13 goals.
Born: Glasgow 1876.
Career: Benmore, Queen's Park, Newcastle United, Rangers, Queen's Park.
When R S McColl first arrived at Queen's Park as an 18-year-old wearing his school cap, the doorman would not believe he was a player, telling him that he was too young even to carry the hamper.
McColl, however, became known as the 'Prince of Centre-forwards' by the many who admired his speed, courage, uncanny swerve and ruthless finishing shot. It was rumoured that he could put 'side' on the ball to send it swerving past goalkeepers. He made his international debut at 19 and scored prolifically, registering three hat-tricks in five internationals at the turn of the century. In 1902 he captained Scotland in the Ibrox Disaster match.
After spells as a professional with Newcastle and Rangers, he was reinstated as an amateur with Queen's Park in August 1907, one of the few players to have been permitted to return to the club after playing professional. After an absence of six years he was recalled to the Scotland team in 1908, helping Jimmy Quinn collect four goals against Ireland.
He scored six in a game for Queen's Park as late as 1910, and that same year, he formed the R.S.McColl chain of confectioners which has spread nationwide and still exists today.

offside enough times to hold out. Meechan came back, the Scots rallied, and the game was saved, in the last minute.

The England game at Celtic Park attracted a huge crowd which proved difficult to control. Spectators spilled on to the track, and sections of the crowd threw missiles at those around the pitch. This served to get the fans back on to the terraces — something not achieved by 150 police and 150 Gordon Highlanders.

Two Aston Villa players — Jimmy Cowan (Scotland) and James Crabtree (England) — had travelled overnight, and

for Scotland this highlighted a future problem of selecting Anglo-Scots for home matches.

Willie Lambie's early goal gave the Scots a fine start, and Jack Bell added a second to give them a 2-0 interval lead. It was a much-improved England in the second half. John Goodall scored and England pressed strongly to the final whistle. Scotland thanked Neil Gibson for a sterling wing-half display.

BELL'S TRIUMPH

1896-7 The inclusion of Anglo-Scots and the acceptance of professionalism in Scotland reaped its reward in that the Scots scored a fine win over England at The Crystal Palace. But Scotland were now running into difficulties in the 'minor internationals'.

Before the draw at Wrexham in March 1897, the Welsh had managed two draws and 19 defeats in 21 games against Scotland, and the Scots had scored 76 more goals. It now appeared, however, that Scotland would have to put out stronger, more representative teams if they were to continue their undefeated record against the improving Welsh.

It was noticeable that, in contrast to the previous year, Oswald was allowed by Rangers to play against Wales even though they were playing in the Scottish Cup final on the same day.

At the Racecourse, a ground criticised for its lack of cover and for having no banking, the Welsh equalised twice before a Scottish 'goal' was disallowed for offside in the last minute.

The Ireland game was not so close. At half-time, Scotland led 4-0 — the pick of the goals being McPherson's dazzling long-range shot — and the Scottish goalkeeper enjoyed an untroubled first 45 minutes: 'Dickie played with his coat on and only once was he called upon to defend'. In the second half, Ireland had the wind at their backs and were not completely outclassed.

The game at The Crystal Palace was a triumph for Jack Bell and Nicol Smith, stars of the Scotland team. England were handicapped by an injury to centre-half Crawshaw early in the game. Nevertheless, they took the lead through Bloomer before Tom Hyslop, the 6ft 3in Scottish forward, equalised soon afterwards. The same player created the winning goal. Hyslop's shot was blocked by Robinson, but Jimmy Miller knocked in the rebound.

Jimmy Miller was knocked unconscious while scoring the goal that beat England in 1897.
"Are you all right?" asked an anxious Neil Gibson.
"Did I score?" enquired Jimmy.
"You did."
"Then I'm all right."

NICOL SMITH

1897 to 1902: Right back, 12 caps.
Born: Darvel, Ayrshire, 1873.
Career: Darvel, Rangers.
Nicol Smith played with Rangers for 12 years before his tragic death from enteric fever in January 1905, when he had just turned 31 years of age.
From the same lace-making town as his namesake Alec, a later Scottish international, Nicol Smith first displayed his international credentials in 1896 when he produced a superhuman display for the Scottish League against the Football League. For Rangers he had a legendary partnership with Jock Drummond, although the two rarely appeared in the same Scotland team. Smith was a tremendous tackler, swift in recovery, and he possessed a powerful shoulder-charge.

COWAN'S DISGRACE

1897-8 Wales and Ireland were dealt with severely, but Scotland came unstuck against England in front of their own supporters. After the 3-1 defeat, there was much speculation about the condition of Scotland centre-half Jimmy Cowan, although allegations that the player was the worse for drink were unproven.

Against Wales, the right-wing pair of Gillespie and Miller 'fell into each other's styles' but neither played for Scotland again after the 5-2 win. Gillespie thus had the rare distinction of scoring a hat-trick in his only international.

In fact only Higgins, in 1885, Dickson, in 1888 and Morris, in 1949, have also scored hat-tricks on their debuts and yet were never selected again.

For the game in Ireland, Bob Kelso was recalled. It was 13 years since his first cap and ten since his previous appearance in a Scotland shirt. The Irish had managed only one draw in 14 encounters and some cynics suggested that Scotland players should be selected on the basis of their stomach for sailing across the Irish Sea.

This trip to Belfast turned out to be a calm passage. The Scots arrived on a Friday morning, and next day they took a 2-0 half-time lead before winning 3-0.

England were a different proposition, and Scotland's run of eight unbeaten games ended. In front of a much smaller attendance than that of two years previously — and no repeat of those unruly scenes — England deserved their victory. They were two up in 21 minutes, and although Miller pulled a goal back, Bloomer then scored his second of the game.

Cowan was blamed for his poor tackling and eccentric dribbling, both by players and spectators. 'Cowan's play disheartened us all,' said Rangers' Neil Gibson. It appeared that Cowan was suffering from a cold and had been asked to stand down before the game, but he argued that he would be well enough to turn out. However, he played well below par, and explanations were sought. Whatever the circumstances, it was a peculiar business, and Cowan never played for Scotland again.

ALEC SMITH

1898 to 1911: Outside-left, 20 caps, 5 goals.
Born: Darvel, Ayrshire, 1876.
Career: Darvel FC, Rangers.
At one time Alec Smith played 12 consecutive internationals for Scotland. He was a hallmark of consistency, an unselfish provider of chances and the greatest outside-left of his day. He had innumerable colleagues in the Scotland forward line, although his Rangers partner, Finlay Speedie, played inside to him for the three games of 1903.
His span of 21 years with Rangers established a club record which lasted until Dougie Gray broke it. His first game was on 30 April 1894, when he played in a trial match at the recommendation of Nicol Smith who also came from Darvel. Alec Smith was working in a lace mill at the time but he created a good impression in a 3-1 win against Notts County who had just won the English Cup.

A bicycle was promised to the scorer of the first goal in the 1898 Scotland-England game. The prize went to Wheldon of Aston Villa.

HOPES DASHED

1898-9 Scotland at last changed their policy against both Wales and Ireland, fielding their best eleven rather than an experimental team. The result was two staggering victories and the added bonus that players could get used to each other before the England match. The outcome was rather different, however, when Scotland went down 2-1 at the muddy and relatively cramped Villa Park.

The Welsh game began slowly. 'Harricus' of *Athletic News* complained that, in the first 25 minutes, 'there had not been more than half a dozen occasions on which a goal was imminent'. In those days, that signalled a poor game.

A soft goal from Campbell gave Scotland the lead at half-time. Then Wales lost JL Jones with an injury and their ten men were hit by five second-half goals. It might have finished 7-0, but Bob McColl struck a late penalty straight at Jimmy Trainer. Wales ended the match with several defenders limping badly.

Victory over Ireland was even more devastating. Five goals came in the first half, and Ireland's token strike came when Scotland were leading 6-0, early in the second half.

Scottish hopes were high as they approached the match at Villa Park, but their spirits were dampened when they discovered that the pitch measured 101 yards by 71 yards, in contrast to the normal international pitch of 120 by 80.

Aston Villa were disappointed that the Scots had not included their own man, Jimmy Cowan. Cowan had won three caps — all of them against England — before upsetting the selectors in Glasgow 12 months previously. The inclusion of the local man would have added to the Villa Park attendance, but the selectors would not hear of it.

When England scored twice in the first half, it seemed that Scotland were indeed missing Cowan. The Scots hit back to score after the interval, but England held on for a rather fortunate win.

ENGLAND DESTROYED

1899-1900 After two consecutive defeats by the English, Scotland came back in sensational fashion. Wearing Lord Rosebery's racing colours of pink and primrose hoops, the Scottish eleven destroyed England at Celtic Park to complete a season of three wins. The occasion of RS McColl's hat-trick in Scotland's 4-1 win would live as a peak performance, not surpassed until the 'Wembley Wizards' of 1928.

A Cup-tie replay between Hibs and Hearts ruled out four players for the

JACKY ROBERTSON

1898 to 1905: Left-half, 16 caps, 2 goals.
Born: Dumbarton 1877.
Career: Dumbarton junior football, Morton, Everton, Southampton, Rangers, Chelsea (player-manager), Glossop.
A £300 signing for Rangers in August 1899, Jacky Robertson won all his international caps at left-half, although he could move into the forward line to win matches. He captained the great 1900 Scotland team, although he later described the 1928 'Wembley Wizards' as even better. He played seven times against England. Reputedly the person who introduced passing back to the goalkeeper to relieve pressure, Robertson later coached abroad.

Scotland beat Wales 5-2 in February 1900 with seven Rangers players in the team — Matt Dickie, Nicol Smith, David Crawford, Bobby Neill, Jacky Robertson, Bob Hamilton and Alex Smith.

Wales game, but Scotland still took a 4-0 half-time lead. Wales scored twice in reply, and might even have saved the game, but Scotland chalked up another success.

The 3-0 win over Ireland was thoroughly deserved, but the goals were not classics. Smith looked well offside when he scored the second, while the third was a long and hopeful effort from Campbell that somehow found its way over the line. But any adverse memories were soon to pale beside the spectacular Scottish performance against England.

BIGGEST VICTORY

1900-01 Scotland's biggest-ever victory — they could easily have doubled their 11 goals, according to referee Gough — was followed by a fortunate draw with Wales and then a deserved draw with England, who equalised late in the game.

The Irish team which arrived in Glasgow was a mere shadow of that originally selected, and almost 15,000 spectators saw one of the greatest routs in international football history. Scotland scored five in the first half and six in the second.

Seven of the players who destroyed Ireland played in the next game, against Wales, and another annihilation was expected, especially as the Welsh were without several leading players, including the great Billy Meredith. Yet Wales, kicking with the advantage of a strong wind, dominated the first half. It was 30 minutes before their goalkeeper, Roose, made a save.

Scotland held out, and took the lead with 16 minutes to play. A fine 30-yarder from Robertson went in off the underside of the bar. Then Parry equalised for Wales.

Poor weather restricted the attendance for the season's climax at The Crystal Palace. Scotland scored first, through John Campbell, 'a tremendous rocketer which scraped the paint off the underside of the bar'. England equalised through Blackburn, although there was a strong hint of offside about his goal.

Scotland edged 2-1 in front with a goal from Bob Hamilton, a schoolteacher, but England scored a late face-saver. Andy Aitken and Jock Drummond between them fluffed a clearance and Steve Bloomer ploughed through the mud to level the scores.

SCOTLAND 4   ENGLAND 1
7 April 1900, at Celtic Park

A FIRST-MINUTE goal by R.S.McColl, the only Queen's Park amateur in the team, set the course for a resounding victory in the 20th-century's first Scotland-England game. McColl scored three first-half goals, each one more thrilling than the last.

The SFA paid tribute to Lord Rosebery, the sporting peer who later became Prime Minister, by wearing hooped shirts in Rosebery's racing colours.

High prices kept the attendance to below the capacity of Celtic Park, which sported a new grandstand. About 64,000 paid, but thousands more got in for nothing and estimates of the actual attendance ranged from 60-80,000.

McColl's opening goal was fired home from an acute angle, and five minutes later, with England full-back Oakley prostrate on the pitch with a broken nose, Jack Bell scored a second.

After 28 minutes, McColl drove in a third: 'It was the best shot of the day, alike a paralyser to Robinson and to the hope of the Saxon,' commented the *Athletic News*. The paper continued: 'Nothing short of a mound of Limburg cheese, which they say is so strong to smell, would keep the Scots out of the English goal'.

Scotland conceded a goal to Bloomer, but before half-time McColl netted his third and thereafter, it was the Scots against England goalkeeper Robinson.

There were five Rangers players in this great triumph, but the only Anglo-Scot in the team, Liverpool centre-half Alex Raisbeck, deserved special mention. Playing in his first international, Raisbeck dominated the field with his flaxen hair, handsome features and athletic qualities. One of seven collier brothers, he himself raised 14 children. Unlike the pale-faced Bloomer, or the excessively slight Albert Buick, Raisbeck looked every inch a professional footballer.

Captained by Jack Robertson, Scotland had scored a fine victory and afterwards, Lord Rosebery told the players, "I have not seen my colours more worthily worn since Lada won the Derby in 1894." And the secret of success? "Perfect team play," said McColl. "Every man on the side seemed made for his position. I could not imagine a set of eleven men combine more effectively."

SCOTLAND: Rennie; N.Smith, Drummond, Gibson, Raisbeck, Robertson, Walker, Campbell, McColl, Bell, A.Smith.
ENGLAND: Robinson; Oakley, Crabtree, Johnson, Chadwick, Needham, Athersmith, Bloomer, Smith, Wilson, Plant.

Referee: S.Torrans (Ireland)   *Attendance: 64,000*

Although R.S.McColl was the obvious hero of Scotland's fine win over England at Celtic Park, the victory was very much a team effort and one man who had a particularly fine match was the Liverpool centre-half, Alex Raisbeck (left) who was making his international debut. Raisbeck, a native of the Stirlingshire pit village of Polmont, played for Blantyre Brigade, Larkhall Thistle and Hibs before moving into English football with Stoke. He spent 11 seasons at Liverpool before moving back to the Scottish League. Neil Gibson (far left) was another former Larkhall player who shone in the 1900 defeat of England, unlike Raisbeck his career was spent entirely in Scottish football.

THE IBROX DISASTER

CELTIC, Rangers and Queen's Park all competed for the right to stage the 1902 Scotland-England international. Ibrox Park was chosen because Rangers had, two years earlier, spent £20,000 on a ground improvement scheme which included two covered stands and, behind each, magnificent inclined terracing. Ironically, it was one of these terraces which was the setting for a disaster which killed 26 people.

On 5 April 1902, it had been raining, but the weather had done nothing to dampen the spirits of the Scots, who were looking forward to a visit from an off-form England team. Heavy rain was still falling as the game kicked off and the ground was already full.

Yet still more people surged in and many of those already inside began to look for an escape. Hundreds poured from the Eastern Terrace along the side of the pitch and up into the Western Terrace. Up they went, climbing the long, narrow stairways to the very top. And then the crowd began to sway. People at the foot of the terrace spilled on to the grass. And still the rain came pouring down.

Back up at the very top of the terrace, men in the heaving sea of humanity felt the ground trembling under their feet. Rows of steel uprights holding the wooden planking began to groan. Something had to give.

With a sickening crack, the terracing gave way as seven rows of planking disappeared and with them, hundreds of spectators swallowed up in a hole some 50 feet long and 12 feet wide. They dropped 40 feet to the ground, falling on top of each other.

Twenty-six people were killed, hundreds more injured, and yet, incredibly, the game was allowed to continue after an 18-minute hold-up. Later, the reason given was that officials feared an even bigger disaster if the game had been abandoned.

Indeed, many thousands did not realise the gravity of the situation and, as one newspaper put it: 'Nothing could better illustrate the vastness of this stadium than that 400 people should drop through a hole and the rest remain in ignorance'.

Throughout the rest of the game, rescue workers treated the injured and dying, having to cope with the incongruous cheering of the rest of the crowd. Broken wood was used as stretchers and splints as the rescuers prayed that no further disaster would occur in some other part of the jam-packed stadium.

The game, played out with thousands around the touchline making life difficult for the players, ended 1-1. Scotland winger Bobby Templeton remembered until his dying day, having to dribble around spectators as well as England defenders on his way to goal.

The result did not count towards the home championship and a replay was staged at Birmingham the following month. The result was again a draw and Scotland were the new champions.

Aftermath of the disaster. The collapsed wooden terracing through which 26 people fell to their deaths, disappearing along with hundreds of other spectators.

IBROX DISASTER

1901-2 The Ibrox Disaster — and to a much lesser extent, crowd trouble in Belfast — overshadowed a successful playing season. There were resounding wins over Wales and Ireland, against whom the Scots had now scored 100 goals in 19 games.

Scotland met Ireland at Distillery's ground, and the attraction was so great that overcrowding resulted. By kick-off time, spectators were six-deep on the track surrounding the Grosvenor Park pitch.

Scotland led 1-0 at half-time and then sailed four goals ahead without reply. At that point, spectators left in their hundreds. The mood of the crowd was already antagonistic — Scotland's Jock Drummond had upset the Irish fans by tripping Morrison on a few occasions — and now the departing crowd bombarded those who remained with cinders and clinkers. One missile struck Robertson on the head and the Scot was temporarily laid out.

The teams were on the field for over two hours, which indicates the scale of the crowd disturbance. The players remained on the pitch for the half-time interval, and there were numerous stoppages during Scotland's eventual 5-1 victory.

The game against Wales followed a similar course — 1-0 ahead at half-time and an eventual 5-1 scoreline. Albert Buick's 30-yard second-half goal helped to widen the gap between the teams.

If only the game at Ibrox on 5 April 1902, could be remembered solely for the fact that it was the first time both Scotland and England had fielded all-professional teams in this now-famous clash. However, ten minutes after the start, part of the West Stand collapsed, causing the deaths of 26 spectators, while a further 587 people were later compensated for their injuries. The game was resumed after 18 minutes, but the 1-1 draw was erased from the list of official internationals.

The game was restaged at Birmingham in May, the first time that the close-season had been infringed. The proceeds of this game went to the Ibrox Disaster Fund. Scotland took a 2-0 first-half lead through goals by Bobby Templeton and Ronnie Orr, one of three Newcastle players in the team. The second half was a contrast. Two goals in a minute brought England a draw, and they might have turned it into a win.

DEFEAT BY IRELAND

1902-3 After the Ibrox Disaster, there followed a season which included one of Scotland's greatest mishaps on the field — defeat by Ireland at Parkhead. The championship finished in a three-way tie with only Wales left out of the honours.

The game against Wales was played on a Monday and Scotland forced a 1-0 win. The goal came after 25 minutes when Bobby Templeton centred and Morgan Owen miskicked his clearance to allow Finlay Speedie to score. After that, some uncompromising defending kept the Welsh at bay.

A team of Home-Scots was on duty on the historic occasion of Scotland's first-ever defeat at the hands of Ireland. The Irish had lost 4-0 to England, but a ninth-minute goal from the head of Connor shocked Scotland. David Lindsay hit an Irish post, but Scotland conceded a second goal when Kirwan netted near the end. At the 20th attempt, Ireland had beaten Scotland, a feat which the Welsh had yet to achieve.

The Ireland game was played on a Saturday, which made it difficult for Scotland to obtain the release of certain players. Two days later, the customary Home-Scots versus Anglo-Scots trial match was played. For the England game, also on a Saturday, Sunderland released Ned Doig, Andy McCombie and James Watson, although it appears that the players had to fight to get away.

Scottish fortunes appeared to be sinking lower still when England, kicking with the wind, dominated the first half of the game at Bramall Lane, Sheffield. Doig, however, performed miracles in goal, and England's sole reward was a goal from amateur Vivian Woodward.

Then Scotland struck back, scoring twice within two minutes to upset England's hopes of winning their third consecutive game. In the 55th minute, Speedie scored his second goal of the international season, then Bobby Walker hit the winner. By the final whistle, Scotland were undoubtedly the superior team.

HARRY RENNIE

1900 to 1908: Goalkeeper, 13 caps.
Born: Greenock 1873.
Career: Greenock Volunteers, Bellgrove Ramblers, Morton, Hearts, Hibernian, Rangers, Kilmarnock.
Harry Rennie began his career as a successful half-back but from May 1897 he played in goal. He cost Hearts £50 when he moved from Morton and won his first two caps. The rest of his international appearances were as a Hibs player.
Rennie was possibly the first 'scientific' goalkeeper. He studied the technique of narrowing the angle, he practised running sideways and backwards, and his extra training was 'shadow-diving' on the locker room floor. He also built up a theory called 'The Shooting Gesture', watching players closely so that he could predict their intentions from the movements of their feet. Positioning was therefore his great strength and he pioneered the marking of the goalmouth as an aid to judging angles.
Although he played for Scotland for eight years, Rennie appeared against England only three times. Later he coached three generations of goal-keepers including Scottish internationals like Jimmy Cowan.

BOBBY WALKER

1900 to 1913: Inside-forward, 29 caps, 7 goals.
Born: Edinburgh 1879.
Career: Dairy Primrose, Hearts.
"You would think that Bobby Walker had eight feet," Jacky Robertson once said. "You go to tackle him where his feet were, but they're away when you get there."
Bobby Walker was not fast on his feet but fast in his mind and this enabled him to avoid defenders and provide inch-perfect passes during an exceptionally long career with Hearts and Scotland. Until Alan Morton's 30th cap in 1932, Walker was the Scotland record appearance holder. Once described as 'the father of altruistic football', he played a trial for Hearts in 1896, and his last appearance was when he partnered Billy Meredith in the 1915 Belgian Relief Match.
He played 11 times against England, the last in 1913 as a late replacement for McMenemy. He was still slow, as was his style, but just as subtle and therefore not out of his depth. A gas engineer by trade, Walker was the uncle of St Mirren's George Walker who played four games for Scotland in the early 1930s.

Action from the game against England at Sheffield in April 1903. Note the Scottish linesman complete with kilt in picture four.

Goalkeeper Ted Doig punches clear from an England attack at Sheffield in 1903. Doig had a marvellous game and restricted England to one goal.

A SHAKY SEASON

1903-4 After the shock setback against Ireland the previous season, Scotland had a narrow escape when Wales visited Dundee. Reduced to ten men, Scotland held on to a draw, and went on to complete their first season without a single victory.

Wales had five absentees from their selected team when they arrived in Dundee, and during the first half, the Scots looked set for a huge score. Indeed, there was one 20-minute period when the Scottish goalkeeper, Dr Leslie Skene, did not touch the ball.

Scotland led by Bobby Walker's smart fifth-minute goal, but the scorer was then taken ill and missed the second half. Wales soon equalised and, thereafter, the Scots were on the defensive.

At Dalymount Park, Dublin, Scotland staved off a second successive defeat against the Irish, while there was no repeat of the ugly crowd scenes of 1902. In fact, only 5,000 spectators were present. Hamilton gave Scotland the lead, but the Irish rallied in the second half.

The team for the England game was chosen immediately, and only four of the

Scottish eleven on duty in Dublin survived. Only three of them played — there were four late changes — in unfavourable conditions at Celtic Park. A biting wind and heavy snow showers led one newspaper to comment: 'Never has an international been played in worse ground conditions'.

Scotland held their own, kicking into the wind in the first half, and there was no score at the interval. Scotland began the second half by switching wingers, but it was England who took the lead after 64 minutes. Watson miskicked and allowed Bloomer to take the ball through and fire home past Peter McBride. Despite an heroic display by centre-half Alex Raisbeck, the Scots went down.

> *In the mid-1900s, Falkirk outside-right, Jocky Simpson, was selected for Scotland before it was discovered that he was English. His parents were both from Falkirk, but Simpson was born in Manchester. After moving to Blackburn Rovers, Scotland's 'lost' international played eight times for England.*

WALES WIN AT LAST

1904-5 At the Racecourse, Wrexham, on a Monday afternoon, Wales finally succeeded in beating Scotland after 30 years of trying, and the mid-1900s proved to be a period of recession for the Scottish team.

Scotland dominated the first half hour of the Wrexham match, but fell behind to Watkins who took a pass from Morris to score. Two minutes into the second half, Scotland suffered a cruel blow. Morris tried a hopeful shot from way out, goalkeeper Harry Rennie appeared to be blinded by the sun and made no attempt to save the ball, which duly sailed into the Scotland net. Billy Meredith scored a third and all Scotland could manage was a late consolation.

The Scots hit back with a resounding, and more typical, win against Ireland, before losing unluckily to England at The Crystal Palace. England were outplayed but won the game, thanks to a brilliant, swerving long-range shot from Joe Bache ten minutes from time.

SCŌTLAND'S NEW INTERNATIONALS

Crawford.]
G. WILSON
(Heart of Midlothian).

R. Thiele.]
CHAS. THOMSON
(Heart of Midlothian).

Maclure MacDonald.]
J. HAY
(Celtic).

Maclure MacDonald.]
P. SOMERS
(Celtic)

Elbourne.]
T. T. FITCHIE
(Woolwich Arsenal)

Stuart and Winfield.]
P. MacWILLIAM
(Newcastle United).

Furniss.]
J. LYALL
(Sheffield Wednesday).

Starfield.]
A. YOUNG
(Everton).

J. h. Thompson.]
J. HOWIE
(Newcastle United).

Davie Crawford of St Mirren and Rangers won three caps, the first two in 1894 and the third in 1900.

Alex McFarlane of Dundee, capped five times between 1904 and 1911.

Third Lanark's Tom Sloan won one cap, against Wales in 1904.

Scotland, wearing Rosebery colours, press during the game against England at The Crystal Palace in 1905.

The Scotland team that beat England 2-1 at Hampden in April 1906: Back row (left to right): J.K.McDowall (secretary), W.Dunlop, J.Liddel (linesman). Middle row: W.Nunnerley (referee), C.Thomson (reserve), P.McWilliam, D.McLeod, P.McBride, G.T.Livingstone, A.Aitken. Front row: J.Howie, A.Menzies, A.G.Raisbeck (captain), Geo Stewart, A.Smith, J.Wilson (trainer).

ANDY AITKEN

1901 to 1911: Wing-half, 14 caps.
Born: Ayr 1877.
Career: Ayr Thistle, Ayr Parkhouse, Kilmarnock, Newcastle, Middlesbrough (player-manager), Leicester Fosse, Dundee, Kilmarnock, Gateshead (manager).
Andy Aitken started as an inside-forward with Ayr Parkhouse, but his professional career was spent as a right-half or centre-half. Nicknamed 'Daddler', he won a Football League championship medal with Newcastle and twice played in FA Cup Finals for them. He was sold to Middlesbrough for £500 and missed out on Newcastle's rise in the latter 1900s when the Magpies consolidated their position as the finest club side of the day.
Ten of Aitken's caps were won against England, and he would have won more caps if Scotland had not fielded weaker teams against Wales and Ireland. Aitken retired through a groin injury in January 1913 and later became a licensee.

HOWIE SINKS ENGLAND

1905-6 In front of a record Edinburgh crowd, a Welsh team without Billy Meredith completed a second surprise victory over Scotland. A narrow win in Ireland followed, and then the Scots gained an unexpected victory over England.

Wales were represented by 'men of obscure clubs and League reservists' and, not surprisingly, Scotland dominated the game. But the first goal fell to Wales when Raeside let the ball slip through his hands. Scotland slid to a 2-0 defeat.

A staggeringly large crowd of 100,000 converged on 'New' Hampden Park for the game against England. There were seven Anglo-Scots in the team, while England had one player, Jimmy Conlin, who had been raised in Scotland.

The turning point came in the tenth minute when England lost Makepeace. The Everton half-back jumped at Menzies

who ducked, and Makepeace fell awkwardly over his opponent's back. England's ten men held out until a minute from half-time. Then Ashcroft caught James Howie's shot, but the England goalkeeper was adjudged to be over the line.

A second Howie goal, ten minutes after half-time, spurred England to play the 'one-back game'. Bob Crompton stayed on his own, to compensate for Makepeace's absence, and Scottish forwards were persistently caught offside, as three defenders rather than two were required goalside of attackers under the existing offside law.

England pulled a goal back through their young centre-forward Shepherd, but otherwise the England leader was well-shackled by the superb marking and tackling of centre-half Alex Raisbeck.

SELECTORS CRITICISED

1906-7 A third successive defeat by Wales saw the Scottish selectors make nine changes for the next game, against Ireland. And despite the resultant win, there were as many changes for the England game, when a record nine Anglo-Scots played in a Scottish team which was unlucky not to win.

Visiting the Racecourse, Wrexham, was a hazardous business, although the pitch had been levelled. The Welsh had Morgan Owen virtually lame from the start, and the Scots were humiliated by a team comprising only ten fit men. With two minutes remaining, Billy Meredith cut in and passed to Gordon Jones, who in turn fed Morris. Wales were ahead.

After a 3-0 win over Ireland — and a poor overall showing despite the result — the Scotland team was full of Anglo-Scots for the England match at Newcastle. One wag remarked, 'A hansom cab was all that was needed to take the Scotland team to England.' There was serious criticism of the Scottish selectors for overlooking players like Jimmy McMenemy, Jimmy Quinn, Jimmy Sharp and McPherson.

In the event, Scotland might have won. Had Alex Raisbeck been on form, and had not Bloomer chosen this match to score what he always considered was his best-ever goal, then victory could have been theirs. Bloomer's goal was a superbly struck left-foot shot of which Scotland goalkeeper Peter McBride said, 'I had no more chance of stopping it than a snowball would have in Hades.' And England goalkeeper Sam Hardy agreed: 'Aye, it wanted me alongside you, Peter, and then the two of us would have looked silly.'

RECORD CROWD

1907-8 After five years in the doldrums, Scotland recovered her prestige by beating both Wales and Ireland, and drawing with England, whose late equaliser was disputed. Part of the world-record crowd came on to the pitch at full-time to point to the smudge on the crossbar where it had been struck by Windridge's long-range shot. But did the ball cross the line when it bounced down?

Although the Welsh game produced a close result, the Ireland match was described as a fiasco. It was soon apparent that the Scots were the masters and their burly players made light of the heavy conditions. Jimmy Quinn scored four of the five goals.

At Hampden Park, on 4 April 1908, 121,452 people paid for admission to see Scotland meet England, beating the previous record of 110,802 for the 1901 English Cup Final at The Crystal Palace. About 70 people were slightly hurt in the crush and three were admitted to hospital. There

JIMMY QUINN

1905 to 1912: Centre-forward, 11 caps, 7 goals.
Born: Croy, Dunbartonshire, 1878.
Career: Smithston Albion (Croy), Celtic.
Jimmy Quinn, the iron man of soccer, was a Celtic hero for 15 years (1900-15) and ranks alongside McColl, Andy Wilson, Gallacher and McGrory as one of the great centre-forwards of the early 1900s. He was a sturdy, spectacular player with a fine miner's physique, and he would have won more caps but for injuries which resulted from his tearaway style.
Fame arrived when he scored three goals against Rangers in the 1904 Scottish Cup Final. The next year he was sent off in another Cup tie against Rangers and when Celtic fans invaded the pitch, the match was abandoned. He scored some key goals for Scotland, and once hit four in a game against Ireland. His last game was at outside-left against England and in that position he used his weight against Bob Crompton. A man of a thousand injuries, he advertised Boag's Rheumatic Rum, before a knee injury finished his career.

were also many who broke into the ground free of charge and friction among the spectators led to stones and bottles being thrown.

About 5,000 people spilled over on to the touchline, yet the game went ahead, played to the accompaniment of one of Hampden's boisterous winds. Scotland's team of 'veterans' took the lead after 27 minutes when Andy Wilson converted a cross from Jimmy Quinn, who was Scotland's best forward.

Jimmy Sharp had a fine game at half-back, although England winger Rutherford was injured for most of the game. Peter McBride was brilliant in goal, and Charlie Thomson tackled ruggedly in the centre. It looked like Scotland's game until the 75th minute when Windridge hit a rising drive. The ball struck the underside of the crossbar and rebounded to the ground. The referee gave a goal, but it was one which would long be debated.

SLIPPERY START

1908-09 The international season got off to a slippery start at Wrexham, where two inches of snow covered a partly-thawed, treacherous surface. The Scots were 3-0 down at half-time and were certainly not as bad as the scoreline suggests. Then Alec Bennett steamed down his wing and created goals for Bobby Walker and Peter Somers.

The over-elaborate Scots missed the services of the injured Jimmy Quinn in the 3-2 defeat. Quinn, hurt in an inter-League game, also missed the Ireland game which, for the first time, was played on a Monday. Ireland were saved from an even heavier defeat only by Scott's goalkeeping.

There was some doubt as to whether the game against England would take place. The English players' union was discussing various issues with the England internationals, but 'not wanting to disappoint the general public' it was decided to go ahead with the game. The union's statement contained a controversial passage which assured the public that 'the players will be in their places and will do their utmost to win'.

England's players then issued a statement declaring that they always intended to give of their best 'notwithstanding what has appeared in the Press'. Certainly, they proved their dedication with two early goals as the Scots started slowly.

After the goals, the Scots had as much of the play. Their best chance came when Pennington handled, but James Stark struck the penalty straight at Sam Hardy.

For the first time in a Scotland international, the goalkeepers and the referee wore distinctive colours.

DEVINE INTERVENTION

1909-10 Despite a surprising defeat in Ireland, Scotland won the championship. They had to thank a late goal by Archie Devine against Wales, in his only international, and then a stirring performance against England — one of many occasions

CHARLIE THOMSON

1904 to 1914: Centre-half, 21 caps, 4 goals.
Born: Prestonpans, East Lothian, 1878.
Career: Prestonpans FC, Hearts, Sunderland.
Charlie Thomson played centre-forward in the early part of his ten years with Hearts, but it was as a centre-half that his fame grew. He never lost the ability to attack, but as a defender he was relentless with remarkable stamina. 'Big, brawny and brave,' it was once said of him.
'Thomson was a great bustler,' wrote a journalist after the 1911 game with Ireland, 'and like John Walker was not too particular in his tackling, but he covered a great deal of ground and showed no signs of tiring.'
He developed into an inspirational captain – he captained Scotland 13 times – and responsible penalty-taker for Scotland, although he missed one against Ireland in 1908. He was captain against England three times, which equalled the achievements of Charles Campbell and Jacky Robertson. Thomson's value is indicated by the structure of the deal which took him to Sunderland in April 1908 when he was nearly 30. There was a £350 transfer limit, so Sunderland paid Hearts £700 for Thomson and a makeweight player.

that the Scots have raised their game after being virtually written-off beforehand.

In the last of the two internationals ever played at Kilmarnock, Devine scored his goal in the 75th minute with a 20-yard shot, after Jimmy McMenemy, who had missed 20 minutes through injury, laid on the chance.

Scotland produced an indifferent display in Belfast and went down to Thompson's second-half goal. Quinn was mastered, and Elisha Scott, the Irish goalkeeper, saved everything that came his way.

Several changes were necessary for the England game. Perhaps the most significant were the alterations to the half-back line. Andy Aitken, Charlie Thomson and Peter McWilliam were outstanding. It was the third time that this combination had been fielded — the other two games had been lost — and this was their finest hour and a half.

Two goals came in the first 30 minutes. Bobby Templeton beat several players in a terrific run, Quinn's shot was blocked by Hardy, McMenemy pounced on the loose ball and poked it into the empty net.

Alec Bennett set up the second for Quinn, who bowled Pennington over and charged the ball and Hardy into the net for a typical Quinn goal. Hampden's 110,000 spectators saw Scotland top the championship.

UNBEATEN RUNNERS-UP

1910-11 In contrast to the previous season — when four points were good enough to win the championship despite the shock defeat in Ireland — Scotland found that the same number of points gave them only runners-up spot, despite being unbeaten.

The venue for the Wales game — Ninian Park, Cardiff — was relatively new to international football. Soccer was gaining a growing following in South Wales, hence the move from Wrexham, but Ninian Park, the home of then Southern League club Cardiff City, was criticised as being a 'primitive ground'. Its limited accommodation was a contrast to the Glasgow grounds and the narrow Cardiff pitch cramped the players, while a bumpy playing surface caused errors, and some players complained of glass on the pitch.

On this difficult ground, Scotland's saviour was RC Hamilton, a late replacement on the left wing. Hamilton's previous ten caps had brought him 12 goals from the three inside-forward positions. It was seven years since he had last played for Scotland, and this was not one of his best games. But his last-minute goal, his second equaliser of the game, earned Scotland a draw.

Part of the only barrier around the pitch — a simple wooden paling — gave way early in the game, but there were no serious consequences. Peter McWilliam was off the field injured when Granville Morris gave Wales a 2-1 lead midway through the second half. In the last minute, John Walker lofted a free-kick into the Welsh goalmouth. Injured goalkeeper Roose fell while fisting away, and Hamilton got his vital touch in the scramble which followed.

Ireland were outclassed in the next game, but Scotland had to settle for two goals. Billy Reid hit the first with a powerful drive, and Jimmy McMenemy made the fullest use of Alex Smith's accurately flighted corner.

England had won their opening two

games, so the championship rested on the result of the match at Liverpool. Scotland struggled during the first half and fell behind to Stewart's goal. Just before half-time, Alec Bennett centred and Higgins and Smith both went up for the ball which crashed against a post. Scotland claimed a goal, but the referee waved play on.

It would have been a grave injustice if Scotland had lost, and with three minutes remaining, Smith flighted over a corner and Higgins rose high above the English defence to steer it home.

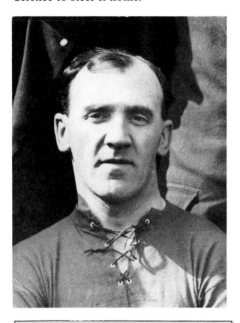

JIMMY McMENEMY

1905 to 1920: Inside-forward, 12 caps, 5 goals.
Born: Rutherglen, Lanarkshire, 1880.
Career: Rutherglen Glencairn, Celtic, Partick Thistle, Stenhousemuir, Partick Thistle (coach), Celtic (trainer-coach).
The football field was his chessboard, they said of Jimmy McMenemy, who dictated the play with his perfect passing. He schemed and plotted, setting the pace to suit himself and appearing to walk through a game as he made the ball do the work. He was the general, hence his nickname of 'Napoleon'.
At Celtic (1902-20) he helped his club to 11 championships and six Scottish Cup successes. Celtic gave him a free transfer, thinking him finished, but his style was timeless. He came into Partick Thistle's injury-hit team as a 40-year-old and they created a major upset by beating Rangers 1-0 to take the Scottish Cup in 1921.
As he was a contemporary of Bobby Walker, McMenemy won less caps than he deserved, but as late as 1919 he was a perfect partner for a winger, in this case Alan Morton. McMenemy never played on a losing Scotland side in official internationals. He was the father of several footballing sons, including John (Motherwell and Scotland) and Harry (Newcastle).

HERO JOHN WALKER

1911-12 A share of the championship was achieved by a late winner against Wales, a comfortable victory over a depleted Irish side, and a fighting draw against England at an overcrowded Hampden Park.

The game against Wales increased in excitement and effort as it progressed, and the only goal came from Jimmy Quinn in the closing moments. Scotland went in for long, swinging passes, whereas the Welsh demonstrated closer skills, particularly their wingers, the veteran Billy Meredith and the young Ted Vizard. There was no doubt, however, that the Scots deserved their win.

At the time of the Ireland game, the Irish FA were in dispute with several of their senior clubs, who not only boycotted the international, but went as far as arranging a rival match elsewhere in the city. This alternative game attracted 10,000 spectators.

Ireland were also handicapped by the absence of four players not released by Everton and Bradford City. Scotland's star was Wattie Aitkenhead who scored the first two goals, both from Sinclair crosses. McKnight made it 2-1 with a late penalty, but Scotland controlled the second half and added goals through Billy Reid and Bobby Walker.

> *In 1912, the SFA asked Sunderland if they would release Charlie Buchan, should he be selected for the next international. They said they would —because although Buchan's parents were both Aberdonians, he was born in Woolwich, London.*

Bobby Walker, now 33, had one of his greatest afternoons in the match against England. Both the game's goals came in the first 13 minutes, and both followed throw-ins. Jimmy Quinn, chosen on the left wing to use his weight against Bob Crompton, forced England's veteran full-back to kick into touch. Andy Aitken got possession from the throw-in and scored. Holley equalised from close-range and at the end of the match, Scottish fans chaired full-back John Walker, their star defender, from the field.

The atmosphere for this vital game was charged with emotion. Although it was played at the height of a coal-strike, and there were therefore no trains to the ground, the game has so captured the imagination of Scottish fans that many pawned personal items to raise the one shilling admission, and then walked miles to the ground.

Hampden was not equal to the crowds. The official attendance was 127,300, but thousands who could not see the game had their money refunded. Spectators strayed along the touchline, and thousands sat around the edge of the pitch. On one occasion, England's outside-left Wall tumbled into the mass of spectators.

DUBLIN DEBACLE

1912-13 Arthur Adams blew his whistle to end the game in Dublin and the stage was set for some of the most unruly scenes in the history of international football.

Players fought to keep the ball as a souvenir. Scotland's George Robertson reached it first, but a spectator, Patrick Gartland, knocked the ball out of Robertson's hands and Ireland's Andrews grabbed it. In the struggle which followed, Gartland was knocked over and feared badly injured.

Rumours that Robertson had broken the spectator's leg spread through the Irish crowd who were already incensed by Scotland's second goal — there were universal pleas for offside when Alec Bennett scored — and frustrated by Ireland's failure to save the game after dominating the second half.

An angry mob gathered outside the dressing rooms and began smashing windows. For an hour, the Scotland team were virtual prisoners. Referee Adams, busy preparing for his bath, opened a french window to find a huge Irishman rushing

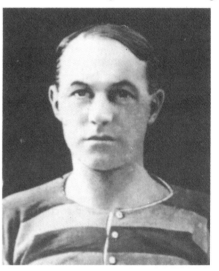

ALEC McNAIR

1906 to 1920: Full-back, 15 caps.
Born: Stenhousemuir, 1883.
Career: Stenhousemuir Hearts, Stenhousemuir, Celtic, Dundee (secretary- manager).
After winning occasional caps at wing-half, Alec McNair switched to full-back in 1912 and he became a fixture in this position. He was Scotland's equivalent of the Englishman Jesse Pennington, unruffled, intelligent and extremely well-respected. Willie Maley of Celtic recorded that McNair was 'a gentleman and a treasure to the club in every way'.
He made almost 600 League appearances for Celtic and represented the Scottish League 14 times. He equalled Alec Smith's Scottish League longevity record of 21 seasons, and he was last capped when 36, although this final appearance was a hazardous one in the Hillsborough mud.

past him brandishing a wooden stake. Fortunately, the Irishman contented himself with damaging the bath.

George Robertson was arrested and taken to the police station. The Irish FA agreed to meet the costs of the injured man, who dropped charges, but the mob pursued the Scottish players to their hotel where full-back John Walker was attacked outside.

One man who missed the match was veteran Bobby Walker, who had injured a leg in the goalless draw with Wales, a game in which the Scots were grateful for their defence.

Against England, at Stamford Bridge, the championship was at stake. England won with an untidy 37th-minute goal. Simpson shot, Brownlie caught the ball, but he was charged over the line by England centre-forward Harry Hampton. Brownlie claimed that he never went over the line, but at least one man disagreed. Scottish referee Alex Jackson, wearing a Norfolk jacket and a three-inch stiff linen collar with tie, awarded the goal.

Brownlie had played well, despite his mistake which allowed the English goal, but it was England goalkeeper Sam Hardy who stole the show in a game which saw Scotland on top for long periods. Scottish centre-half Charlie Thomson developed a feud with Hampton which dragged on into the Sunderland-Villa match in that season's English Cup Final and which eventually led to a month's suspension for each player.

> In 1913, Scotland played in Ireland for the second consecutive year to help the finances of the Irish FA.

SCOTLAND'S REVENGE

1913-14 There was a second successive goalless draw with Wales, and then followed more amazing scenes at the end of the game against Ireland. The home team, down to ten men, rescued a draw with a last-minute equaliser, and Ireland thus won the international championship for the first time. For Scotland, it had been a depressing era — only one outright championship since 1904.

Ireland had beaten both Wales and England, and they needed a point from Scotland to ensure the championship. The Irish set off at a great pace, but incurred setbacks through injury. O'Connell was hurt in a tackle with Andy Wilson. McConnell was also injured and Lacey was forced to move to full-back. Worst of all, goalkeeper McKee collided with Wilson and had to retire just after half-time. McConnell went in goal, O'Connell returned, but Ireland still had only eight fit men and no specialist goalkeeper.

However, the pitch resembled a Kerry bog and was proving a great leveller. Charlie Thomson urged the Scots on through atrocious conditions, and when McConnell made his only mistake, 20

JIMMY BROWNLIE

**1909 to 1914: Goalkeeper, 16 caps.
Born: Blantyre, Lanarkshire, 1885.
Career: Blantyre Victoria, Third Lanark, Dundee United (secretary-manager).**
For six years Brownlie was chosen for all Scotland's internationals and he conceded only 11 goals in 16 appearances, missing the 1911 England game through injury. 'Brownlie was a powerfully built man, with hands of extraordinary size,' it was written of him, 'and when he clutched the ball it seemed completely to disappear'.
A bricklayer by trade, he succeeded Raeside in the Third Lanark goal and became known as 'The Man with the Iron Clutch'. He was brilliant against England in 1909, perhaps even better against Wales at Wrexham in 1913 and when Scotland lost to Ireland in 1910.
In 1910, Brownlie was party to a unique event, when opposing goalkeepers each scored for their own side in a first-class match. Clem Hampton of Motherwell was the other goalkeeper. Brownlie played in the Victory internationals of 1918-19, and when he was 40, he kept goal in an emergency for Dundee United against Hearts in a Cup tie.

minutes from time, Joe Donnachie slipped the ball into an empty net.

It seemed that luck had deserted the Irish in their hour of need and their prospects of a first international title began to ebb away. But in the dying seconds, Alec McNair let Sam Young through and the Irishman crashed the ball into the back of the Scottish net. The crowd swarmed to the touch-line and the immediate post-match scenes were spectacular. In contrast to the previous season, they were of sheer exuberance.

Scotland felt humiliated and they vented their feelings on England at Hampden Park. Jimmy McMenemy and Jimmy Croal treated Hampden to one of its greatest-ever displays of inside-forward play, and early in the game, Charlie Thomson hit a

glorious goal from 20 yards. Harold Fleming equalised for England, but the second half was one-way traffic as Scotland besieged the England goal. McMenemy put the Scots ahead again, and then the same player laid on a third for Billy Reid. The crowd was an estimated 130,000 with the gates closed 20 minutes before the kick-off and with thousands more locked outside. Those lucky enough to gain admission reckoned that Scotland should have had six before the final whistle.

WILSON'S AMAZING TALE

1915-19 Just when Scotland appeared to have found a successful combination, beating England 3-1 in 1914, war was declared and in one of the bloodiest of all conflicts, Scottish footballers, like most young men, suffered. But for one man, Andy Wilson (no relation to his pre-war namesake), it was a case of turning swiftly from casualty to celebrity when international competition resumed in 1919.

The first of four Victory internationals in six weeks was against Ireland at Ibrox. Wilson, injured on army service the previous year, was nursing a shattered left arm in Glasgow's Stobhill Hospital. He went to Ibrox in an ambulance, simply to watch the game.

It was at Ibrox that fact turned out to be stranger than fiction and wrote a script which came straight out of an adventure comic. Two Scots, Monair and McMullan, were stranded by a railway breakdown and although McMullan arrived late to take his place, the other vacancy was filled by Andy Wilson, who scored both Scotland's goals in their 2-1 win.

Both Wilson's goals were disputed. The first was a penalty, and the winner stemmed from a hefty challenge on Irish goalkeeper Scott. Not surprisingly, the Scots began unsteadily, but by the end, they were well on top.

The return in Belfast was a poor match and the goalless draw had only one redeeming feature for Scotland, the fine goalkeeping of Brownlie, who saved a penalty from Rollo.

Scotland rediscovered their touch in the opening 12 minutes of the first England game when they raced into a 2-0 lead. The goals came from crosses by Alan Morton, who looked dangerous every time he got the ball. However, England settled down and Turnbull pulled a goal back on the hour. The equaliser was a brilliant effort from Syd Puddefoot who scored a superb individualist goal with 15 minutes to play.

Scotland found Puddefoot a stumbling block in the return at Hampden a week later, when England gained their first victory in Scotland for 15 years. England led 3-0 at half-time, Grimsdell scoring two from wing-half and Puddefoot the other. Scotland pulled back two — a Wilson penalty and a fine goal by Morton — but Puddefoot scored again and Wilson's second of the match came too late to save Scotland. No wonder that, three years later, Falkirk paid a record £5,000 for Puddefoot, who had guested for them during the war.

The Inter-War Years

NINE-GOAL THRILLER

1919-20 "Two bob to watch a match played on a ploughed park," moaned one Scottish supporter before the game with England at Hillsborough, Sheffield, and his sentiments were echoed by fellow Scots who had made the journey south.

Yet the vile weather provided a setting for one of the most brilliant and exciting matches ever played. Never was a florin better spent than on that April day, when Scotland and England constructed a nine-goal thriller.

Three days of heavy rain in Sheffield had all but destroyed the pitch, and the Scots sensibly abandoned their traditional close-passing game for long, sweeping passes to the wings, from where the afternoon's damage would be done.

> *Immediately after World War One, referees in home internationals were neutral, but each country provided a linesman. Thus Burslem referee Mr J. Mason officiated at the Wales-Scotland game at Cardiff in 1920, while SFA president Mr T. White ran the line.*

For 25 years, the Scotland-England game had been a low-scoring affair. Now England's inside men fed off chances created by wingers Wallace and Quantrill, while Scotland's counterparts were Alex Donaldson and Alex Troup, who played in a special strap to protect a damaged shoulder.

Scotland fell behind, then drew level in the 13th minute when Tom Miller took Troup's cross on to score. Almost immediately, England regained the lead with a goal described as 'a theatrical achievement', Quantrill applying the finishing touch from Wallace's centre.

By half-time, Scotland were 4-2 in the lead and looked set for the win that would give them the international championship, although they had been kept ahead by the brilliant goalkeeping of Kenny Campbell, who had returned to Scotland to play for Partick after being the only Anglo-Scot in the team that had played Wales in February.

In the second half, England moved the ball around, hitting hard, first-time passes over the mud. Bob Kelly made it 4-3 — the only one of nine goals not laid on by a winger — and Alf Quantrill's strong runs set up two more. England led 5-4.

Even when Campbell was injured, and Jimmy Gordon had to deputise in goal for ten minutes, Scotland still looked capable of equalising. But when England goalkeeper Hardy made a superb save from Paterson two minutes from time, the Scots had to accept defeat.

"It was my biggest thrill," exclaimed JC Clegg, the veteran FA chief, at the final whistle. The shame was that only 35,000 spectators had witnessed this magnificent football match, less than the number which

ANDY WILSON

1920 to 1923: Centre-forward, 12 caps, 13 goals.
Born: Newmains, Lanarkshire, 1896.
Career: Cambuslang Rangers, Middlesbrough, Hearts, Dunfermline, Middlesbrough, Chelsea, Queen's Park Rangers, Nimes (France), Clacton Town (trainer-manager), Walsall (manager), Gravesend and Northfleet (manager).
Burly Andy Wilson overcame a bad arm injury, received on military service, to captain Scotland from the position of centre-forward.
After heroic performances in two Victory internationals in 1919, Wilson's first six caps were won with Dunfermline in the rebel Central League, even though he was still registered with Middlesbrough. Back with 'Boro he was the leading English First Division scorer in 1921-2.
In November 1923, Wilson moved to Chelsea for a record £6,000, but he had played his last game for Scotland. His strike rate of 17 goals in 14 internationals (including wartime) rates among the best. On the 1921 tour of North America his scoring rate was sensational. One American admirer, A.C.Sullivan, celebrated his feat in a poem: *Vy Endy Vilsal vill desh down Und greb the ball – beng! beng! He'll shoot so fest he'll score five more As all the other gang.*

had watched Scotland's comfortable 3-0 win over Ireland earlier that year.

The championship went to Wales, who fully deserved their 1-1 draw with the Scots. On the occasion of what the Welsh FA believed was Billy Meredith's 50th international appearance, Wales led for most of the game until Tommy Cairns' header earned Scotland a point.

One shining star in a disappointing game was Alan Morton, who won his first peacetime cap that day. Morton had missed the England game through injury, allowing Troup his chance in the Hillsborough mud.

DAWN OF A GREAT DECADE

1920-1 Scotland won all three internationals to carry off the championship outright for the first time since 1910. This success was the springboard for a tremendous decade and the 1920s belonged almost exclusively to Scotland.

The success was not caused simply by Scotland stumbling upon the right blend and establishing a settled team, but rather by an abundance of fine players, leaving the main problem for the selectors that of who to leave out. In 1920-1, Scotland used 19 players in three internationals. Only Jock Marshall, Jimmy McMullan and Andy Wilson played in all three.

When Scots expressed concern at the state of the Hampden Park turf in 1921, one English writer summed up the state of the British game: 'They should worry...grass grows quicker than players'.

Scotland's first scalp was that of Wales, holders of the crown. At Aberdeen, in front of an unusually quiet Scottish crowd, Alex Troup's fine run led to a 46th-minute winner from Andy Wilson.

Wilson captained the side in Belfast, and his eager shooting brought some fine saves from Scott in the Irish goal. Wilson's penalty gave Scotland a first-half lead and Joe Cassidy added a second after half-time.

Hope was high when Wilson's side faced the English at Hampden, and 85,000 spectators ignored increased admission charges and the inconvenience of Glasgow's trains being cancelled during an industrial dispute. The players had to cope with Hampden's seemingly statutory strong wind, which was to prove the downfall of England goalkeeper Gough.

Wilson's 20th-minute goal meant that the Scottish centre-forward had now scored in five successive internationals, an achievement that has been equalled, but never bettered, in the years since.

Wilson's goal was created by Morton who, partnered by Andy Cunningham, began to weave freely down the left wing. Two minutes from half-time, Morton's shot-cum-centre from the touchline was turned into the net by Gough. Ten minutes later, Cunningham's header beat the England goalkeeper and Scotland had crowned a fine season.

JIMMY McMULLAN

1920 to 1929: Wing-half, 16 caps.
Born: Denny, Stirlingshire, 1895.
Career: Denny Hibernian, Third Lanark, Partick Thistle, Maidstone United, Partick Thistle, Manchester City, Oldham Athletic (manager), Aston Villa (manager), Notts County (manager), Sheffield Wednesday (manager).
Master tactician Jimmy McMullan won seven caps against England and only one game was lost. Slightly built, cultured and classy, McMullan's greatest day came when he captained the 1928 'Wembley Wizards'. His passes to Alan Morton did much of the damage. McMullan won a Scottish Cup-winners' medal with Partick in 1921, and shortly afterwards Thistle turned down £5,000 from Newcastle for him. He went to non-League Maidstone for two years and Partick got nothing. Eventually Manchester City paid £4,700 for him. McMullan's spell with Maidstone meant that he missed international matches for two seasons, but he lost none of his skill and was soon reinstated, captaining the side for the first time in 1924.

John McPherson, a Scotland international between 1879 and 1885, once took English journalist Jimmy Catton to show him the ground where the first international took place. Catton could see nothing resembling a football pitch and asked where he should be looking. "Why there mon," replied McPherson. "That's Bannockburn."

TITLE RETAINED

1921-2 The championship was retained with wins over Ireland and England, while the defeat by Wales was on a Wrexham pitch reckoned to be in worse condition than for any previous international.

Snow and sleet fell for hours before the Wrexham match and continued throughout the game. The *Wrexham Leader* summed up the conditions thus: 'Play had not been in progress three minutes before the players were slipping and sliding about in all directions, and at every revolution the ball gathered so much snow that it resembled a Christmas pudding covered in white sauce'.

About 10,000 hardy souls braved the blizzard — the Racecourse ground had covered accommodation for only 2,000 of them — and the referee borrowed a broom to sweep clear the 18-yard lines at half-time.

Despite the levelling conditions, the Scots dominated the second half. Peers, the Welsh goalkeeper, was forced into three breathtaking saves at Andy Wilson's feet. On the last occasion, Peers injured a knee and Stanley Davies had to take over in goal.

Scotland, missing Andy Cunningham, went down 2-1, despite a heroic defensive performance by Middlesbrough full-back Jock Marshall. Alan Morton was still the star forward, but there were seven new caps in the side.

Centre-half was one problem position, and for the game against Ireland, the selectors chose their sixth different centre-half in as many games. Scotland were fortunate to win 2-1, Andy Wilson scoring twice in the last 20 minutes. Ireland had the better of the first half and led through Gillespie's 25-yarder, but their injured full-back McCracken had to change places with winger Lacey.

In the summer of 1921, Scotland made an important pioneering two-month tour of Canada and the United States. The 'Scottish Soccerites' as they were dubbed by American newspapers, won all 19 games in Canada, scoring 85 goals, the majority of which fell to Andy Wilson. Their closest scare was a 1-0 win in Montreal when Rankin scored with a late sizzler.
For the six games in the US, Scotland were billed as 'Third Lanark'. After a close game in New York when Bennett scored the winner two minutes from time, they arrived at the 25th and final match of the tour at Fall River with a 100 per cent record. The local team met for 'skull practice' on the eve of the game and 3,682 saw a 2-2 draw. Crowds of this size made the tour a financial success. At Fall River, Scotland ha been guaranteed 75 per cent of the receipts with a minimum of $1,000. On their return, the tour organiser, Glasgow sportswriter Robert Connell, said, "Our trip, the first of its kind ever attempted, will do more to boost this great game than anything else I can conceive of."

Against the Auld Enemy, Scotland won a poor game at Villa Park. It was a sharp contrast to the brilliant play at Sheffield two years earlier, although most Scottish supporters would have thought that winning 1-0 with a freak goal was better than losing a classic match 5-4. Scotland's first win on English soil since 1903 came from a 62nd-minute goal. England goalkeeper Dawson's clearance rebounded off full-back Wadsworth and fell perfectly to Andy Wilson who accepted the gift eagerly.

HAT-TRICK OF CHAMPIONSHIPS

1922-3 A draw against England was the only point dropped and Scotland were clear champions for the third successive season. Andy Wilson had now scored in ten of the last 11 internationals, while the all-Rangers left-wing pair of Tommy Cairns and Alan Morton were proving formidable, and Willie Harper had established himself as Scotland's goalkeeper — at least until he crossed the border to play for Arsenal.

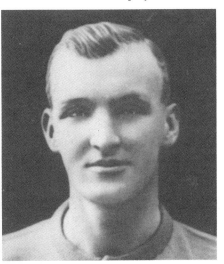

ANDY CUNNINGHAM

1920 to 1927: Inside-forward, 12 caps, 5 goals.
Born: Galston, Ayrshire, 1891.
Career: Newmilns FC, Kilmarnock, Rangers, Newcastle United, Newcastle United (manager), Dundee (manager). The tall, golden-haired Cunningham was 29 when he first played for Scotland, but he went on to establish himself in a manner that was the envy of many younger men. He captained the Rangers teams that won the championship eight times in the 1920s. Key features of his play were excellent close control and fine positional ability.
Despite losing key football years to the war – he played for the Scottish League as early as 1912 – Cunningham had phenomenal success, and as late as 1929 Newcastle reputedly paid £2,500 for his transfer. He is thought to be the English Football League's oldest debutant, two days after his 38th birthday.

In February 1924, Wales avenged their rugby defeat by Scotland with a 2-0 win over the Scots at Ninian Park. Left: Action from the game. Right: The two captains, Blair (Scotland) and Keenor (Wales), both Cardiff players. Note that they are both wearing the same coloured socks.

In February 1926, Scotland beat Northern Ireland in Glasgow. Left: Play around the Irish goalmouth. Right: Hughie Gallacher scores one of his three goals for Scotland.

Jimmy McMullan leads out the 1924 Scottish team at Wembley.

Things did not look so rosy when Scotland met Ireland in Belfast at the beginning of March. It was the first of the three home internationals which still formed Scotland's complete fixture list. England had ventured abroad as far back as 1908, with a tour of Austria, Hungary and Bohemia, but Scotland were still content with their home opposition.

Andy Wilson scored the only goal of the game against Ireland. It came 20 minutes from the end and was one of the few contributions which the centre-forward had made to the afternoon's play. It was a narrow victory in every sense of the word.

Wales fielded a scratch team for the international on St Mirren's ground at Paisley. Five of the visitors' originally selected team were required by their clubs. Not all were as considerate as Cardiff City, who released Blair for Scotland and Keenor and Len Davies for Wales.

Despite losing Willie Cringan through injury at half-time —Cunningham fell back to play a storming game at centre-half — Scotland were in control. The lethal left-wing pair of Cairns and Morton created a goal for Wilson in each half.

At Hampden Park, the 'two-bob' tariff helped cut the attendance to 71,000 for the big game of the international season. Cunningham again starred, but this time in his orthodox position of inside-right.

It was Cunningham who tapped in a first-half equaliser after Kelly had headed England in front. Scotland trailed 2-1 at the interval, but Wilson's predictable goal came in the 55th minute when Wadsworth missed his chance to clear and the Scottish centre-forward snapped up the opportunity.

Thereafter, it was the Scots versus Taylor, the England goalkeeper. Scotland should, perhaps, have won, but the draw was sufficient to seal another title success.

When Scotland met Wales at Ninian Park, Cardiff, in February 1924, both captains, Blair (Scotland) and Keenor (Wales) were playing on their home club ground. And Scotland had Walean-Scots in both full-back positions. Blair was partnered by burly Jock Marshall, 'the ferro-concrete full-back', who was still considered international quality, although he was playing for non-League Llanelli.

WEMBLEY DEBUT

1923-4 Scotland had not won on a Welsh ground since 1903 and the unsuccessful run continued at Cardiff in February 1924. Wales won 2-0 and their goalkeeper Gray had to face only one shot which caused him concern — an Alan Morton effort when the winger cut in and forced Gray to turn the ball aside for a corner.

Morton was originally omitted for the Ireland game, and then reinstated in place of Adam McLean (Celtic). The game was spoiled by the high wind that often made goalkeeping a nightmare in Glasgow. On this occasion, however, Scotland goalkeeper

ALAN MORTON

1920 to 1932: Outside-left, 31 caps, 5 goals.
Born: Partick, 1893.
Career: Airdrie Academy, Queen's Park, Rangers.
Has there ever been a more exciting left-winger than Alan Morton? He bobbed and weaved, pranced and dummied, wobbled and shimmied as he dribbled with the insides of his feet, searching for the best way to goal. He danced and dallied, and then attacked defenders, switching the ball from one foot to the other.
Morton stood just 5ft 4in, and weighed a mere 9st. To help his perfect balance, he wore only three studs on the sole of each boot, claiming that four might cling to the turf, interfere with pivoting and threaten cartilage injury.
He was naturally right-footed but could take any direction necessary to avoid defenders. "I had a side view not unlike the view a mirror gives a motorist," he once said.
A mining engineer by trade, he was a part-time professional, often working on the morning of an international. He joined Queen's Park to keep his brother Bob company before moving to Rangers in 1920. In 13 years at Ibrox, Morton helped Rangers to nine championships and his 31 caps were a record until surpassed by George Young. No one bettered his 11 caps against England and the 1926 game was known as 'the year that Morton didn't play'. In 1928, after he had tormented England's defenders, a frustrated home fan muttered, 'You little blue devil'. A journalist overheard the remark and mentioned it in his report. Thereafter Morton was 'the wee blue devil'. For 38 years (1933-71) he was a Rangers director.

Willie Harper, who had dropped the ball to present Wales with their second goal in Cardiff, had an easy afternoon. Most of his energy was expended in nerves as he watched his forwards buzzing around Ireland's goal trying to score.

Not until the 85th minute did Andy Cunningham breach the Irish defence, and then David Morris added a second with a header which proved to be almost the last touch of the match.

By the time an experimental Scottish team took the field at the new Wembley Stadium, Wales were assured of the championship. England included Charlie Buchan for his first cap against Scotland and the Sunderland player set up a second-half equaliser in the 1-1 draw.

Scotland, with five new caps, led 1-0 at half-time through a strange goal engineered by Clunas. The wing-half's shot hit an upright, rebounded off goalkeeper Taylor and trickled slowly over the line.

Scotland fielded a strong half-back line, and two sound Ayr United full-backs, while speedy winger Sandy Archibald was the chief danger in the first half. Scotland had used 24 players in these three internationals, yet they were on the verge of one of the most memorable periods in any international team's history.

GALLACHER'S FIRST GOALS

1924-5 Fielding a settled side for the first time since the war — only 14 players were used — Scotland earned three convincing victories. The last of these, against England, was achieved with a team of Home-Scots, although in little more than a year, seven of them were transferred to English clubs.

In the three-match season, Scotland used only one player from outside the Scottish League — Cardiff full-back Jimmy Nelson. A sign of that season's stability was the continued use of Dave Morris, the Raith Rovers centre-half. During the 1920s, Scotland chose no fewer than 19 different centre-halves in 34 internationals, and Morris was the most regular in what was the lynch-pin position. In the days before the 'stopper' centre-half, a player like Morris would be up and down the field, linking defence with attack.

Against Wales, both Alex Jackson and Jimmy Dunn won their first caps, while Hughie Gallacher scored his first goals, both excellently taken, to signal what great days were to come.

Scotland enjoyed one of their best performances for years when they met Ireland. In the fourth minute, Morton's pass provided Davie Meiklejohn with a brilliant goal. Then followed a scintillating spell from Gallacher. First, he hit a post, then he scored a goal, and finally he sent Dunn away for Scotland's third. All this, and only 35 minutes had gone.

Gallacher continued his superb form against England, scoring a goal in each half. In the 36th minute, he took a pass from Tommy Cairns, feinted, side-stepped and then left goalkeeper Dick Pym with nothing more to do, except pick the ball out of the net. Five minutes from time, the

Alan Morton has the England defence on the run at Hampden in 1923.

Below: Scotland's team for the 50th Scotland-England international (1926). Despite the absence of Alan Morton — his deputy Alec Troup is on the extreme right of the front row — this Scotland team was probably as good as the much-acclaimed 'Wembley Wizards'. Captained by big Jock Hutton (front row, third from the right) the players show intense determination as they await the kick-off at Old Trafford. Bottom: Huddersfield's Alex Jackson scores the only goal of the game. Scotland's victory at Old Trafford confirmed them as champions and gave England the wooden spoon.

WILLIE McSTAY

1921 to 1928: Full-back, 13 caps.
Born; Netherburn, Lanarkshire, 1894.
Career: Netherburn Junior, Larkhall Thistle, Celtic, Hearts, Glentoran (manager).
Willie McStay was introduced into the Scotland team in 1921, but it was not until the mid-1920s that he established himself, when he excelled in both full-back positions. He made 550 Scottish League appearances, and when he joined Hearts in 1929 he was succeeded as Celtic captain by his younger brother Jimmy, who became Celtic manager (1940-45). Willie was great uncle to Paul McStay, Celtic star of the 1980s.

centre-forward finished off a cross from Alex Jackson, the 'baby' of the team.

Jackson had a fine afternoon, and about the only time that Wadsworth, the England left-back, beat the young winger was in a race to seize the ball as a souvenir at the final whistle. The Hampden crowd roared for Wadsworth to hand over the ball to the new Scotland star, but the Englishman held on to his prize.

PERFECT DEFENCE

1925-6 For the second successive season, Scotland won all three internationals, this time without conceding a goal, despite the fact that two of the matches were on opponents' grounds.

The Welsh game was played in October — an early-season date may have ensured that clubs were less reluctant to release players than they were during the vital run-in to the season — and Scotland at last overcame their difficulties on Welsh soil.

Fred Keenor, the Welsh captain, dislocated a knee in the second minute, but his ten

During the year after Scotland beat England in 1925, with a team of Home-Scots, seven of the players moved to English clubs. They were: Willie Harper (£4,500 to Arsenal), Phil McCloy (£3,000 to Manchester City), Davie Morris (£4,700 to Preston), Jimmy McMullan (£4,700 to Manchester City), Alex Jackson (£5,000 to Huddersfield), Willie Russell (£3,650 to Preston) and Hughie Gallacher (£6,500 to Newcastle).

colleagues resisted Scotland until the last 15 minutes. After Scotland had opened the scoring through Leicester's 'Tokey' Duncan - one of four new caps - Stan Davies moved from right-back to centre-forward, and the Welsh defence was exposed to two late goals.

Ireland — now really Northern Ireland because the Republic of Ireland had begun separate international matches — had to make four changes from their selected team for the visit to Glasgow in February. The match was a personal triumph for Hughie Gallacher, who scored a hat-trick. His goals came in the 13th, 48th and 65th minute, the last fired into an empty goal after Alex Jackson's dribble had distracted all the opposition, including the goalkeeper.

The 50th official match of the Scotland-England series was played at Old Trafford, and an estimated 10,000 Scottish supporters travelled south for the game. *The Times* commented: 'A stranger in Manchester on Saturday night might well have fancied himself in Glasgow. Inside the ground, there was the same impression of Scottish enthusiasm and comparative indifference on the part of the English spectators'.

The Scots won 1-0, which meant that England had not beaten them since the 1920 Sheffield quagmire. Inevitably, the 36th-minute goal involved Gallacher and Jackson. The winger gave goalkeeper Taylor no chance with a shot that shook whitewash from the post on its way into the net.

BRILLIANT McMULLAN

1926-7 Success against Wales and Ireland in the first two games of the season took Scotland's remarkable run to nine wins and a draw in ten matches. That meant 19 points out of 20, the last seven won without conceding a goal, but at Hampden, England's 'Dixie' Dean broke through the Scotland defence at last with two late goals, giving England their first win in Scotland for 23 years.

Prompted by the brilliant wing-half play of Jimmy McMullan, Scotland beat Wales convincingly, with Jackson's second goal being the highlight. But Ireland had hopes of a draw until the 89th minute when Morton made it 2-0 with his second goal of the game.

Although Scotland included three new caps for the game against England, they still began favourites and needed only a draw to take their sixth outright championship in seven years. Their chances

increased dramatically when England lost centre-half Hill with an eye injury. And Scotland's victory seemed a certainty when Morton turned home Adam McLean's centre to give Scotland the lead against ten men.

Then England's weakened side struck twice to silence Hampden. Hill had returned with a heavily-bandaged head, to play outside-right, and suddenly Andy Cunningham was looking more like a veteran. Young 'Dixie' Dean twice beat Jack Harkness to the ball to score killer goals, and so ended Scotland's run of keeping a blank sheet. Four Scottish goal-keepers — Willie Harper, Willie Robb, Allan McClory and Harkness — had, between them, held out for over 747 minutes, by far the longest spell of successful defensive containment in Scotland's history.

Scotland's record in the 1920s was phenomenal — 24 wins and five draws in 34 internationals. During the record 747-minute spell of defensive contain-ment (February 1925 to April 1927) Scotland scored 20 goals without reply.

DAVIE MEIKLEJOHN

1922 to 1933: Right-half or centre-half, 15 caps, 3 goals.
Born: Govan, Glasgow, 1900.
Career: Maryhall Juniors, Rangers, Partick Thistle (manager).
Many would say that there has been no finer captain of Rangers than Davie Meiklejohn, and he was also a giant among Scotland skippers. An unruffled and versatile player, 'Meek' made 635 appearances for Rangers (493 in the League) and scored 54 goals. Perhaps his most famous goal was the coolly taken penalty which broke the deadlock in the 1928 Scottish Cup Final, paving the way for Rangers' first Cup success for 25 years. He twice captained Scotland against England.

AFTER 23 YEARS: ENGLAND WINS ACROSS THE BORDER.

A SECTION OF THE ENORMOUS CROWD OF 110,000 PEOPLE AT HAMPDEN PARK, GLASGOW, WHO SAW THEIR TEAM LOSE BY 1 GOAL TO 2.

SCOTLAND'S ONLY GOAL SCORED BY MORTON (SEEN WITH ARMS RAISED).

DEAN, OF EVERTON, RAIDS SCOTLAND'S GOAL.

ALEX JACKSON.

CIGARETTES

Scotland went to Canada in 1927. On 19 June, they gained their seventh win in eight matches when they beat Hookalls, a touring Austrian side, 4-1, although the game in Winnipeg was marred by violence. On 11 July, in Toronto, the Scots beat the Ulster United National League team 3-0. There was one surprise when Toronto beat a Scottish XI 3-2, although the Scots later had their revenge with a 10-0 win against the same team.
Full tour record:
P 18, W 17, L 1, F 99, A 17.

WEMBLEY WIZARDS

1927-8 When the season started, Scotland were in a position to boost a sensational post-war record — their 24 games since 1919 had produced 17 wins, three draws and four defeats — but their superior status took a knock with dismal results against Wales and Ireland, before they regained prestige with a stunning performance at Wembley.

In many ways, Scotland's 5-1 win over England in March 1928 was the peak performance of a fine era, but the rest of this splendid period in Scottish international history should not be forgotten.

However, early-season games with Wales and Ireland were not particularly memorable. Against the Welsh, Scotland were two goals ahead inside 15 minutes, but then came a Welsh revival. Despite Jimmy Gibson's fine performance as Scotland's centre-half, Wales forced a 2-2 draw.

There were four changes from the team originally selected to meet Ireland. The one new cap, prolific scorer Jimmy McGrory, had a frustrating baptism. The Scots had 90 per cent of the play, but Elisha Scott played a sterling game in the Irish goal. Scotland lost 1-0 to a goal from Chambers after ten minutes, after McClory had fumbled a centre.

Referee for the 1928 'Wembley Wizard' match was a Scot, Willie Bell, and he was sensible enough to wait until a fellow Scot, goalkeeper Jack Harkness, was in possession before ending the game. Harkness stuffed the ball from this famous victory under his jersey and darted to the safety of the dressing room. Years later, he handed the ball to the safekeeping of the SFA.

Scotland beat a Norwegian XI 4-0 in an unofficial international before 12,000 people in Oslo on 27 May 1929, with goals from Rankin (2), Fleming and Nisbet.

HUGHIE GALLACHER

1924 to 1935: Centre-forward, 20 caps, 24 goals.
Born: Bellshill, Lanarkshire, 1903.
Career: Bellshill Academy, Bellshill Athletic, Queen of the South, Airdrie, Newcastle United, Chelsea, Derby County, Notts County, Grimsby Town, Gateshead.
In February 1925, a small but slippery centre-forward ran through the Tynecastle mud, sending Welsh defenders slithering. He ran from the halfway-line and with only goalkeeper Gray to beat, dribbled around him and tapped the ball into the net. Hughie Gallacher had established himself as Scotland's number-one centre-forward.
In his heyday (1924-30) Gallacher won 18 caps. Of these games, 16 were won and only one lost. In 1934 he returned for two more caps but both games were lost. His scoring record was outstanding. His 22 goals in the home championship is a Scottish record and will now stand as a permanent tribute to his goalscoring genius.
Newcastle signed Gallacher from Airdrie for £6,500 in December 1925 and he skippered their championship-winning team when he was only 24. His speed in front of goal brought him plenty of rewards and he scored 387 goals in 543 Scottish and English League games. But his temper was also quick and there were dark days for him off the field, particularly when he divorced his first wife. In those days divorce was an expensive business which carried much social stigma. In 1957, Gallacher committed suicide, throwing himself in front of a train, while awaiting a charge of ill-treating his daughter.

ALEX JACKSON

1925 to 1930: Outside-right, 17 caps, 8 goals.
Born: Renton, Dunbartonshire, 1905.
Career: Renton School, Dumbarton Academy, Renton Victoria, Dumbarton, Aberdeen, Bethlehem Steel (USA), Aberdeen, Huddersfield Town, Chelsea, Ashton National, Margate, Nice (France).
Alec Jackson, who only once played in a losing Scotland team, was one of the big attractions of his generation. Handsome in every respect, he was a raiding right winger who had a happy knack of scoring by running on to left-wing centres. He was known as the 'Flying Scotsman' or 'Gay Cavalier'.
Aberdeen paid £100 for him in 1923 but Jackson and his brother, Wattie, spent a season in America where their elder brother was making good. He moved to Huddersfield when Herbert Chapman, the most successful English manager of the inter-war period, paid £5,000 for him.
Jackson's hat-trick for the 'Wembley Wizards' in 1928 was his greatest Scotland success, and two days later he scored a remarkable goal to win Huddersfield an FA Cup semi-final replay.
By the time he joined Chelsea in September 1930, Jackson was worth £8,500 but his career petered out in the big city. He kept a pub in St Martin's Lane, then had a partnership in the Queen's Hotel, Leicester Square. He died tragically in 1946, in a motoring accident.

ENGLAND 1   SCOTLAND 5
31 March 1928, at Wembley

'ON SEVERAL occasions, the little lads in navy-blue shirts took the ball, as if on a string, from one end of the field to the other without an opponent touching it,' wrote a reporter after Scotland had annihilated England.

Yet the Scots were untypically pessimistic. In contrast to the all-tartan team of 1925, only three Home-Scots faced England in 1928.

Experienced men like Hutton, McStay and Meiklejohn were omitted. Cunningham and McPhail were overlooked, and Gallacher was preferred to McGrory despite having just completed a two-month suspension. Tommy Law and 'Tiny' Bradshaw were winning their first caps, Alex James his second. It was a raw-looking team, yet the experimentation could be justified in a game which was to settle bottom place.

On the eve of the game, skipper McMullan looked at Scotland's smallest-ever forward line — only Alex Jackson stood over 5ft 6in — and told them, "Pray for rain."

The rain came and Wembley's greasy surface was ideal for the tiny Scots forwards.

In the first minute, England hit a post. The ball rebounded to McMullan who set up a move between James and Dunn. Morton clipped over a centre and Jackson headed Scotland into the lead.

Just before half-time, James made it 2-0 and Scotland dominated the second half.

James hit the bar and Hufton made fine saves before Jackson made it 3-0. Gallacher set up the fourth for James, and Jackson's hat-trick goal came from Morton.

England's 89th-minute goal came from a free-kick but there was no real chink in Scotland's defence where Bradshaw shackled 'Dixie' Dean. Bradshaw was a 'footballing' centre-half whose one fault was a liking to dribble his way out of trouble. This was his only cap and, sadly, the team of 'Wembley Wizards' came together for only one memorable afternoon.

McMullan said later that England's wing-halves had allowed the Scottish inside men too much room. Whatever the reason, the memory was a long and sweet one for Scots.

ENGLAND: Hufton; Goodall, Jones, Edwards, Wilson, Healless, Hulme, Kelly, Dean, Bradford, Smith.
SCOTLAND: Harkness; Nelson, Law, Gibson, Bradshaw, McMullan, Jackson, Dunn, Gallacher, James, Morton.

Referee: Mr Bell (Scotland)   *Attendance: 80,868*

Hughie Gallacher throws himself at the ball as Scotland attack yet again.

The Duke of York, later King George VI, meets the Scotland team (left), and (right) he watches the 'Wembley Wizards' while seated between the King and Queen of Afghanistan.

Hughie Gallacher is just beaten to the ball by England goalkeeper Hacking at Hampden in 1929.

CHEYNE'S LAST-KICK WINNER

1928-9 "It's a curious thing," mused Peter Wilson of Celtic before the 1928 Scottish Cup Final, "but in an everyday, bread-and-butter type of game, you seldom find the wind blowing at Hampden. But when it comes to the big time, then you can bet on a swirl."

In the last seconds of the game with England on 13 April 1929, the Hampden wind blew one of its most famous gusts to play a leading role in a piece of famous Scotland-England drama.

Picture the dying seconds of the game: Scotland are grateful for the 0-0 scoreline because they have lost Alex Jackson with a dislocated elbow, following a collision with England's Ernie Blenkinsop. New cap Alec Cheyne — a late replacement at inside-right for Tommy Muirhead — has been told by skipper Jimmy McMullan to stay out wide and attempt to hold the ball on the wing 'where we can come to no harm'. In Scotland's last attack, Cheyne holds the ball and wins a corner.

Cheyne takes the corner himself. The 110,512 spectators watch breathlessly as the Aberdeen player places the ball carefully at the corner-flag and then sends it sweeping over the heads of the waiting, watching players. The ball flashes into the goal-area, and then seems to slow and hover in the wind until it is taken up and carried on. A gust has swept it into the corner of the net as bewildered Englishmen look on helplessly.

Cheyne's corner was the last kick of the international season and it gave Scotland the championship by two points from an England team that looked set to share the

honours until that heart-stopping moment.

This was Scotland's busiest and most successful season to date. Not only did they win the three home internationals, but they were unbeaten in a four-match tour of the Continent from 21 May to 6 June.

The forwards were in superb form. Although Wales scored an early goal, three from Gallacher gave Scotland a commanding 3-1 lead soon after half-time. Wales were let off lightly as the Scots, who had amateur William King at centre-half, served up some of their best post-war football.

> *Alex Cheyne's goal in the 1929 Scotland-England game — two years after the law was changed to allow goals direct from corners — was not the only unusual incident of the match. An indirect free-kick was awarded under the new law concerning the goalkeeper not being allowed to carry the ball more than four steps. Confusion reigned and the Scottish defenders initially lined up behind the ball, rather than on their own goal-line. Eventually, they managed to clear their lines.*

Gallacher's display in the resounding win over Northern Ireland was even more spectacular — a hat-trick in the first 15 minutes and four altogether. Jackson did almost as he pleased on the right flank and he created five of Scotland's seven goals.

This meant that Scotland had scored 16 goals in three games, but Jackson's first-half injury against England put the Scots on the defensive and ruled the winger out

of the close-season tour, an event which included none of the 'Wembley Wizards'.

Fourteen players set off for Norway, in the charge of trainer Andy Reid (St Mirren). The first game produced a convincing 7-3 victory, although it might not have seemed likely when the Scots led only 3-2 at half-time.

A 4-0 win against a Norwegian X1 led to the big game of the tour, against Germany. Willie Imrie's header gave the Scots a first-half lead, but a 50th-minute equaliser limited Scotland to a highly creditable draw.

BROADER HORIZONS

1929-30 Although there were three excellent victories — against Wales, Ireland and France — a 5-2 defeat at Wembley soured the proceedings somewhat. Hughie Gallacher missed the England game, but his six goals in the three wins made it an excellent season for him, until he upset the Scottish selectors with his activities in Paris.

Gallacher scored twice in the first 20 minutes against Wales, then hit a post after the Welsh had pulled the game round to 2-2. Scotland won their 50th encounter

> *Although only seven capped players were included in the 1929 Scottish touring party, the trip proved a success in many ways. A crowd of 42,000 saw the game in Berlin, and there were 24,000 to watch Scotland in Amsterdam, thus convincing the SFA that there was much-needed revenue to be had in certain European cities.*

Scotland were held to a draw in Glasgow by Wales in October 1930. Here, Len Evans, the Cardiff City goalkeeper, back-punches a corner by Greenock Morton winger Danny McCrorie.

with Wales by 4-2, thanks to two goals in the last eight minutes. The first of these came from one of the many long-range efforts by Alex James, the second was registered by Jimmy Gibson from 25 yards. Fittingly, the goals went to Scotland's star schemers.

There were the usual reminders of the lasting problem of availability of players. McDougall might have won a cap against Wales, had his club, Sunderland, consented to release him as a replacement for the injured Meiklejohn. Sunderland refused, so yet another centre-half, this time Johnstone of Hearts, came in for his international debut.

Then Scotland faced an Ireland team which had beaten an 'unrepresentative' Welsh side 7-0, so there was no guide to current form. The hard, sandy Celtic Park pitch, and occasional foggy intervals, also made the outcome uncertain. Scotland dominated the second half and goals from Hughie Gallacher and George Stevenson improved the 1-1 half-time scoreline and saw the Scots home.

England's win at Wembley was some revenge for their defeat two years previously, although it could never dim the memory of those 'Wembley Wizards', especially as Scotland had so much play in the 1930 game.

There were necessary last-minute changes, caused by the withdrawal of Gibson and Gallacher, who was aiding a struggling Newcastle side.

England outside-right Sammy Crooks gave Tommy Law a nightmare first half as the home team scored four goals in the 33 minutes preceding the interval. Scotland, with six Rangers players, fought back with Fleming's two goals.

The game with France was Scotland's first *official* international with a foreign country. An easy victory and healthy receipts were followed by a leisurely week of sight-seeing. Scotland now had an appetite for foreign opposition and a tour of Austria, Italy and Switzerland was arranged for the following year.

> Rangers contributed six of the team which played England in 1930 — Dougie Gray, Jock Buchanan, Davie Meiklejohn, 'Tully' Craig, Jimmy Fleming and Alan Morton.

A FAMOUS VICTORY

1930-31 Following an outcry surrounding the previous season's Scotland-England game, when Gallacher was playing for Newcastle while opponents Arsenal released Jack and James, the Football League placed a ban on its clubs releasing players to any country other than England.

This severely hampered the progress of Scotland, Wales and Ireland. Even when players were released, the association involved usually had to beg, giving three weeks' notice, and pay an insurance premium and a week's wages. The decision by the

BOB McPHAIL

1927 to 1938: Inside-left, 17 caps, 7 goals.
Born: Barrhead, Renfrewshire, 1905.
Career: Braehead Ashgrove, Glasgow Pollok, Airdrie, Rangers.
In the days when inside-forward trekked up and down the field, attacking and defending, Bob McPhail was the epitome of the all-round player. Not only was he hard-working but his career aggregate of 305 League goals (for Airdrie and Rangers) is second only to Jimmy McGrory.
McPhail joined Rangers in April 1927 for £5,000 from Airdrie, who had been forced to sell Gallacher and McPhail inside 18 months. By the time McPhail retired, in January 1941, he was the proud possessor of seven Scottish Cup winners' medals, eight Charity Cup medals, seven Glasgow Cup medals and nine League championship awards. And he is still the holder of the Rangers career goalscoring record.
McPhail's greatest moments for Scotland came late in the 1937 game against England when his two goals excited the record crowd to fever pitch and swung the game in the Scots' favour.

Football League undoubtedly proved a watershed between the all-conquering Scottish teams of the 1920s, and the merely successful teams of the 1930s.

Fielding 'all-tartan' teams, Scotland used 25 players in three home internationals, starting the season disastrously with a home draw against Wales.

Unable to call upon any First Division players, and limited to players from Welsh clubs, Wales fielded the most 'scratch' team in their history. It comprised Fred Keenor and ten others, three of whom were amateurs.

It seemed simply a question of how many Scotland would score. There was a feeling that if Scotland won 20-0, then it would do football a service in highlighting the international farce and bringing the game to its senses.

When Bamford volleyed in a Welsh goal after six minutes, spectators took heart that the visitors might, after all, put up a reasonable show. They did just that and although Barney Battles equalised just before half-time, Scotland struggled in the second half and had to settle for a 1-1 draw.

The selectors made wholesale changes for the game against Northern Ireland, but their reward was another poor result. Scotland won the toss but little else. Goalkeeper John Thomson did not touch the ball until a few minutes before the interval, but the Scottish forwards failed to capitalise on a fierce wind and the outcome was a goalless draw.

Inevitably, there were yet more changes for the England game. Only John Thomson and Alan Morton played in all three home internationals. Tragically, the England match was also to be Thomson's last international. Five months later, the Celtic goalkeeper dived at the feet of Rangers forward Sam English in the Glasgow derby and died in hospital from his injuries.

England were clear favourites to win at Hampden. They had scored a total of nine goals aainst Ireland and Wales, while the troubled Scots tried another much-changed combination. Miller and McNab were surprise choices at half-back, Stevenson was played at inside-right rather than his usual inside-left position, and winger Sandy Archibald, now 33, was brought back after seven years in the international wilderness.

Scotland won the toss and played with the wind in their favour. Despite that advantage, the Scots reached the interval still 0-0 and England looked forward to taking charge in the second half.

But they reckoned without the Hampden Roar. The noise from the majority of the record crowd of 129,810 was deafening as they took up the challenge and willed their team on. For their part, the Scottish players kept the ball on the ground and tried to retain possession at all costs, denying England the chance to sweep forward with the wind gusting at their backs.

Scotland won a debatable corner, Archibald miskicked and the ball flew off Blenkinsop. Goalkeeper Hibbs got a hand to it, but succeeded only in knocking it to George Stevenson, and the delighted Scot whipped it into the back of the net. Jimmy McGrory got a second and the 'veteran' Scots had won a famous victory.

If only Scotland could have taken the Hampden Roar with them on their summer tour. In Vienna, Liddell and McNab were

A not so happy visit to Wembley. Top: Scottish goalkeeper Tommy Hamilton watches as England hit a post during the 1932 international. Bottom: In the same match, which Scotland lost, Hamilton collides with 'Pongo' Waring.

injured — Liddell had to leave the field — and Scotland tumbled 5-0, their first defeat by foreign opposition.

In Italy, the roar was 'Duce, Duce,' as Mussolini saw his country's footballers win easily (3-0), although he rated Danny Blair as the best player on the field.

The poor results might have been explained by staleness after a long season, or the unaccustomed heat, or the absence of players from Rangers, Celtic and Motherwell. Another reason was that British football still underrated foreign opposition. One critic wrote that the home game was too insular, and too content to let the world go by. And although some damage was repaired against the Swiss, the summer tour of 1931 was a colossal shake-up for Scottish football.

GEORGE STEVENSON

1927 to 1934: Inside-forward, 12 caps, 4 goals.
Born: Kilbirnie, Ayrshire, 1905.
Career: Lochwinnoch Viewfield, Kilbirnie Ladeside, Motherwell, Motherwell (manager).
At Motherwell, George Stevenson formed a brilliant left-wing partnership with Bob Ferrier. Aided by free-scoring centre-forward Willie McFadyen, they helped Motherwell to their first-ever championship in 1931-2. Unfortunately, Stevenson never played in a Scotland team with either Ferrier or McFadyen. Ferrier was English by birth, while McFadyen's two caps were when Stevenson was out of the team. Stevenson was an inside-left, although he occasionally played inside-right for Scotland. He made 513 Scottish League appearances, and his son-in-law, Jim Forrest, was a Motherwell and Scotland player in the 1950s.

MORTON'S RECORD

1931-2 Scotland and England came to contest their Wembley international each with maximum points. Alan Morton broke a Scottish record by winning his 30th cap, but the Scots went down, rather unluckily, 3-0 with a depleted 'all-tartan' eleven.

Against Northern Ireland, Hepburn of Ayr took over from the much-lamented John Thomson, and although Davie Meiklejohn missed a penalty, Scotland still won easily.

It was a penalty by Curtis of Wales that put Scotland behind in the next game. The Scots recovered from that 15th-minute set-back to take the lead before half-time. McGrory escaped the Welsh offside trap in the second half, and a Scottish win was never in doubt, despite a typically Welsh onslaught near the end.

At Wembley, Scotland were without the injured McPhail and Meiklejohn, and Anglo-Scots like Gallacher were also missing. At centre-forward was Neil Dewar, a prolific scorer with Third Lanark.

In the early stages, Scotland threatened with their short passing and Morton almost deceived goalkeeper Pearson with a lob. George Brown was forced into an unfamiliar defensive role, but the Scots were unlucky with England's first two goals. Waring's header rolled slowly over the line, and Barclay's shot went in off a defender. England's third goal, from winger Crooks, came two minutes from time.

Dewar's big breakthrough came in France where the centre-forward scored three times in the first 35 minutes before France pulled one back from the penalty spot.

HUMILIATION AT TYNECASTLE

1932-3 There were two good wins — against Northern Ireland and England — but in between came a humiliating rout at the hands of the Welsh, whose win at Tynecastle was achieved with only ten fit men for much of the game.

Welsh outside-right Phillips was carried off with an injured left leg after his team went ahead through Jock Thomson's own-goal. Phillips resumed, limping badly, but almost unbelievably, his side led 4-0 at half-time.

Phillips did not return for the second half, but that did not deter the Welsh who scored a fifth within a minute of the restart when O'Callaghan netted his second of the game. For Fred Keenor, playing his last international for Wales, the Tynecastle match had been a triumph.

Scotland could only point to the absence of Gallacher, McPhail and Massie from a team which included only one Anglo-Scot — Derby's 'Dally' Duncan — and no player with more than seven caps.

There were nine changes for the England game. Only the wingers retained their places, and Alex James said that he was unfit and pulled out, only to play for Arsenal on the day of the international. The ignominious defeat by Wales proved to be his final appearance in a Scottish shirt. James, the master of midfield, and

JIMMY McGRORY

1928 to 1934: Centre-forward, 7 caps, 6 goals.
Born: Glasgow, 1904.
Career: St Roch's (Glasgow), Celtic, Kilmarnock (manager), Celtic (manager).
When he was signed by Willie Maley in 1922, Jimmy McGrory was hailed as a second Jimmy Quinn, whom he resembled in build and courage. However, McGrory established a far superior reputation with 397 goals in 378 League games for Celtic, and well over 500 in all first-class games. McGrory was not as skilful as some players, but his strength, stamina and alertness worried defenders. He converted chances with either foot and especially with his head. He came to the fore just as the offside law was changed and in one game against Dunfermline in 1928, he scored eight goals.
He was a Scotland legend but his international appearances were limited by the presence of Gallacher in the Scotland team at a crucial time. His winning goal against England in 1933 set off one of the earliest – and loudest – Hampden Roars.

the man famous for his baggy shorts, was well and truly out of favour.

Bob Gillespie was included at centre-half, despite having virtually retired. A late replacement for Meiklejohn, Gillespie captained the team and, like Jimmy Crawford, was an amateur. It was the first time that two amateurs had appeared in the same Scotland team since Alex Christie and RS McColl, 34 years previously.

At Hampden, given the spirit of the Scots and a roaring record crowd, the

HIBBS, IN GOAL FOR ENGLAND, WATCHES A SHOT BY McGRORY CROSS THE LINE. AN ENGLISH DEFENDER LOOKS ROUND AT THE REFEREE, ANXIOUS TO KNOW WHETHER A CORNER WILL BE AWARDED.

134,170 People see Scotland beat England.

Superior play beats the Sassenach at Glasgow.

It was Scotland's day for football last Saturday. At Dublin they were winning the Rugby championship at the expense of Ireland, while at Hampden Park, Glasgow, they overcame the England soccer eleven by two goals to one. The attendance at Glasgow, 134,170 people, was the greatest football crowd of which there is any official record. When Arnold of Fulham had an equalising goal at his mercy he shot outside and though later on England made it one all, Scotland had by then got through an anxious time and were playing the sounder football. On the whole the English full-backs were not equal to their task.

A VIEW FROM THE AIR OF HAMPDEN PARK, GLASGOW, THE HOME OF THE FAMOUS RANGERS: NOTE THE COMPARATIVE ABSENCE OF COVERED SEATS.

THE FIRST OF SCOTLAND'S TWO GOALS: McGRORY, THE SCOTTISH CENTRE-FORWARD, IS BEATING HIBBS IN THE ENGLISH GOAL. McPHAIL, THE SCOTTISH FORWARD WHO WITH DUNCAN HAD A SHARE IN THIS DAZZLING GOAL, IS SEEN RUNNING FORWARD TO CONGRATULATE McGRORY.

JOE NIBLOE

1929 to 1932: Full-back, 11 caps.
Born: Cockerhill, Renfrewshire, 1904.
Career: Shawfield Juniors, Rutherglen
Glencairn, Kilmarnock, Aston Villa,
Sheffield Wednesday.
When Joe Nibloe was 27, Aston Villa
paid Kilmarnock £1,900 for his transfer,
and this effectively stopped him winning
further international caps. He was
capped at left-back and is one of the
few men to have won both a Scottish
Cup winners, medal (with Kilmarnock),
and an FA Cup-winners' medal (at
right-back with Sheffield Wednesday).

Welsh debacle was swept aside and England were beaten 2-1, both goals coming from Jimmy McGrory.

'Magrorious,' shouted one fan, eight minutes from time, after the centre-forward had collected McPhail's subtle pass and shot the winner. The goals ensured McGrory lasting fame in the annals of Scottish international football, but the man who was the Scottish League's most prolific goalscorer, suffered from being a contemporary of Gallacher and won only seven caps. Like James — and like Celtic's stylish wing-half Peter Wilson — he was generally recognised as being 'undercapped' considering his ability. Wilson in particular was ever in the shadow of Meiklejohn, but was still a superb wing half.

DARK DAYS

1933-4 Nobody could remember such a bad season. All three home internationals were lost, and the fortunate draw with Austria was achieved in a tough encounter, an early example of the ill-feeling which has dogged Scotland-Austria matches over the years.

The selectors called on no less than 34 players for the season's four games, but no combination gave satisfaction. Northern Ireland's veteran goalkeeper Elisha Scott saved a Scottish penalty and Northern Ireland took a 2-0 lead by half-time. Despite Bob McPhail's reply, Northern Ireland secured their fourth victory in 46 encounters with Scotland.

The Scottish League had already lost to the Irish League, so Scottish football was on trial when Wales won the game at Cardiff. Scotland started well against an exceptional Welsh team — Jimmy Easson hit a post and Welshman Ben Ellis cleared off the line from his own back-pass — but trailed 3-0 after only 57 minutes. Two late consolation goals did little to ease the pain.

> *Harry McMenemy, son of 'Napoleon', was named in the Scotland team to meet Wales in October 1933, but he was injured and his brother John was called up to replace him. It was John McMenemy's only international, while Harry was never capped.*

Tempers flared at Hampden after Platzer, the Austrian goalkeeper was shoulder-charged in typically British fashion by Willie McFadyen. Early in the game, the Scots looked likely winners, with McPhail and Duncan reproducing the fine form that had destroyed England's right flank the previous season. Scotland took the lead twice, but in the end they were glad of the draw.

A little Scottish pride was restored in the second half of the game at Wembley. England led by a first-half Bastin goal, but the Scots pressed strongly in the first half hour of the second period. Then came a 25-yard free-kick from Brook, and England were two ahead. Two minutes from the end, Bowers headed a third past 'Jakey' Jackson, the Scotland goalkeeper who had been called up from Chelsea Reserves.

> *The last amateur to captain Scotland was Bob Gillespie who led the team against England in 1933.*

GOALKEEPING PROBLEMS

1934-5 Following the previous poor season, Scotland suffered one of their most humiliating blows in Belfast when Northern Ireland's ten men beat them. But victories over England and Wales turned the tide, and the slump of the mid-1930s was over.

Scotland's temporary demise had coincided with changing roles on the field. To counteract, Big Jimmy Simpson was introduced as Scotland's first 'stopper' centre-half, and his international debut was marked by an upsetting incident when Ireland's goalkeeper Elisha Scott suffered a split head saving from Jimmy Smith, and did not reappear after half-time.

Ireland were trailing to a goal from Hughie Gallacher's deflected shot, so with wing-half McMillan in goal, and playing with four forwards, the Irish looked out of luck.

Yet Scotland found the going harder against ten men. The Irish crowd roared

JOE KENNAWAY

> *Before playing for Scotland in 1934, Canadian-born goalkeeper Joe Kennaway played for Canada (against USA in 1928) and for USA (against Canada in 1930). He is the only Scottish international to have played for two other countries and one of the very few footballers to have been capped by three different nations.*

their approval as McMillan pulled off a string of remarkable saves, then in the 80th minute, Martin equalised from close-range. Scotland temporarily lost Stevenson, and in the final minute they lost the game. Gowdy lobbed the ball into a crowded goalmouth and Coulter scored to earn Ireland an astonishing victory.

In changing more than half their team, Scotland called on their fifth goalkeeper in five games when they met Wales. The kick-off was scheduled for 2.20pm on a Wednesday, typical of the problematical arrangements in these pre-floodlight days. The outcome was Scotland's best performance for years.

The late introduction of Tommy Walker meant that Bob McPhail was not missed, especially as Charlie Napier, the man they called 'Happy Feet', helped Duncan form a devastating left-wing. Scotland were never in danger of losing, and their three goals were all initiated by Duncan. First came a deflected shot, then two perfect crosses for Napier to score.

This game ended a run of five official internationals without a win, the longest

CHARLIE NAPIER

barren spell known to Scotland at this time.

Even though Napier was moved to outside-right for the game against England, he still combined sensationally with Duncan. Two Napier corners were headed home by the left-winger, one in each half. The gates had been closed 40 minutes before the start, but this was a poor England team and a sub-standard international. Wrote one journalist: 'Three well-known football writers and myself fought our way to Hampden Park, and we were all unlucky. We got in'.

> Scotland won all 12 games of their 1935 four-week tour to North America, beating Hamilton 10-1, and scoring nine goals against both Calgary and Kitchener. Matches were also played against Philadelphia, New York, Toronto, Chicago, Winnipeg and Montreal. The Scotland trainer was Arthur Dixon.

PENALTY THRILLER

1935-6 Fifteen minutes from the end of an uplifting, entertaining match at Wembley, England were leading 1-0 when Eddie Hapgood clattered Johnny Crum, and Scotland were awarded a penalty. It was a moment of high drama, because Scotland needed a goal to clinch the home championship.

The duty fell to young Tommy Walker, who placed the ball on the spot and stepped back, only for the wind to blow the ball its own circumference from the mark. Walker replaced the ball and stepped

> When Scotland toured North America in 1935, American journalists dubbed Tommy Walker 'the Babe Ruth of British Soccer'. In 1921 they had called Andy Wilson by the same title. Scotland won all 13 games, beating the United States 5-1 and 4-1. The first game, at the New York Polo Grounds, attracted the biggest US soccer crowd for nine years and they saw a fine display by 6ft 4in American goalkeeper Stanley Chesney keep the score down.

back again. Again the wind shifted the leather from the spot.

Behind the goal, Crum was watching in pain, receiving treatment. Half the Scottish team were not watching at all, having not dared to look as Walker made his third attempt at the penalty. This time the wind obligingly dropped, and the ball stayed on the spot long enough for Walker to take a short run and shoot fiercely past Sagar's right hand.

That made the score 1-1 and gave Scotland the championship with just four points. Their 4-2 victory over England early in the season, in a match arranged to swell Glasgow's contribution to King George V's Jubilee Fund, had nothing more at stake than pride. One feature of this unofficial international was England's use of an outfield substitute — Smith for Bray at half-time — for the first time.

Wales surprised the Scots in the first championship game. Both teams played the 'third-back' game, and the Scots took the lead, but Wales equalised before half-time.

The Ireland game proved a reversal of the previous season. This time, the Irish took the lead (Kelly from 20 yards in the 49th minute), Scotland equalised (a wonderful shot from Walker) and then came the Scots' turn for a last-ditch winner when Duncan made it 2-1 in the dying seconds.

Then Walker's penalty raised a mighty roar from the tens of thousands of Scots at Wembley. "The Scots were in seventh heaven, but it was amusing to note grown men kissing each other," wrote Trevor Wignall in the *Daily Express* "Hugging and hand-shaking and kissing at a football match — is it any wonder that foreigners deny we of our race can keep our emotions in hand?"

GERMANY AT HAMPDEN

1936-7 One of the busiest seasons to date was also one of the most successful, and the only defeat in six matches was an unlucky one against Wales, who went on to win the championship.

The first game of the season, against Hitler's Germany, caused much controversy before it finally took place. Owing to traffic congestion, the German team arrived late at Hampden and the start was delayed for 18 minutes. The crowd were irritated, and then frustrated as the German defence held out for an hour before Jimmy Delaney snapped up a lucky rebound. Ten minutes

from time, the same player cut in and scored a splendid goal. Delaney collided with the goalkeeper and had to leave the field, but returned and almost completed a hat-trick.

More prestige was recovered when Scotland fought back from a one-goal deficit to beat Ireland convincingly. A record Windsor Park crowd meant that police reinforcements were needed to deal with gate-crashers, but there were no encroachments on the field.

> **GEORGE BROWN**
>
> **1931 to 1938: Left-half, 19 caps.**
> **Born: Glasgow, 1907.**
> **Career: John Street School (Glasgow), Glasgow Ashfield, Rangers.**
> George Brown took over the left-half position a couple of years after Jimmy McMullan's international career had ended, and the two men had similar qualities. Both were placid, skilful and fine tacticians. Brown never thumped the ball, but always stroked his passes. He came into his own against continental opposition, playing brilliantly against Austria (1933) and Czechoslovakia (1937).
> Brown was a schoolmaster by profession, a graduate of Glasgow University, and he succeeded in combining two careers, although this was not always easy. When Scotland played Wales on a Wednesday afternoon in 1934, he had to arrange leave from his 'scholastic duties'.
> Brown, fair-haired and of gentle manner, was a silky player whose finesse was well-suited to Alan Morton, but the two overlapped all too briefly at the end of Morton's career. For a long period, Brown prompted McPhail and Duncan, while at club level he won a remarkable seven championship medals as Rangers dominated the 1930s. He later became a director at Ibrox.

Then came the unfortunate defeat by Wales. Bobby Ancell was injured soon after the start, while Willie Mills (playing in place of the injured Napier) and Tommy Walker both hit a post, and there was disappointment for the 23,858 who watched the first international to be played in Dundee for 28 years (and which proved to be the last). The reshuffled Scottish team had Ancell on the left wing in the second half. Although they equalised, Scotland lost to Glover's 80th-minute goal.

An agreement, reached in the summer of 1934, had slightly eased the availability of Anglo-Scots, and there were four in the team to play England at Hampden. A world record crowd of 149,547 roared Scotland to victory. "If ever a match was won and lost by a roar, it was this game," said Stanley Matthews, the new England outside-right.

> A member of the 149,000 crowd for the 1937 Scotland-England game at Hampden Park told Bob McPhail later: 'I didn't have room to move.' I was almost squeezed to death.' McPhail replied, "You should have been where I was, I had plenty of room." McPhail scored two late goals to give Scotland victory.

ALEX MASSIE

1931 to 1937: Right-half, 18 caps, 1 goal.
Born: Possilpark, Glasgow, 1906.
Career: Peterhill, Glasgow Benburb, Glasgow Ashfield, Partick, Ayr United, Bethlehem Steel (USA), Dolphin (Dublin), Hearts, Aston Villa, Aston Villa (manager), Torquay United (manager), Hereford United (manager). Alex Massie started as an inside-forward, but Hearts converted him to wing-half and in that position he won all his caps. He never lost his flair for attack, however, and his superb ball control tempted Villa to pay £5,000 when they signed him from Hearts in December 1935.

Steele's 40th-minute goal was poor reward for England's dominance of the first half, but Scotland's recovery was an epic. Pipers paraded at the interval and the Scots delayed their entrance on to the field. Referee McLean (Northern Ireland) walked impatiently up and down the half-way line, the England players kicked their heels, and then came the deafening roar which signalled that the Scottish team were on their way. From then on, the sheer atmosphere of Hampden seemed to will the ball towards the England goal.

Frank O'Donnell quickly equalised Steele's goal, then George Brown, Tommy Walker and Bob McPhail found each other with seemingly magnetic accuracy. The others joined in and victory was only a matter of time. Eventually, two goals in the last 12 minutes, both from McPhail, saw that justice was done. One was a 15-yard shot, the other a header.

Scotland were in buoyant mood when they left to play Austria for the third time, and Czechoslovakia for the first. Austria, managed by Hugo Meisl, the 'Herbert Chapman' of European football, were formidable opponents, especially when Massie pulled a muscle after ten minutes. Scotland's ten men took the lead, but drew 1-1 with Massie limping on the wing.

Everyone in the touring party was given a game, and the left-wing trio of Brown, McPhail and Torry Gillick starred in the comfortable win over the Czechs.

WALKER STARS

1937-8 Scotland's bad run against Wales continued — the Scots had won only once in the last six meetings — but defeat in Cardiff was the only black mark on an otherwise successful season.

Wales played the offside trap to counter the delicate skills of inside-forward artists Walker and McPhail. The Scots trailed 2-0 and Alex Massie's late goal was the only consolation in a revival against a Welsh side reduced to ten men for the last 20 minutes.

Ireland and Scotland then virtually eliminated each other from the championship by playing out a draw in Aberdeen. The men who caught the eye were inside-forwards Peter Doherty, wearing a number ten on his back, and Tommy Walker, whose shirt-back was blank.

Doherty scored after 15 minutes and hit a post as Ireland dominated the first-half. Walker laid on Jimmy Smith's 48th-minute equaliser. McPhail was missing for 15 minutes of the second half after being stretchered off, but he returned to limp on the left wing. It was his last international appearance.

Czechoslovakia had run England to 5-4 a week previously, but the Scots scored in the first minute. Goalkeeper Planicka mishandled Buchanan's centre, and Andy Black shot home. There followed an hour's defence, then Dave McCulloch's goal began a 5-0 avalanche.

The Anglo-quota was raised to eight — FA Cup Finalists Preston provided four

— when England were beaten on their own soil in a poor game. Fittingly, the only goal went to Tommy Walker, who breasted down Frank O'Donnell's back-header, swerved past his marker and drove the ball high into the net.

This was Scotland's first shut-out at Wembley — there has only been one since (1981) — and was achieved by goalkeeper Dave Cumming, who was winning his only peace-time cap.

In the final game, the first official international against Holland, Walker headed in Alex Munro's cross to give his side a 3-0 lead. After a goalless first half, Scotland cruised to a 3-1 win.

WALKER'S SCREAMER

1938-9 Scotland were now *the* team to beat. Victories over Northern Ireland, Wales and Hungary meant six successive wins, and the stage was set for a remarkable finále to the season. England had not won at Hampden for 12 years and they found the pitch there like a gluepot after a heavy

DOUGLAS 'DALLY' DUNCAN.

1932 to 1937: Outside-left, 14 caps, 7 goals.
Born: Aberdeen, 1909.
Career: Aberdeen Richmond, Hull City, Derby County, Luton Town (player-coach, then manager), Blackburn Rovers (manager).
Dally Duncan had the ideal blend for a winger. He could dally, hence his nickname, and demonstrate his skills on the ball, but he could also speed down the wing and finish with a perfect centre or ruthless shot. He scored over 100 Football League goals, a particularly good figure for a winger, while for Scotland he averaged a goal every other game. Two he remembers best were from headers in front of nearly 130,000 people at Hampden.

Two England players, Sam Barkas and Eric Brook, were involved in a car accident on their way to play against Scotland at Newcastle on 2 December 1939. Replacements had to be found at the ground and a Scot, Newcastle's Tommy Pearson, turned out for England in place of Brook. Pearson, who later played for and managed Aberdeen, represented Scotland after the war.

TOMMY WALKER OBE

1934 to 1939: Inside-forward, 20 caps, 9 goals.
Born: Livingstone, West Lothian, 1915.
Career: Livingstone Violet, Broxburn Rangers, Linlithgow Rose, Hearts, Chelsea, Hearts (asst. manager, then manager), Dunfermline (administration manager), Raith Rovers (manager, then secretary).
Starting with a schoolboy cap, Tommy Walker went on to become one of Scotland's greatest internationals, yet he never won a medal in his 14 years at Hearts, or during his brief spell with Chelsea who he joined for £8,000 in 1946.
But for the war he would most likely have beaten Alan Morton's record number of caps. Walker played in 11 Wartime or Victory internationals, and on one occasion he apparently kitted out an entire Scotland wartime side with a collection of his pre-war international shirts.
He played mostly at inside-right, ice-cool, and a gentleman on and off the field. His passing and dribbling were as good as anyone of his era, his shooting probably harder, and in the 1930s, Hearts rated him as priceless.
His intention to become a minister was probably frustrated by the war and instead he became a highly successful football manager. In 15 years at Hearts he steered them to two championships, while the international players under his wing included the 'terrible trio' of Alfie Conn, Willie Bauld and Jimmy Wardhaugh, as well as Dave Mackay, Alex Young, Davie Holt, Willie Wallace, Jimmy Murray and Jim Cruickshank. Awarded the OBE in 1960, Walker was later a Hearts director for six years.

JERRY DAWSON

1934 to 1939: Goalkeeper, 14 caps.
Born: Falkirk, 1909.
Career: Camelon Juniors, Rangers, Falkirk, East Fife (manager).
Christened James, but nicknamed Jerry after a famous Burnley and England goalkeeper (Jeremiah Dawson), Jerry Dawson had excellent positional sense and agility. He was a safe rather than spectacular goalkeeper, although he did have a peculiar curving run when taking goalkicks.
Dawson succeeded Tom Hamilton at Ibrox, and in his first 'Old Firm' game he was the Rangers goalkeeper when John Thomson of Celtic received a fatal injury in the other goalmouth. Thomson might have held the Scotland position for years, but Dawson got his chance in 1934 and became undisputed first-choice, known as the 'Prince of Goalkeepers' when he retired at his peak.
His display at Hampden in the first half of the 1937 England game kept Scotland in with a chance and set them up for one of the most memorable second halves. He continued to play for Scotland until April 1943.

JIMMY SIMPSON

1935 to 1937: Centre-half, 14 caps 1 goal.
Born: Ladybank, Fife, 1908.
Career: Auchtermuchty Bellevue, Newburgh West End, Dundee United, Rangers.
Lanky Jimmy Simpson was a pioneer of the change to the 'third-back game' whereby the centre-half stayed back rather than acted as a conveyor belt between defence and attack. He played in all 14 internationals that took place between October 1934 and November 1937, becoming established as Scotland's captain. His son, Ronnie Simpson, kept goal for Queen's Park, Third Lanark, Newcastle United, Celtic and Scotland after the war, and played in the Celtic team which won the 1967 European Cup. Jimmy Simpson captained Scotland 13 times, which at the time equalled Charlie Thomson's record. However, Simpson's leadership was a continuous period, bettered since only by George Young (captain in 32 consecutive internationals) and Eric Caldow (15). A serious ankle injury caused Simpson to miss the game against Czechoslovakia (Dec 1937) and thus end his run.

Scotland first wore numbered shirts for the game against England on 14 October 1944. Earlier that year, a proposal to introduce them had been defeated on the chairman's casting vote. He said, 'Numbers are all right for horses and greyhounds, but not for humans.'

Scotland goalkeeper Dave Cumming and his defenders keep England at bay in April 1938. Although he kept a clean sheet it was Cumming's only peacetime cap.

downpour which persisted throughout the match.

Midway through the first half, Hampden's green scarred by ugly black weals where the players had slipped and slid, Scotland went ahead. The ball was played across the face of the England goal, stuck in the mud, and Dougall raced in to hammer it past the helpless Woodley.

In the second half, both sides defied the gusting wind and driving rain to produce a soccer classic. With 20 minutes to play, England drew level when Beasley of Arsenal cracked a wonderful drive past the groping fingers of Jerry Dawson, arguably Scotland's greatest goalkeeper since Jack Harkness.

The rain was now getting even worse and the players found it increasingly difficult to control the ball. Yet, urged on by the mighty Hampden Roar, they continued to snap at each other's throats, searching for the goal which would surely settle the international championship.

Two minutes from the end, it came. Matthews took a Goulden lob, ghosted past McNab, rounded Cummings, and curled the ball on to the head of Lawton who was waiting to bullet it past Dawson.

It had been a superb game and Matthews, the man who had laid on the winner, recalled afterwards: "The England team shook hands like a bunch of school kids, while Hapgood danced on the pitch, and in the dressing room a few minutes later, tossed his boots in the air in sheer exuberance."

Hapgood said, "I've played all these years and this is the win I've longed for. I could have jumped over the moon in delight." Perhaps that was the first time a footballer confessed that he was 'over the moon'.

In their first three games of the season, Scotland had shown superiority, although they began slowly against Wales and trailed to a superb goal by Astley. In the 83rd minute, with the score at 1-1, the crowd were treated to two pieces of vintage Tommy Walker. First, he beat two men

BOS

ANDY ANDERSON

1933 to 1938: Right back, 23 caps. Born: Airdrie, 1909. Career: Baillieston Juniors, Hearts. Andy Anderson was a sure-footed, reliable full-back who broke the existing Scottish record for consecutive international appearances. He played 16 times without a break, surpassing the previous best of 12 held jointly by Alec Smith, Bobby Walker and Andy Wilson. Anderson, a joiner by trade, was with Hearts for ten years before retiring in 1939.

Conditions were so bad at Hampden on 15 April 1939, that both teams changed their shirts at half-time. England borrowed a set from Queen's Park.

and scored with a screamer; then he hit one from fully 30 yards.

When Walker scored from the penalty spot in the 19th minute of the Hungary game, he equalled Andy Wilson's record of scoring in five successive internationals. The penalty came after a trip on Andy Black, who afterwards intercepted a clearance by the Hungarian goalkeeper and scored from 30 yards. But then Black broke his collar-bone and Scotland, a man short, were pulled back to 3-1.

In the summer of 1939, with war in Europe looming, Scotland toured Canada and the USA.

Scotland's close season tour to North America saw them win 13 of their 14 games, with one drawn. One game in Vancouver was played under floodlights, and a match against the American League was the first time that a Scottish team had been involved in extra-time. With the score at 2-2, another 30 minutes were played and Jimmy Carabine, who had scored an equaliser, completed his hat-trick and Scotland won 4-2. Another outstanding achievement was Archie Garrett's seven goals in St Louis. In Detroit, Scotland were losing 1-0 at half-time to a Michigan team. They pulled back to win 7-1.

When Ben Ellis of Motherwell played for Scotland on the 1939 North American tour, he had already received six Welsh caps in the 1930s.

Looking Back ....

Bob McPhail Remembers

MY FIRST schoolboy international was at Swansea, and the trip down was the first time I'd been on a train with a restaurant. Schoolboy games were under-14 in those days. They put a second crossbar on the goals, a foot below the other. The badge I got for that schoolboy international I treasure most of all. It's in a casket at Ibrox now, along with my other medals, over 30 of them.

I won a Scottish Cup badge at Airdrie, where I also won my first cap — a boy amongst men. At the time there was an old fellow, the Queen's Park trainer, who went around with a wee thimbleful and gave a drop to each Scottish player. I thought, if it's good enough for Jimmy McMullan, Hughie Gallacher, Alan Morton and the like, then it's good enough for me. I think it was port, or perhaps brandy. Anyway, I'd never tasted either. What with the excitement and the thimbleful....

I played with Hughie Gallacher at Airdrie. Hughie had a great understanding with an outside-right called Jimmy Reid who used to drop them at the far post for him. One day I got there first and headed a goal. Hughie gave me a real tongue-lashing: "That's my job. You've no right to be there." He was a real character.

At Rangers I played with Alan Morton, a small man with a long stride. He could gallop and he could dodge players. Morton gave you the ball, not when he'd finished with it, but when he wanted to start with it.

· One day I slammed a ball a foot over Morton's head. He didn't jump an inch, just looked at me and said, "Big fellow, the game is called FOOT-ball." There was no answer to that.

One day, playing for the Scottish League against the English League, George Male had been clattering me. Alan Morton called for the ball, pushed it through Male's legs, went back —and did the same again. That quietened the big fellow.

I preferred inside-left — though I once had to move over to inside-right to accommodate Alex James in a representative game. I had more options at inside-left because I liked to use my right foot best.

Andy Cunningham was at inside-right, a big fellow who was all left foot. He had a terrific shot in it. It was opposite to what you might expect, but it worked.

Jimmy McGrory was a marvellous man to have in your side. If you mishit a ball, made a bad pass, it never seemed like a bad pass because there was nothing hopeless for Jimmy. He chased it and lots of times it came off. His heading was terrific. He was strongly built with a thick-set neck.

We had lots of fun in those days. Alan Morton would say, "See if your pal's here today, Bob." I'd kick the ball over the bar into the crowd and a voice would call out: "Hard luck, Bobby. Try again, Bobby. Better luck next time." I'd say to Alan, "Aye, he's there. I'll be alright today."

George Brown was a fine player. He wouldn't go into a tackle unless he was dead sure. We played Partick and they had Peter McKenna — 'Ma Ba' McKenna — who was all the rage at that time.

George Brown said, "Leave him to me." George never let McKenna over the halfway line. He took him all the way across the pitch, from left touchline to right.

Dally Duncan Remembers

EVEN though I won an FA Cup winners' medal with Derby, playing for Scotland was the top honour in my career. That's the reason I went to Derby, to get into the Scotland side, because they had a lot of internationals at the Baseball Ground, and I reckoned my best chance of recognition lay there alongside so many fine players.

I was dedicated to football. I played for Aberdeen Schoolboys at 11 and I always went along to watch the Dons whenever I could. It paid off and I played in all three matches for Scotland Schoolboys in 1923-4.

After playing for Aberdeen Richmond, I was invited to Hull for a trial. It was the first time I'd been to England but I soon settled and in 1930, when Hull reached the FA Cup semi-final, scouts were buzzing around me and that's when I moved to Derby.

I was soon in the Scotland team, playing my first game against Wales at Tynecastle. Although I scored, we got beat 5-2 and I thought, oh dear, that's the end of me. But I never looked back and played right up to the war.

Bob McPhail was a fine player, a big fellow who could shift — and who could hit a ball, too.

Charlie Napier fitted in like a glove. He had a great burst of speed over 20 or 30 yards, and I was supposed to be the same. Charlie also had a terrific shot.

Once, against England, Hughie Gallacher needed two goals to beat some record. We scored two — but it was me, not Hughie, who got them. They were two headers, both from Napier corners. You'd never dream that Charlie could play outside-right — his left foot was his best — but the selectors couldn't leave him out because he'd played a blinder against Wales at Aberdeen in the previous international.

Hughie called me a few names that day, but overall I got on with him very well. I know he had a reputation, but when he was sober, you couldn't have wished to meet a more charming fellow.

I was overjoyed with those headers against England. I never stood still at corner kicks. I made people move with me, then I'd dart forward at the last minute. The real secret was a good spring off the ground. I just nicked one of them. I can see it now, going away from Harry Hibbs in the England goal.

After the game against England for King George V's Jubilee Trust, the SFA presented each of us with a solid-silver 'Quaigh' Scottish loving cup.

Another golden memory is of 1935, when we went across to New York in a beautiful ship called the Aquitania. It was a P&O liner with two swimming pools, cinema, everything. Not bad for a lad from Aberdeen.

Scotland defending at Hampden in 1929 when they beat England 1-0. This ended an era which had seen Scotland win six and draw two of nine games against the auld enemy.

A Scottish forward is beaten to the ball by the French goalkeeper in Colombes in the 1932 international. Scotland won 3-1. This fixture was part of the more 'worldly' approach of the inter-war period, when there were tours to North America (1921, 1927, 1935 and 1939) and games against Continental opposition.

WAR GAMES AGAIN

1939-46 Wartime football is a relatively neglected period of study, which is perhaps as well for Scotland, who came off second-best for most of World War Two. Between 2 December 1939 and 14 April 1945, Scotland won just three and drew two of 16 games against England.

When the war was won, Scotland were unbeaten for five games in 1945-6, which included a moment that would live forever in the memory of every Scotsman who saw it. A game aganst England at Hampden was nearing its conclusion, and what seemed an inevitable 0-0 scoreline, when Husband put over a free-kick. Every Scot in the stadium seemed to jump for it as Willie Waddell's head knocked it on to Jimmy Delaney. A thousand 'bunnets' went up in the air as Delaney scored the winner.

This 1-0 success ended a run of seven England victories, during which Scotland conceded 36 goals. They faced a fine England team which showed strength in the half-back line of Britton, Cullis and Mercer, and which had irrepressible forwards like Matthews, Carter and Lawton.

> On 14 October 1944, against England at Wembley, Bob Thyne (Darlington) was a late choice for Scotland. Badly injured in the fighting in Normandy a week after D-Day, Thyne had been invalided home and had resumed playing just five weeks before his international appearance.

Scotland never achieved the same consistency in team selection, although Jerry Dawson, Jimmy Carabine, Tommy Walker, and Jimmy Caskie played in more than half the matches.

The problem of club or country was replaced by the difficulty of players being needed for military service and probably being stationed miles from where they were required to play football. Attendance figures were slightly smaller, and gate receipts went towards Red Cross and other charities. But the games themselves were as good as any peacetime internationals, despite the fact that they have never counted towards 'official' caps.

A header by Clifton won England the first wartime game, played at Newcastle, but Scotland appeared to have revenge the following May, when Dave McCulloch found the back of the net in the last minute. However, the referee went across to the injured Sproston and indicated an infringement. The game ended 1-1 and there followed a storm of booing from the crowd. And the 'Hampden Boo' can be every bit as ferocious as the Hampden Roar. In fairness, Scotland's equaliser had been disputed.

The February 1941 game, again at Newcastle, was won by Scotland. Lawton's 40th-minute goal gave England a 2-1 lead, but two from Wallace — the second a 20-yarder — brought victory.

England won the next three, and the only goal that Scotland could muster was the one which crept under Swift's body at Hampden.

A hat-trick by Jock Dodds helped Scotland to a 5-4 victory which temporarily halted England's spell of dominance. This Hampden game saw the international debut of Billy Liddell.

A goalless draw led into England's most prolific spell of goalscoring. They scored four at Hampden and then inflicted what

BILLY LIDDELL

1946 to 1955: Outside-left, 28 caps, 6 goals.
Born: Dunfermline, 1922.
Career: Kingseat Juveniles, Lochgelly Violet, Liverpool.
An exciting, direct forward who packed a powerful shot in either foot, Billy Liddell was exceptionally popular both on and off the field. During his 22 years as a Liverpool part-time professional, Liddell worked in an accountant's office and his extra-curricula activities included youth work, being a Sunday School teacher and serving as a JP.
The son of a Fifeshire miner, Liddell played for Scotland Schoolboys before joining Liverpool where his first land-lady was the widow of the old Scottish international goalkeeper Ned Doig. Soon after he turned professional in April 1939, war was declared. Liddell played eight times for Scotland in wartime games. It would have been more but for a broken leg in 1943.
Liddell and Stanley Matthews were the only two players to play for Great Britain in both 1947 and 1955. Liddell moved to centre-forward for his club and carried them so much that they became known as 'Liddellpool' for a time. Nearly 39,000 watched his testimonial in 1960.

> Tommy Bogan's international career lasted for about one minute and he did not touch the ball while wearing a Scotland shirt. Bogan collided with goalkeeper Frank Swift in Scotland's first attack in the game on 14 April 1945. He left the field with knee-ligament damage and Leslie Johnston substituted.

is still Scotland's record margin of defeat, by eight goals at Maine Road, Manchester. It was an exceptional England team. Bill Shankly said: "When I heard the team I said two prayers, one of thanks to the Scots for leaving me out, and one on behalf of Adam Little, who had taken my place." Matthews gave Scotland's left flank a torrid time, and Lawton scored four goals from centre-forward. Scotland centre-half George Young later commented, "I thought Lawton must have brought a ladder with him as he climbed into the air to nod the ball this way and that." That same day, Crozier saved a penalty from Carter who had also missed a spot-kick against Dawson at the start of the war.

Scotland had to suffer two more defeats, the second coming at Hampden in front of a record wartime crowd of 133,000.

At Wembley, in October 1944, the Scots took a 1-0 lead through Milne and held it until the 56th minute. Then came a further goal spree and another Lawton hat-trick as Scotland went down 6-2.

Scotland chose four Liverpool players for the game at Villa Park the following February, but their star was the Queen's Park amateur goalkeeper Bobby Brown, who was described as 'a human octopus'. Mortensen's winning goal for England was delayed until 13 minutes from the end.

Matt Busby was carried off on a stretcher in that game, but a few weeks later, he was fit enough to play an important part in the drama at Hampden. Scotland were 3-1 down when they were awarded a penalty. Busby stepped up to face his old Manchester City team mate Frank Swift. Perhaps 'Swifty' remembered something from their Maine Road days, for he dived the right way and saved the shot.

After Busby's penalty miss, Scotland went on to lose the game 6-1. But peacetime football was just around the corner. In August 1945, Japan surrendered and the war was finally over. The 1945-6 season saw a return to normality with Victory internationals against Wales, Northern Ireland, Belgium, England and Switzerland.

> Only a last-minute penalty-kick by Jimmy Delaney against Belgium at Hampden on 23 January 1946 preserved Scotland's unbeaten home record against foreign opposition. Although Switzerland took a first-half lead at Hampden on 15 May, they too failed to win, all Scotland's goals in their 3-1 success coming before half-time.

> In August 1946, Scotland drew 2-2 with England at Maine Road, Manchester, in a game played in aid of the Bolton Disaster Fund. Stanley Matthews laid on two first-half goals for Welsh, while Waddell created two for Thornton after the interval. This was one of only four occasions when Rangers' famous and feared Waddell-Thornton combination was on show in a Scotland team.
> Scotland: Miller (Celtic); D.Shaw (Hibernian), J.Shaw (Rangers), Campbell (Morton), Brennan (Newcastle U), Husband (Partick T), Waddell (Rangers), Dougal (Birmingham C), Thornton (Rangers), Hamilton (Aberdeen), Liddell (Liverpool).

ELEVEN STRANGERS

1946-7 There were celebrations to end the war, but little to celebrate in the Scottish football camp as the selectors called on 26 men for the three home internationals, none of which was won. The two-match summer tour opened disastrously against Belgium, but recovery came against Luxembourg when the Scots won by a six-goal margin, their biggest win since Ireland were beaten 11-0 in February 1901.

Scotland now had only one win this century to show for eight visits to Wrexham. For the first time since 1939, caps were awarded to players, but the clothing-coupon situation held up the time-honoured custom of presenting each player with his international jersey.

The Scotland team played like 11 strangers, and when Willie Waddell put them ahead with a second-half penalty, it served only to stir the Welsh fire. Bryn Jones equalised, Frank Brennan's misjudgement let in Trevor Ford after 79 minutes, and Jimmy Stephen diverted Ford's shot into the net near the end. The defeat shook everyone in Scottish football.

> The Dakota carrying the Scotland party to Belgium in 1947, overshot the runway at Brussels, and the pilot had to lift the aircraft back into the air. The game was played in the Heysel Stadium, then in poor condition following its use as a German tank park, and the shaky Scots lost.

A draw against Northern Ireland was a fair result, but the Scots might have won, had Feeney not made a spectacular goal-line clearance when Billy Liddell lobbed the ball towards an empty goal just after half-time, or had Jimmy Duncanson's shot not hit a post, minutes later. Ireland hit a post too, and then the latter stages of the game were enveloped in the fast-gathering gloom.

There was a bright day ahead, however, when Scotland scored a moral victory over what one leading English journalist

described as 'England's best-ever team'. The untried Willie Woodburn came in at centre-half, Archie Macaulay and Alex Forbes strengthened the wing-half positions, and Scotland might have been three up by half-time. Instead they had to settle for a 1-0 lead through an early goal by Andy McLaren, who ran on to Delaney's pass.

Carter equalised, and in the 75th minute, the same player might have scored the winner, but someone in the crowd blew a whistle. Carter hesitated and the chance was lost.

In Belgium, an estimated 80,000 crowd saw Anoul twice give the home side the lead — the second occasion three minutes from the end — but pride was restored in Luxembourg, where Alex Forbes crowned a fine display with a pitch-length run to score the sixth goal. Scotland had eased off after scoring three in the first half.

> On 28 May 1947, Scotland played the BAOR side in Germany. George Young, playing centre-forward, opened the scoring but Scotland lost 4-3. They were thwarted by a goalkeeper soon to be a Scottish star, Jimmy Cowan. Pearson scored the other two Scottish goals. The team was: Miller; Shaw (D), Shaw(J), Brown, Woodburn, Husband, MacFarlane, Flavell, Young, Steel, Pearson.

'WORST DISPLAY EVER'

1947-8 The post-war football boom was at its peak, and the SFA was organising more games against foreign opposition, yet Scottish international football reached a low point in its history.

In this immediate post-war period, almost every selected team received harsh criticism. There was even a theory that the selectors should choose the 'iron curtain' defence from Rangers — Brown, Young, Shaw, McColl, Woodburn, Cox — and the rampant 'famous five' attack of Hibernians' Smith, Johnstone, Reilly, Turnbull and Ormond.

Depression sank in when Scotland lost all three home internationals. Northern Ireland scored in the 35th and 52nd minutes, both goals coming from Smythe (Wolves), a last-minute replacement for Doherty.

Then the Hampden crowd were 'treated' to what one newspaper described as 'one of the worst displays ever given by a Scottish side'. Wales made Scotland look like 'struggling apprentices' according to another newspaper.

Andy McLaren's header actually gave the Scots an early lead against Wales, but Ford equalised from close-range and then Lowrie scored with a brilliant effort just before half-time.

In the second half, Alex Forbes was stretchered off after being hit by Tommy Jones' free-kick, but the uncompromising red-haired Scotland wing-half was soon back — and he finished the game in goal. Six minutes from time, goalkeeper Willie Miller was carried off with a cut head.

GEORGE YOUNG

1946 to 1957: Right-back or centre-half, 53 caps.
Born: Grangemouth, Stirlingshire, 1922.
Career: Kirkintilloch Rob Roy, Rangers, Third Lanark (manager).
The 6ft 2in, 15st George Young was a giant of the game. He captained his country a record 48 times, created a new record for the number of caps (subsequently passed by Denis Law and others) and his 34 consecutive appearances was a record until Kenny Dalglish beat it in March 1980.
For one so big, Young was incredibly light of step. Skilful, though his play gave scope for a few skyscraper clearances, Young's continued presence when Scotland were ringing changes is a tribute to his consistency. He was extremely hard but fair. His 16 year first-class career was spent with Rangers and his international debut was in 1943 when he faced a daunting bombardment from the English. Young first captained Scotland in 1948 and the following season he stamped his authority on the English, helping Scotland to win the home title. One of his proudest moments came at Wembley in 1949 when Scotland led 3-0 and went on to a famous victory. Young carried a lucky champagne cork, hence his nickname 'Corky'.
Young, who was Scottish Player of the Year in 1955, played 22 times for the Scottish League. Having captained Scotland to two wins in their 1957 World Cup qualifying group, he was surprisingly dropped. He swiftly retired and concentrated on his business interests, leaving many who felt that he finished when still of international standard.

One of the most surprising international withdrawals in history came before Scotland's game against France in May 1948, when Billy Campbell found that the toecap of one of his boots was broken. He tried boots belonging to three reserves, but none fitted and so Sammy Cox played instead.

Delaney and Govan also received touchline treatment so Scotland deserved some sympathy.

And so to the game against England at Hampden, by which time the selectors, seeking a drastic measure, called up goalkeeper Ian Black, who had only three months' experience of professional football with Southampton.

The game was littered with free-kicks, and the only piece of magic came from an Englishman, Tom Finney. Just before half-time, he cut inside Govan and struck a beautiful shot from the corner of the penalty area. Finney always reckoned that it was the best goal of his career.

Hardwick and Scott, the England full-backs, both cleared from the line with their goalkeeper Swift beaten, before a second England goal ended a fine Scottish rally. Swift was injured when Liddell bundled him into the net 20 minutes from time, while Hardwick limped on the England left wing for nearly half the game.

There were complaints about some of the Scottish tackling, as well as team selection and poor results, so this was possibly the point at which Scottish football reached its lowest ebb.

A win over Belgium followed, and after this game, 14 players were selected for the summer tour. They all got a game, but two defeats meant that there were still plenty of problems to solve.

Scotland led against Switzerland, but the home team equalised in first-half injury time. George Young, in his book *Captain of Scotland*, wrote: "The one-sidedness of this official really showed itself at its worst when Switzerland scored their second goal, for to the amazement of us Scots, he jumped into the air with joy — and then shook hands with the goalscorer."

BILLY STEEL

1947 to 1953: Inside-left, 30 caps, 12 goals.
Born: Denny, Stirlingshire, 1923.
Career: Denipace Thistle, Bo'ness Cadora, Leicester City, St Mirren, Morton, Derby County, Dundee, Los Angeles Danes (USA), Hollywood FC (USA).
Billy Steel was probably the most skilful player of the immediate post-war era. Small, but strong and speedy, he packed a powerful shot in his size-five boots. Nicknamed 'Mr Perpetual Motion', he was a tenacious player who was on his feet almost before he hit the ground. Defenders found him difficult to dispossess.
Steel came from obscurity to fame in a matter of weeks. A Scottish cap against England in 1947, after a handful of Scottish League games, was followed by a spectacular goal for Great Britain against the Rest of Europe. In June 1947, Derby broke the British transfer record by paying £15,000 for him, the first five-figure fee ever to pass over the border.
From his first cap, Steel missed only seven of 37 internationals and at one time played 19 consecutive Scotland games. Halfway through that period, Dundee paid a Scottish record £23,000 for his services.
Steel was an individualist who often reserved his best for internationals. He was the first Scotland player to be sent off in an international, but also the first for over 21 years to score four in a game, against Northern Ireland in November 1950. In 1951-2, an ankle injury restricted his appearances.

GORDON SMITH

1946 to 1957: Outside-right, 18 caps, 4 goals.
Born: Edinburgh, 1924.
Career: Montrose, South Esk School, Kirriemuir Juveniles, Roselea, Dundee North End, Hibernian, Hearts, Dundee, Drumcondra.
Gordon Smith had a fantastic career lasting 23 years. He scored over 300 senior goals, won League championship medals with three clubs and entertained thousands with his style. His graceful, loping stride concealed deceptive speed, and his immaculate conversion of half-chances showed that he had begun as a centre-forward.
Smith joined Hibs in 1941 and was with them for 18 years, being named Scottish Player of the Year in 1951, and once scoring five goals in a game against Third Lanark in 1947-8. 'Gay Gordon of Hibernian' deserved more caps but had to withdraw from games through injury.
After one injury he moved to Hearts where he played in a championship team in his mid-30s. Two years later, at Dundee, he guided the Dens Park club to their first title. These later successes were as an architect rather than raiding winger, but Smith's familiar style and rhythm were still present.

Twice in 1948, against Belgium and Switzerland, Scotland included five Hibernian players — Jock Govan, Davie Shaw, Gordon Smith, Bobby Combe and Eddie Turnbull.

This was only part of it. There were pre-match disputes about the use of substitutes and the lightweight Swiss football; and there were post-match complaints about injured players and the heavyweight Swiss tackling. Gordon Smith was convinced that one of his efforts was over the line but the referee waved play on.

There were no ready excuses, however, after the defeat by France. After Eddie Turnbull had hit the French crossbar, three second-half goals sealed the Scottish fate, and the poor results continued —just the sort of time when Scotland international teams are at their most dangerous.

ENGLAND 1 SCOTLAND 3
9 April 1949, at Wembley

IN THE first 20 minutes, the strong and fearless Jimmy Cowan cut out centre after centre, saved shot after shot, and dived at onrushing feet to help set up Scotland for a famous victory.

Gradually, the early England blitz was weathered and Scotland took control. Full-backs George Young and Sammy Cox held England wingers Matthews and Finney, and Willie Woodburn took a strong hold on the middle. The first goal was Scotland's — a Lawrie Reilly centre and a snap-shot from 5ft 5in schemer Jimmy Mason.

At half-time, centre-forward Billy Houliston asked Willie Thornton, the Scotland reserve, how he thought he was doing. "You're doing great," replied Thornton, admiring the way the Queen of the South man was challenging Frank Swift when the England goalkeeper tried to clear.

It was a Houliston tackle that earned Scotland their second goal. The ball broke to Billy Steel who scored comfortably.

Now there was a roar of expectation from Scottish fans every time winger Willie Waddell got the ball, but the third goal came from the other wing. It was the first of six which Lawrie Reilly scored against the English in his career. Although England scored a consolation through Milburn, it was a wonderful Scottish victory.

At the final whistle, the fans rushed on and acclaimed goalkeeper Cowan. When the team returned to Glasgow Central Station, appropriately aboard the Royal Scot, a tumultuous reception greeted them. More than 10,000 people chanted for Cowan.

Ironically, on the same day Cowan performed so gallantly at Wembley, he was missing his club's vital relegation battle with Albion Rovers.

Cowan missed a further bonus from Scotland's win. SFA secretary George (later Sir George) Graham had promised a seven-week tour of America for the players if they beat England.

It was a wonderful offer — a cruise on the Queen Mary and £50 spending money each in a country free of food and clothes rationing — but Cowan, the hero of Wembley, was prevented from going by his mother's illness.

ENGLAND: Swift; Aston, Howe, Wright, Franklin, Cockburn, Matthews, Mortensen, Milburn, Pearson, Finney.
SCOTLAND: Cowan; Young, Cox, Evans, Woodburn, Aitken, Waddell, Mason, Houliston, Steel, Reilly.

Referee: M. Griffiths (Wales)   *Attendance: 98,188*

England's Frank Swift is beaten by little Jimmy Mason for Scotland's first goal.

HERO JIMMY COWAN

1948-9 "Get on with scoring," skipper George Young told his forwards. "We'll hold these fellows without your help." And no one held up the English better than Scotland goalkeeper Jimmy Cowan, who was carried shoulder-high from the field after a tremendous win at Wembley.

Four games, four wins. Scotland were back, although they started timidly, fielding an experimental team against Wales. Seven new caps included two men, Lawrie Reilly and Hugh Howie, who had been deputising for injured men in the Hibs side.

Scotland were worthy of their first win in Wales since 1931, although two of their goals in the 3-1 win could be described as

> *England star Raich Carter described the Hampden Roar that hit him as he was kicking-in before an international: "It began with a murmur, rolling round the ground and mounting up out of nothing into a swelling, terrific roar that came at us from all sides. I wondered what had happened. Then I saw the Scotland team running out in their navy-blue shirts."*

'freaks', the first coming when Welsh goalkeeper Sidlow badly misjudged a long free-kick by full-back Howie. Although Bryn Jones equalised, Willie Waddell scored twice and Scotland had a 3-1 lead by half-time. The Welsh complained that one of Waddell's goals did not cross the line.

There was a terrific climax to the Ireland game. At Hampden, the Irish led 2-0 after only five minutes and all the old post-war doubts were raised. The burly, bustling Billy Houliston — the only Queen of the South player ever capped — pulled one back after half an hour. Then Jimmy Mason equalised in the 72nd-minute in the twilight. Houliston headed a last-minute winner.

The game against England would decide the championship — it was just like old times — and Cowan played brilliantly as England blitzed the Scotland goal in the opening 20 minutes. Sammy Cox had the measure of Stanley Matthews, and Scotland's forwards found the opportunity to attack the home goal, prompted by Billy Steel, the only Anglo-Scot in the side.

The Willie Waddell-Jimmy Mason right wing was a success and the latter gave Scotland the lead with a shot which went in off a post after 29 minutes. Billy Steel's goal, five minutes after the interval, gave Sotland an unassailable two-goal lead — especially with Cowans in such amazing form. The 3-1 victory would go down as 'Cowan's Match'. Afterwards, wives and girlfriends joined in the celebrations and a family atmosphere was created.

Steel was the star of the game against France, when a record midweek crowd of 130,000 saw the visitors' goalkeeper Vignal play brilliantly, even stopping a penalty by Young.

JIMMY COWAN

1948 to 1952: Goalkeeper, 25 caps.
Born: Paisley, 1926.
Career: Paisley schools football, Mossvale Juniors, St Mirren, Morton, Sunderland, Third Lanark.
A centre-forward at school, Cowan was coached as a goalkeeper by the legendary Harry Rennie and blooded in army representative games before making a dramatic entry into Scottish football.
In January 1947, on leave from Germany, he went into the Morton team at short notice and saved two penalties. His call-up was so late that some reports attributed his saves to regular goalkeeper Archie McFeat.
Morton had signed Cowan on a free transfer, but his value grew quickly when he made his name in the 1948 Scottish Cup Final. Further fame came at Wembley a year later. Not long after recovering from a broken arm, Cowan defied England's forwards. His display gave Scottish football a tremendous boost following an indifferent period immediately after the war.
In May 1949, Cowan had to turn down a chance to tour the United States because of his mother's illness. Between April 1949 and November 1951, he made 18 consecutive international appearances. His transfer in June 1953 cost Sunderland £8,000. He died in 1968, shortly after his 42nd birthday.

> *When Scotland won 3-1 at Wembley in 1949, the game was tagged 'Cowan's Match' and the heroic Scottish goalkeeper was chaired through a throng of elated fans. He eventually limped to the dressing room, fell on to a bench and said, "Oh Lord, save us from our friends!"*

SO NEAR TO RIO

1949-50 For the first time, the world's oldest international championship had wider implications. Although the World Cup organising committee annulled their original suggestion — that only the British champions would go to Rio — and invited the top two teams, Scotland announced that they would only compete in the World Cup as British Champions. Now all depended on the last few minutes of the match against England.

A smallpox outbreak in Glasgow had caused a scare and the players stayed out of the city until the day of the match — the Scots at Largs and the English at Troon.

> *When Scotland played England in April 1950, all five forwards were called William — Waddell, Moir, Bauld, Steel, Liddell. No wonder England fielded a goalkeeper called Bert Williams.*

Scotland needed a draw to retain a share of the championship but, in the closing stages at Hampden, they were behind to Bentley's 63rd-minute goal and were being thwarted by England goalkeeper Bert Williams. There were just five minutes to play when Willie Bauld unleashed a ferocious shot which this time beat Williams' despairing fingers. But instead of bulging the back of the England net, the ball thumped against the crossbar and bounced out — some Scots claimed in and out — and over the straining head of Bauld. A minute later, Waddell burst through, but scooped his shot over the bar. England were winners by a single goal and it was they who were South America-bound. Despite much debate, Scotland decided to stay at home.

> *Scotland sailed to America in 1949, aboard the Queen Mary. The Scots lost only one game, but that was a dramatic upset. At Triborough Stadium, in front of 15,000 spectators, Belfast Celtic held on to their 2-0 interval lead. The other eight games were won and more positive features of the tour were Willie Waddell's six goals in Philadelphia, a floodlit game against St Louis All-Stars, and a 4-0 win over the United States. The following year, the Americans beat England in the World Cup.*

The Scotland line-up for the match against France at Hampden Park in April 1949. Back row (left to right): Alex Dowdells (trainer), Willie Waddell, Sammy Cox, Bobby Evans, Jimmy Cowan, Willie Woodburn, George Aitken, Willie Telfer (reserve). Front row: Willie Thornton, Lawrie Reilly, George Young, Billy Steel, Billy Houliston. Scotland playing in Rosebery colours, won the game 2-0, Steel scoring both goals.

Defeat by England ended a run of six successive victories which included a good win against Wales, when Billy Steel seemed to play with twice as much energy as any other member of the Scottish attack, and a spectacular win in Belfast when the Scots took advantage of weak Northern Ireland goalkeeping, and Henry Morris scored a hat-trick in his only international.

Just before the Switzerland game, the executive committee reconsidered their decision not to send a team to the World Cup, but did not change their minds, even though SFA president John Lamb was in favour of the trip. It was no surprise when the Scottish vice-president of FIFA was not re-elected. The only heartening Scottish news from the World Cup was when their oldest and fiercest rivals, England, were sensationally beaten 1-0 by the USA. The Americans even had a Scot, Ed McIlvenny, in their team, and their manager Bill Jeffrey was also a Scot.

The unbeaten home record against foreign opposition was maintained when Scotland sat on their 3-1 interval lead against Switzerland. A draw in Portugal and a win in France, where Liddell missed a penalty, were achieved with teams which showed much more stability than those of the immediate post-war years. In eight successive games, the first three names on the team-sheet had been the same — Jimmy Cowan, George Young and Sammy Cox, while Billy Steel had given the team equal consistency at inside-left.

HOME DEFEAT BY AUSTRIA

1950-51 In a busy season there were outstanding successes — three home international wins, and victories in matches arranged to celebrate the Festival of Britain — but two defeats by Austria raised important questions about the position of Scotland (and indeed Britain) in the world arena.

There were late changes for the Wales game. Gordon Smith and Sammy Cox pulled out, while Eddie Turnbull damaged a muscle in the last minute of pre-match training at Reading. Willie McNaught made an excellent debut at full-back, and another new cap, Bobby Collins, provided the cross for Billy Liddell's goal — a magnificent flying header — after Reilly had scored two that might have been prevented by better goalkeeping.

Scotland were a little flattered by their 6-1 win over Northern Ireland. John McPhail scored twice in the first 14 minutes, but McGarry made it 2-1 just before half-time. Then Billy Steel scored four goals in 26 minutes.

Defeat by Austria at Hampden in December 1950 ended Scotland's home run against foreign opposition — Austria (1933, 2-2); Germany (1936, 2-0); Czechoslovakia (1937, 5-0); Hungary (1938, 3-1); Belgium (1948, 2-0); France (1949, 2-0); Switzerland (1950, 3-1).

On 13 December, Scotland became the first of the home international sides to be beaten on their own soil by foreign opposition. Austria won 1-0 on a cement-hard ground, Melchior's half-hit shot going in via a post in the 25th minute. The frozen pitch made for difficult conditions and the theatrical Austrian goalkeeper Zeman could hardly have relished diving about. The much-revered attacking qualities of centre-half Ocwirk were also restricted.

"At home, we play an attacking centre-half," said Walter Nauch, Austrian selector and coach, "but in these conditions, I told Ocwirk to stay in defence."

One of the season's recurrent issues was the question of substitutes. Scotland and Austria agreed to permit substitute goalkeepers in the event of injury, but the Wembley international with England was marred when Wilf Mannion of England fractured a cheek-bone in a 14th-minute heading duel with Billy Liddell.

Despite the Austrian setback, there was little room for debate in team selection

WILLIE WADDELL

1946 to 1954: Outside-right, 17 caps, 6 goals.
Born: Forth, Lanarkshire, 1921.
Career: Forth Wanderers, Strathclyde, Rangers, Kilmarnock (manager), Rangers (manager).
The image of Willie Waddell accelerating towards goal, sustaining his speed, and then setting up the climax of an attack with a shot, or a centre to the likes of Willie Thornton is sufficient, even today, to excite those who saw him play.
Waddell was a well-built winger with tremendous speed and a lethal shot. His display in Wales in 1948 helped lift Scottish football, and he was brilliant against England in 1949. He made his Rangers debut against Arsenal in 1938, scoring the only goal of the game. He played nine Wartime or Victory internationals, and obviously his number of caps would have been far greater, but for the war.
He is revered for his partnership with Rangers centre-forward Thornton, but the two men appeared in the Scotland team on only four occasions and Waddell suffered from the changing Scottish forward-line selections. In 26 appearances (wartime included) he played with more than a dozen different centre-forwards and even more inside-rights.
After eight years as Kilmarnock manager, he took the helm at Rangers where he steered them to their first European trophy before becoming a director and consultant.

following a string of good results. The only gamble was the introduction of Bobby Johnstone against England, while Willie Redpath was included when Allan Brown dropped out.

Johnstone might have scored twice in the first ten minutes as Scotland dominated, belying later claims that England would have won but for Mannion's injury. Although

Hassall gave England's ten men the lead with a fine goal, Scotland led 3-1 after 52 minutes. England fought back strongly with a goal from Finney and a late penalty claim when Mortensen tumbled. 'The refereeing was poor,' commented one newspaper, 'and there is no football law that says penalties are not allowed in international matches.' But Scotland had just as strong a claim when Blackpool's Harry Johnston appeared to handle just before half-time, and not since 1934 had England beaten Scotland in a full international at Wembley.

A somewhat disappointing display against Denmark was followed by a game against France that was settled 13 minutes from time. Willie Redpath dribbled on and on from his own penalty area, before playing the ball for Reilly to head into the net. For only the fifth time in their history, Scotland had been able to field the same team in consecutive matches.

Hero of the Belgium game was George Hamilton of Aberdeen, who was playing in his first international at the age of 31. Hamilton headed an early goal, laid one on for Jimmy Mason, and then scored two himself in the second half to give Scotland a 4-0 lead. One goal came after Hamilton took the ball half the length of the field before netting.

Then came a heavy defeat against Austria. In the Prater Stadium, 200 long-coated, gun-toting policemen formed a channel for Billy Steel to escape after the Scot was sent off in the 82nd minute. Steel was the first Scot to be sent off in an international.

The atmosphere at the post-match banquet was frosty, one of many sour notes which have punctuated club and country clashes between the Scots and Austrians right up to 1984, when Celtic were involved in the controversial European play-off against Rapid Vienna in Manchester.

GEORGE HAMILTON

AN AMUSING INTERLUDE

1951-2 It was a season of mixed fortunes for an experienced Scottish side that was particularly feared for the hard, determined tackling of players like George Young, Jimmy Scoular, Willie Woodburn, Willie Redpath and Alex Forbes.

Against Northern Ireland, Tommy Orr scored 32 minutes after lining up for his first international, and Bobby Johnstone netted twice against the run of play to put the Scots three goals ahead after an hour.

This victory was followed by two defeats at Hampden. Ivor Allchurch's last-minute header gave Wales a win, after Orr had missed an eighth-minute penalty. Then Finney and Broadis schemed England to their third successive Hampden Park triumph.

England's Stan Pearson scored two left-footed goals — one a well-hit volley, the other a half-hit effort — and all Scotland had to show was a scrambled goal by Lawrie Reilly late in the game.

> In 1951-2, Alan Morton said, "In Scotland today, there is only one international eleven. Before the war, there were sufficient stars for several international teams."

The game against the USA was more an amusing interlude than a full-scale international. Two Scottish goals in the first 11 minutes virtually killed the game as a contest. The score was 4-0 at half-time, then a fifth goal followed a miskick by O'Connell, who had earlier put through his own goal. Ian McMillan got Scotland's sixth with the last kick of the match.

The USA team were described as 'something close to a good-class Junior Cup team' by 'Waverley' in the *Daily Record*. Their goalkeeper, Borghi, entertained with baseball-type throws to the half-way line. Sammy Cox was stretchered off 12 minutes from time, but recovered for the Scandanavian tour.

In the days before substitutes, touring parties were small. Only 11 players set off from Scotland, although three more joined the party in Copenhagen after club tours.

The opposition was largely amateur, but a close game in Denmark was settled only by Lawrie Reilly's late header. Then followed defeat in Sweden when the home side scored twice in the first three minutes. Liddell pulled one back with a 25-yard free-kick, but a second-half Swedish goal sent the Scots tumbling.

> Despite the favourable April weather when the Americans visited Glasgow in 1952, their centre-half Charlie Colombo wore a pair of leather gloves throughout the game.

WILLIE WOODBURN

1947 to 1952: Centre-half, 24 caps.
Born: Edinburgh, 1919.
Career: Edinburgh Ashton, Musselburgh Athletic, Queen's Park Victoria XI, Rangers.
Willie Woodburn was a brilliant, stylish defender, particularly strong in the air. He was a gentleman off the field, but the stormy side of his career received much publicity. In 1954, after his fifth sending off, the SFA banned him *sine die*. The ban was lifted two years later, but his career was over.
After attending a rugby-dominated school, Woodburn spent 18 years with Rangers, who were fortunate to have two top-class centre-halves, Woodburn and Young, available in the same era.

'LAST-MINUTE' REILLY

1952-3 The old football adage that a game is never won or lost until the final whistle was suitably emphasised by Lawrie Reilly, who salvaged draws against Northern Ireland and England with late goals that earned him the nickname of 'Last-minute' Reilly.

The first of these vital Reilly goals came against Northern Ireland, when he appeared in a packed goal-area to head Young's cross into the net to earn Scotland a 1-1 draw. There was no time to restart play.

Against England, Reilly shot past Merrick to produce his second equaliser of the game. Again it was the last touch of the match.

Against Sweden, it was asking too much of Reilly to pull a match from the fire for a third time, so Scotland deservedly lost 2-1 at Hampden.

Football in the 1950s was often billed as a series of duels. It was who got the better — left-back or outside-right, centre-half or centre-forward, and sometimes, the goalkeeper over the whole opposition. When Scotland met Wales at Cardiff in 1953, Frank Brennan was recalled to wage battle against buccaneering Trevor Ford, while Lawrie Reilly faced Ray Daniel.

Play swung from end to end, with hardly any action in the midfield, and one journalist likened it to watching a tennis match.

easy equaliser, and Steel's brilliant dribble led to Liddell's winner.

Scotland finished on top, and Reilly demonstrated his late finishing powers, having one attempt cleared off the Welsh goal-line, seeing another hit a post, and the next ruled out for hands after he had got the ball in the net.

Reilly's late efforts were more successful when they were most needed, after Northern Ireland had shocked the Scots with an 82nd-minute goal by D'Arcy, and then after 90 minutes of gripping entertainment at Wembley.

Before the England game, there had been criticism that the Steel-Liddell left wing was past its peak, and had a Lofthouse header not been headed off the line by George Young, the Scots would have trailed 3-1. Indeed, the outlook was even bleaker when Sammy Cox left the field injured with 20 minutes still to play.

Cox was already in hospital when he heard the news of the dazzling bout of interpassing between Reilly and Johnstone that led to that last-second goal.

LAWRIE REILLY

1948 to 1957: Centre-forward, 38 caps, 22 goals.
Born: Edinburgh, 1928.
Career: Edinburgh Thistle, Hibernian.
Lawrie Reilly, who went to a rugby-dominated school, created a big reputation for goalscoring, based on his speed, determination and desire to take the shortest route to goal. Physically, he was not a big man, but his goals for Scotland gave him the status of a giant.
A one-club man and Hibs' most capped player, Reilly came within one goal of equalling Hughie Gallacher's record. His last-minute goals were legendary and he scored six goals in seven games against England. He could produce the unexpected. In 1951, a text-book ruling would have been for Reilly to pass to Johnstone, but he went on himself to score against England. Two years later, again at Wembley, he fed Johnstone, took the return, and scored a sensational last-minute goal.
Reilly headed the Scottish League goalscorers for three successive seasons in the early 1950s. In 1954, he had a long lay-off through illness, and in 1957, demonstrated his courage by playing against England with stitches in his left foot after a dressing room accident the previous day.

SAMMY COX

1948 to 1954: Left-back, 25 caps.
Born: Darvel, Ayrshire, 1924.
Career: Queen's Park, Third Lanark, Dundee, Rangers, East Fife.
When Campbell was a late withdrawal in France in 1948, Sammy Cox proved capable of deputising in the number-ten shirt, but the remainder of his caps were won at left-back, where he was one of the few capable of restraining wingers of the calibre of Stanley Matthews.
His greatest success against Matthews came at Wembley in 1949, while his Groucho Marx impression helped entertain colleagues after the game. At that time, Cox was better known as a left-half with his club side, but he won the popular mantle of 'utility player'. His injury at Wembley in 1953 cost him his Scottish Cup Final place, but a year later he captained Scotland against England. In 1959, he emigrated to Canada.

BOBBY EVANS

1948 to 1960: Wing-half or centre-half, 48 caps.
Born: Glasgow, 1927.
Career: Thornliebank Methodist FC, St Anthony's (Glasgow), Celtic, Chelsea, Newport County (player-manager), Morton, Third Lanark (trainer-coach, then player-manager), Raith Rovers.
Bobby Evans' 48 Scotland caps – only five less then George Young's then record – were equally divided between wing-half and centre-half. First, he was a wing-half, red-haired in the tradition of Forbes and Macaulay, thick-set, strong tackling and always at the heart of the action.
Although he was a hero at wing-half in the 1949 Wembley victory, Evans faced stiff competition from McColl, Docherty and Scoular over the next few years. Evans played brilliantly at centre-half in Vienna and Budapest in 1955, but it was not until another tour, two years later, that he established himself in that position. Elected captain, he twice skippered Scotland against England. Although of medium height, Evans was good in the air. His enthusiasm for the game was unceasing, and even when he was handicapped by a back injury (from 1958) he continued to play at the top. When he retired in 1967, he was nearly 40.

Although Ford struck a beautiful goal to open the scoring, debutant George Farm gave a magnificent display in the Scotland goal, and it was the Scots who had the best of the duels. Allan Brown collected an

WORLD CUP FINALISTS

1953-4 As runners-up to England, Scotland qualified once more for the World Cup Finals, to be held in Switzerland, and this time there was never any doubt about them going to compete. How they would fare was, of course, much more doubtful, and six weeks before the Finals, they were slow-handclapped by the Hampden crowd as they scrambled a 1-0 win against Norway.

'On this form, Scotland have no chance in the World Cup tournament,' screamed the headlines.

Even the 3-1 win over Northern Ireland was not especially heartening and the

> *When Scotland met England in a 'B' international at Roker Park, Sunderland, on 3 March 1954, it was the first time that a representative match in Britain had been played under floodlights.*

difference between the two sides was the sharpshooting of Scotland's Charlie 'Cannonball' Fleming of East Fife, who scored twice.

Scotland had the better of a remarkable international against Wales. They led 3-1 until Ivor Allchurch's brilliant goal, and then John Charles equalised with two minutes to play. There was still time for a typical last-minute effort from Reilly, and with a clear passage to goal in the closing minute, he looked certain to score. Welsh centre-half Daniel toppled him on the brink of the penalty area, and the free-kick came to nothing.

When Scotland and England met at Hampden, the prize for the victors was the easier part of the World Cup Finals draw. Woodburn, Young and Reilly were all unfit, and England were the better side.

Broadis brilliantly equalised Brown's seventh-minute goal for Scotland, then second-half headers by Nicholls, Allen and Mullen gave England a 4-1 lead. Right on time, a mix-up between Byrne and Merrick allowed a lob from debutant

Willie Ormond to creep home.

This meant only one win in seven Hampden games, and that was against the USA, so Scottish fans were unusually unsupportive when their team attacked for 90 per cent of the Norway game, and had only a 35th-minute headed goal by George Hamilton to show for it. In fact, the Hampden crowd cheered for the Norwegians in the later stages.

Paddy Buckley injured a knee in the Norway match and missed the summer games and the World Cup Finals. There were experiments in Norway and Finland where 18 players were given the chance to play themselves into the World Cup party.

The display in Norway was a vast improvement, and the home side's equaliser came only two minutes from time.

Lord Rosebery's colours were worn in Finland where goals from two Hibs players, Ormond and Johnstone, gave Scotland the lead. The Finns presented Doug Cowie with a cup — they judged him the best Scotland player — and Bobby Johnstone received a clock for being voted second-best.

WORLD CUP FINALS ⚽ 1954

SCOTLAND'S first visit to the World Cup Finals was a failure. Lack of preparation was indicated in the chaos surrounding the Scottish camp. Games against Austria and Uruguay were lost, and Scotland finished bottom of the four-nation group. When they returned, one selector said, 'Never mind, just as long as we beat England.' It summed up the parochial outlook of the day.

At least Scotland had a team manager, albeit on a temporary basis, but Andy Beattie threatened to resign even before he took the players to Ayr for a month's special training. The selectors chose only 13 players for the party, including only one goalkeeper, and among those omitted was George Young, leaving no obvious candidate for the captaincy.

Rangers players were not allowed to go to Switzerland because they were required for the club's trip to the USA.

In Switzerland, the players were forced to train in their club jerseys, which prompted Willie Fernie to describe the Scotland party's appearance as "like liquorice allsorts," while another embarrassing moment came when the Austrian captain Ernst Ocwirk presented Willie Cunningham with a pennant before the first game and the Scotland skipper had nothing to hand back.

Undaunted, however, Scotland played with great spirit against the Austrians. There was the familiar sharp-tackling which was one of the hallmarks of the 1950s — halfbacks Tommy Docherty, Jimmy Davidson and Doug Cowie reigning supreme — and then a magnificent fightback by the forwards after Probst had given Austria a 33rd-minute lead. In the last minute, Neil Mochan almost forced extra-time but his shot was saved by the goalkeeper.

Although Scotland deserved credit for this performance, their outing against Uruguay three days later was one of the biggest humiliations. Uruguay won 7-0 and they might have scored a dozen.

By then there was internal dispute and just before the Uruguay game, Beattie, the manager of Huddersfield, resigned his Scotland duties.

On that disastrous day in Basle, the Scotland players - the same eleven who had faced Austria — had to stand around for over six minutes while the two-part Uruguayan national anthem was played, then run around in unaccustomed heat as the two Uruguayan wingers ran them ragged. In the words of one critic, 'Scotland's defenders stood around like grazing Highland cattle'. Two down at half-time, Scotland conceded three goals in a ten-minute spell just after the break.

This rounded off a poor season for British soccer. With England being hammered twice by Hungary, there was talk of a Great Britain team being entered for the next World Cup.

McKenzie beats Austria's Halla to the ball as Scotland lose 1-0 in Zurich in the Group Three match.

A pool of 22 players was selected before the 1954 World Cup Finals, but only 13 travelled to Switzerland. They were: Martin (Aberdeen), Cunningham (Preston), Aird (Burnley), Docherty (Preston), Davidson (Partick T.), Cowie (Dundee), McKenzie (Partick T.), Fernie (Celtic), Mochan (Celtic), Brown (Blackpool), Ormond (Hibs), Evans (Celtic), Hamilton (Aberdeen). Bobby Johnstone (Hibs) was originally one of the 13 but withdrew through injury. Hamilton replaced him, and the eight on stand-by were Anderson (Leicester), Henderson (Portsmouth), Mathers (Partick T.), Wilson (Portsmouth), Binning (Queen of the South), Combe (Hibs), Copland (Raith Rovers), McMillan (Airdrie). No Rangers players were released.

WEMBLEY MISERY

1954-5 More misery came when England won 7-2 at Wembley — goalkeeper Fred Martin had conceded 18 goals in three games by then — but the season ended with hope when the Scots finally beat Austria, albeit in a bruising battle, and then turned in a praiseworthy performance against the all-conquering Hungarians.

Yet it was obvious that some of the suggested remedies would have to be considered — Under-23 and 'B' international teams, trial games, changes in selection methods, more pre-match training sessions, and, perhaps most important of all, a full-time national team manager.

All of these suggestions were eventually adopted — some taking longer to invoke than others — and, meanwhile, the Scots relied on their tough-tackling defenders to produce some immediate results.

The good record at Ninian Park continued when Tommy Ring robbed Roy Paul and centred for Paddy Buckley to score. It was 17 years since Scotland had lost in Cardiff.

There was a different tale when Northern Ireland visited Hampden. Although Jimmy Davidson's free-kick gave Scotland the lead, the Irish scored twice before half-time. It was left to an Irish defender to put through his own goal to give the Scots a point. Bobby Johnstone fluffed his shot and Norman Uprichard had it covered until it came off McCavana's shin.

Scots Joe McDonald (left-back), Bobby Johnstone (inside-right), and Billy Liddell (outside-left), played for Great Britain against the Rest of Europe in Belfast in 1955. The British side lost 4-1 in a game which celebrated the 75th anniversary of the Irish FA.

Scotland prepared for the Hungary game with three full-scale practice matches against Scottish League club sides. Only two Anglo-Scots were included in the team, and Lawrie Reilly was back after a long lay-off through illness.

Bill Liddell (left) watches anxiously as Lawrie Reilly and Schmeit, the Austrian goalkeeper, challenge for the ball during the game in Vienna in May 1955.

Initially, Hungary, captained by Ferenc Puskas, threatened to do what they had done to England and run up a hatful of goals. They led 2-0 through Boszik and Hidegkuti after half an hour. Tommy Ring's 40th-minute left-footer raised Hampden spirits, although Sandor restored the two-goal margin.

The second half was tense. Johnstone scored on the restart, and the Hampden Roar was now much in evidence. Ring and Jimmy Wardhaugh had chances to make it 3-3, even though Willie Cunningham was missing for ten minutes after being carried off. Then, in failing light, Kocsis scored a fourth and a few seconds later, the referee blew for full-time.

Some Europeans criticised Scotland's 'hard tackling' against Hungary, singling out Tommy Docherty, John Cumming and Lawrie Reilly, the latter for his charge of Farago that laid out the goalkeeper.

Before their fine performance in Hungary in 1955, Scotland played a friendly against a local side, Semmering. Tommy Younger came on at centre-forward in the second half and bet Gordon Smith that he would score a hat-trick. Younger won his bet.

At Wembley, goalkeeper Freddy Martin froze with nerves, 40-year-old Stan Matthews gave Harry Haddock perhaps the biggest runaround of his life, and England's Dennis Wilshaw scored four goals — then a Wembley record — in England's 7-2 win.

That was perhaps the lowest point of the 1950s. Victory over Portugal followed, then Scotland twice fought back to equalise against Yugoslavia. The Yugoslavs changed their goalkeeper in the second half, but Tommy Gemmell had to stay on the field, despite an ankle injury.

The 4-1 win over Austria was a fine result, but the match was one of the roughest, bruising, blistering battles in soccer history. On the field, fist fights broke out every few minutes, and the pitch was twice invaded by hundreds of the 65,000 shrieking, whistling spectators. Scotland captain Gordon Smith had to have police protection during the game, while special police escorted the entire Scotland team to their coach after the game. Amazingly, only one player, Austria's Barschandt, was sent off following a series of fouls on Gordon Smith.

The game took place four days after Austria had concluded a state treaty with the wartime occupying powers, restoring Austrian independence. Archie Robertson scored his first goal for Scotland, after just 30 seconds, and a Scottish victory was always likely. The fourth goal came from Reilly, almost inevitably, in the last minute.

Scotland followed up the Austria match with a worthy performance in Hungary. In the 42nd minute, Gordon Smith used his speed to break clear and give Scotland a half-time lead — a goal greeted with total silence by the crowd. Three Hungarian goals inside 23 minutes turned the game. Billy Liddell had two chances, but shot wide from the penalty spot — perhaps affected by ear-splitting whistling from the crowd as he ran up — and then hit the post when he might have found the net.

ALL-SQUARE

1955-6 For the first time in the 72-year history of the home championship, all four countries finished level. Scotland were denied an outright title by a last-minute England goal at Hampden.

Haynes controlled Byrne's cross and hit the equaliser, though there were claims for hands. Haynes said later: "Hampden's fantastic roar had been a bit off-putting all through, but the silence at that moment

Scottish despair as Johnny Haynes levels the scores with a disputed goal at Hampden Park in April 1956.

was even more unnerving. It was like the end of the world had come. The only sound was Young and Younger roaring at the referee that I had handled."

The standard of the international championship was not high, and the emphasis was on spirit rather than skill. Scotland lost in Belfast, thanks mainly to the daring and brilliance of Irish goalkeeper Norman Uprichard, who was chaired from the field by spectators.

Bobby Johnstone brightened up a poor international against Wales and his world-class skill brought two goals in the first 24 minutes. Even so, some of the Hampden crowd streamed out before the end.

South African international John Hewie was introduced at left-back against England as the Scots attempted to end the run of Hampden defeats against their old rivals. Wright and Finney had been in the England team on the four post-war occasions that their country had been successful at Hampden, where England had also triumphed in 1939.

Scotland went ahead after an hour when Hewie's cross found Graham Leggat, who fired past Reg Matthews. England pressed, but the Scots looked to have weathered the storm until that fateful last minute when Haynes scored his disputed goal.

In the final match of the season, Austria returned to Hampden for the first time since upsetting Scotland's unbeaten home record against foreign teams. The Scots gained some revenge with a 1-1 draw.

WORLD CUP QUEST

1956-7 Off on the World Cup trail which led to Sweden, Scotland found themselves in a qualifying group with Spain and Switzerland, the first time that their World Cup fortunes had rested with matches

against foreign opposition. The season ended with Scotland needing to win their final match, against Switzerland at Hampden, to qualify.

It was a season of inconsistent performances. First came a scrambled draw against Wales, a result that hinged on a controversial penalty awarded for hands when Welsh centre-half Daniel fell on the ball when challenging Lawrie Reilly. It was the first point that Wales had reaped from Scotland at Ninian Park for 19 years.

Alex Scott had a dream start to his international career when he scored a fine 25th-minute goal against Northern Ireland. By then, Scotland had Doug Cowie limping after one of Tommy Casey's rugged tackles. After half an hour, Cowie left the field for good and Scotland's ten men fought bravely to win.

The game with Yugoslavia was a victory for might over mind, with Tommy Docherty 'mightier' than most. The Yugoslavs were hailed as 'soccer-educated', but the Scots took the lead after 37 minutes with a header from inside-forward Jackie Mudie, who was normally employed as a centre-forward with Blackpool.

The second goal came when Sammy Baird headed against the bar, then hit the rebound home ten minutes after half-time.

Defensive wing-half Docherty was to figure in a key incident in the Wembley international. His tackle on Preston team-mate Tom Finney resulted in the England star being carried off in the 52nd minute.

At that point the Scots led through Tommy Ring's shock first-minute goal, but Derek Kevan equalised and Duncan Edwards shot a ferocious late winner. Willie Fernie did have the ball in the England net, but Reilly was adjudged to have fouled the goalkeeper. Scotland were criticised for falling back on the defensive with their 1-0 lead.

BOBBY JOHNSTONE

1951 to 1956: Inside-forward, 17 caps, 9 goals.
Born: Selkirk, 1929.
Career: Newtongrange Bluebell, Selkirk, Hibernian, Manchester City, Hibernian, Oldham Athletic.
The youngest member of the Hibs 'Famous Five' forward-line, Bobby Johnstone was a Scotland international when only 21. He was a stunning dribbler who possessed a powerful shot that brought him a haul of goals which would have made any centre-forward proud.
After his transfer to Maine Road for £22,000 in March 1955, Johnstone became the first man to score in successive Wembley FA Cup Finals. He appeared in six successive Scotland-England fixtures in the 1950s, and in 1955, he was selected for Great Britain against the Rest of Europe.

The opening World Cup qualifying game, against Spain, was a tough and uncompromising affair. Scotland led through Mudie, allowed Spain to draw level, and then went in front again from a John Hewie penalty. The South African was playing because Alex Parker was unfit.

Two late Mudie goals, who thus completed his hat-trick, gave Scotland a fine start in the competition. Mudie was not especially tall, but he was an excellent header of the ball.

A win over Switzerland meant four points from two World Cup games, but the match in Basle was a contrast to the fighting performance against Spain. Vonlanthen put the Swiss ahead and Scotland had to thank the 'mighty midgets' Mudie and Collins, for their goals. Again Docherty was a hero.

Within a few days, Scotland were back to their best, humbling World Cup holders West Germany on their own soil. George Young was rested and Bobby Evans' display as skipper meant that Young had, in fact, played his last game for Scotland.

Tommy Ring — then playing in the Scottish Second Division with Clyde — tortured his marker and laid on goals for Collins and Mudie. The thrill of the night came in the 56th minute when Collins scored his second to put Scotland 3-0 ahead.

This high spot was met with typical inconsistency. Four days later, in Madrid, a team showing two changes was run ragged by Di Stefano and Kubala, as Spain took a 3-0 lead after an hour and went on to win 4-1. It was fortunate that the Spanish had drawn a game against Switzerland, leaving the Scots needing two points to ensure their passage to Sweden. The crucial game was scheduled for the start of the following season.

DOUG COWIE

1953 to 1958: Left-half, 20 caps.
Born: Aberdeen, 1926.
Career: Caledonian Juveniles (Aberdeen), Aberdeen St Clement's Dundee, Morton, Raith Rovers (manager).
Doug Cowie made his Scotland debut in 1953 at Wembley when he had the task of marking Ivor Broadis. Cowie moved to centre-half for the next match, and again represented Scotland in that position a year later, though by that time he was first-choice left-half. Late in 1956, he lost his place to Tommy Docherty, but a surprising recall 18 months later saw Cowie re-establish himself in time for the World Cup Finals.

ON TO SWEDEN

1957-8 When Willie Fernie streaked through the Swiss defence and gave Jackie Mudie the chance to put Scotland 2-1 ahead against Switzerland at Hampden, the last major obstacle along the path to the World Cup Finals was removed. Scotland went on to win 3-2 and qualify, but a disastrous home championship season, followed by tough encounters with Hungary and Poland, was hardly the best preparation.

The first scare was against Northern Ireland, but Mudie strode past Jackie Blanchflower to provide Graham Leggat with the goal that rescued a point.

Tommy Docherty played a big part in the first two goals of the Switzerland game. He set up an easy chance for Archie Robertson, but then sliced a clearance for Riva to equalise. In the 50th minute, the erratic Fernie justified his selection with his part in Mudie's goal, but the Scots had to thank Tommy Younger, who scrambled the ball away from Chiesa after the Swiss outside-right had beaten virtually everyone else on the pitch.

Scotland made it three through Alex Scott, who had come in for the injured Gordon Smith, and then they survived a frenetic last 20 minutes.

Wales had more of the Hampden game played in front of an unusually subdued crowd. For the first 15 minutes, a Scotland victory looked likely, but after Collins gave them the lead, the game changed. Wales lost Mel Charles for ten minutes, but Medwin equalised and Jones hit a post ten minutes from time.

After the 1-1 draw against Wales, nobody tipped the Scots against England, and the less said about the game the better. Tommy Younger helped keep the score down to 4-0 and thousands streamed out before the final whistle.

Bobby Collins leaps for joy after scoring against Switzerland in the World Cup.

Only four players were retained from this debacle for the Hungary game three weeks later. After a brilliant Mudie header had given Scotland an early lead, the 54,400 drenched spectators saw a cruel game. Younger was crippled, Cowie hobbling, and Mudie strapped up. Fenyvesi earned Hungary a draw with a second-half goal.

The final warm-up match for Sweden was another rough-and-tumble affair, but the 2-1 victory in Poland was encouraging. Bobby Collins provided the highlights. His first goal hit the goalkeeper, an upright and the goalkeeper again, before cannoning into the net. Collins' second was bent beautifully into the net from around 40 yards. Cieslik scored a late reply, but the performances of players like Collins, Younger and Eddie Turnbull meant that the Scots now had an outside chance in Sweden.

Scotland's 22 for the 1958 World Cup Finals in Sweden were: Younger (Liverpool), Brown (Dundee), Caldow (Rangers), Hewie (Charlton), Parker (Everton), Haddock (Clyde), Turnbull (Hibs), Evans (Celtic), Cowie (Dundee), Docherty (Preston), McColl (Rangers), Mackay (Hearts), Leggat (Aberdeen), Murray (Hearts), Mudie (Blackpool), Collins (Celtic), Imlach (Nottingham Forest), Scott (Rangers), Baird (Rangers), Coyle (Clyde), Robertson (Clyde), Fernie (Celtic).

DENIS LAW'S DEBUT

1958-9 The convincing 3-0 win against Wales was significant for two reasons. Matt Busby made his debut as Scotland team manager, and Denis Law played his first game for Scotland. The youngest player this century to have made a Scotland debut, Law crowned a fine game with a

IAN McCOLL

1950 to 1958: Right-half, 14 caps. Born; Alexandria, Dunbartonshire, 1927.
Career: Vale of Leven Academy, Vale of Leven Juniors, Queen's Park, Rangers, Scotland team manager, Sunderland (manager).
Part of Rangers' famous 'Iron Curtain' defence, Ian McColl won his first cap in 1950 against England, in a team which had five Rangers players. McColl failed to hold a regular place and, rather surprisingly, he was overlooked for more than five years after playing in the 5-0 win over Belgium in 1951. When he returned in 1956-7 it was as a member of one of Scotland's most successful teams. All his international appearances were at right-half, although he proved his versatility with Rangers. In 1960, he was brought back to play in the Scottish Cup Final. He performed brilliantly and took his fifth Scottish Cup-winners' medal.

goal, albeit a fortunate one when an attempted clearance hit him and the ball rebounded into the net from the crossbar.

Dave Mackay was the new Scotland captain, but the inspiration was Tommy Docherty who had displaced Welsh captain Dave Bowen from the Arsenal team.

Scotland looked to be cruising to the international championship when they took a 2-0 lead against Northern Ireland. In a devastating spell just after half-time, David Herd shot a brilliant goal and Bobby Collins added a second. Scotland might have led 3-0, but Collins missed the chance.

The last 20 minutes provided a complete reversal. An own-goal by Eric Caldow and an 83rd-minute effort from Jimmy McIlroy enabled Northern Ireland to draw.

Three months after taking up his appointment, Matt Busby realised that he was not fit enough to combine the duties with those of Manchester United manager. He resigned his Scotland post, and when the team went south to Wembley in April, Andy Beattie was in charge.

Fielding a small but hardy defence — only goalkeeper Bill Brown was over 5ft 8in — Scotland had most of the play, but the limelight was stolen by two England players. Billy Wright was winning his 100th cap, and a young Bobby Charlton headed the only goal of the game.

Scotland had relied largely on older players for the England game — Willie Ormond was now 34 — but the next game, against West Germany, saw the introduction of young attacking players like John White, Andy Weir and Ian St John, who was a late replacement. Five goals came in the first half-hour, with Scotland setting the pace. White and Weir both scored in the first seven minutes.

The final ten minutes were particularly nerve-wracking as Scotland held out the Germans. One dangerous opponent was young Uwe Seeler, who had already scored a goal.

WORLD CUP FINALS ⚽ 1958

"SCOTLAND learned nothing, absolutely nothing, from the World Cup Finals of 1954," wrote John Camkin. "Every mistake made in Switzerland four years ago, was repeated in Sweden in 1958."

Again, Scotland were the only country without a manager, but this time it was due to tragic circumstances. In January, the SFA had appointed Matt Busby, the Manchester United boss, on a part-time basis, but Busby had been seriously injured in the Munich Air Disaster. Scotland trainer Dawson Walker was left in charge of the players.

Scotland were drawn in a group with Paraguay, France and Yugoslavia, who they had beaten at Hampden the previous season. As in 1954, Scotland produced a fine start to the World Cup Finals, but a poor finish.

Their first opponents were Yugoslavia. Stewart Imlach pulled a muscle in the third minute and Scotland were further handicapped when Patakovic gave the Yugoslavs the lead soon afterwards.

Then came a great fight-back. Murray headed an equaliser just after half-time, and in the 70th minute came the incident which changed the course of Scotland's World Cup. Yugoslavian goalkeeper Beara let slip a cross and the ball bounced off Mudie and into the net. But the referee gave a foul against the Scotland

player and the result was 1-1.

By the time Scotland met Paraguay, it was clear that the South Americans' game was based more on brawn than skill, yet Scotland fielded a lightweight team, including Robertson and Fernie on the left-wing.

As with their first-ever South American opponents — Uruguay in 1954 — Scotland were given a hard time. Aguero's shot went through Younger's legs to give Paraguay the lead, and later in the game, the goalkeeper dropped a corner for Parido to make it 3-1. Despite a 20-yard goal from Collins, Scotland lost to the weakest team in the group. Paraguay had conceded seven to France, Scotland's final opponents, and only a miracle could keep the Scots in the competition.

Having started the tournament as captain, Younger had now played his last game for Scotland and Bill Brown came in for the France match. France's prolific scorer, Just Fontaine, laid on a first-half goal for Raymond Kopa, and then scored one himself. In between, Hewie hit a post with a penalty and it was the 67th minute before the Scots pulled a goal back when Sammy Baird's shot went in off a post. It was too little too late and Scotland finished bottom of their group.

The summer tour began with a startling shock against Jutland, a team that could hardly be called first-class opposition. The youthful Scotland team were lucky not to be beaten. They led 2-0 at half-time, but allowed Jutland back into the game. Scotland led again at 3-2, before Jutland scored a 76th-minute equaliser.

Victory in Holland was a fine performance. The Dutch led at half-time, and Graham Leggat's winner was a magnificent effort. But the success was marred by the sending-off of Bertie Auld, who received much sympathy when he was dismissed in the third minute of injury time.

In Portugal, as in Holland, spectators rained cushions on to the pitch, and there was not much action apart from Matateu's 25th-minute winner for the Portuguese.

BOBBY COLLINS

1950 to 1965: Inside-forward, 31 caps 10 goals.
Born: Govanhill, Glasgow, 1931.
Career: Polmadie Hawthorn Juveniles, Glasgow Pollok, Celtic, Everton, Leeds United, Bury, Morton, Ringwood City (Australia), Hakoah (Australia), Oldham Athletic (player-coach, later assistant manager), Huddersfield Town (manager), various coaching posts, then Barnsley (manager).
Only Denis Law and Jimmy McMenemy have had longer Scotland international careers than Bobby Collins, who made his debut on 21 October 1950 against Wales, and played his last game, against Poland, on 23 May 1965. During that time, Collins, just 5ft 4in tall, changed from a diminutive winger into a stockier midfield general.
He proved himself as an inside-forward in Yugoslavia in 1955, tenacious in both defence and attack, and in the late 1950s he scored more Scotland goals than anyone else.
When Everton sold him to Leeds for £22,500 in March 1962, many predicted his career was on the wane, but his greatest personal triumph was still to come. He took Leeds to Division One and in 1965 was the first Scot to be elected Footballer of the Year in England. Recalled to the Scotland team in 1965, after a six-year absence, Collins won three more caps before a broken thigh bone ended his international career later that year. However, he played for Oldham Athletic as late as April 1973.

TOMMY YOUNGER

1955 to 1958: Goalkeeper, 24 caps.
Born: Edinburgh, 1930.
Career: Hutchison Vale, Hibernian, Liverpool, Falkirk (player-coach), Stoke City, Leeds United, Hibernian (PRO), Scottish FA president 1983-4.
Big and burly Tommy Younger came into the Scotland team after the 7-2 defeat at Wembley in 1955. He held his place for 24 consecutive matches which is still a record for a goalkeeper, and six of those 24 matches were lost.
This was remarkable for such a courageous goalkeeper who had to withstand much injury. Against England in 1957, for instance, he played with a bandaged hand.
After eight years with Hibs, Younger joined Liverpool in 1956 for £9,000. He earned a high reputation in England, but probably played even better for his country. Younger captained Scotland during the 1958 World Cup.
As a Hibs director, Younger progressed on the administrative side of football. In 1983, he succeeded Willie Harkness as SFA president, but died in January 1984, when in his early 50s.

TOMMY DOCHERTY

1951 to 1959: Wing-half, 25 caps, 1 goal.
Born: Glasgow, 1928.
Career: Shettleston Juniors, Celtic, Preston North End, Arsenal, Chelsea (player-coach), Chelsea (manager), Rotherham United (manager), Queen's Park Rangers (manager), Aston Villa (manager), FC Oporto (manager), Hull City (assistant manager), Scotland manager, Manchester United (manager), Derby County (manager), Queen's Park Rangers (manager), Sydney Olympic (Australia, manager), Preston North End (manager), South Melbourne (Australia, manager), Wolves (manager).
Raised in the Gorbals, Tommy Docherty developed into a wing-half with a deadly tackle who captained Scotland and later managed the national team. His first job was in a bakery and he played for St Paul's Guild. After service with the Highland Light Infantry, with whom he played football in Palestine, Docherty was signed for Celtic by Jimmy McGrory. At Parkhead he was in the shadow of Bobby Evans and his success came with Preston and Arsenal, who signed him for £28,000 after the 1958 World Cup when Docherty was in dispute with Preston who wanted him for a club tour to Switzerland.
Docherty did not play in the Finals – after being captain he lost his place – but he was soon back the next season. Then he broke an ankle playing against Preston and thereafter became a more defensive player. What followed was an eventful managerial career, including an exciting spell in charge of the Scotland team.

JOHN HEWIE

1956 to 1960: Left-back, 19 caps, 2 goals.
Born: Capetown, South Africa, 1957.
Career: Arcadia (South Africa), Pretoria (South Africa), Charlton Athletic.
John Hewie is one of very few South African-born Scottish internationals. His father hailed from Yarrowfield, near Selkirk, and had emigrated to South Africa.
Charlton manager Jimmy Seed discovered Hewie on one of his many recruiting drives to that country and Hewie turned into one of Charlton's most valuable players in the post-war era. He played in nine different positions for them, including goalkeeper.
In 1955-6, Seed chose a team of South Africans to play Scotland in a game to raise funds for the 1956 Melbourne Olympics. Scotland won 2-1, watched by 50,000 at Ibrox, and Hewie starred for the Springboks.
Nicknamed 'Long John' because of his height and slim build, Hewie played against England at Wembley in 1956, eligible because of his father's birthplace. All but three of Hewie's caps were won at left-back, but he was renowned as a wing-half in club football.

HAMPDEN'S WICKED WIND

1959-60 For the first time in four years, Scotland had a hold on the home championship, sharing the title with Wales, but not since 1951 had they won the crown outright. Against overseas opposition there was a series of setbacks, indicating that work still had to be done before the next World Cup.

The 4-0 success in Belfast was Scotland's biggest win against a British team for nine years. After so long in the doldrums,

Scotland returned to scoring form with a counter-attacking style that brought four goals in the first 53 minutes. Wing-halves Dave Mackay and Bert McCann inspired a forward line that had an average age of 22, but the contest might have been closer if Northern Ireland's Jimmy McIlroy had converted a penalty when the score was 1-0.

Wales were saved from defeat at Hampden by a defence that was well-marshalled by John Charles, who had 'escaped' from Italy to play centre-half. Wales took a seventh-minute lead from Charles' free-kick and then lost full-back Mel Hopkins with facial injuries soon afterwards. Scotland had 20 corners, compared to Wales' three, but the only tangible outcome came when Leggat put home Auld's centre just after half-time. Bill Brown missed the last 15 minutes of the match with a head injury, and Mackay went in goal.

Spurs refused to release Brown, Mackay and White for the England game, so Alex Young and Frank Haffey won their first caps, while John Cumming came out of the international wilderness. There were nine Home-Scots on show plus Hibs' Joe Baker who played for England.

The wicked Hampden wind played havoc with the spectacle and the game was littered with free-kicks and throw-ins. England had two penalties and Charlton scored one and missed the other. In fact, Charlton missed it twice, Haffey having moved before the ball was kicked to save his first effort. The major controversy came when Baker charged Haffey into the net. The referee ruled 'no goal'.

In May, Poland won at Hampden, then Scotland flopped badly in Austria and were losing 4-0 until Mackay's 71st minute goal.

A week later, Scotland bounced back with a thrilling 3-3 draw with Hungary. English referee Arthur Ellis was jostled by Hungary's goalkeeper Grosics at the end of an eventful game.

Grosics' main complaint concerned Scotland's third goal, scored by Alex Young. Appeals for offside went unheeded and Scotland, now 3-2 ahead, looked like winning until Hungary's injury-time equaliser.

This tremendous performance — the half-back line, in particular, did exceptionally well — was followed by a dramatic defeat in Turkey. Scotland arrived in Ankara in the midst of a military coup. The 25,000 crowd was composed almost entirely of armed soldiers. There was no room for officials, and journalists had to squat on the running track.

The atmosphere was tense and the setting most unlikely for a sporting event. Eric Caldow's penalty equalised an early Turkish goal, but the Turks' outside-right, incongruously named Lefter, scored twice in three minutes before half-time. In boiling heat, on a bumpy pitch, Turkey led 4-1 before Alex Young headed Scotland's second.

Four players went on the summer tour but did not play a game — Niven (Rangers), Parker (Everton), Higgins (Hearts), Gabriel (Everton).

GRAHAM LEGGAT

1956 to 1960: Outside-right, 18 caps, 8 goals.
Born: Aberdeen, 1934.
Career: Aberdeen schools, Banks o' Dee, Aberdeen, Fulham, Birmingham City, Rotherham United.
Graham Leggat was a brave, fast-raiding winger who was also famous for his goalscoring deeds. For Aberdeen, he scored 29 goals in 1956-7 – and once scored five in a match against Airdrie – while his goal against England, on his Scotland debut in 1956, would have been the winner but for a last-minute equaliser from Haynes.
After his £16,000 move to Fulham in 1958, Leggat played anywhere in the forward line and averaged a goal every two games in over 250 Football League appearances. This versatility may have cost him his place on Scotland's right wing, and he was also unfortunate with injuries.

On 29 May 1960, Alex Young became Scotland's first-ever substitute when he came on after 12 minutes of the game against Austria, replacing the injured Denis Law.

MANAGER McCOLL

1960-61 Just before Wales beat Scotland for the first time in ten years, Andy Beattie decided that his club side, Nottingham Forest, needed him more than Scotland. Beattie was replaced by Ian McColl. Scotland beat Northern Ireland 5-2, but then suffered a record defeat at Wembley.

Scotland's team against Wales in 1960-61. Back row (left to right): McKay, Gabriel, Leslie, Caldow, Martins, Mackay. Front row: Herd, White, Young, Hunter, Wilson.

Eric Caldow and Johnny Haynes lead out their respective teams for the Scotland-England match at Wembley in April 1961.

In World Cup qualifying games there were two easy victories over Eire, but a heavy defeat against Czechoslovakia — Paddy Crerand was sent off — left the Scots needing to win the return against the Czechs to force a play-off.

The season started with Scotland's lightweight forward-line floundering in the Cardiff mud. Surprise was expressed at the omissions of Law and Leggat, and when Beattie decided not to travel with the team — a decision which staggered many people — it raised the question of whether a full-time manager was needed.

Beattie's replacement — still part-time — was 33-year old Ian McColl, who was still a Rangers player. His first game in charge was against Northern Ireland, who had lost their last five matches and who were having to scratch around for a team.

Jackie Plenderleith and Jim Baxter were introduced into the half-back line, and Ralph Brand scored twice, despite being parted from his Rangers scoring partner Jimmy Millar. Leggat was still out of favour, but Law returned to star alongside deep-lying Alex Young.

There were seven changes for the Wembley match. The average age of the Scotland team was 24, but the height of the forward line sparked rumours that Snow White had been drafted on to the selection committee. Older fans reminded people that the 'Wembley Wizards' were no giants.

The unusual scoreline of 9-3 will always be associated with the game at Wembley in April 1961. It was a particularly unfortunate

afternoon for goalkeeper Frank Haffey, who on another day might have saved four of the goals. The scoreline gave rise to a joke at the goalkeeper's expense: 'What's the time?' asked one fan. 'Nine past Haffey,' smirked another.

Scotland gained some credit for fighting back from 3-0 to 3-2 before a disputed 56th-minute goal. The Scots protested that Jimmy Greaves took a free-kick too quickly when Bryan Douglas put England 4-2 ahead. Although Scotland pulled back to 5-3, and nearly 5-4, they capitulated in the Wembley sunshine and only new-cap Billy McNeill earned high praise.

After this debacle, 15 players were hastily selected for the World Cup games with Eire. Law and Mackay were left out, but Scotland achieved two comfortable victories, despite David Herd's late withdrawal from the Dublin game.

Paddy Crerand was a star at Dalymount Park, but in Czechoslovakia, the Celtic wing-half was sent off along with Kvasnak in the 35th minute of the vital World Cup game. Scotland were losing 2-0 and Jim Baxter had been held responsible for both goals. Herd badly damaged a knee in the 70th minute to add to the depression. Scotland now needed to beat the Czechs at Hampden to progress.

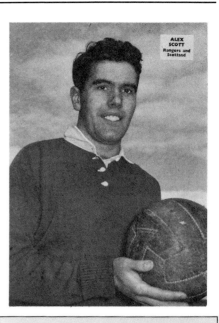

Rangers supplied six players against Czechoslovakia in May 1961 — Bobby Shearer, Eric Caldow, Jim Baxter, Ian McMillan, Alex Scott and Davie Wilson.

SO NEAR TO CHILE

1961-2 In the 83rd minute of the vital World Cup game against Czechoslovakia, with the score at 2-2, Denis Law swerved away from two lunging tackles, veered to the left-hand side of the penalty area, and then cut back his shot just inside the right-hand post.

Law's memorable winning goal earned a play-off in Brussels, but Czechoslovakia won 4-2 after extra-time and ended Scotland's hopes of going through to the World Cup Finals in Chile.

It was the one bleak spot in a season when the Scots conclusively won the home title, their first outright success for 11 years.

Law was the star of the Czechoslovakia game — Scotland twice equalised under Hampden's new floodlight pylons — but Torino refused to release him for the next two internationals.

Even so, Scotland chalked up confidence-boosting victories against Northern Ireland — all six goals coming from Rangers players — and Wales before the World Cup qualifying play-off in the Heysel Stadium.

There was an unsettling prelude to the game when confusion reigned over whether Law would be released to play, and then hasty measures to insure the player when he was allowed to appear. There were squabbles over the order of the national anthems, which balls should be used, and

Goalkeeper Frank Haffey after conceding nine goals at Wembley.

ALEX SCOTT

1956 to 1966: Outside-right, 16 caps, 5 goals.
Born: Falkirk, 1936.
Career: Camelon Thistle, Bo'ness United, Rangers, Everton, Hibernian, Falkirk.
Alex Scott's teenage progress was quite remarkable. On his Scottish League debut, he scored a hat-trick for Rangers against Falkirk, his home-town club. Eighteen months later, Scott, then 19, scored the only goal in his first international, against Northern Ireland. Scott, who won League Championship and Cup-winners' medals in Scotland and England, was on the winning side in 11 of his 16 internationals, but apart from a spell in 1961, he never enjoyed a sustained run in a Scotland shirt. In October 1961, he scored a hat-trick against Northern Ireland, when all six Scotland goals came from Rangers players.
Scott's younger brother, Jimmy Scott, was also a Scotland international. Both played for their country in 1966, but not in the same team.

whether Lawrie Leslie of West Ham could be included, even though he was not in Scotland's original list of 22 players submitted ten days in advance.

Scotland, troubled by injuries, included two new caps, Eddie Connachan and Hugh Robertson, and played Ralph Brand out of position rather than introduce a third new player. Three Dundee players were included in a youthful team.

Had Ian St John converted a good chance in the 66th minute, Scotland would have been 2-0 ahead. Instead, four minutes later, Hledik, the Czech right-back, headed in a corner. St John immediately slid in Ralph Brand's free-kick, but Scherer equalised with just eight minutes to play. The referee ruled that the ball had gone in and out of the net, rebounding off a stanchion.

In extra-time, John White hit the bar from 20 yards before the Czechs scored twice more. The door to Chile was closed, but it was no disgrace to lose to Czechoslovakia, who went on to the 1962 World Cup Final.

Although England qualified for the Finals, there was no doubt that Scotland were the best British team. A few weeks after Davie Wilson had scored a hat-trick against the English in an inter-League match, the winger opened the scoring at Hampden. His 15th-minute shot flew into the England net off Swan's right foot as the centre-half tried a goal-line clearance.

St John headed against the bar in the first-half, but midway through the second period, England claimed an equaliser when a shot from Haynes hit the bar and bounced down somewhere around the goal-line. Two minutes from time, Caldow sealed victory with a penalty. Scotland's three home internationals had produced ten goals for and only one against.

One game remained. It was a chance to avenge the Uruguay defeat of 1950. There was no Law and White, and only two days before, St John had played for Liverpool in the euphoric atmosphere of their Second Division championship success. It must be said, though, that the touring Uruguayans also had players claimed by clubs.

Soon after half-time, Uruguay were coasting 3-0 and in the 53rd minute, a scuffle broke out. Scotland rallied late in the game and Brand's brilliant last-minute goal was worthy of a better setting.

> In October 1962, Denis Law (Huddersfield, Manchester City, Torino and Manchester United) emulated the feat of Hughie Gallacher (Airdrie, Newcastle, Chelsea and Derby) of being capped while with four different clubs. No Scottish player has since repeated this achievement.

AUSTRIAN FIASCO

1962-3 Scotland confirmed their position as the top British team with a 100 per cent record in home internationals. They had revenge for the 9-3 Wembley mauling, though victory against England was marred by a tragic collision between Eric Caldow and England centre-forward Bobby Smith.

Then came a series of upsets when a violent clash with Austria was abandoned and Norway and Eire inflicted unlikely defeats, before the Scots ended the season in glory. Over the years, it has been a hallmark of the Scottish team that they can bind together when least expected. The 6-2 win in Spain was just such an occasion.

Ian Ure was a little fortunate to get his initial chance against Wales — Billy McNeill was injured — but he established himself at centre-half. Another regular was Rangers' teenage outside-right Willie Henderson, who crowned his debut with a spectacular 80th-minute goal against Wales.

Stormy scenes against Uruguay at Hampden Park.

Henderson might have played on the left-wing against Northern Ireland, but Steve Chalmers, included at outside-right, went down with influenza and had to wait a further two years for his first cap. The Irish game was dominated by Denis Law, who had scored four for Manchester United on the Saturday and who now hit four more.

Strangely, there was a stage in the game when Northern Ireland, leading through Billy Bingham's early goal, looked as though they might win at Hampden. But after Law's 40th-minute goal, the floodgates opened. Henderson and George Mulhall got the ball into the penalty area and Law's lightning reaction did the rest.

Only five minutes of the game at Wembley had gone when a tackle left Eric Caldow with a fractured leg, while England's Bobby Smith hobbled on the left wing with a knee injury.

Mackay was prepared to drop back to full-back, but manager McColl nominated Davie Wilson, who agreed to play left-back if McColl watched him from the touch-line. So Wilson took Caldow's place and played magnificently. Jim Baxter strode elegantly and arrogantly into the vacant spaces.

Baxter scored both Scotland's goals, first robbing Armfield to net from an angle, then calmly converting a penalty. England made a late rally and Douglas scored, but it was destined to be Scotland's day. 'Bewhiskied Scots weaved on to the field and kicked their tartan bonnets into the goals and planted their standards on the greenest turf in Britain, and impatient policemen chased them,' wrote John Rafferty in the *Scotsman*.

Over the years, Scotland-Austria games had not been suited to those with faint hearts, but the most volatile came in May 1963 when referee Jim Finney felt forced to abandon play after 79 minutes to prevent anyone being seriously hurt.

The international boiled over from the 16th minute when Finney allowed Scotland's first goal, despite a linesman's raised flag. After the second goal, ten minutes later, Austrian centre-forward Nemec protested so much that he was sent off. Five noisy minutes passed before Nemec left the

ENGLAND 1   SCOTLAND 2
6 April 1963, at Wembley

AFTER Scotland team manager Ian McColl had made a key decision — moving Davie Wilson to left-back to replace the injured Eric Caldow in the fifth minute — ten Scotsmen fought magnificently and played skilfully to win the game. On his first Wembley appearance, Jim Baxter stole the show with two goals, and his encore was to stuff the ball up his jersey at the final whistle and keep it as a souvenir.

It was a new-look Wembley that year. A roof of aliminium and glass had been fitted, but far from the Scots being overawed, they found that the new roof aided the acoustics — and tens of thousands of cheering Scottish fans made full use of it. "I knew they'd rebuilt Wembley — I didn't know they'd shifted it to Glasgow," said Jimmy Greaves as the teams emerged.

After five minutes, the mood changed when a cumbersome tackle by the burly England centre-forward Bobby Smith left Eric Caldow with a badly broken leg. Manager McColl arrived just as trainer John Harvey was helping Caldow on to a stretcher and Dave Mackay was preparing to play left-back.

"On my way down from the Royal Box, I'd been wondering what was the right move," recalls McColl. "Even though only five minutes had gone, I could see that our half-back line of Mackay, Ure and Baxter had settled. I didn't want to disturb that situation, perhaps because I'd been a wing-half myself.

"I also had to think of Dave Mackay. His international career had been full of upset and he hadn't played to his true form, so I didn't want to move him.

"I knew Davie Wilson very well, so I asked him to play left-back. He agreed, on one condition — that I stayed by him on the touch-line."

Wilson played brilliantly, while the man immediately in front of him, Jim Baxter, scored twice. The first was struck left-footed past the right hand of England's debutant goalkeeper Gordon Banks; the second, from the penalty spot after Ron Flowers had fouled Willie Henderson, sent Banks the wrong way.

Bryan Douglas scored a second-half goal for England, but the Scots passed the ball around and kept possession to win the home title.

ENGLAND: Banks; Armfield, Byrne, Moore, Norman, Flowers, Douglas, Greaves, Smith, Melia, Charlton.
SCOTLAND: Brown; Hamilton, Caldow, Mackay, Ure, Baxter, Henderson, White, St John, Law, Wilson.

Referee: L. Horn (Holland)   *Attendance: 98,606*

Jim Baxter scores, from the penalty spot, one of his goals in the 2-1 win for Scotland against England at Wembley in April 1963.

ERIC CALDOW

1957 to 1963: Full-back, 40 caps, 4 goals.
Born: Cumnock, Ayrshire, 1934.
Career: Cumnock Academy, Glenpark Juveniles, Muirkirk Juniors, Rangers, Stirling Albion, Corby Town (player-manager), Hurlford United (manager), Stranraer (manager).
Between April 1957 and April 1963, Eric Caldow missed only two internationals, but then at Wembley, on his 40th appearance, he fractured a leg in a collision with England's Bobby Smith. Caldow was especially quick on the turn. Although wingers might get by him, he was a hard man to leave behind, and once he won his chance in the Scotland team, he was an automatic selection. He captained the team for three years after taking over from Bobby Evans, and he took responsibility for penalty kicks.
His famous club partnership with Bobby Shearer represented Scotland four times, but Caldow also teamed up with John Hewie, Alex Parker, John Grant, Dunky McKay and Alex Hamilton.

pitch, then Law gave Scotland a 3-0 half-time lead.

The countries had agreed on substitutes for this 'friendly' — goalkeepers at any time and outfield players up to half-time — but when Austria lost Rafreider on a stretcher, it was just after half-time. They were forced to continue with nine men and Law zipped through to make it 4-0.

Linhart scored for Austria, then Hof was sent off. Almost immediately, Law avoided a flying boot, and then retaliated. Linhart crumpled to the floor and referee Finney decided that enough was enough.

"What could I do?" asked Finney afterwards. "I felt that I had to abandon the match or somebody would have been seriously hurt. I ordered Nemec off for spitting, and Hof for a diabolical tackle at waist-height."

The three-match tour of Europe gave Scotland a chance to look at new goalkeepers because Bill Brown preferred to tour with Spurs. Adam Blacklaw conceded two goals in the last ten minutes in Norway to give the amateurs a shock win, although Scotland had been forced to replace the injured Mackay, while Davie Gibson was hobbling by the end of the game.

Five days later, Tommy Lawrence conceded a sixth-minute goal when Noel Cantwell was first to a bouncing corner-kick to put Eire in front. This setback in Dublin occurred on a concrete-hard pitch and was aided by some concrete-hard Irish tackling.

Rather than bring in Brown (Partick) to face Spain, Scotland switched McNeill to full-back. The Scots started nervously and conceded a goal. Law's 15th-minute equaliser started an incredible burst of three Scottish goals in three minutes.

Ure fed Wilson in the 34th minute and Scotland led 4-1 against a Spanish side that was rebuilding after the great Real Madrid era. The Scots led 4-2 at half-time, and ten minutes later, St John raced from the halfway line to set up Henderson for the fifth. St John's late goal made it 6-2.

PROLIFIC LAW

1963-4 Scotland had a wealth of individual talent and, if it could all be put together at the right time and in the right place, then there seemed no limit to what could be achieved with the abundant skills available. Missing Baxter, Law and Wilson, there was a shock defeat in Belfast, but thereafter, the Scots were unbeaten in a season which promised much.

"Non-triers, it's as simple as that," explained Ian McColl after the defeat by Northern Ireland. There was also a need for a goalscorer, so Alex Scott and Denis Law came back into the team, and Alan Gilzean was included at centre-forward.

At the time, Law was playing well enough to solve any goalscoring problems on his own. Four goals against Norway took his tally to 15 in his last eight internationals. The Norway game was arranged for a Wednesday, but postponed because of fog. Frantic negotiations permitted the game to be played the following evening.

Norway took an early lead, but the Scots were in rampant mood. Law's close-range reflex finishing combined with Mackay's long-range rocket shots to bring six goals.

When Gilzean went around the Welsh goalkeeper and presented Law with an easy goal in the next game, it not only gave Scotland a 2-0 lead but also meant that Law had scored 21 goals in 22 games (including the abandoned Austria match and another against Austria when he was on the field for only 11 minutes). Law, only 23, was within sight of Gallacher's 23-goal record for Scotland.

DAVE MACKAY

1957 to 1965: Wing-half, 22 caps, 4 goals.
Born: Edinburgh, 1934.
Career: Slateford Athletic, Newtongrange Star, Hearts, Tottenham Hotspur, Derby County, Swindon Town (player-manager), Nottingham Forest (manager), Derby County (manager), Walsall (manager), Arabic Sporting Club, Kuwait (manager).
Dave Mackay won virtually every honour in the game: caps at Schoolboy, Under-23 and full levels; Scottish League, League Cup and Cup-winners' medal (with Hearts); Football League and FA Cup-winners' medals (with Spurs); Second Division championship winners' medal and joint Footballer of the Year (with Derby); and the first player to represent the Scottish League against the Football League and the Football League v Scottish League.
At first glance it is strange that Mackay won only 22 caps, for he was a driving force behind great teams. He had attacking attributes such as a powerful shot – against Norway in 1963, he hit a goal with each foot from 25 yards – a delicate chip and a long throw. But he was better known for his tough tackling defensive work.
Yet his early international appearances coincided with some failures (Spain 1-4 and England 3-9) and he spent two years out of favour in the early 1960s. Just as he was re-establishing himself as captain, he was hit by injury in 1963. A twice-fractured leg sidelined him for 21 months. His reappearance, against Northern Ireland in 1965, was perhaps premature, for he was well below the form that he later displayed.

Unlike Scotland, England now had a full-time manager in Alf Ramsey, who was introducing his team to the 4-2-4 system. After a tactical workout against Ayr United — "It's the second time I've played against England and not won a cap," said Ayr wing-half Willie Toner — England suffered their third successive defeat against Scotland.

Including nine players from Scottish League clubs, Scotland were stirred to one of their best post-war displays. The 1964 game was decided 18 minutes from time when Gilzean's head reached a corner before Banks and Norman could get to the ball. One English journalist commented that England had slavishly adhered to the 4-2-4 system 'that wouldn't have beaten Scotland even if it had been 40-20-40.'

Scotland, the British champions, seemed a good bet for the 1966 World Cup Finals when they forced a draw in a friendly with West Germany in the intense heat of Hanover. The Scots were 2-0 down after 32 minutes — Seeler scored them both — and it was not until the sun dipped below the stands midway through the second half, that Scotland hit back. A smart Gilzean header reduced the deficit. Six minutes from time, Law forced the ball against a post and Gilzean snatched the equaliser. West Germany had yet to beat Scotland in an international.

At Ibrox, on 24 February 1964, a Scotland team beat the Scottish League 3-1 with goals from McBride (2) and McIlroy.

CRAZY OPENING

1964-5 The 1966 World Cup Finals were to be staged in England. The Scots, drawn in a qualifying group with Finland, Poland and Italy, made a fine start with two victories over the Finns and an excellent draw in Poland. There was, however, still a long way to go and only one team would qualify.

Scotland controlled the game in Wales, but lost when Ken Leek scored twice in the last four minutes. This heralded an unbeaten run of six games that saw out the season, a run which equalled the best performance since the war.

With Ure, Yeats and McNeill unfit, John McGrory came in at centre-half to face the Finns, who fielded only one professional. Law headed a first-minute goal and Scotland raced to a 3-0 half-time lead. Scott had pulled a leg muscle and Finland came back into the game.

The Hampden duel with Northern Ireland had a crazy opening 31 minutes during which time all the game's five goals were scored. Best's shot went in off Irvine's head, Davie Wilson followed up John Greig's shot to equalise, Alan Gilzean celebrated his return from injury with a goal, Irvine's flying header kept the Irish in the game, and Wilson's spectacular right-foot shot ended the scoring. And there was virtually an hour still to play. The team at Wembley was dominated

BILL BROWN

**1958 to 1965: Goalkeeper, 28 caps.
Born: Arbroath, 1931.
Career: Arbroath Cliftburn, Carnoustie Juveniles, Carnoustie Panmure, Dundee, Tottenham Hotspur, Northampton Town, Toronto Falcons.
After 24 successive nominations as reserve to Tommy Younger, Bill Brown finally received his chance against France in 1958, when he was still with Dundee. He joined Spurs for £16,500 in June 1959 and became a member of the Tottenham team which won the Double in 1960-61. Brown did not miss a game as Spurs became the first club this century to lift both English League Championship and FA Cup. Lean and agile, Brown won Schoolboy and Under-23 honours. He broke Jimmy Cowan's record of caps for a goalkeeper and held it until surpassed by Alan Rough.**

---

by Anglo-Scots. Three of them — Brown, Crerand and Collins — were recalled after long absences, six years in Collins' case. Eddie McCreadie was winning his first cap.

Scotland were criticised for not making light work of an England team reduced to nine fit men for the second half. England took a 2-0 lead by the 35th minute, through deflected shots by Bobby Charlton (off Alex Hamilton's knee) and Jimmy Greaves (off the post) but Scotland came back with a strange goal by Law five minutes before half-time.

Law hit a dipping shot from 30 yards, Banks misjudged it, kicked wildly at the ball and sliced it into the net. 'The goal was historic on two scores,' wrote John Rafferty. 'It made Law Scotland's highest-ever goalscorer and it was the first time that a goalkeeper had been 'yorked'.'

Either side of half-time, England lost Wilson (rib injury) and Byrne (cartilage)

but St John's 59th-minute shot produced the only goal of the second half.

Three changes meant a better blend against Spain — John Hughes and Billy Bremner made their debuts — in a game played on a Saturday evening. It was yet another windy Hampden venue. The players had trouble controlling the ball, and the referee had trouble controlling the players. Willie Henderson came in for some rough treatment, and Reija of Spain was sent off.

Then came two World Cup qualifying games in five days, preceded by a sensation. While the Scotland team were at Largs, preparing for the trip, Ian McColl was deposed as manager and the SFA temporarily appointed Jock Stein, who was steering Celtic to glory.

Spectators in the 100,000-seater stadium in Chorzow's Park of Culture had their spirits dampened by dreadfully wet conditions. Law saved the precious point with a goal 12 minutes from time. Collins' cross was knocked out, Henderson headed it back in, and Law did the rest.

After a 13-hour journey by bus, train and aeroplane, there was a good result in Finland, although it was not without its worries. Hyvarinon put the Finns ahead in the fifth minute, and Law hit the inside of a post with a 15th-minute penalty.

Undeterred, Law made the equaliser when his cross was cunningly dummied by Willie Hamilton for Wilson to shoot home. Law was voted man of the match — the prize was a silver spoon — but it was left to John Greig to show the white-shirted Scottish forwards how it should be done. Greig's 25-yarder won the game.

ECSTACY AND GLOOM

1965-6 The long, drawn-out qualifying route to the World Cup Finals sharpened the feelings of Scottish fans. There was satisfaction for most of the game with Poland as Scotland led 1-0, then despair as the Poles scored twice in the last ten minutes. Frustration as Italy dogged Scotland in a game they had to win was followed by a moment of ecstasy when Greig's 88th-minute thunderbolt sealed victory. Finally, gloom shrouded Scottish football when the depleted Scots went down in Naples.

The 1966 World Cup Final was fought out between England and West Germany, two sides that Scotland had outclassed two years earlier, and the Scottish season petered out with some disappointing results.

In Belfast, Law damaged his shoulder in the fifth minute, and Scotland lost 3-2 to an 88th-minute goal following a twice-taken free-kick.

Hughes, Mackay and Baxter were left out of the side to play Poland, while Willie Johnston, 18, was the surprise inclusion. Skipper Billy McNeill opened the scoring following a 14th-minute corner, and Scotland should have had more to show for their first-half dominance.

In the second half, Willie Henderson began limping, then Liberda scored an 84th-minute equaliser. The tragic transformation continued in the next minute

DAVIE WILSON

1960 to 1965: Outside-left, 22 caps, 9 goals.
Born: Glasgow, 1939.
Career: Baillieston Juniors, Rangers, Dundee United, Dumbarton, Dumbarton (asst manager, later manager), Kilmarnock (asst manager).
After the 1950s had seen a steady stream of left-wingers – ever since Billy Liddell retired – the problem was solved by the advent of Davie Wilson, a direct winger who could cut in and shoot. Among his goals for Scotland was the key strike against England in 1962, while the following year, at Wembley, he excelled in the unfamiliar left-back position, a switch caused by Caldow's injury.
To score nine goals in 22 internationals is a fine achievement for a winger, and Wilson's scoring prowess was also demonstrated in other football. He once hit three for the Scottish League against the Football League and scored six for Rangers against Falkirk in a 1962 game. A leg fracture received in a Scottish League Cup semi-final caused him to miss three internationals in 1963, but he came back to lay on the winning goal against the English later that season.

IAN ST JOHN

1959 to 1965: Centre-forward, 21 caps (1 as sub), 9 goals.
Born: Motherwell, 1938.
Career: Motherwell Bridge Works FC, Douglas Water Thistle, Motherwell, Liverpool, Coventry City, Coventry City (asst. manager), Motherwell (manager), Portsmouth (manager).
Ian St John's selection as Scotland's centre-forward was received with some criticism in the early 1960s, but the selectors kept watching him and had it not been for injuries, he might have won more caps. He was an energetic leader, relying on a springy leap to compensate for a lack of inches.
St John was a creative player, but some of his goalscoring achievements are also memorable, including the quickest hat-trick in Scottish football (2 minutes for Motherwell) and four goals for the Scottish League (against the Irish League at Ibrox in 1959). It is sad that his two goals against Czechoslovakia in Brussels in 1961 did not win Scotland a place in the World Cup Finals.
At Liverpool he was worshipped. One story suggests that a religious hoarding 'Jesus Saves' provoked the response, 'But St John knocks in the rebound'.

JOHN WHITE

1959 to 1964: Inside-forward, 22 caps, 3 goals.
Born: Musselburgh, Midlothian, 1937.
Career: Musselburgh Union, Bonnyrigg Rose Athletic, Alloa Athletic, Falkirk, Tottenham Hotspur.
John White was slim and appeared frail, but he was one of the most skilful, scheming inside-forwards of all time. At Tottenham they knew him as 'the White Ghost', or 'the Ghost of White Hart Lane', because he flitted about the field, appearing unexpectedly, delicately prompting the flow of attacks.
In 1959, Falkirk, who had bought White from Alloa for £3,300 two years earlier, made a huge profit by selling him to Spurs for £20,000. His skills helped Tottenham create their Double-winning team. White scored on his Scotland debut, after which there was little doubt that he would be the rightful number eight. But he missed some internationals through club commitments, and his untimely death – struck down by lightning on a golf course in 1964, aged 27 – cut him down in his prime. Like James Dunlop, John Thomson and Peter Scarff, he died a young man with all Scotland mourning.

A common problem when Scotland played continental opposition was the need to negotiate a satisfactory arrangement regarding the use of substitutes. Against Finland, in May 1954, for instance, Andy Beattie thought the teams had agreed on no substitutes but found the Finns had spare goalkeepers changed before the game. Someone had to be sent back to the Scots' hotel to collect Fred Martin's boots. Not until May 1969 was a substitute used against a British country — Jim Herriot against Wales.

Seven post-war Scottish internationals have qualified through parentage rather than birthplace — Alex Cropley, David Harvey, John Hewie, Bruce Rioch, Bob Wilson, Andy Goram and Richard Gough.

Denis Law and Jim Baxter played in the Rest of Europe team which met Scandinavia on 20 May 1964 in Copenhagen. Law scored a goal as the Rest of Europe won 4-2. The match celebrated the 75th anniversary of the Danish FA.

"That the 1966 World Cup Finals were being held in England meant that we just had to qualify, such were the advantages of playing in Britain,"said Jock Stein.
"Before the Naples game we had two injured goalkeepers and on the Saturday before the game I went to watch Adam Blacklaw of Burnley. That same day, Law and Henderson were injured. Until then it had been a good year — we'd beaten Italy at Hampden in one of the best internationals for ages — but by the time we got to Naples, we stood no chance."

when Sadek's bouncing shot deceived Brown and gave Poland victory.

Scotland's two remaining World Cup games were against Italy, who led the group with seven points from four games. Scotland, needing to win the game at Hampden, completely reshaped their defence with Greig at right-back.

Bill Brown played more than half the game with a pulled leg muscle, but most of the action centred around Italy's padlocked defence. Scotland attacked relentlessly and, just when it seemed that they had been denied victory, came glory. Baxter glided through and curled the ball into the path of Greig whose powerful shot won the game. Jock Stein was so overjoyed that he jumped fully-clad into the bath to join his team.

Greig scored a late-goal in the next game, against Wales, but this time it was not decisive, merely sealing a 4-1 victory. All the game's other goals had come in the first 20 minutes with Henderson's solo effort and Bobby Murdoch's volley particularly memorable for Scotland, who played in all-white.

Injuries had meant four new caps against Wales, but the game in Italy proved an even bigger headache. McNeill, Law, Baxter Henderson and Willie Stevenson were all ruled out, and Stein plumped for a defensive performance in the hope of forcing a play-off. Liverpool stopper Ron Yeats wore the number nine but dropped back as an extra centre-half.

With such tactics, Scotland could not afford McCreadie's 38th-minute miskick which allowed Pascuti to put Italy ahead. Late goals by Faccheti and Mora underlined the Italian victory, and Scottish fans had nothing but the eventual consolation of Italy suffering humiliation at the hands of North Korea in the Finals.

Jock Stein resigned after the Naples game and the SFA advertised for a part-time manager: '.....the job might suit a man with other business interests'.

After Willie Waddell and Eddie Turnbull had turned down the post, the job went to the uncapped John Prentice who had a tough baptism in the international arena.

Another new-look team went down 4-3 to England at Hampden. Highlights were Law's leap and near-post header which cut England's lead to 2-1, and a fight-back that brought two goals for Willie Johnston and which almost saved the game when Willie Wallace's shot was headed off the line by Stiles.

Five Rangers stars played their third match in a week when Scotland were humiliated 3-0 by Holland, then a late Portugal goal inflicted Scotland's third successive defeat.

All was forgotten, however, when an understrength Scotland took a first-minute lead against Brazil. The Brazilians equalised after 15 minutes when Jair crossed from the right and Servillo scored at the far post, but a 1-1 draw was an excellent result against a team with experienced Bellini and Zico, the up-and-coming Gerson and Amarildo, not to mention a phenomenon called Pele.

DENIS LAW

**1958 to 1974: Inside-forward, 55 caps, 30 goals.
Born: Aberdeen, 1940.
Career: Aberdeen Schools, Huddersfield Town, Manchester City, Torino (Italy), Manchester United, Manchester City.**
When Denis Law arrived at Huddersfield as a skinny 15-year-old wearing thick glasses, it is claimed that he was missed by those waiting to meet him at the station. But people soon found it impossible to take their eyes off the man who became one of football's most brilliant goalscorers.
He would stroll, then dart, chase and tackle. And he hit goals from all heights and with either foot. Many of them were the culmination of a soaring leap and a salmon-like twist of head and body. He was not a great dribbler, nor did he possess a hard shot, but he was probably a better snaffler of half-chances than any other player.
He was Scotland's youngest debutant in modern times. He scored on his debut, in Wales, and his Hampden debut was devastating. He was 'Denis the Menace', or simply 'the King'. In the early 1960s, he was sometimes overlooked, and there were times when he was unavailable, especially after his £100,000 transfer to Italy, the first six-figure fee involving a British club.
In 1962-3, Law scored 11 goals in seven games, gave a brilliant display at Wembley, and had a short spell as captain though still only 23. Next season he scored for the Rest of the World against England and stole the show.
In the late 1960s, Law overcame a bad knee injury and re-established himself in the Scotland team in 1971-2. A free transfer from Manchester United at the end of the next season did not halt his international career. He re-signed for Manchester City and achieved his ambition of playing in the World Cup Finals. Law broke George Young's appearances record and he held the scoring record for 18 years. Today, his influence lives on in the players who admired him such as Kenny Dalglish and Asa Hartford.

WORLD CHAMPIONS DEFEATED

1966-7 The relevance of the home championship was now being questioned, but the competition assumed a new dimension when it was announced that it would serve as a qualifying round for the European Nations Cup. Scotland made a fine start and by the halfway stage they had five points from three games, including a win over World Cup holders England at Wembley.

In a season of only four international matches, Scotland had two managers. Kilmarnock boss Malcolm MacDonald was caretaker for the first two games before Bobby Brown became Scotland's first full-time team manager.

It was a strange, subdued Ninian Park which greeted Scotland for the Wales game. Black armbands were hardly sufficient to describe the previous day's disaster at Aberfan where a slag mountain had come sliding through the morning mist and buried the village school.

The game itself was not memorable. Scotland played 4-2-4 with Bremner and Baxter in midfield, and the striking combination of Joe McBride and Denis Law saved them with two minutes to play. Sprake partially saved from McBride and the ever-alert Law snapped up the chance to equalise Ron Davies' breakaway goal of eight minutes earlier.

After six games without a win, Scotland scored a tortuous 2-1 victory over Northern Ireland who were without George Best. The Irish scored with their first shot, Nicholson deceiving Ferguson with a dipper. Scotland equalised, also from long-range, with a shot from Bobby Murdoch, whose record of five goals in 12 internationals ranks with that of some strikers.

Scotland's winner came from Bobby Lennox, who hooked the ball over his shoulder late in the first half.

After Jimmy Cowan's spectacular display in 1949, Wembley had proved something of a goalkeeping graveyard for Scotland at six-year intervals — Martin in 1955 and Haffey in 1961 had every reason to forget those games — so the more superstitious held their breath when 36-year-old Ronnie Simpson was called up for his first cap in 1967 — at Wembley.

It was Bobby Brown's first game in charge and it proved to be an overwhelmingly successful debut for the new Scotland boss. Willie Wallace was a late replacement for club mate Jimmy Johnstone, while Baxter, Bremner and Jim McCalliog formed a midfield which dominated the match.

Scotland took a 2-0 lead, sent on their way, as usual, by Law's opportunism at snapping up a rebound. England fielded ten of the side which had won the World Cup Final ten months earlier, but they had to wait until the last ten minutes for their two goals. Jack Charlton limped at centre-forward for much of the game — only goalkeepers could be substituted — but that took nothing away from a fine Scotland performance.

Ronnie Simpson, son of pre-war Rangers stopper centre-half Jimmy Simpson, used

ENGLAND 2 SCOTLAND 3
15 April 1967, at Wembley

TEN members of England's World Cup-winning team were on the field the day that Scotland took the Auld Enemy apart at Wembley. It was Scotland's own World Cup Final, and it ended England's unbeaten run of 19 games.

England had achieved their success with Sir Alf Ramsey's well-drilled 4-3-3 system. Now the Scots found a system to match, a 4-3-3 formation with added flair. It was the first Scotland team selected by Bobby Brown.

"We had a problem in goal," recalls Brown. "I brought in Ronnie Simpson for his first cap. He'd been highly successful with Celtic, and he was the ideal man in a crisis, a calming influence. He was also a reliable goalkeeper.

"I chose the club partnership of John Greig and Ronnie McKinnon for the back. I thought we needed a midfield ball-player — Baxter — and a ball-winner — Bremner — but it was a question of who to play between them. We needed someone who could get a goal, but who could defend when necessary. I chose Jim McCalliog, who could do both. He was not pacey, but he was an intelligent player who could follow instructions."

It worked a treat. Denis Law, who often tended to drift into midfield, stayed up front and had one of his best games, scoring Scotland's opening goal.

Bobby Lennox made it 2-0 before the injured Jackie Charlton — who turned out to be England's best forward after limping into attack — pulled one back. Jim McCalliog got a third at the near post, and Scotland were home and dry.

"Bremner and Baxter were magnificent," said Brown. "We were right on top of England and would have won 5-2 but for Gordon Banks."

Scotland demonstrated their supremacy, not so much by the scoreline, but by their manner. Baxter was the master victor. He calmly walked away from one ball, knowing that Law would get there first, he played 'keepie-uppie' on the edge of his own penalty area, and he helped weave passing patterns through midfield as Scotland became self-annointed 'world champions'.

ENGLAND: Banks; Cohen, Wilson, Stiles, J.Charlton, Moore, Ball, Greaves, R.Charlton, Hurst, Peters.
SCOTLAND: Simpson; Gemmell, McCreadie, Greig, McKinnon, Bremner, McCalliog, Law, Wallace, Baxter, Lennox.

Referee: G.Schulenburg (West Germany)   Attendance: 99,063

The oldest player on the pitch, Ronnie Simpson (36), is congratulated by the youngest, Jim McCalliog (20), after Scotland's victory over the 'World Champions' in 1967. Both players were making their international debut. But whereas Simpson was the ninth Celtic player to wear a Scotland shirt in only three internationals, McCalliog was the first Sheffield Wednesday player to be capped for 47 years.

ALEX HAMILTON

1961 to 1965: Right-back, 24 caps.
Born: Bo'ness, West Lothian, 1939.
Career: Westrigg Bluebell, Dundee.
In 1961-2, Dundee took Scottish football by storm as they swept to their first title. Against Wales, in November 1961, two defenders sporting crewcuts were brought into the Scotland team. They were Ian Ure and Alex Hamilton. In his second game Hamilton faced the speed of Jelinek in the vital World Cup decider in Brussels. Scotland lost but Hamilton retained his place. In four years he missed only one of Scotland's 25 internationals. Hamilton spent ten years at Dundee, his only professional club. Fast in the tackle and quick to recover, Hamilton was quite adventurous for his day. He played against England four times, each time mastering the threat of Bobby Charlton. Scotland won three and drew one. He appeared as a substitute when the Rest of Europe won 4-2 in Scandinavia.

JIM BAXTER

1960 to 1967: Wing-half, 34 caps, 3 goals.
Born: Hill O'Beath, Fife, 1939.
Career: Beath High School, Halbeath Youth Club, Crossgates Primrose, Raith Rovers, Rangers, Sunderland, Nottingham Forest, Rangers.
During a career liberally sprinkled with brilliance and controversy, Jim Baxter will best be remembered by Scottish fans for his displays at Wembley in 1963 and 1967. England players were the bulls to his taunting matador act and Baxter's unhurried left-footed attacking play was world-class. Raised in a miners' row in Hill O'Beath, Baxter left school to work as a cabinet-maker in Dunfermline, then at Fordel Colliery. He became a part-timer at Raith Rovers before Rangers signed him for £20,000 just before he joined the Black Watch as one of the last National Service conscripts. Baxter's five years with Rangers brought him a tremendous haul of medals – three Championships, four League Cups, three Scottish Cups. His progress was temporarily halted by injuries including a flaked ankle bone against Wales and a broken leg playing for Rangers in Vienna, but there seemed to limit to what 'Slim Jim' could achieve.
Baxter was Ian McColl's first signing at Sunderland (£72,500 in May 1965) and two and a half years later, Nottingham Forest paid a six-figure fee for him. By then, Baxter's lifestyle was affecting his physique. Before he was 30, Forest gave him a free transfer.

BILLY McNEILL MBE

1961 to 1972: Centre-half, 29 caps (1 as sub), 3 goals.
Born: Bellshill, Lanarkshire, 1940.
Career: Blantyre Victoria, Celtic, Clyde (manager), Aberdeen (manager), Celtic (manager), Manchester City (manager), Aston Villa (manager), Celtic (manager).
Billy McNeill came into a struggling Celtic team as a 19-year-old and enjoyed a one-club career that brought him more honours than any other player in British football history – nine Championships, seven Scottish Cup wins, six League Cup wins. He played in 24 major cup finals and he was the first British player to receive the European Cup.
The tall McNeill was superb in the air, and his winning goal in the 1965 Scottish Cup Final is considered by many as a turning point in Celtic's history. That year he captained Scotland in six successive internationals, but injuries cost him caps in his early career, and eventually one such injury lost him his place to Ron McKinnon.

On 19 May 1967, Scotland Under-23s beat Leeds United 3-2 at Hampden Park. Leeds fielded nine of the team which played in the European Cup Final nine days later. They had five Scottish internationals in their team, Harvey, Bremner, Lorimer, Jordan and Eddie Gray, as well as Frank Gray who was capped later.
Craig, Conn and Forsyth scored for the Under-23s whose team was: Rough (Partick T.); Forsythe (Man U.), Houston (Man U.), McCluskey (Celtic) (sub Miller of Aberdeen), Young (Aberdeen), Narey (Dundee U.), Conn (Spurs), Pettigrew (Motherwell), Pearson (Everton), Gray (Dundee U.), Craig (Newcastle).

In the summer of 1967, the Scottish team played matches in Israel, Hong Kong, Australia, New Zealand and Canada. They won all nine games, including 7-2 victories over Canada and a New Zealand Under-23 team.

Twice in 1967, against Northern Ireland and USSR, Celtic provided six of the Scotland team. First there were John Clark, Tommy Gemmell, Bobby Murdoch, Steve Chalmers, Joe McBride and Bobby Lennox; against Russia, the six Celts were Ronnie Simpson, Gemmell, Clark, Billy McNeill, Jimmy Johnstone and Lennox. And when Willie Wallace substituted for Denis Law in the Russia game, Celtic had seven men on the field.

his considerable experience with Celtic and Newcastle to calm any Wembley nerves. On his next appearance, however, Simpson found that he was the younger of two goalkeepers because Russia's Lev Yashin was 37. Two breakaway Soviet goals beat Simpson, the first lofted over his head by his own full-back Tommy Gemmell, the second a 25-yard effort from Medvid.

In the summer of 1967, a world tour gave new manager Bobby Brown an opportunity to see some of the young players on the fringe of international selection. Results were excellent and all nine games were won, but there were setbacks when a game with a Chinese XI was cancelled, while injuries meant that extra players, McLean and McGrory, had to be flown out.

EUROPEAN DREAMS SHATTERED

1967-8 A third successive defeat in Belfast was a setback to hopes of reaching the European Championship Finals, and victory over England at Hampden was needed. When John Hughes headed an equaliser just before half-time in the final qualifying match, Scotland looked set. But the Scots could not wrest the initiative and the resultant draw meant that England went through while the Scots were left to reflect on shattered dreams.

The real damage had been done in Belfast where George Best finally came good in an emerald green shirt. Scotland were missing three players through suspension and only three of the team beaten 1-0 by the Irish retained their places for the next match against Wales.

A goal by Durban, scored on the break, gave Wales a 2-1 lead after 55 minutes. Gilzean equalised ten minutes later — his second beautifully headed goal of the match from a Bobby Lennox cross. Scotland's winner came 15 minutes later, a volley by Ron McKinnon for his first international goal.

Gilzean was a late withdrawal, through injury, when England came to Hampden for Scotland's first February fixture since 1931.

Had a goal been allowed when Lennox put the ball in the England net — it was ruled out because of a foul on Banks — the result might have been different. But a minute later, Peters put England ahead, and Ramsey's superbly drilled defence kept control in the second half.

There were limited playing resources available for the trip to Amsterdam, where five players — Doug Fraser, Bobby Moncur, David Smith, Bobby Hope and George McLean — made their debuts. A sixth new cap, Jimmy Smith, came on for the injured Hope after 15 minutes. John Greig played as link-man.

ALAN GILZEAN

1963 to 1971: Centre-forward, 22 caps (2 as sub), 12 goals.
Born: Coupar-Angus, Perthshire, 1938.
Career: Coupar-Angus Juveniles, Dundee Violet, Dundee, Tottenham Hotspur, Stevenage Town (manager).
In the early 1960s, Alan Gilzean scored 122 Scottish League goals for Dundee in just over four years, seven of them coming in one match against Queen of the South. He starred when Dundee won the League and embarked on the European Cup. Towards the end of his Dundee days, Gilzean was capped and formed an immediately successful partnership with Denis Law.
'Gilly' was both strong and subtle in his heading, and he was skilful on the ground. He was not on a losing Scotland side until his seventh international and during that run he headed in Davie Wilson's cross for the only goal of the 1964 game against England.
In December 1964, he joined Spurs for £72,500 and enjoyed ten years of glory, narrowly failing to score a century of League goals for Spurs. His partnership with Jimmy Greaves created many more goals and later, Greaves developed a television partnership with Ian St John, the man Gilzean displaced from the Scotland team in 1963.

EIGHT AGAINST CYPRUS

1968-9 There was an excellent start to a hectic campaign to qualify for the 1970 World Cup Finals in Mexico — seven points from four games — but success hinged on trips to West Germany and Austria the following season.

Meanwhile, defeat at Wembley ended a run of nine internationals without defeat, only one victory short of Scotland's best

record this century and the best since that initiated by the Wembley Wizards in 1928. Nevertheless, manager Bobby Brown had his critics amongst Scotland supporters.

Captained by Billy Bremner, Scotland started with a warm-up friendly against Denmark. The Scots had 80 per cent of the play but the deciding goal was delayed until the 70th minute. Lennox's left-foot shot followed Scotland's 11th corner of the match.

After the experiments of previous matches, there was a view that the team to face Austria was the best that Scotland could muster. In the seething Hampden atmosphere, Austria took a third-minute lead — Starek hit a wind-assisted goal — but Law leaped high to head a swift equaliser. Soon after the fair-haired striker had been substituted, Bremner's determination forced the ball over the line for the winner with 15 minutes to play.

Scotland's next World Cup game involved an unenviable trip to Cyprus. There was a nightmare journey, a dreadful pitch, and all the usual problems about players' availability. Three Celtic men (Johnstone, Hughes and Gemmell) were injured, and Gemmell's named replacement, Jim Craig, was a dental surgeon who had patients booked for the day of the game, so he too was unavailable.

The Nicosia pitch resembled a concrete playground, but Scotland's players set manfully about their task and scored five times in the first-half against a team that had held West Germany until injury-time.

Next came the West Germans themselves, one of the world's strongest teams. A typical piece of opportunism by Muller gave them the lead just before the interval. Scotland's experienced team battled away and five minutes from time came one of the many memorable moments of the 1960s. Substitute Charlie Cooke, who was not in the Chelsea first team at the time, held the ball, dummied the defence, and rolled a perfect pass for Bobby Murdoch to slam in the equaliser. A draw was a good result, but many feared that it would be insufficient.

The rescheduling of the home championship to the end of the season improved players' availability, though there were still problems for the World Cup games. The new dates also had a drastic effect on attendances. There were fewer than 19,000 at Wrexham when Scotland's attack out-scored the Welsh aerial strikeforce of Ron Davies, Wyn Davies and John Toshack.

Three days later, an abysmally small crowd of 7,483, the smallest ever to watch a Hampden international, created a desolate atmosphere on a rainy evening. Colin Stein's header forced a draw against Northern Ireland in an overall poor Scottish performance.

Saturday evening of the same week was another dismal time for Scottish fans. They lost 4-1 to England and on the same evening, West Germany beat Austria to make Scotland's World Cup chances slimmer.

Like the previous season, the England game produced a promising period of Scottish play just before half-time when

Stein's header reduced the deficit to 2-1. Then Greig and Peters clashed, England were awarded a penalty and Scottish hopes were gone. This was the first time that Scotland's clash with the Auld Enemy had been televised live.

Scotland answered their critics in the best possible way, scoring eight against Cyprus. It was their biggest victory margin since 1901 and some felt that Stein could have been entrusted with the penalty which might have helped him equal Hughie Gallacher's record of five goals in an international.

AN HONOURABLE EXIT

1969-70 World Cup progress depended on events in Hamburg. The Scots fought magnificently and honourably, and in the 62nd minute, Gilzean rose perfectly to head

in McKinnon's cross and make the score 2-2. Scotland now appeared to have every chance of gaining the victory which was vital to their hopes, but Libuda's 79th-minute goal meant that West Germany topped Group Seven at a crucial time.

Scotland prepared for the vital West Germany game by playing a friendly in Dublin on a Sunday, just 24 hours after six of the team had played in a Rangers-Celtic clash at Ibrox. Stein scored an early goal but, not surprisingly, the Scots were jaded. Ernie McGarr was injured, and Jim Herriot's first touch as substitute goalkeeper was to block a shot by Givens, who hit home the rebound to give Eire a draw. In the second half, Callaghan raced 50 yards and nearly stole a winner for the home side.

West Germany's success in Hamburg was the first time that a German side had beaten Scotland in six attempts. Wolves forward Hugh Curran might have won his first cap, but illness denied him at the last moment.

Eddie Gray's 25-yard shot was stopped by Maier, but Jimmy Johnstone put in the rebound to give Scotland a dream start. Fitchel equalised late in the first half, then Tommy Gemmell and Billy Bremner both hit a post and it was West Germany who took the lead. Beckenbauer took a free-kick, Seeler headed goalwards and Muller shot home a brilliant goal. A similar move proved too good for England nine months later.

Despite Gilzean's header, Scotland went down, losing Gemmell who was sent off for retaliation in the last minute. Manager Brown blamed Swiss official Gilbert Droz for weak refereeing.

There was nothing at stake when Scotland visited Austria for the final match in Group Seven. Ernie McGarr was back in goal, Curran and Francis Burns won their first caps, but goals from Redl, one in each half, gave Austria a 2-0 win.

The switch of the home internationals to the end of the season now began to cause just as many availability problems because clubs like Leeds, in European or domestic competitions, declined to release players. Nevertheless, Scotland went unbeaten and shared the crown in a three-way tie.

For the first time since 1926, Scotland kept a clean sheet against each of the other three home nations, although this was a sign of the defence-dominated times rather than Scotland's own supremacy. Their only goal came from John O'Hare against Northern Ireland, a game which saw George Best sent off after throwing mud at referee Eric Jennings.

Against England, there were strong Scottish claims for a penalty when Colin Stein went toppling over Labone. Two minutes from time, England's Hurst netted but was ruled offside. England were fortunate to escape with a draw, the first goalless game between the two countries (excluding wartime) since they first met in 1872.

After the game with Wales, Bobby Brown signed a new four-year contract as Scotland manager.

BROWN'S NIGHTMARE

1970-71 Three away defeats in the European Nations Championship qualifying group — in Belgium, Portugal and Denmark — meant that further interest in the competition was academic. And without a win in the home internationals, Scotland had a poor season. Defeat at Wembley saw Scottish fans call for manager Brown's head, and the last match of the season, in Moscow, proved to be the manager's last in charge. His 28 internationals had seen nine won, eight drawn and 11 lost.

Even the season's only victory brought anxious moments. O'Hare headed through the Danish goalkeeper's legs following

EDDIE McCREADIE

1965 to 1969: Left-back, 23 caps.
Born: Glasgow, 1940.
Career: Drumchapel Amateurs, Clydebank Juniors, East Stirlingshire, Chelsea, Chelsea (manager), Memphis Rogues (manager).
Eddie McCreadie was one of Tommy Docherty's best signings as Chelsea manager. Starting as a wing-half, but developing into one of the best British full-backs, he was both strong-tackling and brilliant at creating moves. McCreadie started fairly cautiously for Scotland, then displayed the adventurous overlapping qualities he produced for his club. He never scored an international goal, but came close, such as when his shot was brilliantly saved in Poland in 1965.

RON McKINNON
1965 to 1971: Centre-half, 28 caps, 1 goal.
Born: Glasgow, 1940.
Career: Glasgow Benburb, Dunpace Juniors, Rangers.
Ron McKinnon started as a wing-half then succeeded Bill Paterson as Rangers centre-half. His first international chance came in 1965 when Billy McNeill had to pull out of the Italy game. McKinnon's performance established him in the team, giving rise to the debate: who was better – McKinnon or McNeill? Both were superb stoppers, reliable big men in the centre. One solution was to play them together, which happened twice. Generally, McKinnon held pole position until he broke his leg in Lisbon in November 1971. His twin brother, Don McKinnon, was Partick Thistle's centre-half.

Johnstone's 13th-minute centre, and that was the only goal of the match.

This was a reasonable start to the task of qualifying for the European Finals, but the next game, in the fiery atmosphere of Liege, was a hurdle Scotland could not overcome. Belgium included six Standard Liege players and their local knowledge proved invaluable on a bone-hard pitch which had rainwater lying on it to give an unpredictable bounce.

> *On 27 January 1971, a Scotland XI met a Rangers-Celtic team, which included George Best, for dependants of the Ibrox Disaster victims. Scotland won 2-1 at Hampden in front of 81,405 with goals from Gemmill and Lorimer. Team: Cruickshank; Hay, Gemmell, Stanton, McKinnon, Moncur, Lorimer, Gemmill, Stein, O'Hare, Cooke (subs: Craig and McLean).*

WILLIE HENDERSON

1962 to 1971: Outside-right, 29 caps, 5 goals.
Born: Ballieston, Glasgow, 1944.
Career: Airdrie Schools, Edinburgh Athletic, Rangers, Sheffield Wednesday, Hong Kong Rangers, Airdrie.
At 17 Willie Henderson was in Rangers' team and at 18 he was capped by Scotland. They called him 'Scotland's Garrincha', fast and tricky and seemingly defying gravity as he raided from the right wing.
Henderson stood only 5ft 4in and wore contact lenses, but he excited crowds and before his 23rd birthday he had won 21 caps. After that, injuries and an operation for bunion trouble put him out of the reckoning for long periods, but he took part in Scotland's biggest win this century – 8-0 against Cyprus in 1969. Henderson also won Scottish Schoolboy caps and in 1975 he captained the Hong Kong national team.

Scotland stayed on the defensive — only O'Hare and Stein were up front — but in the 36th minute, McKinnon was caught by the treacherous pitch and turned Van Himst's cross past his own goalkeeper. In the second half, Van Himst scored twice more, one from a free-kick, the other from a penalty.

Victory in Portugal was crucial, but Scotland fell behind to another own-goal. Nene crossed and Pat Stanton, marking Eusebio, sliced the ball past Bobby Clark from ten yards. McCalliog missed a good chance soon afterwards, and Scotland conceded a second goal late in the game. Eusebio tapped the ball home after Clark had dived at Nene's feet.

Scotland included seven Anglo-Scots against Wales, and none from Rangers although Greig came on as substitute. It was another difficult pitch — rain on top of what had been a dust-bowl — but Wales kept the ball in the air, aiming for Davies and Toshack. "I thought they were coming down on parachutes," said Bobby Clark after keeping a clean sheet to earn Scotland a draw.

Northern Ireland's first-ever win at Hampden was achieved through yet another Scottish own-goal. It came in the 14th minute when Derek Dougan darted to the near post for a corner, back-headed the ball and turned to see Greig knock it into his own net. In nine games Scotland had scored three in their own net and only two in their opponents'.

Hugh Curran scored at Wembley but England won 3-1 and the wave of criticism reached tidal proportions. Paddy Crerand had spoken out on television and in newspaper articles and now Scottish fans called for the manager's blood. Sir Alf Ramsey put a consoling arm around Brown's shoulders as the two managers left the Wembley pitch.

Brown must have felt that the whole world was against him when he lost nine players from the pool selected to travel to Denmark and Russia in June. In Denmark, Scotland's reputation sank further when Laudrop scored from a free-kick just before half-time and the largely amateur Danes went on to win 1-0.

Scotland's second-ever meeting with the Russians produced a highly commendable Scottish performance, given the scratch nature of the side, but it still added to a horrendous run. Between 22 October 1969 and 13 October 1971, Scotland had scored only three goals in 12 internationals.

SEND FOR THE DOC

1971-2 New manager Tommy Docherty had a flying start to his interim period in charge with wins against Portugal and Belgium, and in November, he was appointed on a more permanent basis.

Docherty named nine Anglo-Scots in his 16-man pool for the Portugal game. Two of the pool, Bob Wilson and Alex Cropley, were born in England and qualified under the new rule which allowed a player to appear for a parent's country of birth if

the player was not claimed by his own country.

Both men played against Portugal, the first English-born footballers to play for Scotland in over 98 years. "I have always thought it ridiculous that, just because I spent the first three years of my life in England, I was considered English," said Cropley.

Despite the seemingly mandatory 4-3-3 formation, Docherty's team served up everything traditional to Scottish football. Little men like Billy Bremner and Archie Gemmill combined skill and wholehearted commitment, Johnstone and Cropley took on men down the flanks. Scotland led at half-time through O'Hare's header. Although Rodrigues unleashed a free-kick equaliser, Gemmill popped up to head the winner less than a minute later.

TOMMY GEMMELL

1966 to 1971: Full-back, 18 caps, 1 goal.
Born: Glasgow, 1943.
Career: Meadow Thistle (Wishaw), Coltness United, Celtic, Nottingham Forest, Dundee, Dundee (manager), Albion Rovers (manager).
'Big Tam' Gemmell pioneered a new era of full-back play. Behind him lay the days when managers panicked if a full-back took a step over the halfway line or took an eye off the winger. In front were the days of 'total football' when full-backs could be adventurous. Gemmell was foremost a defensive player, but his overlapping runs and powerful shooting were exciting. Some of his goals became as legendary as those of any forward – a goal in each of the 1967 and 1970 European Cup Finals, and a last-minute effort against Kilmarnock in 1969 which brought Celtic a fourth successive championship.
Gemmell, who bore a facial resemblence to actor Danny Kaye, represented Scotland on both right and left flank.

COLIN STEIN

1968 to 1973: Centre-forward, 21 caps (6 as sub), 10 goals.
Born: Philpstoun, West Lothian, 1947.
Career: Broxburn Strollers, Armadale Thistle, Hibernian, Rangers, Coventry City, Rangers.
In the late 1960s, Colin Stein scored ten goals in his first seven internationals and there was talk of a new Denis Law. Rangers paid £100,000 in October 1968, the first six-figure fee between Scottish clubs. In one of his first games for Rangers, Stein scored three in three minutes against Arbroath. He was capped, although missed the West Germany game at Hampden (April 1969) because of a 28-day suspension. Stein was top scorer in the Scottish First Division in 1969-70 – the previous season he had scored four against Cyprus – and he scored in Rangers' 1972 European Cup-winners' Cup Final. But he started to find goals harder to come by, especially after October 1972, when £90,000 took him to struggling Coventry.

The next game, against Belgium, was the last in the European Nations qualifying round. Played in Aberdeen, it was the last time a Scotland home game has taken place outside Glasgow and three Dons players were in the side for a famous victory. The only goal came in the fifth minute when Johnstone weaved a pretty pattern through the Belgian defence and crossed for O'Hare to glide the ball in off the left-hand post. The match heralded the international debut of Kenny Dalglish, who came on as a substitute.

Docherty was confirmed as manager and his next game saw an excellent display against the fast-emerging Dutch side. Johann Cruyff put Holland ahead, but George Graham equalised from Bremner's free-kick. Gemmill came close to putting Scotland ahead — the ball rolled tantalisingly outside a post — before Hulsoff scored the Dutch

winner three minutes from time.

The friendly with Peru came when club commitments were reaching their peak. Amazingly, there were no Rangers or Celtic players in the side although Derby County allowed the release of O'Hare and Gemmill, despite their championship-decider with Liverpool a few days later.

Denis Law, now 32, was recalled after a three-year absence. With typical verve and cheek he dominated the proceedings. O'Hare touched in Willie Morgan's free-kick to give Scotland the lead just before half-time, then Law capped his return with a goal midway through the second half.

It was Law who broke the deadlock against Northern Ireland. With Best 'gone missing', the Irish resorted to a nine-man defence and held out for 86 minutes until Law hooked in a ball at hip level. The Irish crumbled and Leeds United's Peter Lorimer hit a second.

The game against Wales looked destined to be a goalless draw, but was rescued by Lorimer. With 18 minutes to play, Bremner poked the ball forward, Tony Green helped it on and Lorimer, possessor of one of the hardest shots in football, struck it superbly.

For the first time since Hampden was enlarged in 1931, there were less than 120,000 people to see England. The English, with Storey and Hunter in midfield, were hardly attractive opposition at this time, but they won 1-0 with a goal from Ball. Ball's shot trickled into the net and Tommy Docherty called it 'a comic cuts of a goal'.

Scotland went to Brazil to play in the Independence Cup, a tournament that went on into July. The first game, against Yugoslavia, was played in a temperature of 80 degrees, but Willie Morgan set up two goals for Lou Macari and the Scots earned a 2-2 draw. Morgan himself missed a 77th-minute penalty and the Yugoslavs snatched a point with a last-minute goal.

After drawing with Czechoslovakia, Scotland produced a brilliant display in front of 150,000 in Rio de Janeiro. Alex Forsyth was outstanding in defence against a Brazilian team that was adding a physical side to the brilliant skills which had won the 1970 World Cup. Scotland battled magnificently and Graham hit the bar before an 80th-minute header from Jairzinho proved the difference between the two sides.

Next day, Brazilian newspapers acclaimed Scotland as one of the best European sides in years. Forsyth was a superstar, they said, and Docherty the great strategist.

CENTENARY CELEBRATIONS SOURED

1972-3 Two wins against Denmark gave Scotland four points before Czechoslovakia, the third member of their World Cup qualifying group, had kicked a ball. But the season ended with four consecutive defeats and earlier, England had won 5-0 at Hampden in a game to celebrate the centenary of the Scottish Football Association.

Joe Harper made a spectacular debut in a Scotland shirt when he came on as substitute in Copenhagen with the game

BOBBY MONCUR

1968 to 1972: Central defender, 16 caps.
Born: Perth, 1945.
Career: West Lothian Schools, Newcastle United, Sunderland, Carlisle United (player-manager), Hearts (manager), Plymouth Argyle (manager). Not especially tall, but a skilful sweeper, Bobby Moncur won his caps alongside commanding figures like Ron McKinnon and Billy McNeill. He captained Newcastle to their 1969 Fairs Cup Final win, scoring three times in the two-legged final with Ujpest Dozsa. Moncur was only 25 when he took over as Scotland captain, and in 1970-71 he skippered the Scots in seven out of eight games, although results were not too good and injury the following season restricted his appearances. Moncur twice won the English footballers golf championship.

against Denmark poised at 2-1 to Scotland. Willie Morgan dribbled through, Lou Macari backheeled a pass, and Harper scored. Three minutes later, Harper hit the post, then Lorimer centred for Morgan to net the fourth.

When the Danes came to Hampden, Tommy Docherty made two changes from the team that finished the game in Copenhagen, and Leeds goalkeeper David Harvey, born in England of Scottish parents, won his first cap. The Scots were given a fine start — Dalglish's second-minute goal was his first of many for Scotland — but there were setbacks towards the end of the 2-0 win. Lorimer, scorer of the second goal, was sent off together with his 'marker' Roentred. Morgan missed his second penalty for Scotland, this time shooting over the bar.

Against a background of controversy, Tommy Docherty resigned in order to take over at Manchester United, and Willie Ormond was appointed in his place.

The actual date of the SFA formation was 13 March 1873, but St Valentine's Day was chosen to celebrate the centenary, a date perhaps selected in order to help stem the physical side of recent Scotland-England games. The frozen surface at

far post to score one of his 'goals from nowhere'. With five minutes to play, Shilton made a fine save to deny Dalglish.

Scotland had been urged on by thousands of their supporters at Wembley, but the trip to Switzerland was a miserable affair. After Celtic's George Connelly had 'disappeared' at the airport before the outward flight, Scotland were beaten by a 30-yard goal, although Joe Jordan almost saved the game with a late header.

A second centenary celebration game was played at the end of June when Brazil, now even more physical, came to Hampden. According to *The Scotsman*, the ball was in play for only 43 minutes, compared with 75 minutes for an average Brazilian game in the 1970 World Cup.

A 1-0 win for Brazil meant four successive Scotland defeats, yet the season ended on a hopeful note. On 2 May, Czechoslovakia had stumbled to a 1-1 draw with Denmark. If Scotland beat the Czechs at Hampden the following September, they would qualify for the World Cup Finals.

BOBBY CLARK

**1967 to 1973: Goalkeeper, 17 caps.
Born: Glasgow, 1945.
Career: Glasgow YMCA, Queen's Park, Aberdeen.**
Son of Clyde director who became SFA treasurer, Bobby Clark played for Scotland at all levels. He was capped for the Youth and Amateur teams at Queen's Park, then he was one of Eddie Turnbull's first signings at Aberdeen. At that time, in May 1965, Clark was at Jordanhill College, training to become a PE teacher.

He played over 500 games for Aberdeen, including a few as an outfield player, and his lightning reflexes took him into Scotland's team against Wales in November 1967. Over three years passed before Clark became first-choice, a position he held until the heavy defeat at Hampden in February 1973. Until then, Clark had conceded only 13 goals in his first 16 internationals.

Hampden, with its uncertain bounce, was hardly conducive to good football. England, playing long through-balls that were ideal for the conditions, scored three times in the first 15 minutes and gave Ormond the worst possible start.

For the Wales game, Ormond introduced five new caps — Peter McCloy in goal, Danny McGrain, Jim Holton and Derek Johnstone in defence, and Derek Parlane up front. Parlane made an impression although restricted by injury, while George Graham had probably his best game for Scotland.

The next match was greeted by all manner of problems. Northern Ireland scored twice in the first 17 minutes at Hampden and then Morgan and Pat Stanton were injured. Scotland's only reply came in the final minute, Dalglish calmly steering home McGrain's cross.

The injury list grew. McCloy, Willie Donachie, Stanton, Graham and Parlane all missed the England game when the only goal followed Ball's free-kick. Chivers feigned and Martin Peters stole in at the

WILLIE MORGAN

**1967 to 1974: Midfield, 21 caps (1 as sub), 1 goal.
Born: Glasgow, 1944.
Career: Alloa Schools, Fishcross FC, Burnley, Manchester United, Burnley, Bolton Wanderers, Minnesota Kicks, Blackpool.**
With his Beatle-style haircut and number-seven shirt, Willie Morgan was likened to a Scottish George Best when he was at Burnley, but after switching to midfield with Manchester United, Morgan achieved far more than Best in late career.

In August 1968, United paid £117,000 for him, setting what was then a British record not involving a player-exchange. Morgan had been capped once while with Burnley – the 1967 Northern Ireland game when Best starred – and he had to wait almost five years for another chance. He established himself on the 1972 tour of Brazil and his skill and vision played a vital part in taking Scotland to the 1974 World Cup Finals.

JIMMY JOHNSTONE

**1964 to 1974: Outside-right, 23 caps (1 as sub), 4 goals.
Born: Viewpark, Lanarkshire, 1944.
Career: Viewpark FC, Celtic, San José Earthquakes, Sheffield United, Dundee, Shelbourne, Elgin City, Blantyre Celtic.**
Jimmy Johnstone, a Parkhead ballboy in the late 1950s, emerged as a major star in the mid-1960s, especially in 1967 when he helped Celtic win the European Cup. By then, red-haired 'Wee Jinky' was already an established international.

His international caps were restricted by injuries and the suspensions he received from both Celtic and the SFA. His talents deserved more caps and one of football's more breathtaking sights was that of Johnstone attacking a full-back, his hips swaying as he beat players almost without touching the ball, then finally showing a remarkable burst of speed. The Wembley programme of 1967 said that Johnstone was 'showing more tricks than any stage conjuror'.

His longest run in the Scotland team was only four matches, starting with a brilliant display against Wales in 1974. Even then controversy was not far away and in the celebrations afterwards his colleagues helped him, literally, to push the boat out too far.

Six years earlier, Johnstone had refused to act as linesman in a Scotland-Celtic practice match. He was left out of the team to meet England and the phrase widely quoted at the time was 'not mentally attuned'.

BILLY BREMNER

1965 to 1975: Wing-half, 54 caps (1 as sub), 3 goals.
Born: Stirling, 1942.
Career: St Modan's School (Stirling), Gowanhill Juniors (Stirling), Gowanhill Juniors (Stirling), Leeds United, Hull City, Doncaster Rovers (manager).
Tiny by football standards, but exceedingly skilful, tough and energetic, red-haired Billy Bremner was a powerful driving force for Leeds United and Scotland, and he was captain in almost half his 54 internationals.
His League debut was at outside-right, partnered by future England manager Don Revie, but his fame was won on the right side of midfield, and when he became a regular in the Scotland team in the late-1960s, his country rarely lost. He first captained the team in November 1968.
Then came a spell when he won less caps, partly because Leeds were so successful. Bremner was English Footballer of the Year in 1970-71, then captained Scotland in the 1974 World Cup Finals where his display against Brazil won him world acclaim. Bremner's fiery spirit, the hallmark of his success, also brought him controversy and an incident with Keegan in the 1974 FA Charity Shield match at Wembley cost him a 34-day suspension and £500 fine. An incident in Denmark ended his international career, one short of Denis Law's record number of Scottish caps.

WORLD CUP FEVER

1973-4 Twelve years, almost to the day, after the fabulous win at Hampden had taken Czechoslovakia to a World Cup play-off, Scotland again conquered the Czechs. This time, victory saw them qualify for the 1974 Finals. And even when Alex Forsyth conceded a 16th-minute penalty to give the Czechs victory in Bratislava, it did not really matter. Scotland were Britain's sole representatives in the World Cup

extravaganza that was about to unfold in West Germany.

Two friendlies were arranged with West Germany, favourites to become world champions. At Hampden, Jimmy Smith formerly with Aberdeen and now with Newcastle United, reappeared in the Scotland team after a six-year absence, and Scotland took a fifth-minute lead through a Jim Holton header laid on by Law. It might have been 2-0 in the 77th minute but substitute goalkeeper Maier saved Bremner's penalty. Five minutes later, Hoeness headed home to salvage a draw for the Germans.

West German team manager Helmut Schoen was in no doubt about the quality of the Scottish team: "They are the best side we have met this year. And that includes Argentina, Brazil, France, Russia and Czechoslovakia."

With half their team missing, Scotland failed to repeat the performance in West Germany. Frank Munro and Holton were suspended, Connelly injured, and the Leeds players denied by the prospect of a League game that never materialised. Celtic's Steve Murray preferred to stay at home with his family.

Scotland named three new caps, including Eric Schaedler whose father had played with Moenchengladbach before becoming a PoW in Scotland where he met and married a girl from Leadhills.

West Germany, meanwhile, fielded eight of their 1972 European championship-winning team. Dominating the first half, they took a 2-0 lead, but after an hour, Scotland introduced Bobby Robinson and Donald Ford. The Scots came more into the game and Dalglish ran on to Tommy Hutchison's through-ball to pull back a goal.

Denis Law won his 54th cap in the next game, against Northern Ireland. Law thus beat George Young's record, but when a Cassidy goal gave the Irish a 1-0 victory, it left the Scotland striker with little to celebrate. Northern Ireland had now won six of their last 11 matches against the Scots with one drawn.

Moreover, Scotland had scored only five times in their last nine internationals and manager Ormond made his players watch a video-tape of the Irish game, illustrating that forwards could have been released more quickly. The next two games each brought excellent 2-0 victories.

Dalglish's header and Jardine's penalty accounted for Wales when Scotland were prompted by Ford and Johnstone. The victory was slightly tarnished when police were called at six o'clock the following morning after Johnstone had drifted out to sea in a small boat, the result of a silly prank.

England had their problems when Stan Bowles disappeared from their camp, and then they lost at Hampden, the first time in ten years that Scotland had beaten the auld enemy at home.

John Blackley, told that he was playing only two hours before the England game, starred as Scotland won with two first-half goals. Jordan's shot was deflected in by Pejic after four minutes, and then Todd

turned in Dalglish's effort. Scotland shared the home championship.

As the build-up to the World Cup grew apace, Scotland's squad demanded payment for a group photograph. More than one national newspaper carried pictures of the rows of empty chairs to underline that this World Cup, with all its attendant commercial activities, was far removed from those of the 1950s.

Scotland's preparation continued in Belgium and Norway. Defeat in Belgium, to a controversial late penalty, awarded when Dalglish collided with Van Himst, was followed by a near embarrassment in Norway. The home team led at half-time with a goal by Lund, who ran on to a long kick from Dunfermline goalkeeper Geir Karlsen. Fifteen minutes from the end, Jordan headed an equaliser and the same player made the 88th-minute winner for Dalglish.

It was Scotland's fourth win on the continent in 12 years and was followed by more controversy. Billy Bremner and Jimmy Johnstone were ordered to their rooms by Willie Ormond after being discovered late at night in the hotel bar. There was talk of sending them home, but after a severe reprimand they were allowed to stay.

PETER LORIMER

1969 to 1975: Outside-right, 21 caps (5 as sub), 4 goals.
Born: Dundee, 1946.
Career: Dundee Schools, Leeds United, Toronto Blizzard, York City, Leeds United.
Famed for his ferocious long-range shooting with his right foot, Peter Lorimer was always a potential match-winner in an era when goals were relatively scarce. Joining a defensive wall to face a Lorimer free-kick was always a dangerous move.
He is one of three players to have appeared in over 500 League games for Leeds, while he holds two club records – most goals in a career and youngest debut (15 years 289 days in 1963). By 1985, he was playing in midfield, even though he was older than his manager, the former Scottish international Eddie Gray.

SCOTLAND 2   CZECHOSLOVAKIA 1
26 September 1973, at Hampden Park

WITH 15 minutes to play and the score at 1-1, all Scotland tried to will in the goal that would secure a place in the World Cup Finals. Besides 100,000 at Hampden — a restriction recommended by the police — there were hundreds of thousands watching the game live on television. Even *Coronation Street* had been pushed forward five minutes.

Skipper Billy Bremner, urging his team forward, crashed a shot against a Czech post. The ball rolled agonisingly along the goal-line before being scooped out. It fell to Willie Morgan who turned it back into the middle where Joe Jordan, who had been on the field for only 11 minutes, rose around the penalty spot to head the winning goal.

Scotland were missing Colin Stein and Derek Johnstone through injury, but on this night they found 12 heroes. Law found the energy of a teenager to go with his peerless skills. George Connelly was making his international debut three months after his walk-out. And Tommy Hutchison thrilled with his runs.

The desperate early stages showed what was at stake. The Czechs massed their defence and Bremner's header, Jardine's free-kick and Morgan's shot were all well saved.

In the 34th minute, Czechoslovakia stunned Hampden by taking the lead. Nehoda tried a hopeful shot from out on the right and although Ally Hunter got both hands to it, the ball went in.

Roared on, Scotland pulled one back before half-time when centre-half Jim Holton soared above a crowd of players to steer a powerful header into the back of the Czech net.

The Czechs blamed Bremner for an injury to Kuna, but undaunted, the Scottish captain continued to play an inspiring role. After 64 minutes, Ormond brought on Jordan for Dalglish and the striker made an immediate impression in the air.

The jubilant team paraded around Hampden at the final whistle. Bremner ran off to find Ormond and Scotland's team manager was chaired from the pitch. The Scots had reached the World Cup Finals for the first time for 16 years.

SCOTLAND: Hunter; Jardine, McGrain, Bremner, Holton, Connelly, Hay, Law, Morgan, Dalglish(Jordan), Hutchison.
CZECHOSLOVAKIA: Victor; Zlecha, Samek, Pivarnak, Beldl (Capkovic), Adamec, Kuna(Dobias), Bicovsky, Nehoda, Stratil, Penenka.

Referee: H.Oberg (Norway)   *Attendance: 100,000*

Billy Bremner and the rest of the Scotland team accept the cheers of a 100,000 Hampden attendance after Scotland had reached the World Cup Finals for the first time in 16 years.

WORLD CUP FINALS ⚽ 1974

SCOTLAND were drawn in a group with Brazil, Yugoslavia and Zaire. The unknown African side were the key to the group and Scotland's first opponents. It was obvious that Scotland would have to go all out for goals, and after David Hay had hit a post, Scotland scored twice in six minutes.

Jordan headed back McGrain's cross and Lorimer volleyed in the first. Jordan's bouncing header sent in Bremner's free-kick for the second.

Then the lights went out and the players gathered in the centre-circle while an electrician was found. The lights were mended but the delay had sent the Scots off the boil. Zaire goalkeeper Kazadi made some world-class saves and although Lorimer hit the crossbar, there were no more goals. Many felt that 2-0 was hardly enough, and some newspapers blamed Bremner for not urging his side on in search of further goals.

Against World Cup holders Brazil, Scotland withstood an early battering. Harvey saved Rivelino's 30-yard free-kick, and Brazil hit an upright and then had a shot cleared off the line by Jardine. After weathering the storm, Scotland fought back well and though there were no goals, they could claim a moral victory.

Bremner was the star as Scotland pressed forward, Hay almost scoring with a 20-yarder and Jordan's heading ability worrying the Brazilian defence.

Assuming that the Brazilians would beat Zaire by at least three clear goals — the Africans had lost 9-0 to Yugoslavia — Scotland needed to beat the Slavs to ensure a place in the next round.

The white-shirted Scots gave a good account of themselves. Substitute Hutchison laid on a last-minute equaliser for Jordan. Now all depended on the Brazil-Zaire result.

As the teams left the field, all eyes turned to the giant electronic scoreboard which blazed out the message that Brazil had won 3-0. A late goal had sent the Scots out on goal difference. It turned out to be a farcical goal too, scored when a low cross crept under the Zaire goalkeeper's body.

Four points from three games were not enough, yet Scotland were the only unbeaten team in the 1974 Finals. West Germany, the eventual winners, lost to East Germany in their first-round group.

The Scotland party flew back home to a tremendous reception. There were 10,000 fans at Abbotsinch Airport to meet what was arguably the best pool of players that Scotland have ever taken to the World Cup Finals.

Scotland's 1974 World Cup Squad. Back row (left to right): McQueen, Stewart, Harvey, Allan, Hutchison. Middle row: Ormond (manager), Schaedler, McGrain, Smith, Hay, Jardine, Jordan, Blackley, Holton, Buchan, Lorimer. Front row: Allan (trainer), Ford, Dalglish, Bremner, Law, Morgan, Johnstone, and McKenzie (trainer).

DISTURBING DEFEATS

1974-5 The exhilaration of the World Cup carried on into a season of nine internationals, most of which produced excellent results, but the season's two defeats were disturbing — 2-1 to Spain at Hampden in a European Championship qualifier, and 5-1 at Wembley.

The problem of availability had not lessened and Willie Ormond was resigned to losing players. Newcomer Graeme Souness sparkled in the friendly with East Germany, whose hard tackling led to two penalties after Jim Holton had been stretchered off following a serious foul by Weise. It was Holton's last Scotland appearance after a hurricane international career of 15 caps in 18 months.

Jordan's penalty hit the goalkeeper's leg, but Hutchison scored the next spot kick to give Scotland the lead. Two more goals meant that Scotland had scored three at Hampden for the first time in over five years.

The route to the European Finals started against Spain at Hampden — the group also included Romania and Denmark — but a surprise defeat meant that Scotland would struggle to survive. Bremner gave them a tenth-minute lead, then Hutchison's penalty was saved by Iribar and before half-time, Quini equalised. The same player scored the winner, a shot which David Harvey might normally have saved.

Charlie Cooke, 32, was brought back for the return in Valencia. His superb first-minute pass led to a headed Jordan goal after Hutchison had hit the bar. After 65 minutes, Spain drew level with a controversial goal. Martin Buchan handled on the line and after Belgian referee Alfred Delcourt had first awarded a penalty, he changed his mind and gave the goal. Paul Wilson came on to experience what was to be a 15-minute international career in a torrid and aggressive environment.

When he came on as substitute against Sweden, Billy Hughes was the fourth new cap blooded in that game. Another debutant, Ted MacDougall, saved the game with three minutes to play, sweeping in a Dalglish pass.

A total of 29 players took part in the Portugal game — Scotland used three substitutes, the Portuguese four — but an own-goal was the sum of the scoring. Gordon McQueen's 43rd-minute header was parried by goalkeeper Damas, full-back Artur tried to clear but succeeded only in putting the ball into the net.

Bruce Rioch played against Portugal but it was in the next match, against Wales, that Scottish fans saw the full extent of his shooting power. He raced on to a square pass to blast a 20-yard equaliser. Wales had led 2-0 at half-time before Colin Jackson's header started the comeback, during which time McQueen's header struck the bar.

Speedy Arthur Duncan impressed against Northern Ireland when Scotland scored three for the second time that season. Scottish supporters were now confident enough to cry, 'Bring on the English'.

JOHN GREIG MBE

1964 to 1975: Defender, 44 caps, (1 as sub), 5 goals.
Born: Edinburgh, 1942.
Career: Edina Hearts, Whitburn, Rangers, Rangers (manager).
In his early years John Greig was a loyal Hearts fan, but his 18-year playing career was spent entirely with Rangers. He started as an inside-forward and first made his name on a tour of the Soviet Union in 1962, making his debut against Locomotiv in Moscow. The following season he dropped back to wing-half when Harold Davis was injured. Greig was in the Scotland team at 21, the start of an uninterrupted run of 21 internationals. His powerful tackling balanced Baxter's attacking flair, but in November 1965, yet another aspect of this versatility was discovered. In his first senior match at right-back, Greig scored a dramatic winner against Italy.
For the return World Cup game against Italy, Greig was captain, a role he held for almost three years (and again on one occasion in the 1970s). He skippered Scotland three times against England, including the famous 3-2 1967 Wembley triumph. Later he settled at full-back and in 1975-6 was elected Scottish Footballer of the Year for the second time. In 1977 he was awarded the MBE in the Jubilee Honours List.
Greig played 857 senior matches for Rangers and 65,000 saw his testimonial against a Scottish select team. He retired in May 1978 and was immediately appointed manager, a position he held until October 1983.

But Wembley proved to be the end of a another promising young international goalkeeping career. Stuart Kennedy, who had been performing well up to then, lost two goals in the first seven minutes against England. After a 25-yard shot from Francis and a header from Beattie, England took total control. Rioch's penalty made the score 3-1 just before half-time, but a deflected Francis free-kick killed any hopes of a Scottish revival.

The last game of the season was played in the almost unbearable heat of Romania, but when the sun went down, Scotland came alive. Trailing 1-0, they stunned the 80,000 crowd with a last-minute goal. McQueen hooked a left-foot shot into the net and Scotland secured their second point in three European qualifying games.

DAWN OF AN EXCITING ERA

1975-6 Scotland enjoyed their first unbeaten season since 1948-9, and the first-ever with as many as seven matches. Six games were won, one drawn and although there was much still to do in order to qualify for the European Championships, Scotland took the home title outright for the first time since 1967. An exciting three-year period was underway, climaxing in the 1978 World Cup Finals in Argentina.

Scotland needed to beat Denmark twice to keep European hopes alive. Fielding a more subtle and skilful forward line than usual, the Scots won in Denmark with a 51st-minute goal from Joe Harper. Possession football enabled them to hang on to the slender lead.

However, celebrations were cut short when the SFA suspended five players — Billy Bremner, Joe Harper, Willie Young, Arthur Graham and Pat McCluskey — following off-the-field incidents. Scotland trainer Ronnie McKenzie resigned following an incident with Bremner and, although the ban on the players was lifted in July 1977, the Copenhagen match proved to be Bremner's last in a Scotland jersey.

To fill the captaincy, John Greig, 33, was brought back for the visit of the Danes. At half-time, the Hampden crowd were left wondering how their team could be 1-0 down after dominating the first 45 minutes. In fact, Harvey's first touch of the ball was to pick it out of the net following Bastrup's 22nd-minute header. But three goals before the hour — from Dalglish, Rioch and MacDougall — saw that justice was done .

Chances of qualifying disappeared when Spain drew in Romania, and Scotland's last group match, against the Romanians at Hampden, had nothing at stake. It was a big night, though, for new boy John Doyle, and for Jim Cruickshank, 34, recalled after a five-year absence.

A miserably cold evening restricted the size of the crowd and a goal by Rioch, another free-kick from the edge of the penalty area, was matched by a late Romanian equaliser.

For the friendly with Switzerland, Ormond lost eight of his original 18-strong party and five new caps took the field. One of

WILLIE JOHNSTON

1965 to 1978: Outside-left, 22 caps (2 as sub), 1 goal.
Born: Glasgow, 1946.
Career: Lochare Welfare, Rangers, West Brom, Vancouver Whitecaps, Birmingham City (loan), Rangers, Hearts.
A former Fife pit boy, Willie 'Bud' Johnston won a Scottish League Cup-winners' medal at 17, then jumped from the Scotland Youth team to a World Cup match against Poland in six months. It was not a happy debut because although Johnston did well, two late goals brought Poland victory, but he made nine appearances in the next five years, the first seven at Hampden.
In December 1972, he moved to West Brom for £135,000 and produced much of his best football, dazzlingly skilful on the left wing. Yet he was missing from international football for over six years before being selected against Sweden in 1977. Ally MacLeod used him regularly in the World Cup build-up.
Sent off no less than 20 times in his career, Johnston found controversy in Argentina when he was sent home after being found guilty of using a proscribed drug. His international career was over, but Johnston was still entertaining Hearts fans in his 39th year before retiring in 1985.

LOU MACARI

1972 to 1978: Forward, 24 caps (8 as sub), 5 goals.
Born: Edinburgh, 1949.
Career: St Michael's Academy (Kilwinning), Kilmarnock Amateurs, Kilwinning Rangers, Celtic, Manchester United, Swindon Town (player-manager).
Lou Macari, raised partly in England with an Italian side to his background and married to an American, is wholly Scottish in his cheeky, confident, skilful approach to soccer. He started as a striker and later moved to midfield where his talent for scoring goals still abounded.
Macari lived in London for all but six months of his first ten years. He played for Scotland Schoolboys before joining Celtic, where he won his first six caps. He was the only Celtic player who agreed to go to Brazil for the 1972 tournament, and he scored twice against Yugoslavia.
Celtic received a Scottish record £200,000 for him in January 1973 when he joined Manchester United, whom he served for over 11 years. Willie Ormond used him regularly for a time, but when Ormond left him out again, Macari criticised the decision in an English newspaper and found himself out of favour. Eventually he was part of World Cup plans, under new manager Ally MacLeod.

MARTIN BUCHAN

1971 to 1979: Central defender, 34 caps (2 as sub).
Born: Aberdeen, 1949.
Career: Aberdeen Boys Brigade, Banks O'Dee 'A', Aberdeen, Manchester United, Oldham Athletic, Burnley (manager).
In February 1970, Eddie Turnbull chose Martin Buchan, then 20, to captain Aberdeen. The manager was rewarded a few months later when Buchan lifted the Scottish Cup as the mature and composed skipper of the Dons. They were qualities he never lost.
His father, also called Martin Buchan, was an Aberdeen player. Buchan, junior, won Youth and Under-23 caps and the former Gordon College pupil was one of the few footballers to understand foreign languages on tour.
He was Scottish Footballer of the Year in 1970-71, the youngest ever, and the inevitable full international cap came the following season. Surprisingly, only one of 34 caps came against England.
Buchan was sidelined with a nasty thigh injury in 1976-7, but he ended that season by collecting the FA Cup for Manchester United, who he had joined for £125,000 five years earlier. The following season, he declined to captain Scotland in Argentina, but his unassuming effectiveness in the national team made him an unsung hero for many years. He retired in October 1984, and had a spell of 110 days as manager of Burnley.

In pure statistical terms, Willie Ormond's reign as Scotland manager shows the value of an extended run. Scotland lost nine of Ormond's first 14 games in charge, but lost only three of the last 24 under his control.

After losing 5-1 to England at Wembley in May 1975 Scotland embarked on an unbeaten run of eight British Championship games — the best since the 1920s. This period brought two British Championship titles. When the Championship was discontinued in 1984 Scotland had 24 outright wins and 18 shares in the title.

'Six foot two, eyes of blue, Big Jim Holton's after you.' Such was the battlecry of the 1974 World Cup, focussed on awesome centre-half Jim Holton. Willie Ormond once said he'd have no injuries in training — he was playing everybody on Holton's side. But, unfortunately, Holton was not indestructible, and his international appearances were limited by injury.

referee Palotai had blown for half-time a second before.

Scotland had not long to wait for a goal. Four minutes into the second half, Clemence allowed a shot from Dalglish to dribble through his arms and off his knees into the net. It was a 'gift', yet there was little doubt that Scotland, with their best side for a decade, deserved the victory. Tom Forsyth, hero of the hour against England, had recently been called a 'cart-horse' by Tommy Docherty in comparison with 'thoroughbred' Martin Buchan.

Rangers, centre-backs Colin Jackson and Tom Forsyth had enjoyed a fine season with their club, Masson, Gemmill and Rioch had proved a superb midfield trio, and the goals were now beginning to flow.

> *Eddie Gray missed the game with Switzerland in April 1976, and so was denied the opportunity to play in the same Scotland side as his brother Frank. The Scotland team did include two Grays — Frank and Andy — but they are not related.*

'EASY, EASY'

1976-7 In another hugely successful season, Scotland clinched their second consecutive home title, this time under the managership of Ally MacLeod. Willie Ormond became manager of Hearts after steering Scotland through one of their most successful eras, and the vociferous MacLeod took over a well-balanced team.

A 6-0 win over Finland was Scotland's biggest goals tally since 1969, and it meant nine games without defeat. The sparse crowd cried, 'Easy, easy,' as they watched some fine goals — a 35-yarder from Rioch, Masson's penalty, Dalglish's back-flick following a flowing build-up, Andy Gray's header, a fifth from Eddie Gray, and a finale from Andy Gray, a well-struck volley.

Andy Gray's first international on foreign soil was not so successful. He was sent off in the 43rd minute of the game with Czechoslovakia, along with home captain Anton Ondrus, as Scotland made a poor start in their bid to qualify for the World Cup Finals. Gemmill, McQueen, Donachie and Buchan were booked, and Scotland were sunk by two goals in three minutes, just after half-time.

Although several players were missing for the next group game, against Wales, Scotland scored a victory. A clever backheel by Dalglish was deflected in by Welsh defender Ian Evans.

At the mere mention of the word 'friendly', the number of players who were suddenly unavailable seemed to escalate. However, the game against Sweden gave an opportunity to Ronnie Glavin, and allowed the recall of Asa Hartford and the long-absent Willie Johnston. Hartford opened the scoring with a 25-yarder that went in off a post and goalkeeper Hellstroem's back; and when

DAVID HAY

1970 to 1974: Defender or midfield, 27 caps.
Born: Paisley, 1948.
Career: St Mirin's Boys Guild, Celtic, Chelsea, Motherwell (manager), Celtic (manager).
A player of remarkable talent and versatility who could play anywhere in the back-four or midfield, David Hay was one of Scotland's 1970s players who could have stepped into any international team. He had a superb World Cup in 1974, but his luck turned after his £225,000 move to Chelsea in July 1974. Then 26, and committed to a poor Chelsea team, he lost his place in the Scotland side, and later suffered serious injuries. At Stamford Bridge, Hay had five operations including two on an eye. He retired in September 1979, leaving some wondering what might have happened in Argentina the previous year, had a fit David Hay been there.

---

them, Willie Pettigrew, scored after 90 seconds. It was also the first appearance of goalkeeper Alan Rough.

Scotland took the home championship by storm and for the first time for years, they had something approaching a settled team. The accurate passing of debutant Don Masson paved the way for an easy win over Wales. Pettigrew broke the deadlock, Rioch headed in Masson's free-kick and after a Welsh penalty, Eddie Gray, making a welcome return after injury, headed in Jordan's cross to make it 3-1.

Masson was again in fine form when Northern Ireland were trounced 3-0. He scored the second goal just after half-time and five minutes later, ghosted past two defenders to lay on a goal for Dalglish. Only 16 seconds into the half, Rioch had missed a penalty when Jennings tipped it on to the post and Dalglish slammed the rebound against the bar.

Headers from Channon and Masson meant that Scotland were drawing 1-1 with England when Clemence brought down Dalglish in the 18-yard area. There was no penalty, however, because Hungarian

---

SANDY JARDINE

1970 to 1979: Right-back, 38 caps (4 as sub), 1 goal.
Born: Edinburgh, 1948.
Career: United Crossroads, Edinburgh Athletic, Rangers, Hearts (asst. manager).
Sandy Jardine, like John Greig an Edinburgh man who made his name with Rangers, was originally an inside-forward and wing-half, and even had a spell at centre-forward for Rangers in 1968-9, averaging better than a goal a game.
Rangers then switched him to full-back, the position he filled for Scotland. The Jardine-McGrain full-back partnership represented Scotland in 19 internationals.
Born across the road from the Hearts ground and christened William Pullar Jardine — his nickname supposedly arises from Rangers trainer Davie Kinnear's comment that 'he runs as though he's running through sand' — he made his debut for Rangers the week after they had lost to Berwick Rangers in the Scottish Cup.
One of his early Scotland games was against Portugal and he helped to block Eusebio who did not reappear for the second half. Jardine turned down Tommy Docherty's invitation to tour South America in 1972, after an arduous Rangers season. In 1974-5, he was Scottish Footballer of the Year. And more than ten years later he was still going strong as Hearts sought the Premier League Championship. Late in 1985 he played his 1,000th senior match, against Rangers. Another example of how players relying on skill, anticipation and soccer intelligence last the longest.

Scotland regained the lead, it was through another peculiar goal when Dalglish's shot also went in via a post and a defender, while Dalglish's boot sailed after the ball.

On 5 May, Willie Ormond, after 38 internationals in charge (18 won, 12 lost), resigned. The SFA looked first to Jock Stein, who decided to stay at Celtic, and then at Aberdeen boss Ally MacLeod, who took the job.

Initially, MacLeod stuck with Ormond's

squad, playing 4-4-2 against Wales. The back-four (especially McQueen) gained more praise than the midfield quartet, one of whom, Bruce Rioch, became the first English-born player to captain Scotland. Although the 0-0 draw set Scotland on the road to retaining the home title, most people had to admit that it was not as important as the World Cup game scheduled for Cardiff the following October. That competition dominated the football landscape and Ally MacLeod said that he wanted to prove himself 'the best manager in the world'.

With Joe Jordan recovered from injury, Scotland overcame a nervous half-hour against Northern Ireland and then set about their task with a neat goal from Dalglish. The same player got a third after McQueen's had extended Scotland's lead.

When Scotland went to Wembley, Alan Rough showed that he was in no mood to follow in the footsteps of less fortunate Scottish goalkeepers. Rough's display in Scotland's 2-1 win meant that he had conceded only six goals in his 11 internationals, two penalties and four efforts which would have beaten any goalkeeper.

Sadly, the victory was marred by tragedy when an Edinburgh gas board worker died of head injuries after diving 15 feet into two feet of water in the Trafalgar Square fountain. And after the game, hundreds of Scottish fans invaded the Wembley pitch and caused £150,000-worth of damage, tearing down goalposts and tearing up the pitch. Wembley, like Hampden, would have to put up fences, and on that day, Scottish football hung its head in shame.

Scotland won the game through McQueen's header, and a goal from Dalglish, who finished off a fine move involving Hartford, Johnston, Rioch and Macari. England's goal came from a late Channon penalty, and at the final whisle, Rioch was carried shoulder-high from the field.

Here, at last, was a Scotland *team* which was experienced in all quarters. Not since the 1950s had a goalkeeper kept his place as regularly as Rough; McGrain and Donachie had been the full-back pairing in 11 internationals; and Dalglish had now played 44 times for his country, half of them alongside Joe Jordan.

Scotland's next test was a tour of South America. The SFA risked a hot political issue by taking a team to play in Chile, where the 1973 military coup had ousted a democratically-elected government.

The Scots had to overcome freezing cold dressing rooms, a start delayed by the lingering Chile national anthem, and a bumpy pitch. They did so with three first-half goals, the last a brilliant run and shot from Hartford. The 4-2 victory was Scotland's first-ever win in South America.

Another left-winger, Willie Johnston, claimed injustice after the Argentina game. He was supported by manager MacLeod and many neutrals after he was sent off in the 56th minute. Masson's 77th-minute penalty gave Scotland the lead after Dalglish had been felled by the aptly named Daniel Killer. Four minutes later, Oscar Trossero acted out a trip and Passerella equalised from the penalty. One recalls the mock

TOM FORSYTH

1971 to 1978: Defender, 22 caps (2 as sub).
Born: Glasgow, 1949.
Career: Stenhouse Thistle, Motherwell, Rangers, Dunfermline (manager), Motherwell (asst. manager).
A £40,000 signing from Motherwell, where he won his first cap, Tom Forsyth of Rangers captained Scotland in only his third international, against Switzerland in 1976. As a defender he was more destructive than creative, his earth-shaking tackle earning him the nickname of 'Jaws'. Forsyth won 14 of his caps under Ally MacLeod who considered him Scotland's most consistent player during this fluctuative period. A fearless six-footer, he was forced to retire through injury in March 1982.

advertisement recruiting European referees for South America: 'Good pay, good lodgings...and a decent burial'.

Despite defeat in Brazil, where Zico's second-half free-kick broke the deadlock, Scotland could look back on fine performances against the European champions, Czechoslovakia, and against Argentina, who would win the 1978 World Cup. They did not realise it at the time, but Scotland had reached their peak 12 months too soon.

Joe Craig scored a goal with his first touch in international football. Coming on as substitute for Kenny Burns in April 1977, Craig scored immediately with his head.

TARTAN ARMY ON THE MARCH

1977-8 'Ally's Tartan Army' marched on towards Argentina with victory over Wales at Anfield, a success which ensured them a place in the World Cup Finals. For the second successive time, they were the only British team to reach the Finals.

A friendly in East Germany heralded

the new season and the hero was Leeds goalkeeper David Stewart, whose saves included a 75th-minute penalty. But even Stewart's brilliance, in what proved to be his only international, could not stop Schade Doerner's 66th-minute goal. Up until then, Scotland had enjoyed more of the game against an uncompromising East German side.

World Cup preliminaries resumed with a Hampden game against the Czechs, who were exhausted by a journey made more difficult by an air-traffic controllers' strike. Even an all-night train journey was not the last of the Czechs' problems. Their Under-21 goalkeeper Macak was fined for shoplifting in Littlewood's store in Argyle Street, Glasgow.

Aerial dominance earned Scotland three goals at 18-minute intervals, through Jordan, Hartford and Dalglish. Jordan's was a superb header following a Johnston corner; Hartford's was followed by a moment's hesitation from the referee who perhaps wondered if Jordan's challenge was unfair before allowing the goal. A late Gajdusek effort sneaked home from 35 yards, but the crowd stayed on to chant, 'We want Ally,' and 'Bring on Wales'. Two late goals against the Welsh gave Scotland the victory that made qualification certain.

Although there was much activity on financial planning — the SFA appointed a Glasgow public relations man, Bill Wilson, as its first full-time commercial consultant — on the playing side the build-up to Argentina was initially very quiet. In the next seven months, Scotland played only one game. Fielding a team without a single Rangers or Celtic player, the Scots got the winner against Bulgaria five minutes from time through substitute Ian Wallace, who ignored appeals for offside and tucked away his shot.

Favourites for the home title, Scotland used the three matches to experiment before Argentina. Derek Johnstone's header brought an equaliser against Northern Ireland, and the same player gave Scotland the lead over Wales with another fine headed goal.

The last five minutes of the Welsh match produced two memorable incidents. First Wales' Flynn took a long run-up before striking a penalty against the post; then Donachie accepted a short goal-kick from Jim Blyth, only to roll it straight back past his own goalkeeper for a bizarre own goal. However, the 1-1 draw extended Scotland's unbeaten Hampden run to 16 games, and there had now been only three defeats in 24 internationals.

Ally MacLeod began telling people that if Scotland beat England three times in a row they would get to keep them.

Silence greeted Coppell's late winner for England, but at the end of the game there was great emotion and it is doubtful whether a beaten team has ever received such a reception. The Scottish players returned to the Hampden pitch to a curtain-call of chanting and cheering. Although Scotland had not won a game in the home internationals, the Hampden Roar gave the impression that, in Argentina, anything was possible.

WALES 0   SCOTLAND 2
12 October 1977, at Anfield

WHEN the Scots invaded Liverpool, the noise of the fans was loud enough to drown that of the Royal Welch Fusiliers band. And Scotland's play was enough to overcome stern Welsh resistance as they marched to the World Cup Finals.

The Welsh FA had forfeited ground advantage because Ninian Park's 10,000 attendance limit under the new safety regulations was not viable.

Scotland were missing the injured Bruce Rioch and Danny McGrain, although Wales themselves were struggling and had less depth to cover their injuries. They were without Leighton James and Ian Evans, who had broken a leg ten days previously. Scotland had not lost to Wales since 1964 and were firm favourites.

The Scots might have scored twice in a frenetic opening 20 minutes. According to one journalist, 'players chased the ball like 20 pairs of hands seeking a bar of soap in a bath'.

Wales overcame the early pressure and gained control for a period midway through the first half. A minute after the start of the second half, Willie Donachie was booked, a caution which eventually meant that he missed the first match of the World Cup Finals.

On the hour Toshack got clear for Wales but Alan Rough touched his shot on to the bar. Eight minutes later, it was the turn of Dai Davies to produce heroics. A brilliant save escalated into a goalmouth scramble, but Scotland could not get the ball into the net.

The turning point came in the 79th minute. Willie Johnston took a long throw-in. Joe Jordan jumped with Dave Jones and a hand touched the ball. All eyes turned to the referee and he pointed to the spot. The Welsh protested vigorously, but Don Masson maintained his cool and, after what seemed like an eternity, he stepped up to fire the ball to Davies' right as the goalkeeper dived the other way. The protests would continue for years, with most people concluding that Jordan had had an important hand in Scotland's success.

Three minutes from time, Scotland sealed their trip to Argentina with a stunning goal. Substitute Martin Buchan crossed to the head of Dalglish, who celebrated his 50th cap with a goal on what was now his home ground.

The final whistle was heralded by wild scenes of Scottish joy, but the police advised Ally McLeod not to take his team on a lap of honour for safety reasons.

WALES: Davies; R.Thomas, J.Jones, Mahoney, D.Jones, Phillips, Flynn, Sayer, Yorath, Toshack, M.Thomas.
SCOTLAND: Rough; Jardine(Buchan), Donachie, Masson, McQueen, Forsyth, Dalglish, Hartford, Jordan, Macari, Johnston.

Referee: R.Wurtz (France).   *Attendance: 50,800*

Don Masson opens the scoring with a controversial penalty in Scotland's World Cup game at Anfield.

SCOTLAND 3   HOLLAND 2
11 June 1978, at Mendoza

SCOTLAND needed to win by three clear goals to qualify for the next stage of the World Cup Finals. Could they score three against a Dutch team famed for its 'total football'? "Yes," said Jongbloed, Holland's goalkeeper, "but not in 90 minutes."

He was wrong. In the 68th minute, Archie Gemmill pounced on the ball after Dalglish lost possession. Gemmill weaved into the penalty area, avoiding three defenders. He switched the ball from right foot to left, and shot. Many people believed that it was the best goal of the competition. It made the score 3-1. There was still hope.

Three minutes later, Johnny Rep scored from 25 yards and the Scots were left with a mountainous task. Nevertheless, to beat Holland 3-2 was a stirring performance and Scotland's football reputation was partially restored.

Graeme Souness, playing in his first game of the tournament, made an important difference to Scotland's team. It was his lob that was headed down for Dalglish to pivot and score the equaliser just before half-time. Early in the game, Rensenbrink scored a penalty for Holland, who had Neeskens carried off on a stretcher.

After half-time, Souness was bundled over in the penalty area, and Gemmill erased memories of Masson's missed penalty against Peru, by scoring with a text-book spot kick. An exciting contest was reborn and Dalglish and Jordan both headed inches wide before Gemmill produced his wonder goal.

SCOTLAND: Rough; Donachie, Buchan, Kennedy, Forsyth, Rioch, Hartford, Gemmill, Souness, Dalglish, Jordan.
HOLLAND: Jongbloed; Suurbier, Krol, Poorvliet, Rijsbergen (Wildschut), Neeskens(Boskamp), Jansen, W.Van der Kerkhof, R.Van der Kerkhof, Rep, Rensenbrink.

Referee: E.Linemayr (Austria)   *Attendance: 50,000*

When Scotland set out for Argentina in 1978, they had raced to the top of many people's hit parades, not least the one that referred to popular music:

> *'We're representing Britain*
> *And we've got to do or die*
> *For England cannae do it*
> *'Cause they didnae qualify.'*

Scotland's 22-man World Cup squad in 1978 was: Alan Rough, Sandy Jardine, Willie Donachie, Martin Buchan, Gordon McQueen, Bruce Rioch, Don Masson, Kenny Dalglish, Joe Jordan, Asa Hartford, Willie Johnston, Jim Blyth, Stuart Kennedy, Tom Forsyth, Archie Gemmill, Lou Macari, Derek Johnstone, Graeme Souness, John Robertson, Bobby Clark, Joe Harper and Kenny Burns. The players were numbered 1-22 in that order.

Archie Gemmill turns to celebrate goal number three for Scotland in their 3-2 win over Holland.

WORLD CUP FINALS ⚽ 1978

SCOTLAND arrived in Argentina with hope — engineered by the effervescent MacLeod — of winning the 'Mundial' as it was known in the politically unstable host country. Defeat by Peru, and a humiliating draw with Iran, punctuated internal problems in the Scottish camp and it was only when rock-bottom had been reached that there came a performance of passion, spirit and skill. The 3-2 win over Holland came too late to save Scotland, but it did much to restore the nation's footballing reputation.

When Scotland paraded at Hampden Park in their navy-blue track suits at the end of May, they were given a wildly enthusiastic send-off. Confidence was sky-high and the extrovert Ally MacLeod revelled in it. Someone asked him what he would do when the World Cup was over. "Retain it!" he boomed.

It seemed a relatively simple matter to overcome Peru and Iran, but a few observers pointed to MacLeod's lack of experience at international level, to his experiments in the home internationals, and to the fact that Rioch and Masson were unsettled with their club, Derby County.

McGrain and McQueen, two key players, were injured, but there was no denying that Scotland's party had abundant skills, although Andy Gray was a surprise omission.

As soon as the party arrived at the Sierras Hotel, Alta Gracia, local newshounds, particularly the *Buenos Aires Daily Herald*, began to spread malicious stories about the Scottish players' night-life. Criticism escalated after the opening game against Peru.

For the first 15 minutes, Scotland played well. Peru's eccentric goalkeeper Quiroga, known as 'El Loco', parried Rioch's shot and Jordan put Scotland ahead from the rebound. But the goal-feast never materialised and Cueto equalised just before half-time.

In the 62nd minute, Diaz brought down Rioch in the penalty area. Masson had scored some notable penalties for Scotland, but on this afternoon in Cordoba, his right-footed shot was saved by Quiroga, who almost certainly moved before the ball was struck.

Scotland were a spent force. Cubillas hit two splendid goals in the last 20 minutes. The Scots had missed not having the suspended Willie Donachie available at full-back.

After the match, the World Cup committee carried out a routine drugs test on two Scotland players and one of them, Willie Johnston, was found to have taken some inexpensive yellow sugar-coated tablets usually prescribed for 'mental and physical fatigue'. Johnston was sent home immediately, his international career at an end.

It was ironic that Johnston had had a poor game anyway. Wrote Colin Malam in his book *World Cup Argentina*: "Johnston's performance against Peru had been enough to give stimulants a bad name".

The incident threw the Scottish party into a state of shock. The SFA had issued repeated warnings that players should not take any pills without telling the doctor. However, Johnston admitted taking Reactivan tablets, and seemed oblivious of the possible consequences, as if he thought prescribed pharmaceutical products were not the same thing as drugs. The player was led out of a side-door of the Alta Gracia hotel and taken on a nine-and-half-hour drive to Buenos Aires where he was put on a night flight.

Demoralised Scotland somehow led at half-time against Iran when centre-back Eskandarian turned the ball into his own net in the 43rd minute. Scotland then lost Buchan with a head injury and, on the hour, Danalfar equalised.

Scottish morale hit an all-time low and Chrysler dropped the squad from its advertising campaign. There were cruel jokes about manager and players and yet from this low, Scotland produced one of their best-ever World Cup performances, beating Holland, runners-up in 1974 and, as it transpired, in 1978 too.

Joe Jordan appears to be 'doing a Maradona' as he challenges Jan Jongbloed and Piet Wildschut during Scotland's match against Holland in Mendoza.

Scotland Managers — 1954-1978

ONE of the best ways of charting Scotland's fortunes, and considering post-war changes, is to look at the men hailed as 'witchdoctors' – the managers.

First to the fray was Andy Beattie, who in February 1954 was manager of Huddersfield Town. Beattie had won five caps as a Preston player and also played in five wartime internationals.

After serving a managerial apprenticeship with Barrow and Stockport, he achieved much at Huddersfield, taking them out of the Second Division and then to third place in the English First Division. He also steered Huddersfield to a 3-2 win over Independiente of Argentina, a result that gave him credence on the world scene.

ANDY BEATTIE

It is difficult, however, to imagine two more contrasting managerial jobs. At Huddersfield, Beattie was a full-time employee, dealing with a match every week and with more than 30 players to call upon, whereas he was in charge of only four Scotland games in four months before he was pitched into the 1954 World Cup with a squad of 13 players. He resigned in the middle of the tournament, indicating that things had been made difficult for him.

Almost four years passed without a manager, but when the World Cup Finals in Sweden loomed, there was the appointment of Matt (later Sir Matt) Busby. But in February 1958, Busby was seriously injured in the Munich Air Disaster. He resumed Scotland duties the following September, but decided by the end of the year that being full-time manager of Manchester United was sufficient, considering his health at that time.

Andy Beattie, who had moved to Carlisle United, was given a second chance. But after his next club move, to Nottingham Forest, he found that the Scotland job was restricting his City Ground duties. He asked to be excused on the eve of an international.

Next came Ian McColl, whose fine Rangers playing career was coming to an end. The choice surprised a few people, but the former Rangers man was in control for a relatively stable and successful period of four and a half years.

McColl was appointed on a game-to-game basis. After the first season, the offer was year-to-year. It was a significant move in the evolution of managerial responsibility, but the selectors still held the upper hand.

"To begin with the team was picked by the International and Selection Committee" recalls McColl "position by position...the Chairman calling for a show of hands from the Committee."

"This changed as we had a bit of success...the team picked itself and more and more I found myself being called on to advise and give my opinion if there was any doubt about any player or position. I used to go down to England to watch big games, and I would report to the next meeting of the selection committee."

In the early 1960s, there were plenty of Anglo-Scots to watch — Brown, Mackay and White at Tottenham, St John and Yeats at Liverpool, Crerand and Law at Manchester United — and those chosen still needed permission from their club.

"I had no trouble in getting players released," says McColl. "I had a fantastic relationship with people like Shankly, Busby, Revie, Catterick and Nicholson. None of them could have been more helpful."

IAN McCOLL

In McColl's days, it was rare for the Scotland manager to be interviewed on television, while journalists had only recently become interested in quoting managers rather than describing events.

McColl was not an Ally MacLeod with the media. "Maybe I was a little bit wrong in that way," he reflects now. "You've got to take the media with you. It's possible to live without them — if you win all your games."

In fact McColl had the best win record of any Scotland team manager (16 victories in 27 matches). "One of the special things was that we had a pretty regular team. A lot of the credit should go to club managers. Rangers were always the anchor — Caldow, Baxter, Henderson, Wilson — and Spurs were on a crest. Manchester United were always there, and Leeds were on the way."

By the late 1960s, however, it was becoming more difficult to obtain the release of players as their clubs became heavily reliant on European competition. When McColl was relieved of his duties in May 1965, the next manager, albeit temporarily, was Jock Stein. He ran into tremendous injury problems and the lack of availability when Scotland played in Naples in 1965.

Stein's brief spell was followed by the short reigns of John Prentice and Malcolm MacDonald, neither of whom had won international caps, although both had distinguished playing careers, and MacDonald had played for Scotland in wartime internationals. Prentice had played for Hearts, Rangers and Falkirk.

Prentice, the Clyde manager, was in charge for less than eight months, much of it spent negotiating the terms of his contract. MacDonald, who had a 22-year playing career, mainly with Celtic, was a stop-gap measure. He was Kilmarnock manager at the time.

The next appointment signalled a watershed. Bobby Brown became Scotland's first full-time manager.

Brown was the last amateur to play for Scotland, making six wartime appearances as a Queen's Park goalkeeper, and one as a professional with Rangers with whom he spent ten seasons.

In 1953, Brown won an English FA coaching badge and eventually combined his job of PE teacher with that of football club manager, first at Stirling Albion, then with St Johnstone.

At St Johnstone, he had great success, helping the club to grow from a part-time Second Division outfit to a full-time member of the First Division. In 1967, he was approached by the SFA and took the job on a four-year contract.

By now the Scotland team manager also selected the team. "I was given a 100 per cent free hand," says Brown. "After the routine business, the international committee would call me in. I gave them my team and the reasons for my choice. Questions were invited — a few were asked — but I was never requested to withdraw a player.

"After games, at subsequent meetings, I was always given a fair hearing, even though with hindsight, we can all think of alternatives."

Although Brown's reign began magnificently with a 3-2 win at Wembley, he soon learned of the day-to-day anxieties connected with the job.

"One of the problems is that an international manager can't have a post-match inquest two or three days later," says Brown. "And he's dependent on an unwieldy fixture-list. Saturday night is spent waiting by the telephone, wondering about call-offs. During my time it was important for clubs to be in Europe and there was not always 100 per cent co-operation from club managers.

"There were times when there were so many cry-offs for training weekends that I began to wonder if they were of any benefit. It was a very difficult period."

Brown's period as manager is a reminder that an international team manager is more concerned with motivation than getting players fit. His excellent start was followed by more fine results, then a moderate period, and finally a slump that called for a fresh face.

In the summer of 1970, when Brown renegotiated his contract, the SFA agreed to a six-month break clause. "With hindsight, I might have left in 1970," says Brown. "The break clause was because my hands were tied, not by the selection committee but by the system. I couldn't get players together."

A classic example of this came a year later on the SFA tour to Denmark and Russia. Brown recalls, "We just couldn't get the players, and some who went were out of training. Yet we did wonderfully well against the Russians, who won with a late goal. But Denmark used to be the Cinderellas and that was my swan-song."

The SFA operated the break clause and called for an exciting new face, Tommy Docherty, who had just been appointed assistant manager of Hull City.

TOMMY DOCHERTY

A natural extrovert, Docherty was given a free hand and he steered Scotland to some fine results. After a trial period, he was offered the job full-time.

Only three of the 12 games played under Docherty were lost, but in little over year there came an attractive offer from Manchester United.

The first manager to last more than five years was Willie Ormond, who quietly and efficiently blended the huge pool of talent available to Scotland in the mid-1970s.

Ormond, a player with Stenhousemuir, Hibs and Falkirk, was the second successful St Johnstone manager to be appointed to the post. He led Scotland to the 1974 World Cup Finals and received universal sympathy when the team failed to qualify for the knockout stages.

But the pressure of the job was continuous as supporters' expectations were raised and Scottish nationalism fervent. Disciplinary issues received widespread publicity, but the SFA supported their manager, even when England won 5-1 in 1975.

It was, in the end as always, the system which was the stumbling block to Ormond. Ormond, awarded the OBE in 1975, left to become manager of Hearts, and later Hibs. He died in May 1984, aged 57.

After Ormond left there was sheer drama. The 1978 World Cup Finals were only a year away, the nation and the media were hungry for an optimistic, ebullient and commercial approach.

WILLIE ORMOND

They got one from Ally MacLeod, who became tagged 'Muhammed Ally' by the media as he boasted about what Scotland might do to the world.

Once the media roller-coaster started Ally's Tartan Army marched on and on, until they were ambushed in Argentina by a couple of sniping Peruvian wingers, a self-imposed drugs warfare, and a media 'mutiny'. Ally pulled together some new ammunition to beat Holland, but he had lost the World Cup war. After the Iran game, he joked that his only friend was a stray dog which had strayed into the Press conference and sat on his lap.

MacLeod is the only manager to have attracted 25,000 to Hampden when there was no game — to send the team off to Argentina. When this was pointed out to him, he replied, "Aye, but there were 100,000 waiting for me when I came back."

Quips like that made Ally MacLeod a tonic to the nation, and nothing seemed to dampen his spirits. Soon after the World Cup Finals, he returned to Ayr United where he had spent 11 years serving his managerial and coaching apprenticeship.

MacLeod, raised in the Mount Florida area of Glasgow, was like the messiah coming home to Hampden. His playing career was as an outside-left with Third Lanark, Blackburn Rovers, Hibs, Third Lanark again and Ayr United. He was Ayr manager from April 1966 to November 1975 before he jumped into the limelight as Aberdeen manager.

ALLY MacLEOD *waits for the final whistle against Wales and confirmation that Scotland have qualified for the 1978 World Cup Finals.*

MacLeod had been a salesman in his early managerial days and this showed in his approach to the Scotland job. It was a significant contrast to the pioneering managerial era of Andy Beattie.

In 25 years the nature of the job had altered immensely. In Beattie's first spell, television companies were experimenting with football in an age when relatively few people owned sets. Training was mainly lapping, and football had a domestic focus with substitutes considered the preoccupation of paranoid foreigners. An international manager was expected to turn up on match days to gee up 11 pre-selected players, and then resume his normal job.

By October 1978, all that had changed. The Scotland manager was now a salesman for the nation, the father figure for a network of youth teams, liaising with Scottish players throughout Europe, studying the opposition and developing tactical scenarios that now involved substitutions.

It was all too much for one man, but the SFA tempted the person generally recognised as the senior statesman in Scottish football...Jock Stein.

WILLIE DONACHIE

1972 to 1978: Left-back, 35 caps (1 as sub).
Born: Castlemilk, Glasgow, 1951.
Career: Glasgow United, Celtic, Manchester City, Portland Timbers, Norwich City, Portland Timbers, Burnley, Oldham.
When he was first capped, as a 20-year-old, Willie Donachie had just completed his first season with Manchester City. Switched from midfield to full-back, Donachie embarked on a consistent career.
An ankle injury against Northern Ireland in 1974 lost him his place temporarily - when he was fit again Jardine and McGrain held the full-back berths - and he missed the Czechoslovakia game in 1977 because of a wrist injury, but otherwise he had a long run as first-choice full-back.

JOCK STEIN ARRIVES

1978-9 After defeat in Austria, Ally MacLeod resigned and became Ayr United's manager, and new Scotland manager Jock Stein embarked on a steady reorganisation of resources. An exciting victory over Norway was the highlight of the season, while the Wembley visit was marred by more trouble from 'so-called Scottish football supporters.'

A more subdued MacLeod took the team to Austria, and the game itself was much quieter than some of the previous battles between the two sides, but Scotland were losing 3-0 with little more than an hour played. Then came an excellent fight-back which produced a magnificent goal from McQueen — a diving header — and another goal from Andy Gray. But, despite the heroics, the 3-2 defeat was a disappointing start to the European Championship campaign.

Scotland's other group opponents were Portugal, Belgium and Norway. Norway

When Scotland played Norway on 25 October 1978, the first game after Jock Stein's return as manager, the eleven Scottish players were all with English clubs.

came next and Jock Stein took control of the team once more.

Norway twice took the lead and might have made it 3-1 when Johansen struck the woodwork. Dalglish twice equalised, the second time with eight minutes to play. In a dramatic finale, Graham was fouled and Gemmill drove the penalty to the goalkeeper's right, with the 'keeper diving to the left, perhaps recalling where Gemmill had put his penalty against Holland in the World Cup.

The injured Souness and Graham missed the trip to Portugal. Alberto scored a 29th-minute winner and defeat left Scotland with much to achieve if they were to qualify for the European Finals for the first time.

There was little joy in the home internationals. With virtually a new defence, Scotland lost heavily at Ninian Park, the first time in 15 years that Wales had beaten Scotland. The game was a personal triumph for three-goal John Toshack.

Victory over Northern Ireland was only Scotland's third in 11 matches. Jordan and McQueen returned to make important contributions, but there were only 14 minutes to play when Arthur Graham scored from close-range.

Goalkeeper George Wood had kept a clean sheet against the Irish, but he had a dismal time at Wembley. John Wark's 21st-minute goal for Scotland looked like the first of many, but just before the interval, Barnes crept a shot through the defence and past an unsighted Wood.

After 64 minutes, Wilkins' shot-cum-centre bounced off Wood's chest and Coppell knocked in the loose ball. England's third, from Keegan, was of a much higher class.

A week later, Hampden was the stage for the skills of Argentina's 18-year-old Diego Maradona. In the 33rd minute, he ran from his own penalty area to create an easy goal for Luque. The new South American star surpassed even this in the 70th minute with an incredible goal. He weaved through and then cheekily put the ball in at the near post for his second of the game. Scotland were thus trailing 3-0 when Arthur Graham scored with the visitors appealing for offside.

Stein plumped for experience in the season's final game, the European Championship match in Norway. He was rewarded with four Scottish goals in the 20 minutes either side of half-time. Yet how different it might have been, had a shot from Aas gone in, rather than hit the bar just before Scotland's first goal.

ONE GLORIOUS MOMENT

1979-80 Interest in the home championship soon diminished with a draw against Austria and two defeats by Belgium. Victory over Portugal temporarily lifted spirits, but otherwise, goals were scarce. A point of near humiliation was reached when Northern Ireland won their first home international for five years.

Sandy Jardine returned as captain against Peru — since he last skippered the side,

BRUCE RIOCH

1975 to 1978: Midfield, 24 caps, 6 goals.
Born: Aldershot, 1947.
Career: Cambridge Schools, London Schools, Luton Town, Aston Villa, Derby County, Everton, Derby County, Birmingham City (loan), Sheffield United (loan), Seattle Sounders, Torquay United (player-coach, then manager), Middlesbrough (manager).
Bruce Rioch was an exciting midfielder with pace, power and a blistering left-foot shot. He captained Scotland in magnificent displays (against England and Czechoslovakia in 1977 and Holland in 1978), but, along with others, he was criticised for displays in Argentina in 1978.
Rioch was first called up in October 1972, but promotion-chasing Aston Villa refused to release him. This led to rumours that he might play instead for England, but Rioch himself was in no doubt that he was Scottish.
His father, a Great Britain hammer-thrower of the 1930s, was a Scots Guard stationed at Aldershot when Rioch was born. He was raised a Scot in England and in 1975, Willie Ormond called him up. Two years later, Rioch skippered Scotland to the home title.

Scotland had used nine captains in four years — but the game evoked too many memories of the World Cup game between the two sides. There was an early Scotland goal when a Peruvian defender finished off Hartford's work. Then John Wark missed a penalty and with five minutes to play, Leguia took advantage of a defensive mix-up to equalise.

Against Austria, Alan Rough equalled Bill Brown's record of 28 caps as a goal-

JOE JORDAN

1973 to 1982: Centre-forward, 52 caps (7 as sub), 11 goals.
Born: Carluke, Lanarkshire, 1951.
Career: Blantyre Victoria, Morton, Leeds United, Manchester United, AC Milan, Southampton, Bristol City.
Joe Jordan blended the forceful style of an old-fashioned centre-forward with the speed and strategy of modern-day football. Powerful in the air, the left-footed Jordan has been an imposing and awesome figure, and three missing front teeth add to his aggressive image. Although he is best remembered as a provider, rather than scorer, Jordan is the only Scot to have scored in three World Cup Finals (1974-78-82) and since 1965 only Dalglish has scored more goals.
Jordan has some memorable efforts to his credit, notably his classic headers against the Czechs (twice) and Sweden to help Scotland into three World Cup Final stages. He scored seven World Cup goals, a record until Dalglish's stunner against Spain in 1984.
Leeds signed him from Morton for £15,000 in 1970, and Manchester United paid £350,000 for him, eight years later. He grew in international status in the 1974 pre-World Cup games, and won nine of his caps against England.

midfield trio of Eamonn Bannon, Roy Aitken and John Wark were still eligible for the Under-21 team, and their inexperience showed when Belgium scored three times in the first half-hour. The fans were displeased, but they might have remembered that this was Scotland's first defeat by European opposition at Hampden since 1974. Robertson's second-half free-kick provided one glorious moment.

Belgium's 3-1 win ensured them a place in the final eight of the European Championship, so when Portugal visited Glasgow, a month after the fixture had been postponed because of snow, there was nothing at stake and Scotland's 4-1 win meant that they still finished next-to-bottom of the five-nation group.

For the first time in ten years, Scotland played in Belfast. Only goalkeeper Billy Thomson, in for the injured Rough, had already played at Windsor Park. Scotland, wearing red, included three new caps and one of them, Peter Weir, had played in only 32 Scottish League games. Billy Hamilton's first-half goal gave Northern Ireland the victory that helped them to their first home title for 66 years.

A team with eight home-based Scots beat Wales 1-0, but the scoreline was 'a farce' according to Jock Stein. Willie Miller scored following a one-two with Dalglish, and Gordon Strachan's effort which hit the woodwork was one of many near misses.

When Scotland met England at Hampden, the teams were battling to avoid the 'wooden spoon'. For the third successive season, Steve Coppell scored, putting England 2-0 ahead in the 75th minute. Brooking opened the scoring, forcing the ball past Rough after Mariner had headed down.

A depleted squad went on tour. The first game, against Poland, was lost and Scotland were lucky to escape a heavy defeat. Poland's goal came after 77 minutes when Willie Miller turned Boniek's shot past Rough. The Scots managed only two shots all game, though one of them, from Weir after a fine run, nearly saved the game.

Scotland's game in Hungary was their fifth in 16 days and it was a weary performance on a bitterly cold evening. Torocsic's two goals put Hungary in charge, but Steve Archibald scored with a near-post header. Almost immediately, Kereki made it 3-1 and sealed Scotland's third successive defeat.

ANOTHER WORLD CUP TRAIL

1980-81 Eight points from the first five games in Group Six was a sound base for qualification for the 1982 World Cup Finals, and John Robertson's Wembley penalty sealed a successful season in which Scotland conceded only four goals in eight matches.

The qualifying group included Portugal, Northern Ireland, Israel and Sweden, who were Scotland's first opponents. In Stockholm, Rough's first-half saves from Nilsson kept Scotland level and in the 72nd minute, Strachan put them ahead.

KENNY BURNS

1974 to 1981: Central defender, 20 caps (4 as sub), 1 goal.
Born: Glasgow, 1953.
Career: Rangers, Birmingham City, Nottingham Forest, Leeds United, Derby County, Notts County (loan), Barnsley.
After being released by Rangers, Kenny Burns gained his reputation at Birmingham, mainly as an impetuous goal-scoring forward, but also as a defender. He was versatile enough to play in Birmingham's attack one Saturday, and then in Scotland's defence, against Spain at Hampden, four days later.
After Nottingham Forest signed him, for £150,000 in 1977, Burns settled into defence, while a spell of tremendous success under Brian Clough and Peter Taylor did much to quieten his fiery character. In 1977-8 he was voted English Footballer of the Year.

After a one-two with Gemmill, Strachan scored from a seemingly impossible angle. It was his first goal for Scotland, and a vital one.

Against Portugal at Hampden, Scotland were frustrated by the experienced Portuguese goalkeeper and skipper, Manuel Bento.

A World Cup trip to Israel followed. Israel's most famous player was Avi Cohen, later to sign for Liverpool, and they had already drawn three games in the group, so Scotland's 1-0 win could be considered satisfactory, especially as Israel had the chances to secure a comfortable half-time lead.

Rough was outstanding in goal — Scotland still had to concede a goal in group matches — and Dalglish's opportunism in the 53rd minute won the game. He pounced on a falling ball after McLeish had headed down Robertson's corner.

When Rough finally conceded a goal, to Northern Ireland's Hamilton, he was

keeper. Rough failed to reach a through-ball and Krankl gave Austria the lead after 40 minutes. But Scotland had performed well and Gemmill rescued a point with a 20-yard left-foot shot. McQueen was strong in defence, even tackling a spectator who invaded the pitch.

After a depleted Scottish team lost in Belgium, there remained only early preparation for the World Cup. The return against Belgium saw Scotland field an experimental team, although Danny McGrain made a welcome reappearance after a long absence through injury. The

ARCHIE GEMMILL

1971 to 1981: Midfield, 43 caps (6 as sub), 8 goals.
Born: Paisley, 1947.
Career: Drumchapel Amateurs, St Mirren, Preston North End, Derby County, Nottingham Forest, Birmingham City, Jacksonville Teamen (USA), Wigan Athletic, Derby County, Nottingham Forest(coaching staff).
Archie Gemmill had a tough international baptism – blooded in difficult away games in Belgium and Holland, then publicly criticised by Tommy Docherty for his performance against England in 1972. That same summer, Derby County did not release Gemmill for Scotland's South American tour and he spent three years in the international wilderness.
Not until his second League Championship medal with Derby in 1975, was Gemmill chosen again. His sprightly, indefatigable midfield talents were never questioned again. He was part of a successful team under Willie Ormond, and he excelled in South America in 1977. Even in exhausting Brazilian conditions he covered every blade of grass.
Gemmill, who captained Scotland under three managers (Ormond, MacLeod and Stein), was one of the few Scottish players to return from the Argentina World Cup with his reputation enhanced. Having won a third Championship medal (with Nottingham Forest) he dazzled the world's TV viewers with a stunning goal against Holland.

handicapped by injury and Billy Thomson had to come on without warm-up in the 71st-minute. Earlier, Rough had tipped a Hamilton header on to the post, while Steve Archibald had hit the woodwork. Thirteen minutes from time, Wark made it 1-1 and the depleted Scotland team settled for a draw. Injury to Dalglish meant the end of the Liverpool player's run of 43 consecutive internationals.

The good start to the World Cup campaign continued with a 3-1 win against Israel which extended Scotland's record of 11 undefeated World Cup games at Hampden. They had to look back to October 1965, when two late Polish goals stunned the Hampden crowd, for their last home defeat.

World Cup euphoria meant that the home internationals were perhaps devalued — except for the England game, of course. Several England-based players missed the Wales game and two Ian Walsh goals gave the Welsh a record sixth successive victory, while Joe Jordan was sent off following an incident with Terry Boyle which left the Welsh player with a broken nose and a missing tooth.

Significantly, the Hampden World Cup game with Northern Ireland attracted 78,444 spectators compared to only 22,448 for the home international against the same team. Scotland made seven changes and new cap Tommy Burns fed Ray Stewart for a fifth-minute goal. Five minutes into the second half, Archibald added a second.

For the first time, the home championship would be inconclusive because England and Wales refused to play in Belfast for security reasons. Nevertheless, the England game was just as important to the Scots and, after a nervous start, McLeish and Miller settled down to keep a tight hold on the England strikers. There was an enforced change when Asa Hartford dislocated an elbow. After 64 minutes, Archibald was sent sprawling in the penalty area and John Robertson scored from the spot.

HIGH HOPES

1981-2 Joe Jordan's heading power put Scotland into the 1974 and 1978 World Cup Finals and now another headed goal virtually assured them a place in the 1982 Finals.

John Robertson's 20th-minute free-kick floated into the Swedish goalmouth and up rose Jordan to head Scotland into the lead. Late in the game, Robertson added a second from the penalty spot after Andy Gray had been fouled.

This excellent performance meant that Scotland needed just one point from their two remaining games in order to ensure a passport to Spain. The task was not easy. Scotland had to face the electric atmosphere of Windsor Park, while they had never won in Lisbon.

However, captained by Asa Hartford and inspired by Alan Rough, Scotland managed the point in Belfast, although not before Hartford had cleared off his own goal-line. Nevertheless, Stein could now begin to plot a course towards Spain. His approach would prove to be more cautious than that of MacLeod in 1978.

By the time Scotland played in Portugal, Northern Ireland, too, were assured of a place in Spain. Scotland's 2-1 defeat in Lisbon was followed, three months later, by another defeat on the Iberian Peninsula when they were given a taste of Spain's talent for winning penalties. Scotland conceded two in Valencia, and a late goal gave Spain a 3-0 win.

GORDON McQUEEN

1974 to 1981: Centre-half, 30 caps, 5 goals.
Born: Kilburnie, Ayrshire, 1952.
Career: Largs Thistle, St Mirren, Leeds United, Manchester United, Airdrie (manager).
In February 1978, Manchester United paid Leeds United a British record fee of £450,000 for the services of Gordon McQueen, a 6ft 3in fair-haired left-footed central defender. With two players with fine physiques, McQueen and Jordan, commanding the middle, it was obvious that Manchester United meant business.
McQueen's big chance in the Scotland team came when Jim Holton was badly injured in 1974, but McQueen himself was unlucky with injuries. He missed most of 1975-6, and then against Wales in 1978, he collided with a goalpost and missed the World Cup Finals in Argentina.
Besides his obvious defensive qualities, McQueen had a happy knack of scoring important goals, particularly from set-pieces. His total of five goals for Scotland is more than any other defender.

A glut of injuries preceded the friendly in Holland, when Jim Bett and Alan Evans played their first internationals. Scotland had a whirlwind start, scoring twice in the first 20 minutes. Frank Gray netted from the penalty spot, then Dalglish latched on to Jordan's backheel.

The future of the home championship was in doubt when it kicked off in April. Scotland earned a creditable draw in Belfast, beat Wales, and looked forward to the 100th meeting with England, and the World Cup beyond.

The centenary match against England proved to be one of the most boring. It was won by Paul Mariner's 13th-minute goal after Butcher's header had struck the bar. Despite the traditional fervour of the fixture, both sides seemed to have more important things on their mind.

WORLD CUP FINALS ⚽ 1982

A PATCHY win against New Zealand was followed by defeat to Brazil, leaving Scotland to win their final group match, against Russia, if they were to proceed further. When Scotland led through Jordan's goal, it looked possible, but the eventual 2-2 scoreline meant that Scotland went out on goal difference. It had been a familiar frustrating World Cup.

Scotland had two warm-up games. At Penina, Portugal, they beat Torralto 9-1 and 7-0. Two different sides were used and Archibald and Souness scored hat-tricks in the first game.

Scotland's group was described by manager Stein as a big mountain to climb. Brazil and Russia were the teams to fear, but the first game was against New Zealand when 14 Scottish-born players were on the field.

Brilliant play by Gordon Strachan paved the way for victory over John Adshead's New Zealanders. Strachan's 40-yard run created a goal for Dalglish in the 18th minute. Two goals from Wark gave Scotland a 3-0 half-time lead.

Then came a transformation as New Zealand pulled back to 3-2, through Sumner, who latched on to McGrain's back-pass, and Wooddin. After ten nervous minutes, during which a Kiwi equaliser looked possible, John Robertson scored from a free-kick, then Steve Archibald headed a fifth. Strachan had a hand in four of the goals.

One of the talking points of this World Cup was David Narey's goal against Brazil, beautifully struck with the outside of his right foot from beyond the penalty area. It was a magnificent goal, scored as defenders closed in, although BBC TV's Jimmy Hill incensed Scottish fans by calling it a 'toe-ender'.

Narey's goal was 'Brazilian' in its execution, but Brazil themselves produced some stunning goals in the 90-degree heat. Zico's free-kick levelled the scores, then Peres kept his side on equal terms with a brave save from Archibald. Oscar headed Brazil in front, followed by a breathtaking moment as Eder chipped the ball left-footed over Rough's head. Falcao's late blast from the edge of the penalty area was almost superfluous.

Russia's goal difference was two better than Scotland's and it needed victory to take second place in the Group. It was a brave fight. Archibald set up Jordan for a 15th-minute goal and at half-time Scotland still had their lead.

However, Chivadze equalised and Shengeia scored a second when Miller and Hansen clashed when trying to clear. Three minutes from time, Souness burst through to score an inspirational captain's goal, but it was too late. Scotland had once again failed by a slender margin.

Unlike 1978, however, Scotland achieved a degree of acclaim, particularly for their performance against Brazil. Scottish and Brazilian fans exchanged souvenirs as they marched back to the city together, and Scottish players and officials were applauded by the Spaniards who lined the streets on the way to the team hotel.

Kenny Dalglish falls to the ground after scoring Scotland's first goal against New Zealand in the 1982 World Cup Finals. Strachan (7) and Wark celebrate.

DANNY McGRAIN

1973 to 1982: Full-back, 62 caps (3 as sub).
Born: Glasgow, 1950.
Career: Drumchapel schoolboy football, Celtic.
Danny McGrain, Scotland's second most-capped player, joined Celtic as an apprentice professional and had a spell with Maryhill Juniors (at the same time as Paul Wilson) before Celtic signed him full-time in 1967.
McGrain was a midfield player until Jock Stein switched him to full-back to replace Jim Craig. Throughout his career, however, he retained a midfielder's ability to run a game, even from full-back. McGrain became a world-class player and a fine Scotland captain, effective at right or left-back. But for injury and illness, his impressive number of caps might have been even higher.
In March 1972, a clash of heads with Dougie Somner (Falkirk) brought McGrain a fractured skull. Typical of the man, he recovered quickly and in May 1973 won his first cap.
Shortly after the 1974 World Cup Finals it was discovered that he had diabetes. Again he minimised the handicap and was Scottish Player of the Year in 1976-7. One incident from a World Cup game against Wales sums him up: McGrain won the ball in his own penalty area, raced 70 yards upfield, lost the ball, chased three defenders to win it back, and then forced Welsh goalkeeper Davies to dive desperately at his feet.
A foot injury caused McGrain to miss many caps, but he returned to appear in 16 consecutive internationals.

EXPERIMENTAL SEASON

1982-3 For the first time since 1874, England took the lead in the series — 40 wins to 39 with 22 draws. They edged in front with victory in a novel midweek evening match at Wembley. Poor results in the European Championship qualifiers compounded Scotland's problems in a season which will go down in history as one of transition and experiment as players like Jim Leighton, Richard Gough, Charlie Nicholas and Mark McGhee arrived on the international scene.

The season started brightly enough when virtually the same team which had drawn with Russia in the World Cup was fielded against East Germany in a European qualifying match played at Hampden where reconstruction work had cut the capacity to 57,000.

Atrocious wet and windy weather meant that the restriction was not tested and only 40,355 turned up. They were rewarded with Strachan and Souness repeating their World Cup form. Yet it was the 54th minute before the Germans' 6ft 6in goalkeeper Rudwaleit was beaten, when Wark headed in Robertson's cross. From the same source, Sturrock headed a second, four minutes after coming on as substitute.

It was a fine start, yet hopes of progress to the European Finals, in which Scotland had never appeared, were dashed by the next three games.

The pitch in Switzerland was a quagmire and sleet fell during the game. The Swiss opened the scoring in the 49th minute when Ponte's free-kick hit a post and fell to Sulser; Elgi's header added a second.

Like the Swiss trip, the journey to Belgium was punctuated with a delay while a pressure fault in the aircraft was rectified. The Belgium game was Stein's 39th in charge, one more than Ormond, and it indicated the increased stability in the Scotland camp. Stein himself favoured continuity in his selection and the five changes against Belgium were largely forced on him through injuries. Kenny Dalglish resumed after a three-match absence and and on another rainy night, scored two of his finest goals.

They came in the 12th and 34th minutes, each giving Scotland the lead. But each time the Belgians equalised. Vander Elst, then playing for West Ham, made it 2-2 and in the second half, he put Belgium ahead. Then, in the 78th minute, came a moment of high drama.

Souness was pulled down in the penalty area by Meeuws, and Frank Gray stepped up for the kick. But goalkeeper Pfaff made a magnificent save, deflecting the ball to safety. Scotland felt that the 'keeper had moved before the ball was kicked, but they were left to ponder the fact that Dalglish had scored two brilliant goals and still finished up on the losing side. Nevertheless, the Scots had come closer than most teams to ending Belgium's unbeaten home run of 17 matches.

Dundee United's Paul Sturrock and David Narey were injured when Switzerland played at Hampden, and with four Aberdeen men and three from Liverpool in the side, Charlie Nicholas found himself the only 'Old Firm' representative present.

It was Nicholas who finished off a fine Scottish rally after the Swiss had gone 2-0 ahead after 58 minutes. Wark pulled a

ASA HARTFORD

1972 to 1982: Midfield, 50 caps (5 as sub), 4 goals.
Born: Clydebank, 1950.
Career: Dunbartonshire Schools, Drumchapel Amateurs, West Brom, Manchester City, Nottingham Forest, Everton, Manchester City, Norwich City, Bolton Wanderers (player-coach), Stockport County (player-manager).
Christened Asa after Asa Yoelson, the real name of singer Al Jolson who died the day Hartford was born, Hartford joined the West Brom groundstaff in April 1966. By his 21st birthday, he had played himself into the Scotland reckoning, but the bottom dropped out of his world in one amazing week in November 1971.
Set to join Leeds United for £177,000, Hartford failed a medical which showed that he had a minor heart condition. The transfer fell through and Hartford withdrew from the Scotland squad selected for the Belgium game.
Within months, however, he had proved his fitness and his international worthiness. He earned six caps in ten weeks in 1972, but was then overlooked for more than three years.
Hartford's busy playmaking was soon an essential part of Scotland's plans and in an era of fine midfield players, he won most caps. Although omitted for ten games after the 1979 defeat by Belgium, his international career eventually spanned ten years.

goal back and then Nicholas controlled the ball and lobbed it over Burgener's head, all in one flowing moment.

Interest in the home title was practically at an end and an experimental Scottish side faced Northern Ireland. Narey and Wark were the only regulars and the resultant draw, though disappointing, was hardly surprising.

Nearer to full strength, Scotland won the next game, against Wales. It was their first victory in Wales for ten years and Alan Brazil, playing in his 11th international, scored his first goal in the 67th minute after Southall had fumbled Strachan's lob.

Scotland and England each had three points when they met at Wembley, where England's robust defenders, Neal, Roberts and Butcher, proved too strong. Bryan Robson's 12th-minute goal gave England the lead, and early in the second half, Cowans swerved a left-foot shot past Leighton.

Immediately after the defeat, a Scotland party minus the unavailable Wark and Brazil, left for Canada. Much media attention focussed on the future of Celtic's Charlie Nicholas, and he responded with a stunning goal in Edmonton. The match was also notable for a refereeing mistake which meant that the first half lasted only 41 minutes. Andy Gray scored two first-half goals in Toronto and goalkeepers Billy Thomson and Jim Leighton returned without conceding a goal. The first of these three games against Canada was Scotland's first-ever international on artificial turf.

FRANK GRAY

1976 to 1983: Full-back, 32 caps (2 as sub), 1 goal.
Born: Castlemilk, Glasgow, 1954.
Career: Glasgow Schools, Leeds United, Nottingham Forest, Leeds United.
Frank Gray, a former Parkhead ballboy, played in two major European finals before his 21st birthday. Originally a left-winger, like his older brother Eddie, he played in midfield and then settled at full-back.
Gray did not play in Ally MacLeod's Scotland spell, but Jock Stein called him up immediately. After winning a European Cup-winners' medal with Nottingham Forest, Gray became an automatic Scotland choice, missing only three of the next 28 internationals.

LAST HOME CHAMPIONSHIP

1983-4

100 years after the first four-way home title race — by now known as the British Championship — came the last. In the summer of 1983, Scotland and England declared that they preferred more attractive foreign opposition to that of Wales and Northern Ireland.

The last home championship, one of the closest ever, was won by Northern Ireland who retained the trophy. But had Scotland scored a consolation goal against the Irish, then they would have finished top, not bottom, for that was how close a race it was. For Scotland, this had been a decade of missing out because of goal differences.

The opening game of the season, against Uruguay, was a strange affair. In the first-half the South Americans made a mockery of the term 'friendly'. Frank McGarvey was carried off with a gashed leg, two Uruguayans were cautioned, and a third, Barrios, sent off for allegedly attempting to trip English referee David Richardson. The only goal of the first-half came from a John Robertson penalty after substitute Davie Dodds had been fouled.

Dodds scored the second after half-time. The second-half was in stark contrast and Uruguay seemed to shun the competitive element, leaving Jim Leighton to make just one serious save.

> *Five Aberdeen players — Jim Leighton, Doug Rougvie, Alex McLeish, Gordon Strachan and Peter Weir — played against Northern Ireland in December 1983, while a sixth, Mark McGhee, came on as substitute.*

Belgium knew that they had already qualified for the European Championship Finals when they visited a wet and windy Hampden in October. A goal by Vercauteren gave them a half-time lead before Nicholas and Dalglish combined to give Nicholas a 49th-minute equaliser. The draw was the first time since 1971 that the Scots had gained anything from Belgium who had won four of the matches played between the two countries since then.

East Germany would now decide which of two countries would take bottom place in Group One. Eamonn Bannon received a late call-up to the Scotland party — he only just caught the 'plane — and his goal in the 77th minute put Scotland back in the game. East Germany had scored twice in the first 45 minutes, a 35-yarder from Kreer and a header from Streich, and they hung on to their lead.

Souness hit a post early on against Northern Ireland, and Pat Jennings saved well from Strachan, before Whiteside and McIlroy scored for an Irish team containing two part-timers. The closest scrutiny was reserved for the attendance at 10,000.

Maurice Johnston scored the winner against Wales on his debut, and this left the game against England, who were severely handicapped by withdrawals. Yet Scotland's

JOHN ROBERTSON

1978 to 1983: Outside-left, 28 caps (2 as sub), 8 goals.
Born: Uddingston, Lanarkshire, 1953.
Career: Drumchapel Amateurs, Nottingham Forest, Derby County, Nottingham Forest.
John Robertson was a Scotland Schoolboy and Youth international but his career took off only when Clough and Taylor took charge of Nottingham Forest. He was a star of the Forest team which twice won the European Cup, playing wide on the left wing and being deceptively quick for a thick-set player.
Often he played deep, yet his speed and trickery took him into the heart of the action. His long-range goal won the 1980 European Cup Final.
He was an exceptionally reliable penalty-taker. His spot kick won Forest the Football League Cup in 1978, and he converted four kicks for Scotland. The most dramatic was at Wembley in 1981, when Scotland won 1-0. Examples of his match-winning abilities were also evident against East Germany in 1982.

inability to beat England at Hampden since 1976 continued. Mark McGhee's classic downward header was equalised by Woodcock's long-range drive.

Souness and Dalglish, playing in the European Cup Final, were unavailable for the France game, and Jock Stein fielded four youngsters in his team — Johnston, Nicholas, Malpas and Simpson. They lost 2-0 to the Platini-inspired French, but the way was paved for the studious Stein to appraise every player available, and to aim for the main ingredient — consistent team selection — that might carry Scotland towards the 1986 World Cup Finals.

Talk of replacing the home championship with a regular three-way tournament between Scotland, England and a major football power like Brazil or West Germany was shelved.

BREATHTAKING WINS

1984-5 Three breathtaking wins at Hampden brought elation and optimism, especially after Kenny Dalglish's goal had capped a 3-1 win against Spain. Two defeats changed the mood completely before the season was rescued sensationally: a win against England squared the official series; an 87th minute Jim Bett goal set up a nail-biting finish in Group Seven of the World Cup qualifying programme.

Jock Stein was now assisted by Aberdeen manager Alex Ferguson. There was the unfamiliar sight of the Scots wearing red shirts ... at Hampden too. Opponents Yugoslavia wore white and scored an early goal. Then came six from Scotland to give Stein his best win of his international career. Steve Nicol, wearing '2', played brilliantly, although not an automatic choice for Liverpool at the time.

The result from this friendly was a boost before World Cup games. Also, SFA secretary Ernie Walker had helped negotiate a change in the qualification process of Group Seven. The runners-up would now play-off (home and away) against the winners of the Oceanic group (Australia, New Zealand, Israel or Taiwan) rather than join another mini group.

Kenny Dalglish, now 33, was still in Stein's plans, but the manager was prepared to use him for part of a game if necessary. Dalglish gave 67 magic minutes against Iceland and the World Cup campaign was underway successfully. Teenager Paul McStay scored twice. The first was a header after Davie Cooper's corner, the second from longer range.

Jock Stein chose the same team to play Spain at Hampden. The manager was rewarded with the best Scotland display during his reign. Kenny Dalglish nearly missed the game with a knee injury but he lasted the full ninety minutes, and his superb goal made it 3-1 and equalled Denis Law's record number of goals for Scotland. Two headers from Mo Johnston set up the victory, while Jim Bett enhanced his reputation.

"We were off to a good start, trouncing Yugoslavia and beating Iceland," said Alex Ferguson later. "And Scotland are much better as the underdog. Three months before, Spain were in the European Championship Final against France, and were unlucky not to win, in many people's eyes. The Press were talking about this great Spanish team and that gave us a wee bit of incentive. It's difficult for me to assess that performance in relation to other Scotish performances but it was a marvellous night for job satisfaction. I was totally elated. At the time you keep calm and sane ... but I felt like going round a corner and shouting and screaming. A marvellous night."

This team had everyone excited. Captain Graeme Souness and Kenny Dalglish provided experience, while Johnston, McStay and Nicol had youth. There was stability in the defence which had three Aberdeen players, and Davie Cooper was re-established after a long absence in the early 1980s.

JOHN WARK

From 1979: Midfield, 29 caps (2 as sub), 7 goals.
Born: Glasgow, 1957.
Career: Drumchapel Amateurs, Ipswich Town, Liverpool.
John Wark captained Scotland at Youth level in 1975-6 and was a full international when only 21. His strong running in midfield and ferocious shooting established him as a regular in the Scotland squad.
Wark made his debut for Ipswich in an FA Cup tie against Leeds and after marking Allan Clarke out of that game, he was soon forcing other players to mark him. In 1980-81, he was the English PFA's choice as Player of the Year. In March 1984, Wark joined Liverpool for £450,000.

DAVID NAREY

From 1977: Defender or midfield, 33 caps (4 as sub), 1 goal.
Born: Dundee, 1956.
Career: St John's School (Dundee), St Columba Boys Club (Dundee), Chelsea, Dundee United.
David Narey, the first Dundee United player to play a full international, has proved himself one of the more talented and versatile defenders of recent times. He can play anywhere in the back-four, midfield, even up front.
His club performances have been mainly in defence, partnering Paul Hegarty in the centre. Hegarty and Narey have twice played together for Scotland, against Maradona-inspired Argentina in 1979 and against Northern Ireland in 1983, when four current and one former Dundee United player (Andy Gray) were in the Scotland team.
Narey has already provided one of the lasting memories of the 1980s – his long-range goal against Brazil which gave Scotland a temporary superiority over the brilliant South Americans in the 1982 World Cup Finals. In 1986 he returned to the Scotland team after a 2-year absence. That summer he played two games in Mexico. Against Uruguay he won his 30th cap, a day after his 30th birthday.
The following season, 1986-7, Narey was selected by Andy Roxburgh for three internationals, and he won a UEFA Cup runners-up medal with his club, Dundee United.

Spain in Seville was a tough proposition, made tougher when Dalglish and Nicol succumbed to viruses shortly before the game. Jim Leighton made some fine saves but a 50th-minute header by Spanish debutant Clos separated the teams.

Defeat in Spain was always possible, but defeat in the next game was a considerable surprise. The 1-0 reverse to Wales raised questions about Scotland qualifying for the 1986 Finals in Mexico. Wales had something to prove after their defeat at Anfield in 1977, while the abolition of the Home Championship made them financially insecure.

Wales had forwards in form — Ian Rush and Mark Hughes. Just before half-time came a killer goal. Hughes challenged McLeish — some thought unfairly — and Rush struck a superb shot from 25 yards.

Scotland thus became the first team to lose at home in Group Seven. Two wins and two defeats was not qualifying form. And this was Wales' first win in Scotland for 34 years.

"Before the match I had talked about not getting involved in a physical game... but we should have showed a bit more grit and determination," said Ferguson. "We didn't show fear at Hampden but we were stamped on by Wales. When Scotland did retaliate Souness received a lot of bad publicity for one tackle on Nicholas. Yet Wales were getting 'wellied in', as they say. Nicholas and Hughes had already made lots of those tackles.

The next setback was the switch of the England-Scotland game from Wembley to Hampden. After crowd riots at Luton, officials in England were worried that an unruly crowd would be at Wembley on 25 May... the Whitsun bank holiday weekend. It was presumed the Prime Minister had intervened with pressure for another venue.

At Hampden the two teams played for the newly-inaugurated Sir Stanley Rous Cup. Such were priorities, however, that many considered the World Cup game in Iceland three days later more important than the England fixture. How times change.

Stein was severely handicapped in his choice of players for both games. Four Liverpool players were unavailable, preparing for a tragic European Cup encounter with Juventus. Two Everton players had to play a Sunday League fixture, while Neil Simpson of Aberdeen withdrew, and Arthur Albiston was injured.

Displaying a new style in shorts — a thick navy-blue racing stripe around the groins — Scotland were the first winners of the Rous Cup. A mediocre, frantic game was settled by one highlight. Jim Bett's left-wing cross was met on the six-yard line by Richard Gough, who leaped high to loop a header into the English net.

The Everton pair, Andy Gray and Graeme Sharp, joined the party for the Iceland game. Gray had been absent for two years, while Sharp was winning his first cap.

A late tackle by Graeme Souness — his caution put him out of the key game in Wales in September — caused Iceland's Sigi Jonsson to be carried off on a stretcher, and the Scotland captain was booed the rest of the game. Near half-time Jim

Leighton brilliantly saved a penalty from Thordarsson. Leighton dived so far to his left that some people in the stadium might have questioned whether the ball was going in or hitting the foot of the post.

Leighton made other key saves in the second-half. Only three minutes remained when Gordon Strachan's right-wing cross eluded all except Jim Bett, who scored left-footed at the far post.

KENNY DALGLISH MBE

From 1971: Striker, 102 caps (8 as sub), 30 goals.
Born: Glasgow, 1951.
Career: Glasgow Schools, Drumchapel Amateurs, Glasgow United, Celtic, Liverpool, Liverpool (player-manager).
'Kenny's from Heaven,' read one famous Liverpool banner, in admiration of a man who has produced plenty of heavenly moments for Scotland fans to savour.
First capped at 20, Dalglish took some time to reproduce club form in a Scotland shirt, but then he became one of the most exciting players in world football – shielding the ball from a shadowing defender, feinting a move one way or the other, turning sharply and firing in a shot or setting up a chance. As Tommy Docherty once said: "Sometimes people say to me he lacks a yard in pace but I say to them that he's ten yards quicker upstairs".
By the time he joined Liverpool for £440,000 in August 1977, Dalglish had scored over 100 goals for Celtic and had captained Scotland. Signed to replace Keegan, he did more than that. His goal won the 1978 European Cup Final, he was twice English Footballer of the Year, his championship medals now total ten – four with Celtic, six with Liverpool – and he has won more than a dozen Cup-winners' medals of various sorts. In the summer of 1985 he was appointed player-manager of Liverpool and in his first season he steered them to the coveted English Cup and League Double.
Against Peru in 1978, he broke Law's appearance record for Scotland. Since then, his hunger for the game seems to have increased and his record number of caps for Scotland has set a standard that may last for ever. In March 1986 he became the first Scot and fifth Briton to complete a century of caps. Already awarded the MBE, Dalglish was accorded Freedom of the City of Glasgow.

RICHARD GOUGH

From 1983: Defender, 33 caps, 3 goals.
Born: Stockholm, 1962.
Career: Witz University, Dundee United, Tottenham Hotspur.
Born in Sweden, and raised in South Africa, Richard Gough is the son of Scotsman Charlie Gough, who played four English League games for Charlton Athletic in the mid-1960s. Richard Gough is an all-round player who provokes debate about what really is his best position: full-back, central defence, midfield, or even striker? For Scotland he has generally played on the right side of defence although his attacking bursts have shown his versatility. He had a fine tournament in Mexico in 1986 and proved one of Scotland's best hopes of a goal. He made his Scotland debut in 1983 and played in half the World Cup qualifying games in 1984 and 1985. A little unfortunate to be omitted from the home game with Australia he excelled in the return, when Scotland sealed the trip to Mexico. A player who appears comfortable on the ball anywhere on the pitch, and a threat at set-pieces, Gough's strike record for his country is as good as most recent midfield players. His header against England in 1985 – the only goal of the game – is a particularly sweet memory.

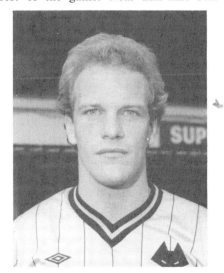

Andy Gray played against Iceland, winning his first cap for two years.

Jock Stein — *Scotland's Father Figure*

"I'VE ALWAYS been aware of the importance of international football in Scotland," began Jock Stein, when we met in the spring of 1985. "Some countries are more concerned with club football but Scotland rallies round for internationals with such wonderful partisan supporters."

Jock Stein managed the national team for seven years and dominated Scottish football of his age, both practically and theoretically. His impact was worldwide. As Ernie Walker, Scottish FA Secretary, said in tribute after Stein's untimely death, he was "the father figure, not only of Scottish football, but of British football".

Stein's life deserves exceptional recognition, far greater perhaps than the CBE he received in 1979. The circumstances of his death provoked an examination of the pressures that football managers are prepared to bear.

Much of Stein's playing career was, by professional standards, quite ordinary. He might have gone down in history alongside a bunch of Albion Rovers players who refused to re-sign in the summer of 1950 (with no disrespect to the likes of Blair, English, Kerr, Jack, Sinclair and Smith) but his career took a resurgence when Celtic signed him in November 1951, ostensibly to play in the reserves.

In eight years with Albion Rovers Stein played 236 games — all except one at centre-half — and scored nine goals, including six penalties. As a 'Bevan Boy', a coal-miner essential to the war effort, Stein was able to stay in Lanarkshire and play for Rovers during the war.

His last appearance for Rovers was in January 1950, against Alloa, and thereafter Stein was in dispute with the club. At 27 he became a full-time player for the first time, with Llanelli in the Welsh League, where he stayed for 18 months. Then came his first association with Celtic.

Celtic found themselves with two injured centre-halves, Jimmy Mallan and Alec Boden, and Stein came into the first team. He graduated to captain and won his only representative honour, against the English League.

Great players do not always make great managers and perhaps marginally successful players, like Jock Stein, think more deeply about football, fathoming its inner world.

Andy Roxburgh, when SFA director of coaching for 10 years ran courses for prospective managers, and is perhaps in a position to generalise on this point: "The great players might not have really studied the game," he says. "They might not have the same sympathy towards learners. Lesser players might have been more frustrated in their playing careers — might have more hunger for success as managers and coaches."

He might have been talking about Jock Stein, who first satisfied his hunger for success, and then sought players who were greedy for more and more success. Rarely has a club manager dominated a national scene as did Stein in his 13 years at Celtic. In one 16-month period, starting November 1966, 12 Celtic players won Scottish caps.

In February 1975, he took charge of the Scotland Under-23 team and there were rumours that Willie Ormond's position was in jeopardy, despite Ormond's success. But in July that year, Stein received serious chest and ankle injuries in a car accident. It was ten months before he resumed his Celtic duties. And that season, 1975-6, Rangers won everything.

In October 1978, the SFA finally appointed Stein as the man to lead the rebuilding programme following the recent World Cup Finals. Five of Ally MacLeod's key players — Masson, Rioch, Macari, Johnston and Tom Forsyth — never played under Stein, who piloted Scotland to the next World Cup Finals in 1982.

"To win the World Cup, preparation is everything," said Stein, "but we had only ten days rest before the start of the campaign. We had a big chance in Spain, with the right players and the right set-up, but we were in a powerful section."

Stein became only too familiar with the problems of preparing for international matches compared with club games. Obviously an international team manager does not see his players on a daily basis and until 1985 no Scotland manager was able to have League matches cancelled, as happened regularly in some other countries. Besides, Scottish players are also scattered across England, and even Europe.

Discipline and man-management were two of Stein's major managerial assets. Used to being in complete control, he exuded authority and commanded respect. Like many managers, he had a touch of steel, and was never afraid to bawl out players when needed. In return, he prepared them for internationals by running through the opposition beforehand, usually for an hour or so, and attending to every detail.

"The Secretary and I go away to check the opposition and the hotels," he said. "We never take an international team to a lower standard hotel. The best players are looked after in the best ways. We'll do nothing detrimental to that to save a penny."

Arrangements were easier in 1985 than during Stein's first period as Scotland team manager, in 1965, but the omnipresent club-country dilemma still remained.

"The first thing to be aware of is club commitments. You have to work hand-in-hand with the club. You don't fight the club, but go alongside. It needs a good three-way relationship — yourself, the player, and his club.

"All clubs start the season aiming to be successful, and the top clubs look to the last eight of the European competitions, which keeps interest from November to March.

"By March, club managers are concerned about the immediate future. They don't want too many distracting commitments. They want their players in the international team — but they also want them fresh."

Nowadays, it is easier to arrange international dates because the European rounds are set well in advance. But players still have to be brought from diverse places.

"The best players are spread around more now — Italy, Spain, West Germany. It is more difficult to keep tabs on players. But then it's good that the natural Scottish playing style is evident in European countries.

"It's always been evident in England, of course. All good teams have a good number of Scots. We commit our young players earlier than most countries, and Scottish players are hungry. Celts are a different breed, and good English teams have the Scots as their driving force. People like Tommy Docherty, Dave Mackay, Denis Law, Pat Crerand.

"We are dependent on Anglo-Scots. Some people say we shouldn't be, but I say, a Scot's a Scot, and he shouldn't be deprived of the opportunity to become a top earner."

Keeping in touch with players across Europe was one reason why Stein needed an assistant, first Jim McLean of Dundee United, then Alex Ferguson of Aberdeen. Scotland managers have always chosen their trainers — Ian McColl worked closely with John Harvey of Hearts, and Bobby Brown valued Hibs' Tom McNiven — and Stein was no exception. After McNiven stepped down through ill-health, Stein relied on Hugh Allan of Kilmarnock and Brian Scott of Celtic, while Jimmy Steel, a masseur, kept the spirit going.

But it needed more, as Stein explained: "You can't watch 20-odd players yourself. If you've got an assistant at club level, it helps to stay in touch, especially now players are in Europe. There used to be just Under-23 and Under-18 international football, though even then it makes you wonder how one manager coped. There must have been times when he was ill and the trainer had to take charge."

And it makes you wonder how Stein coped with the pressures offered by the precarious world of football management. Most of the pressures centre around 'the match' when all wares are displayed. Few businesses have such erratic custom, such well-defined measures of success and such a specific person to be held responsible, particularly by the media.

Nowadays club managers worry not only about their jobs but also about the future of their clubs. With Jock Stein it seemed the spirit of the nation was at stake and six-figure sums determined by the outcome of a few seconds, like Jim Bett's winner in Iceland or Davie Cooper's penalty at Cardiff.

The daily work of management lacks routine. Meal times are fitted in around travel, public engagements and telephone calls. There is always the stressful problem of what to say to whom. The revelation of a piece of trivia can seem akin to a breach of the Official Secrets Act. Sleep might not come easily.

It is an all-consuming world, and a manager's relaxation might be watching two teams under other managers' control. Like other areas of life, the busy grow busier, the underemployed look harder for opportunities.

It used to be that managers picked a team, gave a Friday team-talk and fired up 'the lads' just before kick-off. Then they could sit back and think, 'It's up to them'.

Jock Stein and Bill Shankly, two great Scottish-born managers — and two great figures of world football.

Not so now. The option of substitutions means that managers make decisions every moment of the game. Selecting an international team means choosing 16 players. Whereas Ian McColl used just four substitutes in four and a half years, Bobby Brown began by using a substitute regularly then sometimes two in a game. Willie Ormond used 58 substitutes in 38 games.

"I don't think substitutes at any level are a good thing for managers," said Jock Stein. "Good for the game perhaps. In the beginning, subs were used for injured players and it's good that we're ensured of seeing eleven against eleven . Now they can be tactical, they can waste time, and the crowd can shout about them."

Stein's last tactical decision — the substitution of Cooper for Strachan against Wales — was a masterstroke. Earlier in the World Cup campaign Stein prepared to play Kenny Dalglish for three-quarters of a game and use a substitute as a safeguard.

Stein described Dalglish as "a great professional" and said: "Kenny is an unselfish player. Everyone thought he went to Liverpool to plug the gap left by Keegan, but he actually improved the situation. He took over."

Dalglish takes pride of place for the number of Scotland caps, but Jock Stein was able to look back on other significant influences, like George Young, who had a good liaison with SFA secretary George Graham, Bobby Evans, the red-haired Celtic wing-half, the flamboyant Denis Law, Danny McGrain, Joe Jordan, Asa Hartford.......

1922
Born Burnbank, Lanarkshire.

1938
Signed for Blantyre Victoria. Began work at Hamilton as a miner.

1942
Signed for Albion Rovers.

1942-9
Working in Lanarkshire pits and playing as a part-time professional with Albion Rovers.

1950
Transfer-listed. No Scottish club shows interest. Joins Llanelli (Wales) as full-timer.

Nov 1951
Signed by Celtic to look after reserve side. Two centre-halves injured and Stein goes into first team, becoming captain. Celtic go on to win League and Cup double in 1954.

1955
Becomes Celtic coach after a serious ankle injury.

Mar 1960
Appointed Dunfermline manager. Within a year they win Scottish Cup.

April 1964
Appointed Hibernian manager. Within six months they win their first trophy for 13 years — the Summer Cup.

Feb 1965
Appointed Celtic manager. Within three months they win the Scottish Cup.

May-Dec 1965
Temporary Scotland international manager for World Cup qualifying games.

1965-78
As Celtic manager, he helps club to ten Championships (nine in a row), eight Scottish Cup wins (and three times runners' up), six League Cup wins (seven times runners' up). In 1967, Celtic win all three domestic trophies and become first British team to lift the European Cup.

Aug 1978
Manager of Leeds United after brief period on Celtic board.

Oct 1978
Manager of Scotland international team.

September 1985
Died at Ninian Park, Cardiff, immediately after Scotland-Wales World Cup qualifying game.

Cooper's penalty beat Wales' Southall and Scotland's World Cup hopes are alive again.

1985-6 Tuesday, 10 September 1985 was a night of many emotions. A late Davie Cooper penalty brought a 1-1 draw in Wales and kept alive World Cup hopes....but the tragic death of team manager Jock Stein overshadowed feelings of triumph. Stein collapsed shortly before the end of the game and died soon afterwards.

The home defeat by Wales in March had increased the tension in the group. At that time Stein was still shaking off the effects of the virus that plagued the Scottish party on the February trip to Spain. In the summer the Scotland manager had a prostate operation. And unlike club managers he didn't return to the 1985-6 season with a clean slate. Group Seven was on knife-edge.

Group Seven (morning of 10 September 1985)

Scotland	5	3	0	2	7-3	6
Wales	5	3	0	2	6-5	6
Spain	5	3	0	2	7-7	6
Iceland	5	1	0	4	3-8	2

A win in Wales and Scotland would qualify. A draw meant at least second place and consequent play-off, leaving Wales to sweat over the result of Spain's last game. Defeat for Scotland looked like the end of the road. Spain were expected to defeat Iceland on 25 September.

Wales were in such dire financial straits that they sacrificed their lucky, compact Wrexham setting in favour of playing the game at Ninian Park, Cardiff. The extra receipts ensured solvency for four more years, whatever the result.

Graeme Souness was suspended, while Alan Hansen, Kenny Dalglish and Mo Johnston were missing through injury. This left a nagging doubt: were Wales the better team? The strikeforce Stein selected (Sharp and Speedie) were wonderfully named but lacking in international experience compared with the lean Rush and muscular Hughes. In fact the eleven Scottish players had amassed just six international goals. The Welsh had scored 30.

Ideal ingredients for a gritty Scottish performance. The weather was warm, the chips were down and the spirit was raised.

Scotland supporters wheedled almost half the 40,000 tickets, and as it was the first major test of British spectators since the Brussels disaster there were precautions. Nine pubs were closed. Fourteen off-licences and supermarkets shut at 5.30. A hoolivan toured the streets with surveillance equipment, and 800 police arrived from all over Wales. In fact the fans were boisterous but well-behaved. A theft from H. Samuel was the only reported pre-match incident. Only two people were arrested the whole day.

The first minutes of the game were not so peaceful. Six free-kicks in eight minutes, including three vigorous fouls by Welshman Mark Hughes, who was fortunate to escape punishment. In contrast McLeish was cautioned for one foul on Ian Rush.

A 13th-minute goal for Wales soberised the game. Phillips took a throw-in on the left. Nicol and Aitken went for the ball but Nicholas fought harder. His low cross was met by the swivelling Hughes who shot left-footed past Leighton's left hand from 15 yards.

By half-time the Scots looked down and out. They hadn't looked like scoring and were forced to make a defensive substitution. Alan Rough, now 33, replaced Jim Leighton, who had had a contact lens displaced in a collision with Rush.

The frenetic game resumed. Shortly after half-time one television commentator was moved to comment on a picture of Jock Stein: "Sixty-two years old and Jock has certainly been through the fires but I doubt if many of the fires have had the heat of Ninian Park tonight about them."

In the 54th minute, shortly after Rush had been cautioned for a foul on Strachan, Jock Stein made his last tactical decision. It was a masterstroke, though the mechanics were unwieldy.

For 30 seconds the number '7' was held up to indicate the withdrawal of Nicol. Then '7' was replaced by '8' and Strachan surprisingly made his way to the bench. Even the arrival of Davie Cooper wearing '16' wasn't universally accepted by the fans — some wanted Gray for instance — but Stein took the responsibility and got it right.

Within a few minutes Cooper brought hope. Receiving the ball from a Malpas throw he forced the ball through the legs of the tiring Jones, turned inside Nicholas and then weaved back towards the goal-line. His low left-footed cross was scrambled away. For the first time we thought the Scots might score.

The vital breakthrough came ten minutes from time. Just as it had at Anfield in 1977. And again it was a debateable penalty.

Steve Nicol sent over a cross, Graeme Sharp headed it into the penalty area, David Speedie hooked the ball towards goal. It struck the outstretched arm of Phillips, two yards away, balancing precariously over the penalty spot.

Referee Keizer reached his decision in a split-second. He might have been influenced by earlier incidents, when Cooper and Speedie had been sent tumbling in the penalty area. Also, the second half pressure of the Scots deserved a reward.

Cooper hit the penalty low to Southall's left side. The ball brushed the goalkeeper's hand before it rested safely in the net. 'Que sera, sera,' sang the Scots. 'We're going to Mexico.'

After an eternity, came the final whistle. 'We're going celebrate,' sang the chorus....but fans were unaware at first that a tragedy was unfolding. Jock Stein had collapsed after physically trying to move a photographer.

Some fans soon became aware of an ambulance outside Ninian Park main entrance and stayed around to hear the sad news. Others set off for the city centre, singing, searching for an elusive pub. "There's one round the corner that should be open," said one helpful policeman, "but you buggers drunk it out of beer earlier today."

Then came news of Jock Stein....and there seemed little to celebrate anymore.

On a warm Wednesday evening in Melbourne, Australia, Scotland became the 24th and last nation to qualify for the 1986 World Cup Finals in Mexico. Back home, where it was still Wednesday morning, an estimated 1.3 million in Central Scotland watched the 0-0 draw on television. Having beaten the Australian Socceroos 2-0 on aggregate, Scotland became one of only two countries to play through the last four qualifying tournaments, Poland being the other.

Alec Ferguson was now in charge of the team. Successful manager of Aberdeen for seven years, and Stein's assistant for a year, Ferguson was appointed part-time Scotland manager till the end of the World Cup campaign.

His first game was a friendly against in-form East Germany who had beaten France, Yugoslavia, and were soon to beat Bulgaria. A minute's silence was observed before the start of the

Hampden friendly in memory of the late Jock Stein. Match receipts and players' match fees went towards a Jock Stein Memorial Fund.

Kenny Dalglish and Graeme Souness made welcome returns to the team, and substitute goalkeeper Andy Goram became the first Oldham Athletic player to play for Scotland for 71 years. Goram, born in England, could boast qualification through his father's birthplace.

The East German game itself was frustrating. Scotland had the better of play but failed to score. Midfielder Roy Aitken went closest, and Scotland's goalscoring potential came under scrutiny again. Three goals in six internationals, none from a recognised striker in open play.

Against Australia, at Hampden, Ferguson's strike-force included Kenny Dalglish, making his 99th international appearance in spite of a spell out of the Liverpool team, and debutant Frank McAvennie, a scoring-sensation of the season, West Ham's £340,000 summer signing from St Mirren.

Eliminating Australia was a thankless task. By Scotland's world-soccer standing, Australia should be 'easy meat' — their defenders were certainly meaty enough — but therein lay scope for self-destruction. Remember Zaire, people said, and Iran and New Zealand.

Australian manager Frank Arok, born in Yugoslavia of Hungarian parents, claimed he had been sent off 'at least 17 times' in his own career. His rugged defence was built on five mobile man mountains at the back. "They're all big lads", McAvennie mused after his debut.

Ferguson indicated he would be happy with a 2-0 scoreline, but for 57 minutes the Australians held out. Then Dalglish combined twice in three minutes with McAvennie and Scotland's precious 2-0 result was earned.

First, Dalglish fed McAvennie and the West Ham man was fouled just outside the penalty area. Davie Cooper scored direct from the free-kick, left-footed, low, to goalkeeper Greedy's right.

Next came a long clearance from Alex McLeish. Dalglish slanted a header behind the Australian defence and McAvennie was clear. The first touch was to control the ball, the second touch to lift it past the advancing Greedy.

A moment of goalscoring genius, and older supporters recalled Denis Law in the 1960s. Younger supporters had a simpler message: 'There's only one McAvennie.' Near the end, though, McAvennie might have made it 3-0, when Sharp's shot came back off Greedy.

Two weeks later Scotland met Australia in 70 degree temperatures

West Ham's Frank McAvennie, scorer of Scotland's second goal, breaks clear of Australia's Steve O'Connor and Graham Jennings at Hampden Park.

in Olympic Park, Melbourne. It meant a trip of 11,000 miles, nine days away from home, more than a third of which was spent travelling.

Negotiations with English clubs for the release of players had never been more tactful, and the English Football League revoked their rule that clubs should play full-strength teams. Four key Anglos travelled. Nicol would have made a fifth if not for a family illness. Dalglish and Strachan stayed to help their clubs.

Of the other Scots, Bett was injured, and Gough and Malpas played a UEFA Cup-tie before leaving late. Souness arrived even later, after playing for Sampdoria on the Sunday. Maurice Johnston developed influenza on the trip.

With two quick men up front (Speedie and McAvennie), Scotland hoped Australia would be vulnerable if they played an unnatural attacking game. But the Socceroos were more attacking than anyone realised they could be.

Jim Leighton was the main saviour. His first key save came in the 25th minute when Mitchell crossed and Kosmina headed for goal. Leighton must have seen it late, if he saw it at all, but he beat out the ball.

Souness was cautioned in the 41st minute for a foul on danger-man Oscar Crino. But even when Crino went off, late in the game, there were heart-stopping moments created by substitute Odzakov. The Scots came closest through McStay, and then Speedie, who bounced the ball along the bar near the end. Scotland were grateful for the 0-0 draw.

"I would have preferred to have gone to Mexico with a wee bit better performance," said Alex Ferguson, "but the whole section for us, since the defeat by Wales in March, has been a hard struggle with a lot of tension and nerves."

The overwhelming feeling was relief.

Alex Ferguson had four games before the World Cup Finals to assess his options.

For the Israel game — Scotland's first January international for 102 years — Dalglish, Souness and McAvennie were unavailable, and McLeish was injured. There were four Dundee United players in Ferguson's team, and Sturrock made it five when he came on as substitute.

The only goal against Israel came on the hour, when Paul McStay beat goalkeeper Ran to Jim Bett's cross. It wasn't an impressive Scottish performance but there was satisfaction in extending the unbeaten run, especially as the pitch was bumpy and the small crowd provided a quiet setting for an international.

The next game, against Romania, was an emotional contrast — Kenny Dalglish's hundredth cap. Before the game Dalglish was presented with a solid silver cap, trimmed with gold, by West Germany manager Franz Beckenbauer. During the game Dalglish's touches were mainly golden. He almost provided a first-minute goal for Eamonn Bannon, then assisted in Scotland's two first-half goals. The first (18 minutes) was an 18-yard chip under pressure by the world-class Gordon Strachan, who saw goalkeeper Lung moving away from his goal-line. The second (27 minutes) was a low 20-yard shot from Richard Gough.

Gough's attacking skills were as evident in the second-half. He headed the ball down for Roy Aitken to shoot the third Scottish goal (in the 81st minute) before hitting the bar in the last minute.

Although Romania had their moments during the game — two crossbar smudges and a few missed chances — the 3-0 win was a wonderful fillip considering the East Europeans had only marginally failed to qualify for the World Cup Finals.

Next came the first Scotland-England game at Wembley for three years. Both the day of the week (Wednesday) and the day of the year (St George's Day) were inhospitable to Scottish fans, and the attendance was disappointing.

Both England and Scotland were unbeaten in eight internationals. One of these records would have to go, if only on penalties, since the Sir Stanley Rous trophy would be decided on five penalties (or more) apiece if the scores were level after 90 minutes.

Graeme Souness (centre) and Peter Reid (right) in action during the Scotland-England game at Wembley on 23 April 1986.

Some of the early tackles aroused fantasies of five penalties apiece in normal time. A free-kick to England preceded the first goal Scotland had conceded under Alex Ferguson (in his sixth game in charge). Hodge headed back Hoddle's free-kick, Butcher headed in. This goal also ended a 490-minute spell with the Scottish goal intact — achieved by Leighton, Goram and Rough — second only to the 747-minute spell in the 1920s.

Ten minutes later England made it 2-0 when Alan Rough pushed away Sansom's 30-yard shot and Hoddle headed in. On the hour Butcher hauled down (and injured) Charlie Nicholas, who had to be substituted, and after a considerable delay Graeme Souness converted the resulting penalty. Even so England won 2-1.

Sharp, Strachan and Dalglish missed the England game with injury, and McAvennie was unavailable. These four missed the next game, in Holland. Nevertheless there were eight changes, partly caused by three Celtic players being withdrawn from the squad. Ally McCoist, the Scottish League's top scorer, and Robert Conner won their first caps, and Maurice Malpas played in Souness's midfield role.

The two controversial moments, in a goalless game, came when Paul Sturrock was sent sprawling, first by Wouters (after 15 minutes) and then by Koeman (after 60 minutes). Penalty claims were turned down. But perhaps better that happen in Holland than in Wales.

Scotland had yet to call on five players for a penalty shoot-out, but there were hopes of giving it consideration during June. If Scotland reached the second stage of the World Cup Finals.

GORDON STRACHAN

From 1980: Midfield, 39 caps (5 as sub), 4 goals.
Born: Edinburgh, 1957.
Career: Craigroyston School (Edinburgh), Dundee, Aberdeen, Manchester United.

Gordon Strachan's entry into professional football was as a ground-staff worker at Dundee where he graduated to team captain by the age of 19. In 1977, he signed for Billy McNeill at Aberdeen. The Dons paid £50,000 plus Jim Shirra.

Strachan's energy and exciting skill made him Scottish Player of the Year 1979-80, the season Aberdeen won the championship. The following season, he missed several months' action because of a hernia and intestinal problems. This lay-off occurred just when Strachan was becoming an automatic choice for Scotland. His goal in Sweden gave the Scots a good start on the road to the World Cup Finals and once recovered, he was able to take part in the Finals in Spain. Later in 1982, he played in Switzerland despite having broken a tooth and gashed a gum against Morton four days before.

In 1984, Ron Atkinson signed him for Manchester United and Strachan found great success as United's penalty-taker until a series of misses cost him the job. Strachan helped United to their 1985 FA Cup Final victory.

WILLIE MILLER

1975 to 1986: Sweeper, 52 caps (2 as sub), 1 goal.
Born: Glasgow, 1955.
Career: Eastercraigs FC (Glasgow), Aberdeen.

Willie Miller was playing at centre-forward when Aberdeen first saw him in 1971, and some time went by before he settled into his star role as sweeper. Aberdeen manager Jimmy Bonthrone moved him to centre-half in an injury crisis.

Miller's developing talent paralleled Aberdeen's path to success – no small coincidence – and he was captain when the Dons won the European Cup-winners' Cup in 1983, and, with Alex McLeish, forming Britain's best defensive club pairing. The following season he was Scottish Footballer of the Year.

After intermittent appearances in the 1970s, Miller became a Scottish regular in the 1980s, scoring the only goal of the game against Wales in May 1980. Miller's main assets include his strong tackling, springy leaps to head the ball, and beautifully weighted passing, but he also has tremendous anticipation. Any lack of pace is compensated by his reading of the game, whilst his calmness has contributed to his strength as a leader. He was aptly described by one of his international colleagues as 'the head waiter of British football'.

STEVE ARCHIBALD

From 1980: Striker, 27 caps (6 as sub), 4 goals.
Born: Glasgow, 1956.
Career: Croftfoot United, Fernhill Athletic, Clyde, Aberdeen, Tottenham Hotspur, Barcelona.

A motor mechanic by trade, Steve Archibald was signed by Aberdeen for £25,000 in 1978. Partnering Joe Harper, he scored 23 goals in 1979-80 when Aberdeen won the Premier Division title.

He scored on his international debut, 20 minutes after coming on as substitute against Portugal. His first full appearance came as a Spurs player. Tottenham paid £800,000 for him in May 1980, a record between Scottish and English clubs. He continued to score prolifically and his value increased by the time he left for Spain in the summer of 1984. Under Terry Venables he helped Barcelona to the 1985 Spanish League title.

In the ten years from May 1977 the Scotland international team was under the control of four different managers. Not one of them had won a full international cap as a player.

When Paul Sturrock came on for Graeme Sharp in the 68th minute of the match in Israel in January 1986 it was his ninth appearance as a Scotland substitute — more than any other player. Lou Macari had previously made eight appearances as a substitute.

WORLD CUP FINALS ⚽ 1986

THE last country to qualify and the last to arrive in Mexico (on 1 June), Scotland threatened on occasions to be one of the last to go out of the tournament.

Spirited performances against Denmark and West Germany raised hopes that a win against the aggressive, defensive Uruguayans would enable a third-placed Scotland to qualify from the 'Group of Death' for the last sixteen. Uruguay's Batista was sent off in the first minute but the frustrating 0-0 draw was not enough. Scotland yet again failed to progress from the initial group.

Alex Ferguson had the unenviable task of selecting 22 players for the squad and he chose 14 Scottish League players, surprising some people by omitting David Speedie, Mo Johnston and Alan Hansen. There was a setback when Kenny Dalglish withdrew with a knee injury. Steve Archibald was drafted in.

The squad spent three weeks together — Scotland's longest-ever preparation. Two weeks in Santa Fe, New Mexico, were followed by a few days in Los Angeles, where the team registered a 3-0 win against Los Angeles Heat.

The atmosphere in the squad was good, and Ferguson was relaxed, grateful to be concentrating temporarily on just one of his two demanding jobs, finally admitting that the strain had reached him during the season. Scotland's tournament started at the deep end — against Denmark, favourites to produce the best European challenge.

Ferguson's team, which contained nine Scottish League players, was announced as late as possible. Charlie Nicholas looked sharp and went close three times early in the game. The best chance of the first half came to Scotland, when Richard Gough ran through, fooled the goalkeeper but placed his left-foot shot just too high.

But the pace of the Danish front-runners was a little scary. Willie Miller's last-ditch tackles came to the rescue and one such interception treated Elkjaer to a heavy landing. Elkjaer appeared to be nursing his back, but the next time he ran at Miller he received a fortunate ricochet, ran clear and scored left-footed off the right-hand post.

That goal, by Elkjaer, in the 57th minute, was the only goal of the game. Roy Aitken put the ball in the net but was adjudged marginally offside. And a low cross by Gordon Strachan nearly crept in at the near post. Six minutes from time Berggreen's professional foul tore ligaments in Nicholas's ankle, causing him to miss the next match. The opponents were West Germany, winners in 1974, runners-up in 1966, 1982 and (it transpired) 1986.

Ferguson's selection of one striker raised a few eyebrows, especially as the player was Steve Archibald, who had played only one game in the previous ten weeks, and hadn't scored for Scotland in four years. But Ferguson's tactics later received many accolades, and the entertainment was as good as any World Cup audience could wish to see. At noon, under 90-degree Mexican sun, with hardly any wind, the two teams staged a spectacular game.

First the Germans attacked. Leighton saved an Allofs header, Voller headed against the post, Matthaus shot wide, Magath shot over.

Then the Scots countered. Schumacher pipped Aitken, Malpas clipped the loose ball over the bar, Bannon's left-footer was turned over.

All that by the 18th minute, when the first goal arrived. A left-wing cross was half cleared by the West German defence. Roy Aitken studiously pushed a low pass to Gordon Strachan who shot from the corner of the six-yard box. Schumacher grabbed some air, and the Scots were ahead. The joyful Strachan didn't leap the advertising hoardings South American style, but he seemed to weigh up that option for a moment or two.

Four minutes later Littbarski's perfectly timed through ball enabled Allofs to cover five yards while Gough turned. Voller stumbled the cross into the net. One-one.

The Scotland team that lost to West Germany in June 1986. Back row (left to right): Aitken, Leighton, Nicol, Narey, Gough, Miller. Front row: Souness (captain), Malpas, Bannon, Strachan, Archibald.

The action continued. Leighton saved from Briegel, Nicol volleyed wide, Archibald was shown the yellow card, Souness fired just over, and Bannon's 30-yard free-kick brought Schumacher to his knees at the foot of the right-hand post.

Two minutes before half-time came a heart-stopping moment. Narey's pass to Miller fell short, Voller set off towards goal, but Jim Leighton made an excellent double save.

West Germany scored again in the 50th minute. David Narey was under pressure from Voller and Miller was lured across. An unfortunate turn by Narey saw the ball roll to the unmarked Allofs, whose left foot slid the ball past Leighton's right hand.

Leighton made two more fine saves — from Matthaus and Allofs — before Scotland made a 74th-minute substitution. Davie Cooper came on to win a couple of corners and then send in another dangerous cross six minutes from time. Richard Gough met the ball in mid-air but his header cleared the bar by a foot or two. There was just time for Strachan to drift clear on the right but his cross-cum-shot flew past the far post. It was very hard to criticise the Scotland performance.

Not so the next game. Uruguay. On Friday the 13th. A win would ensure third place in the group and a place in the knock-out stage.

The game took on an air of abnormality after just one minute's play. Uruguay left-back Batista cruelly tackled Strachan from behind and was sent off by the French referee. It was a brave decision by the official but it failed to curb the expected brutality. When Scotland launched their first real attack, in the 11th minute, Sturrock had to hurdle to reach the bye-line.

In the 18th minute Aitken put in a low right-wing cross, Steve Nicol fought off his marker (literally) and played the ball gently towards the vacant net. Goalkeeper Alvez made a brilliant recovery save from what proved to be Scotland's best chance. For the superstitious, Nicol was wearing 'thirteen'.

In a spell around the half-hour mark there was some rough treatment for Sturrock, Strachan and Nicol. Then Uruguay took control in the minutes before half-time. Unfortunately for Scotland, Uruguay had learned a lot about playing with ten men — Bossio had been sent off in the first-half of the previous game against Denmark — and Enzo Francescoli, left alone upfront, nearly scored just before the break.

After half-time the Uruguayans ambled out, and there was some trouble among their supporters. One began to hope any Scotland winner would come later in order in minimise any ugly scenes.

But there was no winner. Scotland were uncreative in dealing with the ten-men opposition, who were skilful if belligerent. The Scotland players needed courage to continue, while it would have taken an unusual managerial decision to bring on an extra attacker early in the game, say after thirty minutes. Graeme Souness, who might have helped set a better pace to the game, wasn't even on the bench as the power had gone from his legs by the end of the West German game. Ferguson had chosen a team and substitutes expecting to play against eleven.

Scotland created some chances. Sturrock vainly put the ball in the net, Alvez saved Gough's volley, struck from an awkward height, Strachan fired in countless right-wing crosses.

Halfway through the second-half Uruguay quelled Scottish pressures with the help of an injured player. And Leighton kept Scotland in the game with a brilliant save from Cabrera's close-range header. As Scotland forced more and more corner-kicks so the time-wasting tactics grew more sophisticated. Diogo was cautioned, and one Uruguayan goal-kick took nearly a minute. In the last few minutes it was left to Scottish defenders. Albiston fired wide, Narey shot over. David Narey was winning his 30th cap on the day after his 30th birthday, and his 30-yard drive almost turned the game for Scotland. One couldn't help but think that thirty was a better number than thirteen.

When referee Quiniou blew his whistle for the last time observers remarked on how his watch must have had no 'stop' on it. Scottish players had their heads down, and supporters were disconsolate. All the hope on seeing Uruguay reduced to ten men had evaporated. It was as though Scotland had lost rather than drawn 0-0. And Alex Ferguson immediately announced it was the last game in his temporary part-time spell as Scotland manager.

After the match there were scenes of acrimony. Uruguay coach Omar Borras called the referee a 'murderer', a reference to the first-minute sending-off. Scottish officials showed they were displeased with the Uruguayans aggressive attitude. Uruguay were punished by FIFA — a 25,000 Swiss franc fine and threat of explusion should the offences by repeated.

Once again there was evidence of history repeating itself. Uruguay had knocked Scotland out in the 1954 World Cup Finals, while the other two games between the countries in 1962 and 1983, had been tempestuous affairs.

Steve Nicol (Scotland) and Klaus Berggreen (Denmark) in action on 4 June 1986 at Neza '86, Nezahualcoyotl, Mexico.

José Batista of Uruguay (on ground) was sent off during the Uruguay-Scotland 0-0 draw on 13 June 1986. Gutierrez (number 2) is seen here protesting to the referee.

Alex Ferguson

JUST after Christmas 1985 four inches of snow fell on the city of Aberdeen and football was temporarily frustrated. "Some weather", said Aberdeen manager Alex Ferguson as he felt the bite of the sub-zero temperatures. "We trained on the beach this morning."

A stark contrast to the prospect five months hence. The 1986 World Cup Finals. Mexico. Scorching heat at 8,000 feet.

After years of pressure for a full-time manager, Scotland were back with a part-timer. This time it was more acceptable. Ferguson's appointment, albeit on a temporary basis, meant continuity after the sudden death of Jock Stein. And it had to be someone who could command respect from experienced players like Graeme Souness and Kenny Dalglish, himself a player-manager.

As Stein's assistant, Ferguson had helped study Scottish players and international tactics, and he had shared the burden of dealing with the Press. But Ferguson also knew that the duties entailed taking ultimate responsibility: "The assistant manager is not only there to play the part of assistant, to be there to bounce ideas off, but to take up the role of manager if necessary."

Ferguson became national manager when 43 years old. His achievements as a manager — St Mirren into the Premier Division, two League titles, three Scottish Cups and a major European title at Aberdeen — were even better than those of Jock Stein at the same age.

Successful football careers are usually founded in communities and families that value the importance of football, and they start with a fantasy experience, like the identification with heroes. Alex Ferguson was no exception. Brought up in Govan, home of Ibrox, he was 'Rangers daft' and he hero-worshipped players like Willie Waddell, Willie Woodburn, Willie Thornton, Sammy Cox and George Young.

"When I first started watching I would collect sets of photos and send away for glossy prints. My heroes were players like Jimmy Mason, Billy Steel and Laurie Reilly — they played in the team that beat England at Wembley in 1949. There were the Rangers players, but there were also Bobby Evans and Willie Redpath in the Scotland team, and Willie Bauld was a great hero of mine."

Coming from Glasgow, Ferguson found it easier to be associated with the Scotland team than did people who lived elsewhere in Scotland. Only one post-war home fixture has not been played at Hampden. Belgium visited Aberdeen in 1971.

"I can remember dodging school to go to the League match at Ibrox in 1951. Scotland won 1-0. They played Inter-League games at Ibrox and full internationals at Hampden. The first full international I saw was in 1954 when England won 4-2. It was pouring with rain. I was lifted over the barrier next to the invalid cars. I stood there and watched the game.

"In those days, for an international in Glasgow, you felt you could fill Hampden two or three times. That's never gone. Scotland have maintained a tremendous following. Unlike other British teams there is great patriotism. There is a political feeling against England going a long way back.'

Alex Ferguson never won full international honours as a player though he went on the 1967 World tour, and he played for Scotland Youth when at Queen's Park in the late 1950s.

"It was an amateur Youth team then," Ferguson recalled, "Selected by a committee taken from the Juveniles, Amateurs, schools and churches. It's different now. When I played against Wales at Llanelli we left by train from Glasgow Central, travelling overnight. But in 1983, when four of my Aberdeen players played in the World Championship in Mexico, they went to Colorado in preparation.

"Travel changed everything. The European Cup changed everything. Before the European Cup all countries were parochial — Scotland used to go to Ireland by boat at one time — and in the 1950s the younger players played only in the British Isles. Now there is no British Youth Championship. It's Europe and the world."

In 1960 Alex Ferguson joined St Johnstone from Queen's Park. Four years later his goalscoring talents were recognised by Dunfermline, for whom he scored 66 goals in 88 league games. During those three seasons Dunfermline came close to major honours, missing the League title by a point in 1964-5.

ALEX FERGUSON OBE

In fact Ferguson's playing career was a series of 'near misses', a reminder that a manager's motivation may be vicarious hunger for success. His two seasons with Rangers were in Stein's Celtic heyday. Then came four years at Falkirk — including two as striking partner to Andy Roxburgh — and a year at Ayr United before injury forced retirement. By then he had prepared for management.

"I did a coaching course in 1965 because at an early age I had an inclination to stay in the game. I knew I needed to prepare for the future. At the age of 26-27 most players have an inkling if they want to stay in the game but they don't necessarily prepare. One minute they're a player, the next a manager. I feel they should be coaches first and given preparation."

Ferguson also felt his varied playing career helped his opportunities to learn: "I played for a big club (Rangers), a good provincial team who were a threat to the Old Firm (Dunfermline), I had a period with an amateur club (Queen's Park), then a yo-yo club (St Johnstone), and I was with a couple of middle-of-the-table clubs (Falkirk and Ayr). My work with the Players' Union also helped in preparation. I was able to take an interest in players' ambitions to better themselves and improve their conditions."

'The biggest change has been freedom of contract. This has taken Scottish players to Germany, Italy, Spain...a bigger platform. It gives Scotland a more worldly position in football. People see players like Souness, Archibald and McGhee and start thinking, 'Must be no bad, Scotland'."

In the 1980s a new international not only has his transfer value increased but is put on a different stage. Clubs throughout

Europe take interest. Ferguson saw that with Aberdeen players like Gordon Strachan and Mark McGhee. There must be mixed feelings for a club manager when a player is called into international duty.

"Clubs worry about the injury thing," said Ferguson. "But players could get that injury elsewhere. They could be injured in training or they could fall over their own doorstep. But for a club like Aberdeen to have six players in a Scotland team, that's great. There's never been such a contribution from a provincial team."

When Ferguson became Scotland team manager there was talk that players of other clubs would be trying harder against Aberdeen in order to impress him. "I'm more concerned with our players. And I'm not looking for one-day wonders."

The choice of an assistant manager with another club, Walter Smith at Dundee United, helped spread the load. The demands of the Press, for instance. Should a Scotland manager show a weakness the Press would be in like sharks for the kill. All eyes seemingly on one man. At one training session in Australia a helicopter came from the sky...to spy.

"The problems of the national job are inherent," Ferguson went on. "You don't have time to prepare. And it's very difficult to be totally successful. Players are a long way away, playing abroad. The ultimate success might be winning the World Cup, but for a small country like ours qualifying for the World Cup is a success."

"It's a success for a small country like Scotland continually to turn out really good players — players with individual class who also become really good team players. Scots have grit. They don't like being beaten. They feel they still have something to prove, particularly down in England. Look at some of the Scottish players of the past: Jim Baxter, Denis Law, Dave Mackay, Billy Steel, Jimmy Mason, and lately players like Kenny Dalglish and Graeme Souness. All top drawer, with tremendous individualism and character. But it's difficult to say how they compare on a world stage. Others like Cruyff and Pele have done it in a World Cup final. One thing, though, going to Mexico is not something we are afraid of. We have a good temperament for it. Our nature is that 'we'll show them'. The underdog tag suits Scotland."

And an 'underdog tag' it certainly was, faced with the same World Cup Finals group as West Germany, Uruguay and Denmark. One much quoted saying of Jock Stein's was that to qualify for the Finals meant wearing working clothes, whereas for the Finals you could look out your best. Alex Ferguson gave his interpretation.

"To qualify for the World Cup Finals, it's like the Scottish Cup battles, where players have to get amongst the mud, getting dirty, fighting their way through. In the Finals all the class can come out on a stage. It's like Shakespearian actors. I'm sure they would perform better in a top London theatre rather than in Perth. Scotland had to do that to qualify."

But the World Cup Finals are still hard work. For the manager there is the thinking about the football and dealing with the Press. For the players there will be the need to cope with the boredom and the length of time away.

"Players have to be prepared to sacrifice, and a manager too has to make sacrifices. Your family is going to suffer from the sacrifice. You need that support. You will all be staying away from home and at times there will be boredom, at times you'll miss the wife and kids....but the World Cup Finals are worth the sacrifice."

No longer was international football simply the game against England, or the British international Championship, or even a test against continental opposition. Scotland now had a place on the world stage.

Scotland fans in Mexico in 1986 for the World Cup Finals.

GRAEME SOUNESS

From 1974: 54 caps (2 as sub), 4 goals.
Born: Edinburgh, 1953.
Career: Tottenham Hotspur, Middlesbrough, Liverpool, Sampdoria, Rangers (player-manager).
Graeme Souness trained with Celtic in 1967 but joined Spurs as an apprentice. After three years in London he left for Scotland, homesick and frustrated by the prospect of ousting any of Spurs' midfield three, Peters, Mullery and Perryman.
In January 1973, Middlesbrough paid £30,000 for his transfer and Souness blossomed under the tutelage of Boro' manager Jack Charlton. In less than two years he was in the Scotland side. After his move to Liverpool in January 1978 – the £352,000 fee was a record between English clubs – he linked up with Kenny Dalglish. As lynch-pin in a magnificent Liverpool team, he dictated the pace and course of many a game, spreading perfect passes from deep, or from penetrative positions.
His long-range shooting could be powerful and his goal against Russia in 1982 following a weaving run is a classic international memory of recent years.
One of the hardest footballers of modern times, Souness has also been one of the most influential. In 1984, he moved to Italy where his midfield talents made him an immediate success and he continued his course as Scotland's captain.

ALAN HANSEN

From 1979: Central defender, 26 caps (3 as sub).
Born: Sauchie, Clackmannanshire, 1955.
Career: Sauchie Juniors, Partick Thistle, Liverpool.
Alan Hansen, an integral part of the highly-successful Liverpool teams, might have won more caps had he not been a contemporary of Willie Miller and Alex McLeish, who had a ready-made partnership at Aberdeen. Unlike many clinical defenders, Hansen always appears to give forwards a chance, but his lengthy stride and skilful ballwork has made him an effective defensive force, and one of the treats of 1970s and 80s has been the sight of him striding into an attacking foray.
Hansen represented Scotland Under-18s at golf, volleyball and squash. His younger brother, John Hansen, is also a Scottish soccer international and they played together for Partick before Alan moved to Liverpool for £100,000 in April 1977.
He was, in some people's eyes, a surprise omission from the 1986 World Cup Finals party.

ALAN ROUGH

From 1976: Goalkeeper, 53 caps (1 as sub).
Born: Glasgow, 1951.
Career: Lincoln Amateurs (Glasgow), Partick Thistle, Hibernian.
Scotland's most capped goalkeeper, Alan Rough has been a model of reliability and an answer to those who claim that the Scots cannot produce a top-class goalkeeper.
He was fifth choice to play against Switzerland in 1976, but then missed only ten games in six years as he smashed Bill Brown's record for goalkeeping caps.
Left-handed Rough was a cool performer and not averse to using his feet – he even took on Keegan in one Hampden dribble. He was the only part-timer in the 1978 World Cup squad, yet he was one of the key performers and his save from Toshack at Anfield was crucial to Scotland's progress. He was also brilliant in Israel as Scotland progressed to the 1982 World Cup Finals. In 1980-81 he was Scottish Player of the Year. In 1985, Rough was still in contention for more caps as the most experienced deputy for Jim Leighton, and in Cardiff he played the second-half in another crucial World Cup game. When he went to Mexico in 1986 it meant he had been in three successive World Cup finals' squad.

WORLD CUP SQUAD 1986

Scotland's 22 for the 1986 World Cup Finals in Mexico were: Leighton of Aberdeen (1), Gough of Dundee United (2), Malpas of Dundee United (3), Souness of Rangers (4), McLeish of Aberdeen (5), Miller of Aberdeen (6), Strachan of Manchester United (7), Aitken of Celtic (8), Bannon of Dundee United (9), Bett of Aberdeen (10), McStay of Celtic (11), Goram of Oldham Athletic (12), Nicol of Liverpool (13), Narey of Dundee United (14), Albiston of Manchester United (15), McAvennie of West Ham United (16), Archibald of Barcelona (17), Sharp of Everton (18), Nicholas of Arsenal (19), Sturrock of Dundee United (20), Cooper of Rangers (21), Rough of Hibernian (22).

SCOTLAND TEAM MANAGERS

Andy Beattie	Feb-Jun 1954	**Bobby Brown**	Feb 1967-Jun 1971
Matt Busby	Jan-Dec 1958	**Tommy Docherty**	Oct 1971-Dec 1972
Andy Beattie	Mar 1959-Oct 1960	**Willie Ormond**	Jan 1973-Apr 1977
Ian McColl	Nov 1960-May 1965	**Ally MacLeod**	May 1977-Oct 1978
Jock Stein	Jun-Dec 1965	**Jock Stein**	Oct 1978-Sep 1985
John Prentice	Mar-Oct 1966	**Alex Ferguson**	Sep 1985-Jun 1986
Malcolm MacDonald	Oct-Nov 1966	**Andy Roxburgh**	Jul 1986-

JIM LEIGHTON

From 1982: Goalkeeper, 35 caps.
Born: Johnstone, Renfrewshire, 1958
Career: Aberdeen.
Jim Leighton spent four years waiting to take over from Bobby Clark, Aberdeen's Scottish international goalkeeper, but when Clark had a cartilage operation Leighton stepped in with some fine displays for Aberdeen. Jock Stein took him to the 1982 World Cup Finals as third-choice goalkeeper and soon afterwards selected him to succeed Alan Rough – against East Germany in October 1982. After conceding nine goals in his first six internationals, Leighton conceded only 15 in his next 26. His overall record places him alongside David Harvey (ten goals conceded in 16 internationals) and Jimmy Brownlie (11 goals in 16) as the most economical of Scottish goalkeepers.
He was one of only three players to appear in all eight qualifying games for the 1986 World Cup Finals – club colleagues Miller and McLeish were the others – and his displays in Iceland and Australia ensured Scotland went the distance. In Mexico his reputation was enhanced. Towards the end of the key game with Uruguay he produced a wonderful reflex save, while his energetic chasing of the ball to quicken the taking of goal-kicks was demonstrative of his overall spirit and inspiration. As an over-age choice for the Under-21 side he showed this fine example, especially his performance in a goalless draw against Italy.
Early in 1986 he missed three internationals with a finger injury, ending a long run when he had left little opportunity for other goalkeepers to gain international experience.

ROY AITKEN

From 1979: Midfield, 30 caps (5 as sub), 1 goal.
Born: Irvine, 1959.
Career: Celtic Boys Club, Celtic.
After disappointments in 1978 and 1982, when he was in Jock Stein's original World Cup pools but not the final 22, Roy Aitken played a key role in the qualification for Mexico in 1986 and was an automatic choice for the three games in the final tournament. A hard-working, wholehearted midfield player. Aitken has an inspirational effect on those around him. His major assets are strength and stamina, while his skill and subtlety are often evident, such as when he set up Strachan's goal against West Germany in Mexico.
He won his first cap in 1979 but did not have a long run in the Scotland team until his performance against England in 1985 earned him a nine-match spell, ended only by his un-availability for the game in Holland. Scotland won five and drew three of those nine games, conceding only three goals in the process. In 1986 he succeeded Willie Miller as Scotland captain.

ALEX McLEISH

From 1980: Central defender, 47 caps (2 as sub).
Born: Glasgow, 1959.
Career: Glasgow United, Aberdeen.
The tall, red-haired Alex McLeish was a pupil at Barrhead High School before he signed for Aberdeen in the summer of 1976 when he was one of chief scout Bobby Calder's many captures. At first he played in defence and midfield, but he settled down in the back-four, forming a famous partnership with Willie Miller at both club and international level.
McLeish made his full international debut against Portugal in March 1980, and said afterwards, "It was marvellous to play for Scotland, but I've got a long way to go before I can consider myself a regular in the team." In fact it was the start of a long run in the side for the popular and easy-going character.
McLeish's courageous challenging for the ball helped Aberdeen to glory in the 1980s. He served a two-year apprenticeship in the Scotland Under-21 team before winning his first full cap.

1986-7 Scotland's regular success in qualifying for the World Cup Finals has never been matched in the European Championship, and so it proved again in 1986-7 when their first five games in Group Seven produced only one win, against Luxembourg.

Scotland's closest to qualifying had been in 1968 when, having won 3-2 at Wembley, they could only draw with England at Hampden, thus finishing second in the group. Otherwise there was little late drama — third, third, fourth and fourth.

Belgium, bugbears on three previous Scotland quests, were favourites again when the countries were grouped together for a fourth time. But Scotland had to play the other three competitors first — Bulgaria, Republic of Ireland and Luxembourg.

Andy Roxburgh needed to restore enthusiasm to a post-World Cup team devoid of stars. When he took over as international coach, Roxburgh was under no illusions: "You can't produce adult players with a magic wand. The long-term answer lies with the nine and ten-year-olds in Scotland, and I hope to develop creative, imaginative players."

It would be a slow process, but much needed, as borne out by the first two games of the season. There was little creativity and imagination. A well-organised Bulgarian defence restricted Scotland to a 0-0 draw, and a well-organised Scotland defence restricted the Republic of Ireland to the same barren scoreline — the third consecutive goalless draw.

Scotland went to Dublin with no Cooper, no McAvennie, no Miller and no McLeish. It was the first time in 32 internationals that the Scots had taken the field without an Aberdeen central defender. New captain, Roy Aitken, led his team on to an over-grassed rugby pitch. Alan Hansen and Jim Leighton played particularly well, Hansen heading off the line from Sheedy, and Leighton saving on the line from McGrath.

By the time Scotland played Luxembourg in November, there were a couple of topical questions: who would succeed Alex Ferguson as Aberdeen manager? And where would Scotland's next goal come from?

Almost inevitably, the next goal came from a penalty — in the 24th minute of the Luxembourg game. Davie Cooper capitalised after Meunier had been convicted of a foul on Pat Nevin, who was starting an international for the first time. Cooper hit a second goal in the 39th minute. Shortly afterwards, Dalglish, playing his 102nd international, was denied the elusive 31st record-breaking goal by Van Rijswijck's save. Mo Johnston headed the third midway through the second half.

The Luxembourg game was the first international in Britain to be sponsored. Whyte & Mackay Distillers had agreed a £350,000 contract for four years' games.

Fortunes slumped in the seventh minute of the return with the Republic of Ireland. Mark Lawrenson headed in Ray Houghton's cross and it was uphill from then ... for the rest of the game ... for the remainder of the European Championship.

For almost an hour of the game in Belgium, Scotland looked the equal of the World Cup semi-finalists — an early goal by Nico Claesen had been swiftly cancelled out by Paul McStay's header

— but the Belgians scored three more. Vercauteren netted one, and Claesen completed a hat-trick.

That left the Rous Cup. This time it was a triangular tournament — Scotland, England and Brazil. England drew 1-1 with Brazil and then visited Hampden. Scotland fielded a double 'double-M' formation — McLeish and Miller at the back, McCoist and McClair at the front — but first-half fun was restricted almost entirely to Butcher-booing. When the game warmed up, Scotland came closest to scoring. Ally McCoist volleyed, and substitute Charlie Nicholas hit the ball against the bar. The crossbars and goal-posts at Hampden, which dated back to 1910, had raised £6,200 in a pre-match auction, and Nicholas, therefore, goes down in history as the last person to prove their solid worth.

As it was, the game was goalless. This was the 24th 0-0 draw in Scotland's history, and 17 of them had come in the last 20 years, seven in the last two seasons. The next day, newspapers covered off-the-pitch news. 'Neds Come North', headlined the *Sunday Mail*, 'English Fans Hell Bent On Trouble'.

Ian Wilson, Brian McClair and Jim McInally were the season's new caps, and every game was plagued with unavailability setbacks. Five Dundee United players missed the England game, hung over from their UEFA Cup Final, but McInally returned to face Brazil.

Brazil were simply Brazil. Scotland had chances in the first half, and Cooper made a noticeable return to the team, but Brazil struck with two second-half goals. Nelsinho hit a deceptive shot from the left-wing, Goram knocked it out and Rai scored. Then came a second goal which was a joy to behold. Mirandinha stroked a 30-yard pass with the outside of his right boot, Valdo collected, duped Miller superbly, turning inside and out, then almost nonchalantly drove the ball past Goram's left hand.

At the end the players exchanged shirts. David Will, President of the Scottish Football Association, presented the Rous Trophy to the Brazilian captain, Geraldo, who was wearing the blue shirt of Scotland. Now there was a scene to stretch the imagination. But the Scottish shirt belongs to the Scot...and always will.

Substitute Charlie Nicholas (falling, far right) sees his almost point-blank shot clip the England cross-bar and fly over to safety in the goalless Rous Cup match at Hampden in May 1987. The three players in the centre, McCoist, Woods and Hodge, have their eyes on the ball, even if the reader cannot spot it immediately.

1949

Trafalgar Square has long been a traditional rallying-point for Scottish fans en route to Wembley. These photographs, taken 28 years apart, show (above) supporters on the eve of the Scots' 3-1 win over England on 9 April 1949 and (below) prior to a 2-1 defeat of the auld enemy on 4 June 1977.

1977

A Lasting Passion ....

AT THE turn of the century Scotland were champions of the world, though admittedly the football world was small.

The annihilation of England in April 1900 crowned a phenomenal period of success. Nine defeats and ten draws in 71 internationals.

When will we see the like again?

I make no excuse for devoting space in this book to the 1800s. Not only for reasons of success, but also because that period formed the backbone for the development of Scottish soccer passion. Scotland gave football to the world from its position on top, and it also exported fine players to English football, where clubs could offer better financial incentives.

International games have often been the catalyst for putting players on a world stage, aiding them to cross national borders and better themselves. Providing the world remains relatively stable, international games will continue to serve this purpose. They will act as a spur to motivate players during club games. They will help raise the transfer value of players for the club. They will excite supporters, and the supportive environment will help create stars. In turn, the stars will be hero-worshipped and copied by the younger generation. The effect will filter through British society.

The exodus of Scottish players to England began in earnest in the 1880s but the effects did not drive home until the 1900s, by which time a generation of youngsters had grown up without being able to watch the best of Scottish players on a weekly basis. How could youngsters copy skills of the 1890s professionals if they were in Birmingham or Blackburn for most weeks of the year and ignored by international selectors? It wasn't until the 1920s that Scotland recovered a position of invincibility, delighting supporters by losing only one game out of ten against England during that decade.

Soccer is still a means for hitting back at the more advantaged country to the south. It is a way of regrouping players who formed part of more recent exoduses to the south. Andy Roxburgh sums it up well: "The game is so important to us. I have to take you into politics: Scotland does not have its own Parliament or its own government. It doesn't have an identity as such. We don't go to war as Scotland. So where is our identity at its best? Well, rugby is more upmarket so it's left to football. Scotland in the World Cup gives the nation an identity. Kilts and tartans travel the world, and football is one of the last great ways of proving this nation exists."

Scotland has retained its identity in each of the last four World

Cup Finals. That in itself is an achievement attributed to consistency. Yet each time Scotland has tantalisingly failed to reach the second stage of the tournament, three times by goal difference and once by a single point.

People could argue that four such successive tournaments cannot be a coincidence. That Scotland are destined to occupy a position on the periphery of the world's top sixteen (as in 1974 and 1978) or top twenty-four (as in 1982 and 1986). But the future is still unpredictable and needs closer scrutiny. Scotland has learned from each recent appearance in the World Cup Finals. The factors are not as consistent as the results would have them appear.

It could be argued that Scotland's pool of players in Mexico in 1986 was not as good or as skilful as some of the previous squads, particularly that of 1974. But in Mexico there were no disasters. There was no Zaire, no Iran, no New Zealand. The team played to the best of its ability.

Arguments will continue about the selection of players — whether Hansen should have been in the final 22 or whether Nicol should have ended playing as a left-sided midfield player — but this time there were reasons for the selection. Nothing was as capricious as, say, 1978, when the injured McQueen was in the party and Andy Gray wasn't.

Scotland's problem in Mexico was known for a couple of years before the 1986 Finals. There was a dearth of goalscorers proven at the international level. There was an organised search for strikers or midfield players who could regularly add to the goal potential. Since 1970, only two players, Kenny Dalglish and Joe Jordan, have scored more than ten goals for Scotland. In Mexico that showed, particularly in the final game. Sadly there was no Dalglish.

Four successive World Cup Finals have provided excellent experience, and Scotland has learned from that experience. The preparation for Mexico has never been bettered. Hotels, training grounds and venues were scrutinised by advance parties, climatic adjustments were planned, a healthy diet was monitored by a doctor who regularly checked the weight of the players, the team manager covered opponents thoroughly and liaised with the best of Scottish coaching talent before making difficult decisions on team selection and tactics. There were pride and discipline. The approach was professional.

Several factors will help Scotland continue the push for the world title held at times in the past. National identity is one, but more important is the long history of football playing an important part in the culture. Boys are encouraged to learn the sport and given opportunity to study heroes as role models. Until there is more similarity in the education and socialisation of the different sexes this will continue.

The individual soccer skills and spirit of adventure learned in the playground has been increasingly blended with know-how and world awareness. Andy Roxburgh's ten years as Director of Coaching has brought stability of planning. Jock Stein and Alex Ferguson have brought more team orientation; more professionalism. Ernie Walker's experience has placed Scotland in a strong administrative and negotiating position. Bill Wilson's commercial experience has been carried through three World Cup Finals which have added to the security of the Scottish Football Association and enabled no expense to be spared in preparing players.

When looking at the strengths of Scotland as a football nation one can't help wonder whether at some point a generation of skilful players can't be fused into a team which can change a series of group results from 0-1, 1-2 and 0-0 to 1-0, 2-1 and 0-0. One of the current Scottish strikers may serve Scotland like Law and Dalglish have in the past. Perhaps.

On the other hand people can debate that there are aspects of the Scottish soccer scene that are drawbacks to Scotland ever winning the World Cup.

Scottish fans in London in 1932 compare fashions with a Billingsgate fish porter.

Maurice Johnston — one of many modern-day strikers compared to Dalglish and Law.

Amateur and Youth international honours for Scotland and played for Falkirk, Partick Thistle, Clydebank and Queen's Park. However, he was never capped at full international level and had never managed a club team.

What is important is that Roxburgh has worked at international level, and, as we have seen in this book, managing an international team is a different proposition from managing a club team. If things don't go well then big names could be brought in at crucial times. If things do go well then Scotland could be another example of how success can be achieved by promoting from within, like Liverpool at club level, or putting faith in coaching, like Argentina's decision to appoint Bilardo, who steered them to the 1986 World Cup.

It is very doubtful whether Scotland could maintain a sustained challenge like world champions Argentina. The best Scotland could do is a short period of success like Holland in the 1970s, France in the early 1980s and possibly Denmark in the late-1980s. That will happen when all key factors come together at the same time.

In the meantime, there is one feature of Scottish international football that remains supreme — the experience. And it is no wonder that supporters are captivated by the spirit, the skill, the flair, the traumas. It is an emotional experience, rich at times, poor at other times, but always intense. A tie that is not easily broken. A tie that has been passed from generation to generation ....for more than a hundred years.

Andy Roxburgh — appointed 'international coach' in July 1986.

Playing through a long cold, wet winter will usually mean adjustments to cope with World Cup Finals venues. And there are question-marks about the Scottish Premier league. Does it give young players the opportunity to develop their skills? Is it too strenuous for the older players? Too many games played at a fast, relentless pace? No time to recover before World Cup Finals? Too much integration with the international fixture-list?

The real answers to Scotland's relative prestige as a football nation can probably be found in the values and attitudes of the society and the resources it has at its disposal. Poor national diet may play a part. A dependence of high fat content can hardly help the general well-being of developing teenagers. But most important will be economic factors. Unless Scotland gains a fairer slice of the national cake, and compares better with other European nations, the investment in football will be limited to what business can afford and what a competent commercial manager can attract. Carlsberg's investment in Danish football is a key factor in that country's rise to football fame. But, like Scotland, its population is small....and doubts are expressed whether Denmark will ever win the World Cup.

One thing is certain. Compared with the 'liquorice allsorts' of the 1954 World Cup Finals, Scotland's organisation is in a different class.

In the summer of 1986 the SFA made two 'in-house' appointments in order to continue the move towards stability and professionalism. Andy Roxburgh, director of coaching for ten years, became international coach. Clyde manager Craig Brown was taken on to the staff, primarily to look after the Under-21 team.

Roxburgh, described by Ernie Walker as "the best coach in the world", seemed surprised by his appointment, but in ten years he has established a reputation with younger players who are growing older all the time. Roxburgh, 42, won Schoolboy,

Educating Internationals

IN THE immediate post-war period, the Scottish selectors occasionally plucked a player from English football and pitched him into an atmosphere charged with tension and new experience. One thinks of Ian Black or Willie Moir, playing against England at Hampden with ten strangers for team-mates.

It does not happen now. Players serve an apprenticeship in international football.

In 1976, UEFA structured a move from Under-23 to Under-21 competition, but learning starts at an even younger age. The Under-19s enter the world-wide FIFA competition; Under-18s have been playing matches for over 30 years and now have an established European competition; the Under-17s play an invitation tournament at Cannes; and there is even an Under-16 team.

A classic example of a player groomed through the system is Paul McStay of Celtic, who captained the Under-18 team which won the European Championship, and the following year led virtually the same team through their group in the 1983 Under-19 World Cup in Mexico. Celtic manager Billy McNeill once joked that the SFA should pay McStay's salary because he was playing that often for his country.

"Nowadays, nobody gets into the international team unless they've come through the system somewhere along the line," says Andy Roxburgh, now Scotland team manager and as SFA director of coaching, a man who originally worked at first hand with the players to Under-19 level. "The players need to be educated. We break the back of that, and the Under-21 does the rest.

"The football aspect is only a small part of it. It's learning about training camps, flying the world, learning to cope with international football and its pressures, learning quickly to blend in with other players, learning different leadership tasks and flexibility, not being upset by travel, relating — albeit superficially — with others, standing for the National Anthem, discipline....we have to get them over the excess of anxiety."

Roxburgh is quick to point out that the teams were only a small part of his job, which was concerned with improving and promoting Scottish football at all levels. The teams offer opportunities to liaise with the clubs and develop methods, but the system goes deeper — training courses for prospective coaches and managers, and, of course, players of all abilities.

Nevertheless, one cannot ignore the achievements of the 1982 Under-18 team which beat Czechoslovakia 3-1 to win the European Championship: Rae (Hibs); Beaumont (Dundee U), Philliben (Stirling), Rennie (Leicester), Rice (Hibs), McStay (Celtic), Bowman (Hearts), McGinnis (Dundee U), Nevin (Clyde), Mackay (Hearts), Dick (Spurs), (Cooper, Black and Gunn were missing from the tournament as Aberdeen were involved in the Scottish Cup, while two Celtic players, McInally and Dobbin, missed the Final through suspension and injury respectively).

McStay is not alone among Under-18 captains who have become full internationals. The list includes Bobby Watson, Bill Dickson, Frank Munro, Tommy Craig, David Narey, John Wark and Ray Stewart.

At Under-21 level, the European Championship has so far proved elusive. The 1982 team, managed by Ricky McFarlane, came closest, losing an exciting semi-final against England by the narrowest margin. Two years later, a goal in extra-time in Belgrade killed off hopes at the quarter-final stage.

A close look at the younger Scotland teams is more than just results; it is a comment on the history of the game and a look to the future.

"It used to be said that you never got into the first team till you were 23," said Jock Stein in 1985. "Lots of kids are now in the first team at 21. Looks at the caps McStay has already, and Nicholas and Johnston....They've all worked their way through. Players like Paul McStay and Neale Cooper have played in riot situations in the Aztec Stadium. Nothing in Mexico would be new to them — but it might be to Kenny Dalglish."

Whatever the outcome of the last quest for the World Cup, the Scottish public is assured that future generations of footballers are queuing up to continue Scottish pride and passion.

Paul McStay, seen here doing battle with Uruguay's Wilmar Cabrera in the 1986 World Cup Finals, is one of a tough new generation of international footballers blooded through the under-age sides.

Terry Butcher (England) and Ally McCoist (Scotland) at Hampden during the 1987 Rous Cup game.

Scotland
Match by Match

1872
Nov 30 v England (Glasgow, Hamilton Crescent) 0-0
Gardner*; Ker, Taylor, Thomson, J.Smith, R.Smith, Leckie, Rhind, W.W.McKinnon, Weir, Wotherspoon.
Att: 4,000   Referee: Keay (Scotland)

1873
Mar 8 v England (London, The Oval) 2-4
Renny-Tailyour, Gibb
Gardner*; Ker, Taylor, Gibb, Robert Smith, Wotherspoon, Renny-Tailyour, Kinnaird, Blackburn, Thomson, W.W.McKinnon.
Att: 2,000   Referee: Lloyd (England)

1874
Mar 7 v England (Glasgow, Hamilton Crescent) 2-1
A.McKinnon, Anderson
Gardner; Hunter, Taylor, Thomson*, C.Campbell, Weir, W.W.McKinnon, Ferguson, A.McKinnon, H.McNeil, Anderson.
Att: 7,000   Referee: Rae (Scotland)

1875
Mar 6 v England (London, The Oval) 2-2
McNeil, Andrews
Gardner; Hunter, Taylor*, McLintock, Kennedy, Weir, W.W.McKinnon, Highet, H.McNeil, Andrews, McPherson.
Att: 2,000   Referee: Stair (England)

1876
Mar 4 v England (Glasgow, Hamilton Crescent) 3-0
McKinnon, McNeil, Highet
McGeoch; Hunter, Taylor*, McLintock, H.McNeil, Highet, W.W.McKinnon, Miller, Ferguson, Baird.
Att: 16,000   Referee: Mitchell (Scotland)

Mar 25 v Wales (Glasgow, Hamilton Crescent) 4-0
Ferguson, Lang, McKinnon, H.McNeil
McGeoch; Taylor, Neill, Kennedy, C.Campbell*, Highet, Ferguson, Lang, W.W.McKinnon, M.McNeil, H.McNeil.
Att: 20,000   Referee: Turner (England)

1877
Mar 3 v England (London, The Oval) 3-1
Ferguson 2, Richmond
McGeoch; Neill, Vallance, C.Campbell*, Phillips, Richmond, W.W.McKinnon, McGregor, McDougall, J.Smith, Ferguson.
Att: 1,200   Referee: Ogilvie (England)

Mar 5 v Wales (Wrexham) 2-0
Campbell, Powell (og)
McGeoch; Neill, Vallance, Phillips, C.Campbell*, J.Smith, McGregor, Ferguson, McDougall, H.McNeil, Hunter.
Att: 5,000   Referee: Unknown

1878
Mar 2 v England (Glasgow, 1st Hampden) 7-2
McDougall 3, McGregor, McNeil 2, McKinnon
Gardner; McIntyre, Vallance, C.Campbell*, Kennedy, Richmond, W.W.McKinnon, McGregor, McDougall, Highet, H.McNeil.
Att: 15,000   Referee: Dick (Scotland)

Mar 23 v Wales (Glasgow, 1st Hampden) 9-0
Campbell, Ferguson 3, Watson, Weir 2, Baird, Lang
Parlane; Neill*, Duncan, Phillips, Davidson, Lang, Weir, Watson, P.Campbell, Ferguson, Baird.
Att: 12,000   Referee: Gardner (Scotland)

1879
Apr 5 v England (London, The Oval) 4-5
McKinnon 2, McDougall, Smith
Parlane; Somers, Vallance, C.Campbell*, McPherson, Beveridge, J.Smith, McDougall, Paton, W.W.McKinnon, H.McNeil.
Att: 4,500   Referee: Wollaston (England)

Apr 7 v Wales (Wrexham) 3-0
Smith 3
Parlane; Vallance, Somers, McPherson, Davidson*, H.McNeil, McDougall, P.Campbell, Paton, Beveridge, J.Smith.
Att: 2,000   Referee: Cooper (Wales)

1880
Mar 13 v England (Glasgow, 1st Hampden) 5-4
Ker 3, Baird, Kay
Rowan; Neill*, McLintock, C.Campbell, McPherson, J.Smith, M.McNeil, Ker, McGregor, Baird, Kay.
Att: 10,000   Referee: Hamilton (Scotland)

Mar 27 v Wales (Glasgow, 1st Hampden) 5-1
Davidson, Beveridge, Lindsay, McAdam, Campbell
Gillespie; Somers, Lang, Davidson*, McIntyre, Douglas, McAdam, Fraser, Lindsay, J.Campbell, Beveridge.
Att: 1,500   Referee: Lawrie (Scotland)

1881
Mar 12 v England (London, The Oval) 6-1
Smith 3, Ker 2, McGuire
Gillespie; Watson, Vallance, C.Campbell*, Davidson, McGuire, Hill, Ker, Lindsay, H.McNeil, J.Smith.
Att: 8,500   Referee: Marindin (England)

Mar 14 v Wales (Wrexham) 5-1
Ker 2, McNeil, 2 (og)
Gillespie; Vallance, Watson, McPherson, Davidson*, J.Smith, H.McNeil, Lindsay, McGuire, Ker, Hill.
Att: 1,500   Referee: Kendrick (Wales)

1882
Mar 11 v England (Glasgow, 1st Hampden) 5-1
Harrower, Ker 2, Kay, McPherson
Gillespie; Watson, McIntyre, C.Campbell*, Miller, Fraser, Anderson, Ker, Harrower, Kay, McPherson.
Att: 10,000   Referee: Wallace (Scotland)

Mar 25 v Wales (Glasgow, 1st Hampden) 5-0
Kay, Ker, Fraser 2, McAulay
Rowan; Holm, Duncan, Kennedy, C.Campbell*, Fraser, Hill, Ker, McAulay(Dumbarton), Kay, Richmond.
Att: 5,000   Referee: Hamilton (Scotland)

1883
Mar 10 v England (Sheffield, Bramall Lane) 3-2
Smith 3
McAulay(Dumbarton); Holm, Paton, Miller, McPherson*, Fraser, Anderson, J.Smith, Inglis, Kay, W.MacKinnon.
Att: 7,000   Referee: Sinclair (Ireland)

Mar 12 v Wales (Wrexham) 3-0
Smith, Fraser, Anderson
McAulay(Dumbarton); Arnott, Holm, Miller, McPherson*, J.Smith, Inglis, W.MacKinnon, Anderson, Kay, Fraser.
Att: 4,000   Referee: Hamilton (Scotland)

1884
Jan 26 v Ireland (Belfast, Ballynafeigh) 5-0
Goudie, Harrower 2, Gossland 2
Inglis; Forbes, Arnott*, Graham, Fulton, R.Brown, Thomson, Gossland, Goudie, Harrower, McAulay
Att: Unknown   Referee: Hindle (England)

Mar 15 v England (Glasgow, 1st Cathkin) 1-0
Smith
McAulay(Dumbarton); Arnott, Forbes, C.Campbell*, McPherson, Shaw, Anderson, Lindsay, J.Smith, Christie, W.MacKinnon.
Att: 10,000   Referee: Sinclair (Ireland)

Mar 29 v Wales (Glasgow, 1st Cathkin) 4-1
Kay 2, Lindsay, Shaw
Turner; Forbes, Paton*, Kennedy, McIntyre, Kay, Lindsay, Shaw, W.MacKinnon, Thomson, R.Brown.
Att: 7,000   Referee: Sloan (England)

1885
Mar 14 v Ireland (Glasgow, 2nd Hampden) 8-2
Higgins 4, Turner, Barbour, McPherson, Calderwood
Chalmers; Niven, McHardy, McPherson*, Kelso, Turner, Lamont, Barbour, Calderwood, Marshall, Higgins.
Att: 3,000   Referee: Harvie (Sheffield)

Mar 21 v England (London, The Oval) 1-1
Lindsay
McAulay(Dumbarton); Arnott, Paton*, C.Campbell, Gow, Anderson, Hamilton, Sellar, Lindsay, Allan, Calderwood.
Att: 8,000   Referee: Sinclair (Ireland)

Mar 23 v Wales (Wrexham) 8-1
Anderson 3, Lindsay 2, Allan 2, Calderwood
McAulay(Dumbarton); Arnott, Paton*, Kelso, Keir, Hamilton, Anderson, Lindsay, Calderwood, R.Brown jnr, Allan.
Att: 4,000   Referee: Sloan (England)

1886
Mar 20 v Ireland (Belfast) 7-2
Heggie 4, Dunbar, Gourlay, Lambie
Connor; McLeod, Thomson, Keir, Cameron, Turner, Heggie, Dunbar, Fleming, J.Lambie, Gourlay.
Att: Unknown   Referee: Woolstewholme (Ireland)

Mar 27 v England (Glasgow, 2nd Hampden) 1-1
Somerville
McAulay(Dumbarton); Arnott*, Paton, C.Campbell, McDonald, Sellar, Hamilton, Somerville, Lindsay, Gray, Aitken.
Att: 11,000   Referee: Hunter (Wales)

Apr 10 v Wales (Glasgow, 2nd Hampden) 4-1
Harrower, Allan 2, McCormick
Gillespie; Lundie, Semple*, Kelso, McCall, Jackson, McCormick, Marshall, Harrower, McGhee, Allan.
Att: 3,000   Referee: Sinclair (Ireland)

Feb 19 v Ireland (Glasgow, 2nd Hampden) 4-1
Watt, Jenkinson, Johnstone, Lowe
Doig; Whitelaw, Smellie, Weir, McMillan, Hutton, Jenkinson, Lambie*, Watt, Lowe, Johnstone.
Att: 1,000   Referee: Unknown

1887
Mar 19 v England (Blackburn) 3-2
McCall, Allan 2
McAulay*(Dumbarton); Arnott, Forbes, Kelso, Auld, Keir, Marshall, Robertson, Sellar, Allan, McCall.
Att: 12,000   Referee: Sinclair (Ireland)

Mar 21 v Wales (Wrexham) 2-0
Robertson, Allan
McAulay*(Dumbarton); Arnott, Forbes, Keir, Auld,
Kelso, Robertson, McCall, Allan, Marshall, Sellar.
Att: 5,000   Referee: Hull (England)

1888
Mar 10 v Wales (Edinburgh, Easter Road) 5-1
Latta 2, Groves, Munro, Paul
Wilson; Hannah, Smellie*, Gourlay, J.Johnston,
McLaren, Latta, McPherson, Groves, Paul, Munro.
Att: 5,000   Referee: Clegg (England)

Mar 17 v England (Glasgow, 2nd Hampden) 0-5
Lindsay; Arnott, Gow*, Kelso, Kelly, Keir, Hamilton,
Berry, Sellar, McCall, Lambie.
Att: 10,000   Sinclair (Ireland)

Mar 24 v Ireland (Belfast, Cliftonville) 10-2
*Dewar, Dickson 4, Aitken, McCallum, Brackenridge,
Wilson (og), A.Stewart*
McLeod; Jackson, D.Stewart*, A.Stewart, Dewar,
Kelso, Gow, Brackenridge, Dickson, Aitken,
McCallum.
Att: 10,000   Referee: Parlane

1889
Mar 9 v Ireland (Glasgow, Ibrox) 7-0
Watt 2, McInnes, Black, Groves 3
Doig; Adams, McKeown, Robertson*, Calderhead,
Buchanan, Watt, McInnes, Groves, Boyd, Black.
Att: 5,000   Referee: Stacey (England)

Apr 13 v England (London, The Oval) 3-2
McLaren, Oswald, Munro
Wilson; Arnott, Smellie*, Kelly, Dewar, McLaren,
Latta, Berry, Oswald, McPherson, Munro.
Att: 10,000   Referee: Sinclair (Ireland)

Apr 15 v Wales (Wrexham) 0-0
McLeod; Thomson*, Rae, Stewart, Auld, Lochead,
Watt, H.Campbell, Paul, Johnstone, Hannah.
Att: 3,000   Referee: Sinclair (Ireland)

1890
Mar 22 v Wales (Paisley, Underwood Park) 5-0
Paul 4, Wilson
Gillespie*; Whitelaw, Murray, McQueen, A.Brown,
Wilson, Watt, J.Brown, Paul, Dunlop, Bruce.
Att: 7,000   Referee: Finlay (Ireland)

Mar 29 v Ireland (Belfast) 4-1
Wylie, Rankin 3
McLeod*; Hunter, Rae, Russell, Begbie, Mitchell,
Wylie, Rankin, McPherson, Bell, Baird.
Att: 4,000   Referee: Stacey (England)

Apr 5 v England (Glasgow, 2nd Hampden) 1-1
McPherson
Wilson; Arnott, McKeown, Robertson, Kelly,
McLaren*, Groves, Berry, W.Johnstone, McPherson,
McCall.
Att: 30,000   Referee: Reid (Ireland)

1891
Mar 21 v Wales (Wrexham) 4-3
Logan, Buchanan, Boyd 2
McCorkindale; Ritchie, Hepburn, McQueen,
A.Brown, Robertson*, Gulliland, Buchanan, Boyd,
Logan, Keillor.
Att: 4,000   Referee: Crump (England)

Mar 28 v Ireland (Glasgow, Parkhead) 2-1
Waddell, Lowe
Gillespie*; Sillars, Paul, Hamilton, Cleland,
Campbell(Kilmarnock), Lowe, Bowie, Fraser,
Clements, Waddell.
Att: 8,000   Referee: Stacey (England)

Apr 6 v England (Blackburn) 1-2
Watt
Wilson; Arnott*, Smellie, Begbie, McPherson,
Hill, Rankin, Watt, Sellar, Berry, Baird.
Att: 8,000   Referee: Morrow (Ireland)

1892
Mar 19 v Ireland (Belfast, Cliftonville) 3-2
Keillor, Lambie, Ellis
Baird; Bowman, Drummond, Marshall, Robertson*,
Dowds, Gulliland, McPherson, Ellis, Keillor, Lambie.
Att: 6,000   Referee: Taylor (Wales)

Mar 26 v Wales (Edinburgh, Tynecastle) 6-1
Thomson, Hamilton 2, McPherson 2, Baird
Downie; Adams, Orr, Begbie, Campbell
(Kilmarnock), Hill*, Taylor, Thomson, Hamilton,
McPherson, Baird.
Att: 1,000   Referee: Reid (Ireland)

Apr 2 v England (Glasgow, Ibrox) 1-4
Bell
McLeod; Doyle, Arnott, Kelly, Sillars, Mitchell,
Sellar*, Taylor, Waddell, McMahon, Bell.
Att: 21,000   Referee: Smith (Scotland)

1893
Mar 18 v Wales (Wrexham) 8-0
Madden 4, Barker 3, Lambie
McLeod; Doyle, Foyers, Sillars*, McCreadie,
Stewart, Taylor, Thomson, Madden, Lambie,
Barker.
Att: 5,000   Referee: Stacey (England)

Mar 25 v Ireland (Glasgow, Parkhead) 6-1
Sellar 2, Kelly, McMahon, Hamilton, (og)
Lindsay; Adams, Smellie, Maley, Kelly*, Mitchell,
Waddell, Campbell (Celtic), Hamilton, Sellar,
McMahon.
Att: 12,000   Referee: Taylor (Wales)

Apr 1 v England (Richmond) 2-5
Sellar 2
Lindsay; Arnott, Smellie, Maley, Kelly*, Mitchell,
Sellar, Waddell, Hamilton, McMahon, Campbell
(Celtic).
Att: 16,000   Referee: Clegg (England)

1894
Mar 24 v Wales (Kilmarnock) 5-2
Barker, 2 Alexander, Chambers 2
Baird; Crawford, Foyers, Johnstone, Kelly*, McBain,
Chambers, Stewart, Alexander, Berry, Barker.
Att: 12,000   Referee: McBride (Ireland)

Mar 31 v Ireland (Belfast, Cliftonville) 2-1
Taylor, Torrans (og)
Barrett; Crawford, Drummond, Marshall*, Stewart,
Longair, Taylor, Blessington, Alexander, Scott,
Keillor.
Att: 6,000   Referee: Phennah (Wales)

Apr 7 v England (Glasgow, Parkhead) 2-2
Lambie, McMahon
Haddow; Sillars, Doyle*, Begbie, McCreadie,
Mitchell, Gulliland, Blessington, McMahon,
McPherson, Lambie.
Att: 46,000   Referee: Reid (Ireland)

1895
Mar 23 v Wales (Wrexham) 2-2
Madden, Divers
Barrett; Sillars*, Glen, Simpson, McColl, Keillor,
Fyfe, Murray, Madden, Sawers, Divers.
Att: 4,000   Referee: Jupe (England)

Mar 30 v Ireland (Glasgow, Parkhead) 3-1
Lambie, Walker, Taylor
McArthur; Doyle, Drummond*, Simpson, Russell,
Gibson, Taylor, Waddell, McPherson, J.Walker,
Lambie.
Att: 21,000   Referee: Mitchell (England)

Apr 6 v England (Liverpool, Goodison Park) 0-3
McArthur; Drummond, Doyle, Russell, Simpson,
Gibson, Lambie, McPherson, Oswald*, Waddell,
Gulliland.
Att: 35,000   Referee: Reid (Ireland)

1896
Mar 21 v Wales (Dundee, Caroline Port) 4-0
Neil 2, Paton, Keillor
McFarlane; McLean, Glen, Gillespie*, Neil, Blair,
Thomson, Paton, McColl, King, Keillor.
Att: 12,000   Referee: McBride (Ireland)

Mar 28 v Ireland (Belfast, Cliftonville) 3-3
McColl 2, Blessington
Anderson; Meechan, Drummond, Gibson, Kelly*,
Hogg, Murray, Blessington, McColl, Cameron,
Lambie.
Att: 8,000   Referee: Cooper (England)

Apr 4 v England (Glasgow, Parkhead) 2-1
Lambie, Bell
Doig; Brandon, Drummond*, Gibson, Cowan,
Hogg, Bell, Blessington, Hyslop, King, Lambie.
Att: 57,000   Referee: Jones (Wales)

1897
Mar 20 v Wales (Wrexham) 2-2
Ritchie (pen), Walker
Patrick; Ritchie*, Gardner, Breslin, Russell, Keillor,
Kennedy, Murray, Oswald, McMillan, J.Walker.
Att: 7,000   Referee: Armitt (England)

Mar 27 v Ireland (Glasgow, Ibrox) 5-1
McPherson 2, Gibson, McColl, King
Dickie; McLean, Drummond*, Gibson, Stewart,
Baird, Low, King, McColl, McPherson, Lambie.
Att: 15,000   Referee: Cooper (England)

Apr 3 y England (London, Crystal Palace) 2-1
Hyslop, Miller
Patrick; N.Smith, Doyle, Gibson, Cowan, Wilson,
Bell, Miller, Allan, Hyslop, Lambie*.
Att: 37,000   Referee: Gough (Wales)

1898
Mar 19 v Wales (Motherwell) 5-2
Gillespie 3, McKie 2
Watson; N.Smith, Scott*, Thomson, Christie,
P.Campbell, Gillespie, Miller, McKie, Morgan,
Findlay.
Att: 10,000   Referee: Stacey (England)

Mar 26 v Ireland (Belfast, Cliftonville) 3-0
Robertson, McColl, Stewart
Anderson; Kelso*, Doyle, Thomson, Russell, King,
Stewart, Campbell (Celtic), McColl, J.Walker,
Robertson.
Att: 7,000   Referee: Lewis (England)

Apr 2 v England (Glasgow, Parkhead) 1-3
Miller
Anderson; Drummond, Doyle, Gibson, Cowan*,
Robertson, Bell, Campbell (Celtic), Maxwell, Miller,
A.Smith.
Att: 40,000   Referee: Robertson (Scotland)

1899
Mar 18 v Wales (Wrexham) 6-0
Campbell 2, McColl 3, Marshall
McArthur; N.Smith*, Storrier, Gibson, Marshall,
King, Campbell (Rangers), Hamilton, McColl,
Bell, Berry.
Att: 6,000   Referee: Sutcliffe (England)

Mar 25 v Ireland (Glasgow, Parkhead) 9-1
*McColl 3, Hamilton 2, Campbell, Bell, Christie,
Berry*
Dickie; N.Smith, Storrier*, Gibson, Christie, King,
Campbell (Rangers), Hamilton, McColl, Bell,
Berry.
Att: 12,000   Referee: Sutcliffe (England)

Apr 8 v England (Birmingham, Villa Park) 1-2
Hamilton
Doig; N.Smith*, Storrier, Gibson, Christie, Robertson,
Campbell (Rangers), Hamilton, McColl, Morgan,
Bell.
Att: 25,000   Referee: Torrans (Ireland)

1900
Feb 3 v Wales (Aberdeen) 5-2
Bell, Wilson 2, Hamilton, A.Smith
Dickie; N.Smith, Crawford, Irons, Neil, Robertson,
Bell, Wilson, McColl, Hamilton*, A.Smith.
Att: 12,000   Referee: Sutcliffe (England)

Mar 3 v Ireland (Belfast, Cliftonville) 3-0
Campbell 2, A.Smith
Rennie; N.Smith, Glen, Marshall*, Orr, Gibson,
Stewart, R.Walker, Campbell (Celtic), Callaghan,
A.Smith.
Att: 6,000   Referee: Sutcliffe (England)

Apr 7 v England (Glasgow, Parkhead) 4-1
McColl 3, Bell
Rennie; N.Smith, Drummond, Gibson, Raisbeck, Robertson*, R.Walker, Campbell *(Celtic)*, McColl, Bell, A.Smith.
Att: 64,000   Referee: Torrans (Ireland)

1901
Feb 23 v Ireland (Glasgow, Parkhead) 11-0
Campbell (Celtic) 2, McMahon 4, Hamilton 4, Russell
McWhattie; N.Smith, Battles, Russell, Anderson, Robertson, Campbell *(Rangers)*, Campbell *(Celtic)*, Hamilton*, McMahon, A.Smith.
Att: 10,000   Referee: Gough (Wales)

Mar 2 v Wales (Wrexham) 1-1
Robertson
McWhattie; N.Smith, Battles, Gibson, Russell, Robertson, Bell, R.Walker, McColl, Campbell *(Celtic)*, A.Smith.
Att: 5,000   Referee: Sutcliffe (England)

Mar 30 v England (London, Crystal Palace) 2-2
Campbell, Hamilton
Rennie; Battles, Drummond, Aitken, Raisbeck, Robertson*, R.Walker, Campbell *(Celtic)*, McColl, Hamilton, A.Smith.
Att: 35,000   Referee: Torrans (Ireland)

1902
Mar 1 v Ireland (Belfast, Grosvenor Park) 5-1
Hamilton 3, Buick, Walker
Rennie; N.Smith, Drummond, Key, Buick*, Robertson, McCartney, R.Walker, Hamilton, Campbell*(Celtic)*, A.Smith.
Att: 12,000   Referee: Bye (England)

Mar 15 v Wales (Greenock, Cappielow Park) 5-1
A.Smith 3, Buick, Drummond
Rennie; Allan, Drummond, Wilson, Buick, Robertson, Campbell*(Celtic)*, R.Walker, Hamilton, McMahon, A.Smith.
Att: 10,000   Referee: McBride (Ireland)

May 3 v England (Birmingham, Villa Park) 2-2
Templeton, Orr
Rennie; N.Smith, Drummond, Aitken*, Raisbeck, Robertson, Templeton, R.Walker, McColl, Orr, A.Smith.
Att: 15,000   Referee: Torrans (Ireland)

1903
Mar 9 v Wales (Cardiff) 1-0
Speedie
Rennie; McCombie, Watson, Aitken, Raisbeck*, Robertson, Templeton, R.Walker, Campbell *(Celtic)*, Speedie, A.Smith.
Att: 6,000   Referee: Kirkham (England)

Mar 21 v Ireland (Glasgow, Parkhead) 0-2
Rennie; Gray, Drummond*, Cross, Robertson, Orr, Lindsay, R.Walker, Porteous, Speedie, A.Smith.
Att: 17,000   Referee: Kirkham (England)

Apr 4 v England (Sheffield, Bramall Lane) 2-1
Speedie, Walker
Doig; McCombie, Watson, Aitken, Raisbeck*, Robertson, Templeton, R.Walker, Hamilton, Speedie, A.Smith.
Att: 36,000   Referee: Nunnerley (Wales)

1904
Mar 12 v Wales (Dundee, Dens Park) 1-1
R.Walker
Skene; Jackson, Sharp*, Orr, Sloan, Robertson, J.Walker, R.Walker, Bennett, McFarlane, Wilson.
Att: 13,000   Referee: Kirkham (England)

Mar 26 v Ireland (Dublin, Dalymont Park) 1-1
Hamilton
Rennie; Jackson, Cameron, Henderson, Thomson, Robertson*, J.Walker, R.Walker, Hamilton, Wilson, A.Smith.
Att: 8,000   Referee: Kirkham (England)

Apr 9 v England (Glasgow, Parkhead) 0-1
McBride; Jackson, Watson, Aitken, Raisbeck, Robertson*, Niblo, R.Walker, A.Brown, Orr, Templeton.
Att: 40,000   Referee: Nunnerley (Wales)

1905
Mar 6 v Wales (Wrexham) 1-3
Robertson
Rennie; McCombie, Jackson*, Aitken, Thomson, Robertson, Templeton, R.Walker, Kennedy, Fitchie, A.Smith.
Att: 5,000   Referee: Kirkham (England)

Mar 18 v Ireland (Glasgow, Parkhead) 4-0
Thomson 2 (2 pens), Walker, Quinn
Howden; McLeod, McIntosh, Gibson*, Thomson, Hay, Mcmenemy, R.Walker, Quinn, Somers, Wilson.
Att: 30,000   Referee: Kirkham (England)

Apr 1 v England (London, Crystal Palace) 0-1
Lyall; McCombie, Watson, Aitken, Thomson*, McWilliam, Walker, Howie, Young, Somers, Wilson.
Att: 40,000   Referee: Nunnerley (Wales)

1906
Mar 3 v Wales (Edinburgh, Tynecastle) 0-2
Raeside; McLeod, Richmond, McNair, Thomson*, Hay, Stewart, McFarlane, Quinn, Fitchie, Wilson.
Att: 25,000   Referee: Lewis (England)

Mar 17 v Ireland (Dublin) 1-0
Fitchie
Rennie; McLeod, Hill, Young, Thomson*, Hay, Hamilton, R.Walker, Quinn, Fitchie, A.Smith.
Att: 8,000   Referee: Bye (England)

Apr 7 v England (Glasgow, Hampden) 2-1
Howie 2
McBride; McLeod, Dunlop, Aitken, Raisbeck*, McWilliam, Stewart, Howie, Menzies, Livingstone, A.Smith.
Att: 102,000   Referee: Nunnerley (Wales)

1907
Mar 4 v Wales (Wrexham) 0-1
McBride; Jackson, Sharp, Aitken, Thomson*, McWilliam, Stewart, Livingstone, Young, Fitchie, A.Smith.
Att: 7,000   Referee: Mason (England)

Mar 16 v Ireland (Glasgow, Parkhead) 3-0
O'Rourke, Walker, Thomson (pen)
Muir; Jackson, Agnew, Key, Thomson*, McNair, Bennett, R.Walker, O'Rourke, Somers, Fraser.
Att: 28,000   Referee: Lewis (England)

Apr 6 v England (Newcastle) 1-1
Crompton (og)
McBride; Thomson, Sharp, Aitken, Raisbeck*, McWilliam, Stewart, R.Walker, A.Wilson, White, G.Wilson.
Att: 40,000   Referee: Robertson (Scotland)

1908
Mar 7 v Wales (Dundee, Dens Park) 2-1
Bennett, Lennie
Rennie; Agnew, Chaplin, McNair, Thomson*, Galt, Bennett, R.Walker, Spiers, McFarlane, Lennie.
Att: 15,000   Referee: Mason (England)

Mar 14 v Ireland (Dublin, Dalymount Park) 5-0
Quinn 4, Galt
Rennie; Mitchell, Agnew, May, Thomson*, Galt, Templeton, R.Walker, Quinn, McColl, Lennie.
Att: 9,000   Referee: Ibbotson (England)

Apr 4 v England (Glasgow, Hampden) 1-1
Wilson
McBride; McNair, Sharp, Aitken, Thomson*, May, Howie, R.Walker, A.Wilson, White, Quinn.
Att: 121,452   Referee: Mason (England)

1909
Mar 1 v Wales (Wrexham) 2-3
Walker, Paul
McBride; Collins, Sharp, May, Thomson*, McWilliam, Bennett, Hunter, R.Walker, Somers, Paul.
Att: 8,000   Referee: Campbell (England)

Mar 15 v Ireland (Glasgow, Ibrox) 5-0
McMenemy 2, McFarlane, Thomson, Paul
Brownlie; Main, Watson, W.Walker, Stark*, Hay, Bennett, McMenemy, Thomson, McFarlane, Paul.
Att: 23,000   Referee: Mason (England)

Apr 3 v England (London, Crystal Palace) 0-2
Brownlie; Cameron, Watson, McNair, Stark*, McWilliam, Bennett, R.Walker, Quinn, G.Wilson, Paul.
Att: 40,000   Referee: Stark (Scotland)

1910
Mar 5 v Wales (Kilmarnock) 1-0
Devine
Brownlie; Law, Mitchell, McNair, Loney, Hay*, Bennett, McMenemy, Quinn, Devine, Robertson.
Att: 18,000   Referee: Bamlett (England)

Mar 19 v Ireland (Belfast, Windsor Park) 0-1
Brownlie; Law, Mitchell, W.Walker, Loney, Hay*, Sinclair, McTavish, Quinn, Higgins, Templeton.
Att: 18,000   Referee: Howcroft (England)

Apr 2 v England (Glasgow, Hampden) 2-0
McMenemy, Quinn
Brownlie; Law, Hay, Aitken, Thomson*, McWilliam, Bennett, McMenemy, Quinn, Higgins, Templeton.
Att: 110,000   Referee: Mason (England)

1911
Mar 6 v Wales (Cardiff) 2-2
Hamilton 2
Brownlie; Colman, J.Walker, Tait, Low, McWilliam*, Bennett, McMenemy, Reid, McFarlane, Hamilton.
Att: 16,000   Referee: Mason (England)

Mar 18 v Ireland (Glasgow, Parkhead) 2-0
Reid, McMenemy
Brownlie; Colman, J.Walker, Aitken*, Thomson, Hay, Douglas, McMenemy, Reid, Higgins, A.Smith.
Att: 32,000   Referee: Bamlett (England)

Apr 1 v England (Liverpool, Goodison Park) 1-1
Higgins
Lawrence; Colman, J.Walker, Aitken, Low, Hay*, Bennett, McMenemy, Reid, Higgins, A.Smith.
Att: 50,000   Referee: Nunnerley (Wales)

1912
Mar 2 v Wales (Edinburgh, Tynecastle) 1-0
Quinn
Brownlie; McNair, J.Walker, Mercer, Thomson*, Hay, Sinclair, McMenemy, Quinn, R.Walker, Robertson.
Att: 31,000   Referee: Mason (England)

Mar 16 v Ireland (Belfast, Windsor Park) 4-1
Aitkenhead 2, Reid, R.Walker
Brownlie; McNair*, J.Walker, Gordon, Low, Bell, Sinclair, R.Walker, Reid, Aitkenhead, Templeton.
Att: 12,000   Referee: Bamlett (England)

Mar 23 v England (Glasgow, Hampden) 1-1
Wilson
Brownlie; McNair*, J.Walker, Gordon, Thomson, Hay, Templeton, R.Walker, McLean, A.Wilson, Quinn.
Att: 127,307   Referee: Mason (England)

1913
Mar 3 v Wales (Wrexham) 0-0
Brownlie; Orrock, J.Walker, Gordon, Thomson*, Campbell, McAtee, R.Walker, Reid, A.Wilson, Templeton.
Att: 6,000   Referee: Baker (England)

Mar 15 v Ireland (Dublin, Dalymount Park) 2-1
Reid, Bennett
Brownlie; Colman*, J.Walker, Mercer, Logan, Nellies, Bennett, Gordon, Reid, Croal, Robertson.
Att: 12,000   Referee: Adams (England)

Apr 5 v England (Stamford Bridge) 0-1
Brownlie; McNair, J.Walker, Gordon, Thomson*, D.Wilson, Donnchie, R.Walker, Reid, A.Wilson, Robertson.
Att: 52,500   Referee: Jackson (Scotland)

1914
Feb 28 v Wales (Glasgow, Parkhead) 0-0
Brownlie; Kelso, Dodds, Nellies*, Pursell, Anderson, Donaldson, McMenemy, Reid, Croal, Browning.
Att: 11,000   Referee: Taylor (England)

Scotland build up a left-wing attack during the 2-0 win over England at Hampden in 1910.

Scotland goalkeeper Harper saves from an England forward at Old Trafford, Manchester, in 1926.

Mar 14 v Ireland (Belfast, Windsor Park) 1-1
Donnachie
Brownlie; Dodds, McNair*, Gordon, Thomson, Hay, Donaldson, McMenemy, Reid, A.Wilson, Donnachie.
Att: 26,000   Referee: Bamlett (England)

Apr 4 v England (Glasgow, Hampden) 3-1
Thomson, McMenemy, Reid
Brownlie; McNair, Dodds, Gordon*, Thomson, Hay, Donaldson, McMenemy, Reid, Croal, Donnachie.
Att: 120,000   Referee: Bamlett (England)

1920
Feb 26 v Wales (Cardiff) 1-1
Cairns
Campbell; McNair, Thomson, Gordon, Cringen*, McMullan, Reid, Crosby, A.N.Wilson, Cairns, Morton.
Att: 20,000   Referee: Mason (England)

Mar 13 v Ireland (Glasgow, Parkhead) 3-0
Wilson, Morton, Cunningham
Campbell; McNair*, Blair, Bowie, Low, Gordon, Donaldson, McMenemy, A.N.Wilson, Cunningham, Morton.
Att: 39,750   Referee: Mason (England)

Apr 10 v England (Sheffield, Hillsborough) 4-5
Miller 2, Wilson, Donaldson
Campbell; McNair*, Blair, Bowie, Low, Gordon, Donaldson, Miller, A.N.Wilson, Paterson, Troup.
Att: 40,000   Referee: Dougray (Scotland)

1921
Feb 12 v Wales (Aberdeen) 2-1
Wilson 2
Campbell*; Marshall, McStay, Harris, Pringle, McMullan, Archibald, Cunningham, A.N.Wilson, Cassidy, Troup.
Att: 20,824   Referee: Mason (England)

Feb 26 v Ireland (Belfast) 2-0
Wilson(pen), Cassidy
Campbell; Marshall, McStay, Harris, Graham, McMullan, McNab, Miller, A.N.Wilson*, Cassidy, Troup.
Att: 35,000   Referee: Ward (England)

Apr 9 v England (Glasgow, Hampden) 3-0
Wilson, Morton, Cunningham
Ewart; Marshall*, Blair, Davidson, Brewster, McMullan, McNab, Miller, A.N.Wilson, Cunningham, Morton.
Att: 100,000   Referee: Ward (England)

1922
Feb 4 v Wales (Wrexham) 1-2
Archibald
Campbell; Marshall*, McKinlay, Meiklejohn, Gilhooley, Collier, Archibald, White, A.N.Wilson, Cunnigham, Morton.
Att: 10,000   Referee: Ward (England)

Mar 4 Ireland (Glasgow, Parkhead) 2-1
Wilson 2
Campbell; Marshall, McKinlay, Hogg, Cringan, Muirhead, Donaldson, Kinloch, A.N.Wilson, Cunningham*, Troup.
Att: 40,000   Referee: Ward (England)

Apr 8 v England (Birmingham, Villa Park) 1-0
Wilson
Campbell; Marshall, Blair*, Gilchrist, Cringan, McBain, Archibald, Crosbie, A.N.Wilson, Cairns, Morton.
Att: 33,700   Referee: Dougray (Scotland)

1923
Mar 3 v Ireland (Belfast) 1-0
Wilson
Harper; Hutton, Blair*, Steele, Morris, McBain, Archibald, White, A.N.Wilson, Cassidy, Morton.
Att: 30,000   Referee: Ward (England)

Mar 17 v Wales (Paisley) 2-0
Wilson 2
Harper; Hutton, Blair, McNab, Cringan*, Steele, Ritchie, Cunningham, A.N.Wilson, Cairns, Morton.
Att: 25,000   Referee: Baker (England)

Apr 14 v England (Glasgow, Hampden) 2-2
Cunningham, Wilson
Harper; Hutton, Blair, Steele, Cringan*, Muirhead, Lawson, Cunningham, A.N.Wilson, Cairns, Morton.
Att: 71,000   Referee: Ward (England)

1924
Feb 16 v Wales (Cardiff) 0-2
Harper; Marshall, Blair*, Meiklejohn, McBain, Muirhead, Archibald, Russell, Cassidy, McKay, Morton.
Att: 26,000   Referee: Andrews (England)

Mar 1 v Ireland (Glasgow, Parkhead) 2-0
Cunningham, Morris
Harper; Hutton*, Hamilton, Kerr, Morris, McMullan, Reid, Cunningham, Gallacher, Cairns, Morton.
Att: 30,000   Referee: Watson (England)

Apr 12 v England (Wembley) 1-1
Taylor (og)
Harper; J.Smith, McCloy, Clunas, Morris, McMullan*, Archibald, Cowan, Harris, Cunningham, Morton.
Att: 65,000   Referee: Dougray (Scotland)

1925
Feb 14 v Wales (Edinburgh, Tynecastle) 3-1
Meiklejohn, Gallacher 2
Harper; Nelson, McStay, Meiklejohn, Morris*, Bennie, Jackson, Dunn, Gallacher, Cairns, Morton.
Att: 25,000   Referee: Ward (England)

Feb 28 v Ireland (Belfast) 3-0
Meiklejohn, Gallacher, Dunn
Harper; Nelson, McStay, Meiklejohn, Morris*, Bennie, Jackson, Dunn, Gallacher, Cairns, Morton.
Att: 41,000   Referee: Watson (England)

Apr 4 v England (Glasgow, Hampden) 2-0
Gallacher 2
Harper; McStay, McCloy, Meiklejohn, Morris*, McMullan, Jackson, Russell, Gallacher, Cairns, Morton.
Att: 92,000   Referee: Ward (England)

Oct 31 v Wales (Cardiff) 3-0
Duncan, McLean, Clunas
Robb; Hutton, McStay, Clunas, Townsley*, McMullan, Jackson, Duncan, Gallacher, James, McLean.
Att: 25,000   Referee: Pinckston (England)

1926
Feb 27 v Ireland (Glasgow, Ibrox) 4-0
Gallacher 3, Cunningham
Harper; Hutton, McStay*, Wilson, McDougall, Bennie, Jackson, Cunningham, Gallacher, McInally, McLean.
Att: 30,000   Referee: Watson (England)

Apr 17 v England (Manchester, Old Trafford) 1-0
Jackson
Harper; Hutton, McStay*, Gibson, Summers, McMullan, Jackson, Thomson, Gallacher, Cunningham, Troup.
Att: 49,000   Referee: Dougray (Scotland)

Oct 30 v Wales (Glasgow, Ibrox) 3-0
Gallacher, Jackson 2
McClory; McStay*, Wiseman, Gibson, Gillespie, McMullan, Jackson, Cunningham, Gallacher, McInally, McLean.
Att: 41,000   Referee: Forshaw (England)

1927
Feb 26 v Ireland (Belfast) 2-0
Morton 2
Harkness; Hutton, McStay*, Muirhead, Gibson, Craig, Jackson, Dunn, Gallacher, Howieson, Morton.
Att: 40,000   Referee: Watson (England)

Apr 2 v England (Glasgow, Hampden) 1-2
Morton
Harkness; McStay*, Thomson, Morrison, Gibson, McMullan, McLean, Cunningham, Gallacher, McPhail, Morton.
Att: 111,214   Referee: Ward (England)

Oct 29 v Wales (Wrexham) 2-2
Gallacher, Hutton(pen)
Robb; Hutton, McStay, Meiklejohn, Gibson, McMullan*, Jackson, McKay, Gallacher, Stevenson, Morton.
Att: 16,000   Referee: Kingscott (England)

1928
Feb 25 v Ireland (Glasgow, Firhill) 0-1
McClory; Hutton, McStay, Muirhead*, Meiklejohn, Craig, Ritchie, Dunn, McGrory, Stevenson, Morton.
Att: 55,000   Referee: Ward (England)

Mar 31 v England (Wembley) 5-1
Jackson 3, James 2
Harkness; Nelson, Law, Gibson, Bradshaw, McMullan*, Jackson, Dunn, Gallacher, James, Morton.
Att: 80,868   Referee: Bell (Scotland)

Oct 27 v Wales (Glasgow, Ibrox) 4-2
Gallacher 3, Dunn
Harkness; Gray, Blair, Muirhead, King, McMullan*, Jackson, Dunn, Gallacher, McPhail, Morton.
Att: 55,000   Referee: Kingscott (England)

1929
Feb 23 v Ireland (Belfast) 7-3
Gallacher 4, Jackson 2, James
Harkness; Gray, Blair, Muirhead, Meiklejohn, McMullan*, Jackson, Chalmers, Gallacher, James, Morton.
Att: 35,000   Referee: Fogg (England)

Apr 13 v England (Glasgow, Hampden) 1-0
Cheyne
Harkness; Crapnell, Nibloe, Buchanan, Meiklejohn, McMullan*, Jackson, Cheyne, Gallacher, James, Morton.
Att: 110,512   Referee: Josephs (England)

May 26 v Norway (Bergen) 7-3
Cheyne 3, Nisbet 2, T.Craig, Rankin
McLaren; Crapnell, Nibloe, Imrie, A.Craig, T.Craig, Nisbet, Cheyne, McCrae, Rankin, Howe.
Att: 4,000   Referee: *Unknown*

Jun 1 v Germany (Berlin) 1-1
Imrie
McLaren; Gray, Crapnell, H.Morton, Imrie, T.Craig*, Nisbet, Cheyne, McCrae, Rankin, Fleming.
Att: 42,000   Referee: *Unknown*

Jun 4 v Netherlands (Amsterdam) 2-0
Fleming, Rankin
McClaren; Gray, Nibloe, H.Morton, A.Craig, T.Craig, Nisbet, Cheyne, Fleming, Rankin, Howe.
Att: 24,000   Referee: Olsson

Oct 26 v Wales (Cardiff) 4-2
Gallacher 2, James, Gibson
Harkness; Gray, Nibloe, Gibson, Johnstone, T.Craig*, Jackson, Muirhead, Gallacher, James, Morton.
Att: 25,000   Referee: McLean (Ireland)

1930
Feb 22 v Ireland (Glasgow, Parkhead) 3-1
Gallacher 2, Stevenson
Middleton; Gray, Wiseman, Gibson, Meiklejohn*, T.Craig, Jackson, Stevenson, Gallacher, James, Morton.
Att: 30,000   Referee: Josephs (England)

Apr 5 v England (Wembley) 2-5
Fleming 2
Harkness; Gray, Law, Buchanan, Meiklejohn*, T.Craig, Jackson, James, Fleming, Stevenson, Morton.
Att: 87,375   Referee: McLean (Ireland)

May 18 v France (Paris) 2-0
Gallacher 2
Thomson; Nelson, Crapnell*, Wilson, G.Walker, Hill, Jackson, Cheyne, Gallacher, Stevenson, Connor.
Att: 25,000   Referee: Van Praag

Oct 25 v Wales (Glasgow, Ibrox) 1-1
Battles
Thomson; Gray, Gilmour, McNab, Gillespie*, Hill, McRorie, G.Brown, Battles, Stevenson, Morton.
Att: 15,000   Referee: Lines (England)

1931

Feb 21 v Ireland (Belfast) 0-0
Thomson; Crapnell, Nibloe, P.Wilson, G.Walker, Hill, Murdoch, Scarff, Yorston, McPhail, Morton*.
Att: 20,000 Referee: Hull (England)

Mar 28 v England (Glasgow, Hampden) 2-0
Stevenson, McGrory
Thomson; Blair, Nibloe, McNab, Meiklejohn*, Miller, Archibald, Stevenson, McGrory, McPhail, Morton.
Att: 129,810 Referee: Atwood (Wales)

May 16 v Austria (Vienna) 0-5
Jackson; Blair*, Nibloe, McNab, McDougall, G.Walker, Love, Paterson, Easson, Robertson, D.Liddell.
Att: 45,000 Referee: Ruoff (Switzerland)

May 20 v Italy (Rome) 0-3
Jackson; Blair, Nibloe, McNab, McDougall*, Miller, Love, Paterson, Boyd, Robertson, D.Liddell.
Att: 25,000 Referee: Bauwens (Germany)

May 24 v Switzerland (Geneva) 3-2
Easson, Boyd, Love
Jackson; Crapnell*, Nibloe, McNab, G.Walker, Miller, Love, Paterson, Boyd, Easson, D.Liddell.
Att: 10,000 Referee: Carraro (Italy)

Sep 19 v Ireland (Glasgow, Ibrox) 3-1
Stevenson, McGrory, McPhail
Hepburn; Blair, McAulay, Massie, Meiklejohn*, G.Brown, Crawford, Stevenson, McGrory, McPhail, Connor.
Att: 40,000 Referee: Caswell (England)

Oct 31 v Wales (Wrexham) 3-2
Stevenson, Thomson, McGrory
Harkness; Blair, McAulay, Massie, Meiklejohn*, G.Brown, R.Thomson, Stevenson, McGrory, McPhail, Morton.
Att: 10,860 Referee: Caswell (England)

1932

Apr 9 v England (Wembley) 0-3
T.Hamilton; Crapnell*, Nibloe, McNab, A.Craig, G.Brown, Archibald, Marshall, Dewar, Napier, Morton.
Att: 92,180 Referee: Thompson (N.Ireland)

May 8 v France (Paris) 3-1
Dewar 3
Harkness; Crapnell, Nibloe, Massie, Gillespie*, Miller, Crawford, A.Thomson, Dewar, McPhail, Morton.
Att: 20,000 Referee: Carraro (Italy)

Sep 17 v Ireland (Belfast) 4-0
McPhail 2, King, McGrory
McLaren; Gray, Crapnell*, Massie, Johnstone, Telfer, Crawford, Stevenson, McGrory, McPhail, King.
Att: 40,000 Referee: Harper (England)

Oct 26 v Wales (Edinburgh, Tynecastle) 2-5
Dewar, Duncan
McLaren; Gray, Blair, Wales, Johnstone*, J.Thomson, Crawford, A.Thomson, Dewar, James, Duncan.
Att: 31,000 Referee: Harper (England)

1933

Apr 1 v England (Glasgow, Hampden) 2-1
McGrory 2
Jackson; Anderson, McGonagle, P.Wilson, Gillespie*, G.Brown, Crawford, Marshall, McGrory, McPhail, Duncan.
Att: 134,710 Referee: Thompson (N.Ireland)

Sep 16 v Ireland (Glasgow, Parkhead) 1-2
McPhail
Harkness; Anderson, McGonagle*, Massie, Lowe, Telfer, Boyd, Venters, McGrory, McPhail, King.
Att: 27,135 Referee: Wood (England)

Oct 4 v Wales (Cardiff) 2-3
Duncan, McFadyen
Harkness; Anderson*, Urquhart, Busby, Blair, McLuckie, McGurk, McMenemy, McFadyen, Easson, Duncan.
Att: 40,000 Referee: Wood (England)

Nov 29 v Austria (Glasgow, Hampden) 2-2
Meiklejohn, McFadyen
Kennaway; Anderson, McGonagle, Meiklejohn*, P.Watson, G.Brown, Ogilvie, Bruce, McFadyen, McPhail, Duncan.
Att: 62,000 Referee: Langenus (Belgium)

1934

Apr 14 v England (Wembley) 0-3
Jackson; Anderson, McGonagle, Massie*, T.Smith, Miller, Cook, Marshall, Gallacher, Stevenson, Connor.
Att: 92,363 Referee: Thompson (N.Ireland)

Oct 20 v Ireland (Belfast) 1-2
Gallacher
Dawson; Anderson, McGonagle, Massie*, Simpson, Herd, Cook, Stevenson, J.Smith, Gallacher, Connor.
Att: 39,752 Referee: Mee (England)

Nov 21 v Wales (Aberdeen) 3-2
Duncan, Napier 2
McClory; Anderson, McGonagle, Massie, Simpson*, G.Brown, Cook, T.Walker, McCulloch, Napier, Duncan.
Att: 26,334 Referee: Thompson (N.Ireland)

1935

Apr 6 v England (Glasgow, Hampden) 2-0
Duncan 2
Jackson; Anderson, Cummings, Massie, Simpson*, G.Brown, Napier, T.Walker, Gallacher, McPhail, Duncan.
Att: 129,693 Referee: Thompson (N.Ireland)

Oct 5 v Wales (Cardiff) 1-1
Duncan
Jackson; Anderson, Cummings, Massie, Simpson*, G.Brown, Delaney, T.Walker, Armstrong, Mills, Duncan.
Att: 35,004 Referee: Caswell (England)

Nov 13 v Ireland (Edinburgh, Tynecastle) 2-1
Walker, Duncan
Jackson; Anderson, Cummings, Massie, Simpson*, Hastings, Delaney, T.Walker, Armstrong, Mills, Duncan.
Att: 30,000 Referee: Nattrass (England)

1936

Apr 4 v England (Wembley) 1-1
Walker
Dawson; Anderson, Cummings, Massie, Simpson*, G.Brown, Crum, T.Walker, McCulloch, Venters, Duncan.
Att: 93,267 Referee: Hamilton (Ireland)

Oct 14 v Germany (Glasgow, Ibrox) 2-0
Delaney 2
Dawson; Anderson, Cummings, Massie, Simpson*, G.Brown, Delaney, T.Walker, Armstrong, McPhail, Duncan.
Att: 50,000 Referee: Nattrass (England)

Oct 31 v Ireland (Belfast) 3-1
Napier, Munro, McCulloch
Dawson; Anderson, Ancell, Massie, Simpson*, G.Brown, Munro, T.Walker, McCulloch, Napier, Duncan.
Att: 45,000 Referee: Thompson (England)

Dec 2 v Wales (Dundee, Dens Park) 1-2
Walker
Dawson; Anderson, Ancell, Massie, Simpson*, G.Brown, Munro, T.Walker, McCulloch, Mills, Duncan.
Att: 23,858 Referee: Barton (England)

1937

Apr 17 v England (Hampden) 3-1
O'Donnell, McPhail 2
Dawson; Anderson, A.Beattie, Massie, Simpson*, G.Brown, Delaney, T.Walker, F.O'Donnell, McPhail, Duncan.
Att: 149,547 Referee: McClean (Ireland)

May 9 v Austria (Vienna) 1-1
O'Donnell
Dawson; Anderson, A.Beattie, Massie, Simpson*, McNab, Delaney, T.Walker, F.O'Donnell, Napier, Gillick.
Att: 63,000 Referee: Langenus (Belgium)

May 15 v Czechoslovakia (Prague) 3-1
Simpson, McPhail, Gillick
Dawson; Hogg, A.Beattie, Thomson, Simpson*, G.Brown, Delaney, T.Walker, F.O'Donnell, McPhail, Gillick.
Att: 35,000 Referee: Bauwens (Germany)

Oct 30 v Wales (Cardiff) 1-2
Massie
Dawson; Anderson, Cummings, Massie, Simpson*, G.Brown, Main, T.Walker, F.O'Donnell, McPhail, Duncan.
Att: 41,800 Referee: Argent (England)

Nov 10 v Ireland (Aberdeen) 1-1
Smith
Dawson; Anderson, Cummings, McKenzie, Simpson*, Hastings, Delaney, T.Walker, J.Smith, McPhail, Reid.
Att: 21,878 Referee: Jewell (England)

Dec 8 v́ Czechoslovakia (Hampden) 5-0
McCulloch 2, Black, Buchanan, Kinnear
Waugh; Anderson*, Cummings, Robertson, Johnston, G.Brown, Buchanan, T.Walker, McCulloch, Black, Kinnear.
Att: 41,000 Referee: Thompson (England)

1938

Apr 9 v England (Wembley) 1-0
Walker
Cumming; Anderson, A.Beattie, Shankly, T.Smith, G.Brown*, Milne, T.Walker, F.O'Donnell, Mutch, Reid.
Att: 93,267 Referee: Hamilton (N Ireland)

May 21 v Netherlands (Amsterdam) 3-1
Black, Murphy, Walker
Dawson; Anderson, Carabine, McKillop, Dykes, G.Brown*, Munro, T.Walker, F.O'Donnell, Black, Murphy.
Att: 50,000 Referee: Argent (England)

Oct 8 v Ireland (Belfast) 2-0
Delaney, Walker
Dawson; Carabine*, A.Beattie, Shankly, Dykes, Paterson, Delaney, T.Walker, Crum, Divers, Gillick.
Att: 40,000 Referee: Mortimer (England)

Nov 9 v Wales (Edinburgh, Tynecastle) 3-2
Walker 2, Gillick
J.Brown; Anderson*, A.Beattie, Shankly, Baxter, Miller, Delaney, T.Walker, McCulloch, R.Beattie, Gillick.
Att: 34,800 Referee: Thompson (England)

Dec 7 v Hungary (Glasgow, Ibrox) 3-1
Black, Walker (pen), Gillick
Dawson; Anderson*, A.Beattie, Shankly, Baxter, Symon, McSpadyen, T.Walker, McCulloch, Black, Gillick.
Att: 23,000 Referee: Nattrass (England)

1939

Apr 15 v England (Glasgow, Hampden) 1-2
Dougall
Dawson; Carabine, Cummings, Shankly, Baxter, McNab, McSpadyen, T.Walker, Dougall*, Venters, Milne.
Att: 149,269 Referee: Hamilton (N Ireland)

1946

Oct 19 v Wales (Wrexham) 1-3
Waddell (pen)
Miller; Stephen*, D.Shaw, Brown, Brennan, Husband, Waddell, Dougall, Thornton, Blair, Liddell.
Att: 30,000 Referee: Evans (England)

Nov 27 v N Ireland (Hampden) 0-0
R.Brown; Young, D.Shaw*, Campbell, Brennan, Long, Smith, Hamilton, Thornton, Duncanson, Liddell.
Att: 98,776 Referee: Reader (England)

1947

Apr 12 v England (Wembley) 1-1
McLaren
Miller; Young, J.Shaw*, Macaulay, Woodburn,
Forbes, Smith, McLaren, Delaney, Steel, Pearson.
Att: 98,200 Referee: De La Salle (France)

May 18 v Belgium (Brussels) 1-2
Steel
Miller; Young, J.Shaw*, Brown, Woodburn, Forbes,
Campbell, McLaren, Flavell, Steel, Pearson.
Att: 85,000 Referee: Laursen (Denmark)

May 24 v Luxembourg (Luxembourg) 6-0
McLaren 2, Steel 2, Flavell 2
Miller; Young, McLaren, Brown, Woodburn, Forbes,
McFarlane, McLaren, Flavell, Steel, Campbell.
Att: 4,000 Referee: Wauters (Belgium)

Oct 4 v N Ireland (Belfast) 0-2
Miller; Young, J.Shaw*, Macaulay, Woodburn,
Forbes, Delaney, Watson, Thornton, Steel, Liddell.
Att: 52,000 Referee: Smith (England)

Nov 12 v Wales (Hampden) 1-2
McLaren
Miller; Govan, Stephen, Macaulay, Woodburn*,
Forbes, Smith, McLaren, Delaney, Steel, Liddell.
Att: 88,000 Referee: Ellis (England)

1948

Apr 10 v England (Hampden) 0-2
Black; Govan, D.Shaw, Campbell, Young*, Macaulay,
Delaney, Combe, Thornton, Steel, Liddell.
Att: 135,376 Referee: Maxwell (N Ireland)

Apr 28 v Belgium (Hampden) 2-0
Combe, Duncan
Cowan; Govan, D.Shaw, Campbell, Young*,
Macaulay, Smith, Combe, Johnston, Turnbull,
Duncan.
Att: 70,000 Referee: Ling (England)

May 17 v Switzerland (Berne) 1-2
Johnston
Cowan; Govan, D.Shaw, Campbell, Young*,
Macaulay, Smith, Combe, Johnston, Turnbull,
Duncan.
Att: 30,000 Referee: Beranech (Austria)

May 23 v France (Paris) 0-3
Cowan; Govan, D.Shaw, Campbell, Young*,
Macaulay, Rutherford, Steel, Smith, Cox, Duncan.
Att: 70,000 Referee: Van Der Meer (Netherlands)

Oct 23 v Wales (Cardiff) 3-1
Howie, Waddell 2
Cowan; Howie, D.Shaw, Evans, Young*, Redpath,
Waddell, Mason, Reilly, Steel, Kelly.
Att: 60,000 Referee: Maxwell (N Ireland)

Nov 17 v N Ireland (Hampden) 3-2
Houliston 2, Mason
R.Brown; Govan, D.Shaw, Evans, Young*, Redpath,
Waddell, Mason, Houliston, Steel, Kelly.
Att: 100,000 Referee: Evans (England)

1949

Apr 9 v England (Wembley) 3-1
Mason, Steel, Reilly
Cowan; Young*, Cox, Evans, Woodburn, Aitken,
Waddell, Mason, Houliston, Steel, Reilly.
Att: 98,188 Referee: Griffiths (Wales)

Apr 27 v France (Hampden) 2-0
Steel 2
Cowan; Young*, Cox, Evans, Woodburn, Aitken,
Waddell, Thornton, Houliston, Steel, Reilly.
Att: 130,000 Referee: Ling (England)

Oct 1 v N Ireland (Belfast) 8-2
Morris 3, Waddell 2, Steel, Reilly, Mason
Cowan; Young*, Cox, Evans, Woodburn, Aitken,
Waddell, Mason, Morris, Steel, Reilly.
Att: 50,000 Referee: Mortimer (England)

Nov 9 v Wales (Hampden) 2-0
McPhail, Linwood
Cowan; Young*, Cox, Evans, Woodburn, Aitken,
Liddell, McPhail, Linwood, Steel, Reilly.
Att:73,782 Referee: Law (England)

1950

Apr 15 v England (Hampden) 0-1
Cowan; Young*, Cox, McColl, Woodburn, Forbes,
Waddell, Moir, Bauld, Steel, Liddell.
Att: 133,300 Referee: Leafe (England)

Apr 26 v Switzerland (Hampden) 3-1
Bauld, Campbell, Brown
Cowan; Young*, Cox, Evans, Dougan, Aitken,
Campbell, Brown, Bauld, Steel, Reilly.
Att: 123,751 Referee: Reader (England)

May 21 v Portugal (Lisbon) 2-2
Brown, Bauld
Cowan; Young*, Cox, Evans, Woodburn, Forbes,
Campbell, Brown, Bauld, Steel, Liddell.
Att: 68,000 Referee: Anzano (Spain)

May 27 v France (Paris) 1-0
Brown
Cowan; Young*, Cox, McColl, Woodburn, Forbes,
Campbell, Brown, Reilly, Steel, Liddell.
Att: 45,000 Referee: Argue (Spain)

Oct 21 v Wales (Cardiff) 3-1
Reilly 2, Liddell
Cowan; Young*, McNaught, McColl, Woodburn,
Forbes, Collins, McPhail, Reilly, Steel, Liddell.
Att: 60,000 Referee: Ellis (England)

Nov 1 v N Ireland (Hampden) 6-1
McPhail 2, Steel 4
Cowan; Young*, McNaught, McColl, Woodburn,
Forbes, Collins, Mason, McPhail, Steel, Liddell.
Att: 75,000 Referee: Griffiths (Wales)

Dec 13 v Austria (Hampden) 0-1
Cowan; Young*, McNaught, Evans, Woodburn,
Forbes, Collins, Turnbull, McPhail, Steel, Liddell.
Att: 68,000 Referee: Ling (England)

1951

Apr 14 v England (Wembley) 3-2
Johnstone, Reilly, Liddell
Cowan; Young*, Cox, Evans, Woodburn, Redpath,
Waddell, Johnstone, Reilly, Steel, Liddell.
Att: 98,000 Referee: Mitchell (Scotland)

May 12 v Denmark (Hampden) 3-1
Steel, Reilly, Mitchell
Cowan; Young*, Cox, Scoular, Woodburn, Redpath,
Waddell, Johnstone, Reilly, Steel, Mitchell.
Att: 75,000 Referee: Evans (England)

May 16 v France (Hampden) 1-0
Reilly
Cowan; Young*, Cox, Scoular, Woodburn, Redpath,
Waddell, Johnstone, Reilly, Steel, Mitchell.
Att: 80,000 Referee: Mortimer (England)

May 20 v Belgium (Brussels) 5-0
Hamilton 3, Mason, Waddell
Cowan; Young*, Cox, McColl, Woodburn, Redpath,
Waddell, Mason, Hamilton, Steel, Reilly.
Att: 65,000 Referee: Fauquemberghe (France)

May 27 v Austria (Vienna) 0-4
Cowan; Young*, Cox, Scoular, Woodburn, Redpath,
Waddell, Mason, Hamilton, Steel, Reilly.
Att: 65,000 Referee: Lutz (Switzerland)

Oct 6 v N Ireland (Belfast, Windsor Park) 3-0
Johnstone 2, Orr
Cowan; Young*, Cox, Evans, Woodburn, Redpath,
Waddell, Mason, Reilly, Orr, Liddell.
Att: 56,946 Referee: Evans (England)

Nov 14 v Wales (Hampden) 0-1
Cowan; Young*, Cox, Docherty, Woodburn, Forbes,
Waddell, Orr, Reilly, Steel, Liddell.
Att: 71,272 Referee: Morris (N Ireland)

1952

Apr 5 v England (Hampden) 1-2
Reilly
R.Brown; Young*, McNaught, Scoular, Woodburn,
Redpath, Smith, Johnstone, Reilly, McMillan,
Liddell.
Att: 134,504 Referee: Morris (N Ireland)

Apr 30 v USA (Hampden) 6-0
Reilly 3, McMillan 2, 1 (og)
Cowan; Young*, Cox, Scoular, Woodburn, Kelly,
Smith, McMillan, Reilly, Brown, Liddell.
Att: 107,765 Referee: Gerrard (Scotland)

May 25 v Denmark (Copenhagen) 2-1
Thornton, Reilly
Cowan; Young*, Cox, Scoular, Paton, Forbes,
Reilly, McMillan, Thornton, Brown, Liddell.
Att: 39,000 Referee: Ahlner (Sweden)

May 30 v Sweden (Stockholm) 1-3
Liddell
Cowan; Young*, Cox, Scoular, Paton, Forbes,
Reilly, Humphries, Thornton, Brown, Liddell.
*Att: 32,000*Referee: Van Der Meer (Netherlands)

Oct 18 v Wales (Cardiff) 2-1
Brown, Liddell
Farm; Young*, Cox, Scoular, Brennan, Aitken,
T.Wright, Brown, Reilly, Steel, Liddell.
Att: 60,000 Referee: Bond (England)

Nov 5 v N Ireland (Hampden) 1-1
Reilly
Farm; Young*, Cox, Scoular, Brennan, Aitken,
T.Wright, Logie, Reilly, Steel, Liddell.
Att: 65,057 Referee: Smith (Wales)

1953

Apr 18 v England (Wembley) 2-2
Reilly 2
Farm; Young*, Cox, Docherty, Brennan, Cowie,
T.Wright, Johnstone, Reilly, Steel, Liddell.
Att: 97,000 Referee: Mitchell (N Ireland)

May 6 v Sweden (Hampden) 1-2
Johnstone
Farm; Young*, Little, Evans, Cowie, Docherty,
Henderson, Johnstone, Reilly, Steel, Ring.
Att: 83,800 Referee: Ling (England)

Oct 3 v N Ireland (Belfast) 3-1
Fleming 2, Henderson
Farm; Young*, Cox, Evans, Brennan, Cowie,
Waddell, Fleming, McPhail, Watson, Henderson.
Att: 58,248 Referee: Bond (England)

Nov 4 v Wales (Hampden) 3-3
Brown, Johnstone, Reilly
Farm; Young*, Cox, Evans, Telfer, Cowie, McKenzie,
Johnstone, Reilly, Brown, Liddell.
Att: 71,378 Referee: Mitchell (N Ireland)

1954

Apr 3 v England (Hampden) 2-4
Brown, 1 (og)
Farm; Haughney, Cox*, Evans, Brennan, Aitken,
McKenzie, Johnstone, Henderson, Brown, Ormond.
Att: 134,544 Referee: Mitchell (N Ireland)

May 5 v Norway (Hampden) 1-0
Hamilton
Martin; Cunningham, Aird, Docherty*, Davidson,
Evans, Johnstone, Hamilton, Buckley, Brown,
Ormond.
Att:25,897 Referee: Clough (England)

May 19 v Norway (Oslo) 1-1
McKenzie
Martin; Cunningham, Aird, Docherty*, Davidson,
Cowie, McKenzie, Hamilton, Henderson, Brown,
Mochan.
Att: 25,000 Referee: Andersson (Sweden)

May 25 v Finland (Helsinki) 2-1
Ormond, Johnstone
Anderson; Wilson, Cunningham*, Evans, Cowie,
Mathers, McKenzie, Johnstone, Brown, Fernie,
Ormond.
Att: 21,676 Referee: Ahlner (Sweden)

WORLD CUP FINALS

Jun 16 v Austria (Zurich) 0-1
Martin; Cunningham*, Aird, Docherty, Davidson,
Cowie, McKenzie, Fernie, Mochan, Brown, Ormond.
Att: 25,000 Referee: Franken (Belgium)

Hampden Park in the 1950s.

The Scotland team against Wales in 1956. Back row (left to right): Parker, McColl, Younger, Hewie, Cowie. Front: Leggat, Mudie, Reilly, Young, Collins, Fernie.

Great show: now o

That's the challenge facing a new generation of talent signed up by the BBC Directors' Academy. John Yorke, the man charged with the task of knocking

T he roads to Hollywood success are steep and strewn with fallen egos, but John Yorke is building a new one that could enable British talent to sit in the director's chair without first having to wait on tables on Sunset Strip.

The new BBC Directors' Academy is about to launch, and later this year its first graduates will already be working on top-rated shows such as *Holby City* and *EastEnders*. Ultimately, they could be making feature films,

Lost classic: the Scotland football team at the 1958 World Cup, with Gary Imlach's father Stewart on [...] right of the [...]

Jun 19 v Uruguay (Basle) 0-7
Martin; Cunningham*, Aird, Docherty, Davidson,
Cowie, McKenzie, Fernie, Mochan, Brown, Ormond.
Att: 40,000   Referee: Orlandini (Italy)

Oct 16 v Wales (Cardiff) 1-0
Buckley
Fraser; Young*, Cunningham, Docherty, Davidson,
Cowie, Waddell, Yorston, Buckley, Fernie, Ring.
Att: 60,000   Referee: Ling (England)

Nov 3 v N Ireland (Hampden) 2-2
Davidson, Johnstone
Fraser; Young*, McNaught, Evans, Davidson,
Cowie, Waddell, Johnstone, Buckley, Fernie, Ring.
Att: 46,200   Referee: Bond (England)

Dec 8 v Hungary (Hampden) 2-4
Ring, Johnstone
Martin; Cunningham*, Haddock, Docherty, Davidson,
Cumming, McKenzie, Johnstone, Reilly, Wardhaugh,
Ring.
Att: 113,146   Referee: Horn (Netherlands)

1955
Apr 2 v England (Wembley) 2-7
Reilly, Docherty
Martin; Cunningham*, Haddock, Docherty, Davidson,
Cumming, McKenzie, Johnstone, Reilly, McMillan,
Ring.
Att: 96,847   Referee: Griffiths (Wales)

May 4 v Portugal (Hampden) 3-0
Reilly, Gemmell, Liddell
Younger; Parker, Haddock, Evans, Young*, Cumming,
Smith, Robertson, Reilly, Gemmell, Liddell.
Att: 20,858   Referee: Gardeazabal (Spain)

May 15 v Yugoslavia (Belgrade) 2-2
Reilly, Smith
Younger; Parker, Haddock, Evans, Young*, Cumming,
Smith, Collins, Reilly, Gemmell, Liddell.
Att: 20,000   Referee: Orlandini (Italy)

May 19 v Austria (Vienna) 4-1
Robertson, Smith, Liddell, Reilly
Younger; Parker, Kerr, Docherty, Evans, Cowie,
Smith*, Collins, Reilly, Robertson, Liddell.
Att: 65,000   Referee: Bernardi (Italy)

May 29 v Hungary (Budapest) 1-3
Smith
Younger; Kerr, Haddock, Docherty, Evans, Cowie,
Smith*, Collins, Reilly, Robertson, Liddell.
Att: 102,000   Referee: Seilpelt (Austria)

Oct 8 v N Ireland (Belfast) 1-2
Reilly
Younger; Parker, McDonald, Evans, Young*,
Glen, Smith, Collins, Reilly, Johnstone, Liddell.
Att: 50,000   Referee: Kelly (England)

Nov 9 v Wales (Hampden) 2-0
Johnstone 2
Younger; Parker, McDonald, Evans, Young*, Cowie,
Smith, Johnstone, Reilly, Collins, Henderson.
Att: 53,887   Referee: Leafe (England)

1956
Apr 14 v England (Hampden) 1-1
Leggat
Younger; Parker, Hewie, Evans, Young*, Glen,
Leggat, Johnstone, Reilly, McMillan, Smith.
Att: 132,817   Referee: Callaghan (Wales)

May 2 v Austria (Hampden) 1-1
Conn
Younger; Parker, Hewie, Evans, Young*, Cowie,
McKenzie, Conn, Reilly, Baird, Cullen.
Att: 80,509   Referee: Bronkhurst (Netherlands)

Oct 20 v Wales (Cardiff) 2-2
Fernie, Reilly
Younger; Parker, Hewie, McColl, Young*, Cowie,
Leggat, Mudie, Reilly, Collins, Fernie.
Att: 60,000   Referee: Mann (England)

Nov 7 v N Ireland (Hampden) 1-0
Scott
Younger; Parker, Hewie, McColl, Young*, Cowie,
Scott, Mudie, Reilly, Wardhaugh, Fernie.
Att: 62,035   Referee: Leafe (England)

Nov 21 v Yugoslavia (Hampden) 2-0
Mudie, Baird
Younger; Parker, Hewie, McColl, Young*, Docherty,
Scott, Mudie, Reilly, Baird, Fernie.
Att: 55,500   Referee: Roomer (Netherlands)

1957
Apr 6 v England (Wembley) 1-2
Ring
Younger; Caldow, Hewie, McColl, Young*, Docherty,
Collins, Fernie, Reilly, Mudie, Ring.
Att: 97,520   Referee: Roomer (Netherlands)

May 8 v Spain (Hampden) 4-2
Mudie 3, Hewie (pen)
Younger; Caldow, Hewie, McColl, Young*, Docherty,
Smith, Collins, Mudie, Baird, Ring.
Att: 89,000   Referee: Dusch (Germany)

May 19 v Switzerland (Basle) 2-1
Mudie, Collins
Younger; Caldow, Hewie, McColl, Young*, Docherty,
Smith, Collins, Mudie, Baird, Ring.
Att: 48,000   Referee: Seipelt (Austria)

May 22 v W Germany (Stuttgart) 3-1
Collins 2, Mudie
Younger; Caldow, Hewie, McColl, Evans, Docherty*,
Scott, Collins, Mudie, Baird, Ring.
Att: 80,000   Referee: Dienst (Switzerland)

May 26 v Spain (Madrid) 1-4
Smith
Younger; Caldow, Hewie, Mackay, Evans, Docherty*,
Smith, Collins, Mudie, Baird, Ring.
Att: 90,000   Referee: Leafe (England)

Oct 5 v N Ireland (Belfast) 1-1
Leggat
Younger; Parker, Caldow, McColl, Evans, Docherty*,
Leggat, Collins, Mudie, Baird, Ring.
Att: 58,000   Referee: Callaghan (Wales)

Nov 6 v Switzerland (Hampden) 3-2
Robertson, Mudie, Scott
Younger; Parker, Caldow, Fernie, Evans, Docherty*,
Scott, Collins, Mudie, Robertson, Ring.
Att: 58,811   Referee: Leafe (England)

Nov 13 v Wales (Hampden) 1-1
Collins
Younger; Parker, Caldow, Docherty*, Evans, Fernie,
Scott, Collins, Gardiner, Mudie, Ewing.
Att: 42,918   Referee: Clough (England)

1958
Apr 19 v England (Hampden) 0-4
Younger; Parker, Haddock, McColl, Evans,
Docherty*, Herd, Murray, Mudie, Forrest, Ewing.
Att: 127,874   Referee: Dusch (W Germany)

May 7 v Hungary (Hampden) 1-1
Mudie
Younger*; Caldow, Hewie, Turnbull, Evans, Cowie,
Leggat, Murray, Mudie, Collins, Imlach.
Att: 54,900   Referee: Clough (England)

Jun 1 v Poland (Warsaw) 2-1
Collins 2
Younger*; Caldow, Hewie, Turnbull, Evans, Cowie,
Leggat, Murray, Mudie, Collins, Imlach.
Att: 70,000   Referee: Sramko (Hungary)

WORLD CUP FINALS

Jun 8 v Yugoslavia (Vasteras) 1-1
Murray
Younger*; Caldow, Hewie, Turnbull, Evans, Cowie,
Leggat, Murray, Mudie, Collins, Imlach.
Att: 9,591   Referee: Wyssling (Switzerland)

Jun 11 v Paraguay (Norrköping) 2-3
Mudie, Collins
Younger*; Parker, Caldow, Turnbull, Evans, Cowie,
Leggat, Collins, Mudie, Robertson, Fernie.
Att: 11,665   Referee: Orlandini (Italy)

Jun 15 v France (Orebro) 1-2
Baird
Brown; Caldow, Hewie, Turnbull, Evans*, Mackay,
Collins, Murray, Mudie, Baird, Imlach.
Att: 13,554   Referee: Brozzi (Argentina)

Oct 18 v Wales (Cardiff) 3-0
Leggat, Law, Collins
Brown; Grant, Caldow, Mackay*, Toner, Docherty,
Leggat, Collins, Herd, Law, Henderson.
Att: 60,000   Referee: Leafe (England)

Nov 5 v N Ireland (Hampden) 2-2
Herd, Collins
Brown; Grant, Caldow, Mackay*, Toner, Docherty,
Leggat, Collins, Herd, Law, Henderson.
Att: 72,732   Referee: Clough (England)

1959
Apr 11 v England (Wembley) 0-1
Brown; McKay, Caldow, Docherty, Evans*, Mackay,
Leggat, Collins, Herd, Dick, Ormond.
Att: 98,329   Referee: Campos (Portugal)

May 6 v W Germany (Hampden) 3-2
White, Weir, Leggat
Farm; McKay, Caldow, Mackay, Evans*, McCann,
Leggat, White, St John, Collins, Weir.
Att: 103,415   Referee: Ellis (England)

May 27 v Netherlands (Amsterdam) 2-1
Collins, Leggat
Farm; McKay, Caldow, Smith, Evans*, Hewie,
Leggat, Collins, White, Law, Auld.
Att: 55,000   Referee: Campos (Portugal)

Jun 3 v Portugal (Lisbon) 0-1
Farm; McKay, Caldow, Smith, Evans*, Hewie,
Scott, Collins, White, Law, Auld.
Att: 30,000   Referee: Zariquiegul (Spain)

Oct 3 v N Ireland (Belfast) 4-0
Leggat, Hewie, White, Mulhall
Brown; Caldow, Hewie, Mackay, Evans*, McCann,
Leggat, White, St John, Law, Mulhall.
Att: 56,000   Referee: Leafe (England)

Nov 4 v Wales (Hampden) 1-1
Leggat
Brown; Caldow, Hewie, Mackay, Evans*, McCann,
Leggat, White, St John, Law, Auld.
Att: 55,813   Referee: Howley (England)

1960
Apr 9 v England (Hampden) 1-1
Leggat
Haffey; McKay, Caldow, Cumming, Evans*, McCann,
Leggat, Young, St John, Law, Weir.
Att:129,193   Referee: Sranko (Hungary)

May 4 v Poland (Hampden) 2-3
Law, St John
Brown; McKay, Hewie, Mackay, Evans*, Cumming,
Leggat, White, St John, Law, Weir.
Att: 26,643   Referee: Holland (England)

May 29 v Austria (Vienna) 1-4
Mackay
Brown; McKay, Caldow, Mackay, Evans*, Cumming,
Leggat, White, St John, Law (Young), Weir.
Att: 60,000   Referee: Deutsch (W Germany)

Jun 5 v Hungary (Budapest) 3-3
Hunter, Herd, Young
Brown; McKay, Caldow, Cumming, Evans*, Mackay,
Leggat, Herd, Young, Hunter, Weir.
Att: 90,000   Referee: Ellis (England)

Jun 8 v Turkey (Ankara) 2-4
Caldow (pen), Young
Brown; McKay, Caldow, Mackay, Evans*, Cumming,
White, Herd, Young, Hunter, Weir.
Att: 22,500   Referee: Steiner (Austria)

Oct 22 v Wales (Cardiff) 0-2
Leslie; McKay, Caldow*, Gabriel, Martins, Mackay,
Herd, White, Young, Hunter, Wilson.
Att: 55,000   Referee: Holland (England)

Nov 9 v N Ireland (Hampden) 5-2
Law, Caldow, Young, Brand 2
Leslie; McKay, Caldow*, Mackay, Plenderleith,
Baxter, Herd, Law, Young, Brand, Wilson.
Att: 34,564   Referee: Howley (England)

Denis Law and Ian St John hover as Jim Baxter (out of picture) scores Scotland's first goal at Wembley in 1963.

◀

With the scoreboard showing a two-goal lead, Law dances around England's Norman in the same game. Players in the background are (left to right) Mackay, Ure, White and Greaves. ▼

1961

Apr 15 v England (Wembley) 3-9
Mackay, Wilson, Quinn
Haffey; Shearer, Caldow*, Mackay, McNeill, McCann, McLeod, Law, St John, Quinn, Wilson.
Att: 97,350   Referee: Lequesne (France)

May 3 v Rep of Ireland (Hampden) 4-1
Brand 2, Herd 2
Leslie; Shearer, Caldow*, Crerand, McNeill, Baxter, McLeod, Quinn, Herd, Brand, Wilson.
Att: 50,000   Referee: Guigue (France)

May 7 v Rep of Ireland (Dublin, Dalymount Park) 3-0
Young 2, Brand
Leslie; Shearer, Caldow*, Crerand, McNeill, Baxter, McLeod, Quinn, Young, Brand, Wilson.
Att: 45,000   Referee: Grandain (Belgium)

May 14 v Czechoslovakia (Bratislava) 0-4
Leslie; Shearer, Caldow*, Crerand, McNeill, Baxter, McLeod, McMillan, Herd, Brand, Wilson.
Att: 50,000   Referee: Steiner (Austria)

Sep 26 v Czechoslovakia (Hampden) 3-2
St John, Law 2
Brown; McKay, Caldow*, Crerand, McNeill, Baxter, Scott, White, St John, Law, Wilson.
Att: 51,590   Referee: Gulliksen (Norway)

Oct 7 v N Ireland (Belfast) 6-1
Wilson, Scott 3, Brand 2
Brown; McKay, Caldow*, Crerand, McNeill, Baxter, Scott, White, St John, Brand, Wilson.
Att: 41,000   Referee: Finney (England)

Nov 8 v Wales (Hampden) 2-0
St John 2
Brown; Hamilton, Caldow*, Crerand, Ure, Baxter, Scott, White, St John, Brand, Wilson.
Att: 74,329   Referee: Holland (England)

Nov 29 v Czechoslovakia (Brussels) 2-4 (aet)
St John 2
Connachan; Hamilton, Caldow*, Crerand, Ure, Baxter, Brand, White, St John, Law, Robertson.
Att: 7,000   Referee: Versyp (Belgium)

1962

Apr 14 v England (Hampden) 2-0
Wilson, Caldow
Brown; Hamilton, Caldow*, Crerand, McNeill, Baxter, Scott, White, St John, Law, Wilson.
Att: 132,441   Referee: Horn (Netherlands)

May 2 v Uruguay (Hampden) 2-3
Baxter, Brand
Connachan (Ritchie); Hamilton, Caldow*, Crerand, (McKay), McNeill, Baxter, Scott, Quinn, St John, Brand, Wilson.
Att: 67,181   Referee: Holland (England)

Oct 20 v Wales (Cardiff) 3-2
Caldow, Law, Henderson
Brown; Hamilton, Caldow*, Crerand, Ure, Baxter, Henderson, White, St John, Law, Wilson.
Att: 50,000   Referee: Dagnall (England)

Nov 7 v N Ireland (Hampden) 5-1
Law 4, Henderson
Brown; Hamilton, Caldow*, Crerand, Ure, Baxter, Henderson, White, St John, Law, Mulhall.
Att: 58,734   Referee: Finney (England)

1963

Apr 6 v England (Wembley) 2-1
Baxter 2
Brown; Hamilton, Caldow*, Mackay, Ure, Baxter, Henderson, White, St John, Law, Wilson.
Att: 98,606   Referee: Horn (Netherlands)

May 8 v Austria (Hampden) 4-1
Wilson 2, Law 2, (Abandoned after 79 min)
Brown; Hamilton, Holt, Mackay*, Ure, Baxter, Henderson, Gibson, Millar, Law, Wilson.
Att: 94,596   Referee: Finney (England)

Jun 4 v Norway (Bergen) 3-4
Law 3
Blacklaw; Hamilton, Holt, Mackay* (McLintock), Ure, Baxter, Henderson, Gibson, St John, Law, Wilson.
Att: 23,000   Referee: Oskarsson (Iceland)

Jun 9 v Rep of Ireland (Dublin) 0-1
Lawrence; Hamilton, Holt, McLintock, McNeill, Baxter, Henderson, Gibson, Millar (St John), Law*, Wilson.
Att: 30,000   Referee: Howley (England)

Jun 13 v Spain (Madrid) 6-2
St John, Wilson, Law, Henderson, Gibson, McLintock
Blacklaw; McNeill, Holt, McLintock, Ure, Baxter, Henderson, Gibson, St John, Law*, Wilson.
Att: 40,000   Referee: Campanati (Italy)

Oct 12 v N Ireland (Belfast) 1-2
St John
Brown; Hamilton, Provan, Crerand, Ure, Mackay*, Henderson, White, St John, Gibson, Mulhall.
Att: 45,000   Referee: Taylor (England)

Nov 7 v Norway (Hampden) 6-1
Law 4, Mackay 2
Brown; Hamilton, Provan, Mackay*, Ure, Baxter (Gabriel), Scott, White, Gilzean, Law, Henderson.
Att: 35,416   Referee: Howley (England)

Nov 20 v Wales (Hampden) 2-1
White, Law
Brown; Hamilton, Kennedy, Mackay*, McNeill, Baxter, Henderson, White, Gilzean, Law, Scott.
Att: 56,067   Referee: Clements (England)

1964

Apr 11 v England (Hampden) 1-0
Gilzean
Forsyth; Hamilton, Kennedy, Greig, McNeill*, Baxter, Henderson, White, Gilzean, Law, Wilson
Att: 133,245   Referee: Horn (Netherlands)

May 12 v W Germany (Hanover) 2-2
Gilzean 2
Cruickshank; Hamilton (Holt), Kennedy, Greig, McNeill*, Baxter, Henderson, White, Gilzean, Law, Wilson.
Att: 75,000   Referee: Poulsen (Denmark)

Oct 3 v Wales (Cardiff) 2-3
Chalmers, Gibson
Forsyth; Hamilton, Kennedy, Greig, Yeats, Baxter, Johnstone, Gibson, Chalmers, Law*, Robertson.
Att: 50,000   Referee: Howley (England)

Oct 21 v Finland (Hampden) 3-1
Law, Chalmers, Gibson
Forsyth; Hamilton, Kennedy, Greig, McGrory, Baxter, Johnstone, Gibson, Chalmers, Law*, Scott
Att: 54,442   Referee: Hannet (Belgium)

Nov 25 v N Ireland (Hampden) 3-2
Wilson 2, Gilzean
Forsyth; Hamilton, Kennedy, Greig, McGrory, McLintock, Wallace, Law, Gilzean, Baxter*, Wilson
Att: 48,752   Referee: Powell (Wales)

1965

Apr 10 v England (Wembley) 2-2
Law, St John
Brown; Hamilton, McCreadie, Crerand, McNeill*, Greig, Henderson, Collins, St John, Law, Wilson.
Att: 98,199   Referee: Zsolt (Hungary)

May 8 v Spain (Hampden) 0-0
Brown; Hamilton, McCreadie, Bremner, McNeill*, Greig, Henderson, Collins, Law, Gilzean, Hughes.
Att: 60,146   Referee: Howley (England)

May 23 v Poland (Chorzow) 1-1
Law
Brown; Hamilton, McCreadie, Greig, McNeill*, Crerand, Henderson, Collins, Martin, Law, Hughes.
Att: 95,000   Referee: Alimov (USSR)

May 27 v Finland (Helsinki) 2-1
Wilson, Greig
Brown; Hamilton, McCreadie, Crerand, McNeill*, Greig, Henderson, Law, Martin, Hamilton, Wilson.
Att: 20,162   Referee: Vetter (E Germany)

Oct 2 v N Ireland (Belfast) 2-3
Gilzean 2
Brown; Hamilton, McCreadie, Mackay, McNeill*, Greig, Henderson, Law, Gilzean, Baxter, Hughes.
Att: 50,000   Referee: Taylor (England)

Oct 13 v Poland (Hampden) 1-2
McNeill
Brown; Hamilton, McCreadie, Crerand, McNeill*, Greig, Henderson, Bremner, Gilzean, Law, Johnston.
Att: 107,580   Referee: Carlsson (Sweden)

Nov 9 v Italy (Hampden) 1-0
Greig
Brown; Greig, Provan, Murdoch, McKinnon, Baxter*, Henderson, Bremner, Gilzean, Martin, Hughes.
Att: 100,393   Referee: Kreitlein (W Germany)

Nov 24 v Wales (Hampden) 4-1
Murdoch 2, Henderson, Greig
Ferguson; Greig, McCreadie, Murdoch, McKinnon, Baxter*, Henderson, Cooke, Forrest, Gilzean, Johnston.
Att: 60,000   Referee: Finney (England)

Dec 7 v Italy (Naples) 0-3
Blacklaw; Provan, McCreadie, Murdoch, McKinnon, Greig*, Forrest, Bremner, Yeats, Cooke, Hughes.
Att: 79,000   Referee: Zsolt (Hungary)

1966

Apr 2 v England (Hampden) 3-4
Law, Johnston 2
Ferguson; Greig*, Gemmell, Murdoch, McKinnon, Baxter, Johnstone, Law, Wallace, Bremner, Johnston.
Att: 134,000   Referee: Faucheux (France)

May 11 v Netherlands (Hampden) 0-3
Ferguson; Greig*, Provan, Stanton, McKinnon, Smith, Henderson, Penman, Scott, Wallace, Johnston.
Att: 16,513   Referee: Dagnall (England)

Jun 18 v Portugal (Hampden) 0-1
Ferguson; Bell, McCreadie, Greig*, McGrory, Bremner, Scott, Cooke, Young (Chalmers), Baxter, Sinclair.
Att: 24,000   Referee: McCabe (England)

Jun 25 v Brazil (Hampden) 1-1
Chalmers
Ferguson; Greig*, Bell, Bremner, McKinnon, Clark, Scott, Cooke, Chalmers, Baxter, Cormack.
Att: 74,933   Referee: Finney (England)

Oct 22 v Wales (Cardiff) 1-1
Law
Ferguson; Greig*, Gemmell, Bremner, McKinnon, Clark, Johnstone, Law, McBride, Baxter, Henderson.
Att: 32,500   Referee: Dagnall (England)

Nov 16 v N Ireland (Hampden) 2-1
Murdoch, Lennox
Ferguson; Greig*, Gemmell, Bremner, McKinnon, Clark, Henderson, Murdoch, McBride, Chalmers, Lennox.
Att: 45,281   Referee: Taylor (England)

1967

Apr 15 v England (Wembley) 3-2
Law, Lennox, McCalliog
Simpson; Gemmell, McCreadie, Greig*, McKinnon, Bremner, McCalliog, Law, Wallace, Baxter, Lennox.
Att: 99,063   Referee: Schulenburg (W Germany)

May 10 v USSR (Hampden) 0-2
Simpson; Gemmell, McCreadie, Clark, McNeill, Baxter*, Johnstone, McLintock, McCalliog, Law (Wallace), Lennox.
Att: 53,497   Referee: Van Ravens (Netherlands)

Oct 21 v N Ireland (Belfast) 0-1
Simpson; Gemmell, McCreadie, Greig*, McKinnon, Ure, Wallace, Murdoch, McCalliog, Law, Morgan
Att: 55,000   Referee: Finney (England)

Nov 22 v Wales (Hampden) 3-2
Gilzean 2, McKinnon
Clark; Craig, McCreadie, Greig*, McKinnon, Baxter, Johnstone, Bremner, Gilzean, Johnston, Lennox.
Att: 57,472   Referee: Finney (England)

1968
Feb 24 v England (Hampden) 1-1
Hughes
Simpson; Gemmell, McCreadie, McNeill, McKinnon, Greig*, Cooke, Bremner, Hughes, Johnston, Lennox.
Att: 134,000 Referee: Van Ravens (Netherlands)

May 30 v Netherlands (Amsterdam) 0-0
Clark; Fraser, McCreadie, Moncur, McKinnon, D.Smith, Henderson, Hope (J.Smith), McLean, Greig*, Cooke.
Att: 20,000   Referee: Riegg (W Germany)

Oct 16 v Denmark (Copenhagen) 1-0
Lennox
Herriot; Gemmell, McCreadie, Bremner*, McKinnon, Greig, McLean, McCalliog (Cormack), Stein, Hope, Lennox.
Att: 12,000   Referee: Carlsson (Sweden)

Nov 6 v Austria (Hampden) 2-1
Law, Bremner
Simpson; Gemmell, McCreadie, Bremner*, McKinnon, Greig, Johnstone, Cooke, Hughes, Law (Gilzean), Lennox.
Att: 80,856   Referee: Loow (Sweden)

Dec 11 v Cyprus (Nicosia) 5-0
Gilzean 2, Stein 2, Murdoch
Herriot; Fraser, McCreadie, Bremner*, McKinnon (McNeill), Greig, McLean, Murdoch, Stein, Gilzean, Cooke (Lennox).
Att: 10,000   Referee: Bonnet (Malta)

1969
April 16 v W Germany (Hampden) 1-1
Murdoch
Lawrence; Gemmell, McCreadie, Murdoch, McKinnon, Greig, Johnstone, Bremner*, Law, Gilzean, Lennox, (Cooke).
Att: 115,000   Referee: Gardeazabal (Spain)

May 3 v Wales (Wrexham) 5-3
McNeill, Stein, Gilzean, Bremner, McLean
Lawrence (Herriot); Gemmell, McCreadie, Bremner*, McNeill, Greig, McLean, Murdoch, Stein, Gilzean, Cooke.
Att: 18,765   Referee: Finney (England)

May 6 v N Ireland (Hampden) 1-1
Stein
Herriot; McCreadie, Gemmell, Bremner*, Greig, Stanton, Henderson, Murdoch, Stein, Law, Cooke (Johnston).
Att: 7,483   Referee: Smith (England)

May 10 v England (Wembley) 1-4
Stein
Herriot; McCreadie, Gemmell, Murdoch, McNeill, Greig, Henderson, Bremner*, Stein, Gilzean (Wallace), Gray.
Att: 89,902   Referee: Helies (France)

May 17 v Cyprus (Hampden) 8-0
Gray, McNeill, Stein 4, Henderson, Gemmell
Herriot; McCreadie, Gemmell, Bremner*, McNeill, Greig, Henderson, Cooke, Stein, Gilzean, Gray.
Att: 39,095   Referee: Coates (Eire)

Sep 21 v Rep of Ireland (Dublin) 1-1
Stein
McGarr (Herriot); Greig, Gemmell (Callaghan), Stanton, McKinnon, Moncur, Henderson, Bremner*, Stein, Cormack, Hughes.
Att: 30,000   Referee: Burtenshaw (England)

Oct 22 v W Germany (Hamburg) 2-3
Johnstone, Gilzean
Herriot; Greig, Gemmell, Bremner*, McKinnon, McNeill, Johnstone, Cormack, Gilzean, Gray, Stein.
Att: 72,000   Referee: Droz (Switzerland)

Nov 5 v Austria (Vienna) 0-2
McGarr; Greig, Burns, Murdoch, McKinnon, Stanton, Cooke (Stein), Bremner*, Gilzean, Curran, (Lorimer), Gray.
Att: 11,000   Referee: Karlo (USSR)

1970
Apr 18 v N Ireland (Belfast) 1-0
O'Hare
Clark; Hay, Dickson, McLintock*, McKinnon, Moncur, McLean, Carr, O'Hare, Gilzean (Stein), Johnston.
Att: 31,000   Referee: Jennings (England)

Apr 22 v Wales (Hampden) 0-0
Cruickshank; Callaghan, Dickson, Greig*, McKinnon, Moncur, McLean (Lennox), Hay, O'Hare, Stein, Carr.
Att: 30,434   Referee: Smith (England)

Apr 25 v England (Hampden) 0-0
Cruickshank; Gemmell, Dickson, Greig*, McKinnon, Moncur (Gilzean), Johnstone, Hay, Stein, O'Hare, Carr.
Att: 137,438   Referee: Horstmann (W Germany)

Nov 11 v Denmark (Hampden) 1-0
O'Hare
Cruickshank; Hay (Jardine), Greig, Stanton, McKinnon, Moncur*, Johnstone, Carr, Stein, O'Hare (Cormack), Johnston.
Att: 24,618   Referee: Linemayr (Austria)

1971
Feb 3 v Belgium (Liege) 0-3
Cruickshank; Hay, Gemmell, Stanton (Green), McKinnon, Moncur*, Gemmill, Greig, Stein (Forrest), O'Hare, Cooke.
Att: 25,000   Referee: Sbardella (Italy)

Apr 21 v Portugal (Lisbon) 0-2
Clark; Hay, Brogan, Stanton (Green), McKinnon, Moncur*, Henderson, McCalliog (Jarvie), Robb, Cormack, Gilzean.
Att: 30,000   Referee: Kitabdjian (France)

May 15 v Wales (Cardiff) 0-0
Clark; Hay, Brogan, Bremner (Greig), McLintock, Moncur*, Lorimer, Robb, O'Hare, Cormack, Gray.
Att: 19,068   Referee: Taylor (England)

May 18 v N Ireland (Hampden) 0-1
Clark; Hay, Brogan, Greig, McLintock (Munro), Moncur*, Lorimer, Green, O'Hare (Jarvie), Curran, Gray.
Att: 31,643   Referee: Thomas (Wales)

May 22 v England (Wembley) 1-3
Curran
Clark; Greig, Brogan, Bremner, McLintock, Moncur*, Johnstone, Robb, Curran (Munro), Green (Jarvie), Cormack.
Att: 91,469   Referee: Dorpmans (Netherlands)

Jun 9 v Denmark (Copenhagen) 0-1
Clark; Munro, Dickson, Stanton, McKinnon, Moncur*, McLean, Forsyth (Robb), Stein, Curran, Forrest (Scott).
Att: 38,000   Referee: Riedel (E Germany)

Jun 14 v USSR (Moscow) 0-1
Clark; Brownlie, Dickson, Munro, McKinnon, Stanton*, Forrest, Watson, Stein (Curran), Robb, Scott.
Att: 20,000   Referee: Marschall (Austria)

Oct 13 v Portugal (Hampden) 2-1
O'Hare, Gemmill
Wilson; Jardine, Colquhoun (Buchan), Stanton, Hay, Bremner*, Cropley, Graham, Johnstone, O'Hare, Gemmill.
Att: 58,612   Referee: Piotrowicz (Poland)

Nov 10 v Belgium (Aberdeen) 1-0
O'Hare
Clark; Jardine, Hay, Bremner*, Buchan, Stanton, Johnstone (Hansen), Murray, O'Hare, Gray, Cropley (Dalglish).
Att: 36,500   Referee: Bostrom (Sweden)

Dec 1 v Netherlands (Amsterdam) 1-2
Graham
Wilson; Jardine, Hay, Bremner*, Colquhoun, Stanton, Johnstone (O'Hare), Gemmill, Dalglish, Graham, Gray (Cormack).
Att: 18,000   Referee: Biwersi (W Germany)

1972
Apr 26 v Peru (Hampden) 2-0
O'Hare, Law
Hunter; Brownlie, Donachie, Carr, Colquhoun, Moncur, Morgan, Hartford, O'Hare, Law*, Gemmill
Att: 21,001   Referee: Partridge (England)

May 20 v N Ireland (Hampden) 2-0
Law, Lorimer
Clark; Brownlie, Donachie, Bremner*, McNeill, Moncur, Johnstone (Lorimer), Gemmill, O'Hare, Law, Graham.
Att: 39,710   Referee: Thomas (Wales)

May 24 v Wales (Hampden) 1-0
Lorimer
Clark; Stanton, Buchan, Bremner*, McNeill, Moncur, Lorimer, Green, O'Hare (Macari), Law, Gemmill (Hartford).
Att: 21,332   Referee: Lawther (N Ireland)

May 27 v England (Hampden) 0-1
Clarke; Brownlie, Donachie (Green), Bremner*, McNeill, Moncur, Gemmill (Johnstone), Hartford, Lorimer, Macari, Law.
Att: 119,325   Referee: Gonella (Italy)

Jun 29 v Yugoslavia (Belo Horizonte) 2-2
Macari 2
Hunter; A.Forsyth (Hansen), Buchan, Colquhoun, Donachie, Bremner*, Hartford, Graham, Morgan, Law (Bone), Macari.
Att: 4,000   Referee: Coerezza (Argentina)

Jul 2 v Czechoslovakia (Porto Alegre) 0-0
Clark; A.Forsyth, Colquhoun, Buchan, Donachie, Bremner*, Graham, Law (Stein), Hartford, Morgan, Macari.
Att: 15,000   Referee: Marques (Brazil)

Jul 5 v Brazil (Rio de Janeiro) 0-1
Clark; A.Forsyth, Colquhoun, Buchan, Donachie, Bremner*, Graham, Hartford, Morgan, Law, Macari
Att: 130,000   Referee: Klein (Israel)

Oct 18 v Denmark (Copenhagen) 4-1
Macari, Bone, Harper, Morgan
Clark; Brownlie, A.Forsyth, Bremner*, Colquhoun, Buchan, Lorimer, Macari (Dalglish), Bone (Harper), Graham, Morgan.
Att: 31,000   Referee: Bahramov (USSR)

Nov 15 v Denmark (Hampden) 2-0
Dalglish, Lorimer
Harvey; Brownlie, Donachie, Bremner*, Colquhoun, Buchan, Lorimer, Dalglish (Carr), Harper, Graham, Morgan.
Att: 47,109   Referee: Corver (Netherlands)

SFA CENTENARY MATCH

1973
Feb 14 v England (Hampden) 0-5
Clark; A.Forsyth, Donachie, Bremner*, Colquhoun, Buchan, Lorimer, Dalglish, Macari, Graham, Morgan (Stein).
Att: 48,470   Referee: Wurtz (France)

May 12 v Wales (Wrexham) 2-0
Graham 2
McCloy; McGrain, Donachie, Graham, Holton, D.Johnstone, Dalglish (Macari), Stanton*, Parlane (Stein), Hay, Morgan.
Att: 18,682   Referee: Lawther (N Ireland)

May 16 v N Ireland (Hampden) 1-2
Dalglish
McCloy; McGrain, Donachie, Graham (Macari), Holton, D.Johnstone, Dalglish, Stanton* (Bremner), Stein, Hay, Morgan.
Att: 39,018   Referee: Burns (England)

May 19 v England (Wembley) 0-1
Hunter; Jardine, McGrain, Bremner*, Holton,
D.Johnstone, Morgan, Macari (Jordan), Dalglish,
Hay, Lorimer (Stein).
Att: 95,950   Referee: Tschenscher (W Germany)

Jun 22 v Switzerland (Berne) 0-1
McCloy; Jardine, McGrain, Bremner*, Holton,
D.Johnstone, Dalglish, Hay, Parlane, Connolly
(Jordan), Morgan.
Att: 10,000   Referee: Verbeke (France)

Jun 30 v Brazil (Hampden) 0-1
McCloy; Jardine, McGrain, Bremner*, Holton,
D.Johnstone, Morgan, Hay, Parlane, Jordan,
Dalglish (Graham).
Att: 70,000   Referee: Burns (England)

Sep 26 v Czechoslovakia (Hampden) 2-1
Holton, Jordan
Hunter; Jardine, McGrain, Bremner*, Holton,
Connelly, Hay, Law, Morgan, Dalglish (Jordan),
Hutchison.
Att: 100,000   Referee: Oberg (Norway)

Oct 17 v Czechoslovakia (Bratislava) 0-1
Harvey; Jardine, McGrain, T.Forsyth, Blackley,
Hay*, Morgan, Jordan, Law (Ford), Dalglish,
Hutchison.
Att: 15,000   Referee: Biwersi (W Germany)

Nov 14 v W Germany (Hampden) 1-1
Holton
Harvey; Jardine, McGrain, Bremner*, Holton,
Connelly, Morgan, Smith (Lorimer), Law (Jordan),
Dalglish, Hutchison.
Att: 58,235   Referee: Taylor (England)

1974
Mar 27 v W Germany (Frankfurt) 1-2
Dalglish
Allan; Jardine, Schaedler, Hay*, Buchan, Stanton,
Morgan, Dalglish, Law (Ford), Hutchison, Burns
(Robinson).
Att: 62,000   Referee: Schiller (Austria)

May 11 v N Ireland (Hampden) 0-1
Harvey; Jardine, Donachie (Smith), Bremner*,
Holton, Buchan, Morgan, Hay, Law (Jordan),
Dalglish, Hutchison.
Att: 53,775   Referee: Jones (Wales)

May 14 v Wales (Hampden) 2-0
Dalglish, Jardine
Harvey; Jardine, Hay, Bremner*, Holton, Buchan
(McGrain), J.Johnstone, Dalglish, Ford, Jordan,
Hutchison (Smith).
Att: 41,969   Referee: Wright (N.Ireland)

May 18 v England (Hampden) 2-0
Jordan, Todd (og)
Harvey; Jardine, McGrain, Bremner*, Holton,
Blackley, Lorimer, J.Johnstone, Jordan, Dalglish,
Hay.
Att: 94,487 Referee: Van Der Kroft(Netherlands)

Jun 1 v Belgium (Bruges) 1-2
Johnstone
Harvey; Jardine, McGrain, Bremner*, McQueen,
Blackley, J.Johnstone (Morgan), Dalglish
(Hutchison), Jordan, Hay, Lorimer.
Att: 12,000   Referee: Ohmsen (W Germany)

Jun 6 v Norway (Oslo) 2-1
Jordan, Dalglish
Allan; Jardine, McGrain, Bremner*, Holton, Buchan,
J.Johnstone (Dalglish), Lorimer, Jordan, Hay,
Hutchison.
Att: 18,432   Referee: Axelsson (Sweden)

WORLD CUP FINALS

Jun 14 v Zaire (Dortmund) 2-0
Lorimer, Jordan
Harvey; Jardine, McGrain, Bremner*, Holton,
Blackley, Dalglish (Hutchison), Hay, Lorimer,
Jordan, Law.
Att: 30,000   Referee: Schulenburg (W Germany)

Jun 18 v Brazil (Frankfurt) 0-0
Harvey; Jardine, McGrain, Holton, Buchan,
Bremner*, Hay, Dalglish, Morgan, Jordan, Lorimer.
Att: 62,000   Referee: Van Gemert (Netherlands)

Jun 22 v Yugoslavia (Frankfurt) 1-1
Jordan
Harvey; Jardine, McGrain, Holton, Buchan,
Bremner*, Dalglish (Hutchison), Hay, Morgan,
Jordan, Lorimer.
Att: 56,000   Referee: Archundia (Mexico)

Oct 30 v E Germany (Hampden 3-0
Hutchison (pen), Burns, Dalglish
Harvey; Jardine*, A.Forsyth, Souness, Holton
(Burns), Buchan, J.Johnstone, Dalglish (D.Johnstone),
Deans, Jordan, Hutchison.
Att: 39,445   Referee: Taylor (England)

Nov 20 v Spain (Hampden) 1-2
Bremner
Harvey; Jardine, A.Forsyth, McQueen, Burns,
Bremner*, Souness, Hutchison (Dalglish), J.Johnstone,
Deans (Lorimer), Jordan.
Att: 92,100   Referee: Linemayr (Austria)

1975
Feb 5 v Spain (Valencia) 1-1
Jordan
Harvey; Jardine, McQueen, Buchan, McGrain,
Bremner*, Cooke, Hutchison, Dalglish, Jordan
(Parlane), Burns (Wilson).
Att: 60,000   Referee: Delcourt (Belgium)

Apr 16 v Sweden (Gothenburg) 1-1
MacDougall
Kennedy; Jardine*, McGrain, Munro, Jackson,
Robinson, Dalglish, Souness (D.Johnstone), Parlane,
MacDougall, Macari (Hughes).
Att: 15,574   Referee: Thima (Norway)

May 13 v Portugal (Hampden) 1-0
Artur (og)
Kennedy; Jardine*, McGrain, Buchan (Jackson),
McQueen, Rioch, Cooke (Macari), Dalglish, Parlane,
MacDougall, Hutchison (Duncan).
Att: 34,307   Referee: Mathewson (England)

May 17 v Wales (Cardiff) 2-2
Jackson, Rioch
Kennedy; Jardine*, McGrain, Jackson (Munro),
McQueen, Rioch, Macari, Dalglish, Parlane,
MacDougall, Duncan.
Att: 23,509   Referee: Wright (N Ireland)

May 20 v N Ireland (Hampden) 3-0
MacDougall, Dalglish, Parlane
Kennedy; Jardine* (A.Forsyth), McGrain, Munro,
McQueen, Rioch, Dalglish, Robinson (Conn),
Parlane, MacDougall, Duncan.
Att: 64,696   Referee: Partridge (England)

May 24 v England (Wembley) 1-5
Rioch (pen)
Kennedy; Jardine*, McGrain, Munro, McQueen,
Rioch, Dalglish, Conn, Parlane, MacDougall
(Macari), Duncan (Hutchison).
Att: 98,241   Referee: Gloeckner (E Germany)

Jun 1 v Romania (Bucharest) 1-1
McQueen
Brown; McGrain, Forsyth, Munro, McQueen*,
Rioch (Hutchison), Dalglish, Miller, Parlane,
Macari (Robinson), Duncan.
Att: 80,000   Referee: Gilek (Turkey)

Sep 3 v Denmark (Copenhagen) 1-0
Harper
Harvey; McGrain, A.Forsyth, Bremner*, McQueen,
Buchan, Lorimer, Dalglish, Harper, Rioch, Hutchison
(Duncan).
Att: 40,300   Referee: Nyhus (Norway)

Oct 29 v Denmark (Hampden) 3-1
Dalglish, Rioch, MacDougall
Harvey; McGrain, Houston, Greig*, Jackson, Rioch,
Lorimer, Dalglish, MacDougall (Parlane), Hartford,
Gemmill.
Att: 48,021   Referee: Nyhus (Norway)

Dec 17 v Romania (Hampden) 1-1
Rioch
Cruickshank; Brownlie, Donachie, Buchan*, Jackson,
Rioch, Doyle (Lorimer), Hartford, A.Gray, Dalglish
(MacDougall), Gemmill.
Att: 11,375   Referee: Prokop (E Germany)

1976
Apr 7 v Switzerland (Hampden) 1-0
Pettigrew
Rough; McGrain, F.Gray, T.Forsyth*, Blackley,
Craig, Dalglish (D.Bremner), Pettigrew (McKean),
A.Gray, MacDonald, D.Johnstone.
Att: 15,531   Referee: Partridge (England)

May 6 v Wales (Hampden) 3-1
Pettigrew, Rioch, Gray
Rough; McGrain, Donachie, T.Forsyth, Jackson,
Rioch, Pettigrew, Masson, Jordan, Gemmill*, E.Gray.
Att: 25,000   Referee: Wright (N.Ireland)

May 8 v N Ireland (Hampden) 3-0
Gemmill, Masson, Dalglish
Rough; McGrain, Donachie, T.Forsyth, Jackson,
Rioch (Hartford), Masson, Gemmill*, Pettigrew
(D.Johnstone), Jordan, Dalglish.
Att: 49,897   Referee: Reynolds (Wales)

May 15 v England (Hampden) 2-1
Masson, Dalglish
Rough; McGrain, Donachie, T.Forsyth, Jackson,
Rioch, Masson, Gemmill*, Dalglish, Jordan, E.Gray
(D.Johnstone).
Att: 85,165   Referee: Palotai (Hungary)

Sep 8 v Finland (Hampden) 6-0
Rioch, Masson (pen), Dalglish, A.Gray 2, E.Gray
Rough (Harvey); McGrain, Donachie, Rioch,
T.Forsyth, Buchan, Dalglish, Gemmill*, A.Gray,
Masson, E.Gray.
Att: 16,338   Referee: Kew (England)

Oct 13 v Czechoslovakia (Prague) 0-2
Rough; McGrain, Donachie, Buchan, McQueen,
Rioch, Dalglish (Burns), Masson (Hartford), Jordan,
A.Gray, Gemmill*.
Att: 38,000   Referee: Michelotti (Italy)

Nov 17 v Wales (Hampden) 1-0
Evans (og)
Rough; McGrain, Donachie, Blackley, McQueen,
Rioch (Hartford), Burns, Dalglish, Jordan, Gemmill*,
E.Gray (Pettigrew).
Att: 63,233   Referee: Biwersi (W.Germany)

1977
Apr 27 v Sweden (Hampden) 3-1
Hartford, Dalglish, Craig
Rough; McGrain, T.Forsyth, Blackley (Narey),
Donachie, Glavin (Jardine), Dalglish*, Hartford,
Burns (J.Craig), Pettigrew, Johnston.
Att: 22,659   Referee: Taylor (England)

May 28 v Wales (Wrexham) 0-0
Rough; McGrain, Donachie, Rioch* (Johnston),
McQueen, T.Forsyth, Masson, Gemmill, Parlane
(Burns), Dalglish, Hartford.
Att: 14,468   Referee: Moffott (N Ireland)

Jun 1 v N Ireland (Hampden) 3-0
Dalglish 2, McQueen
Rough; McGrain, Donachie, T.Forsyth, McQueen,
Rioch*, Masson, Hartford, Jordan (Macari), Dalglish,
Johnson (Gemmill).
Att: 44,699   Referee: Gow (Wales)

Jun 4 v England (Wembley) 2-1
McQueen, Dalglish
Rough; McGrain, Donachie, T.Forsyth, McQueen,
Rioch*, Masson (Gemmill), Dalglish, Jordan (Macari),
Hartford, Johnston.
Att: 98,103   Referee: Palotai (Hungary)

Jun 15 v Chile (Santiago) 4-2
Dalglish, Macari 2, Hartford
Rough (Stewart); McGrain, Donachie, Buchan,
T.Forsyth, Rioch* (Gemmill), Masson, Dalglish,
Macari, Hartford (Jardine), Johnston.
Att: 17,000   Referee: Silvagno (Chile)

Jun 18 v Argentina (Buenos Aires) 1-1
Masson (pen)
Rough; McGrain, Donachie, Gemmill, T.Forsyth,
Buchan*, Masson, Dalglish, Macari, Hartford,
Johnston.
Att: 60,000   Referee: Arpi (Brazil)

Joe Jordan towers above the Welsh defence at Anfield in the vital World Cup qualifying clash of October 1977.

Jun 23 v Brazil (Rio de Janeiro) 0-2
Rough; McGrain, Donachie, Rioch*, T.Forsyth,
Buchan, Masson, Gemmill, Dalglish, Hartford,
Johnston (Jardine).
Att: 61,000 Referee: Saltaro (Brazil)

Sep 7 v E Germany (East Berlin) 0-1
Stewart; McGrain, Donachie, Masson*, McQueen,
Buchan, Dalglish, Hartford (Gemmill), Jordan,
Macari, Johnston (Graham).
Att: 50,000 Referee: Horbas (Czechoslovakia)

Sep 21 v Czechoslovakia (Hampden) 3-1
Jordan, Hartford, Dalglish
Rough; Jardine, McGrain, T.Forsyth, McQueen,
Rioch*, Dalglish, Masson, Jordan, Hartford, Johnston.
Att: 85,000 Referee: Rion (Belgium)

Oct 12 v Wales (Liverpool) 2-0
Masson (pen), Dalglish
Rough; Jardine (Buchan), Donachie, Masson*,
McQueen, Forsyth, Dalglish, Hartford, Jordan,
Macari, Johnston.
Att: 50,800 Referee: Wurtz (France)

1978
Feb 22 v Bulgaria (Hampden) 2-1
Gemmill (pen), Wallace
Blyth; Kennedy, Donachie, Souness, McQueen,
Miller, Dalglish (Wallace), Hartford, Jordan
(D.Johnstone), Macari, Gemmill*.
Att: 65,000 Referee: Partridge (England)

May 13 v N Ireland (Hampden) 1-1
Johnstone
Rough; Jardine, Buchan (Burns), T.Forsyth,
McQueen, Rioch*, Masson, Gemmill, Jordan
(Dalglish), D.Johnstone, Robertson.
Att: 64,433 Referee: Gow (Wales)

May 17 v Wales (Hampden) 1-1
Johnstone
Blyth; Kennedy, Donachie, Burns, McQueen
(T.Forsyth), Gemmill*, Souness, Hartford,
D.Johnstone, Dalglish, Johnston (Robertson).
Att: 70,241 Referee: Wright (N Ireland)

May 20 v England (Hampden) 0-1
Rough; Kennedy, Burns, T.Forsyth, Donachie,
Rioch* (Souness), Masson (Gemmill), Hartford,
Dalglish, Jordan, Johnston.
Att: 88,319 Referee: Konrath (France)

WORLD CUP FINALS

Jun 3 v Peru (Cordoba) 1-3
Jordan
Rough; Burns, Kennedy, Forsyth, Buchan, Rioch*
(Macari), Masson (Gemmill), Hartford, Dalglish,
Jordan, Johnston.
Att: 47,000 Referee: Eriksson (Sweden)

Jun 7 v Iran (Cordoba) 1-1
Eskandarian (og)
Rough; Buchan (T.Forsyth), Jardine, Burns,
Donachie, Macari, Gemmill*, Hartford, Jordan,
Dalglish (Harper), Robertson.
Att: 10,000 Referee: Midiaye (Senegal)

Jun 11 v Netherlands (Mendoza) 3-2
Dalglish, Gemmill 2 (1 pen)
Rough; Donachie, Buchan, Kennedy, T.Forsyth,
Rioch*, Hartford, Gemmill, Souness, Dalglish, Jordan.
Att: 50,000 Referee: Linemayr (Austria)

Sep 20 v Austria (Vienna) 2-3
McQueen, Gray
Rough; Kennedy, Donachie, Gemmill*, McQueen,
Buchan, Dalglish, Hartford, Jordan (Graham),
A.Gray, Souness.
Att: 71,500 Referee: Michelotti (Italy)

Oct 25 v Norway (Hampden) 3-2
Dalglish 2, Gemmill (pen)
Stewart; Donachie, F.Gray, Souness, McQueen,
Buchan, Dalglish, Gemmill*, A.Gray, Hartford,
Graham.
Att: 65,372 Referee: Vojtech (Czechoslovakia)

Nov 29 v Portugal (Lisbon) 0-1
Rough; Kennedy, F.Gray (Donachie), Narey,
McQueen, Buchan, Dalglish, Hartford, Jordan
(Wallace), Gemmill*, Robertson.
Att: 70,000 Referee: Dolflinger (Switzerland)

1979
May 19 v Wales (Cardiff) 0-3
Rough; Burley, F.Gray, Wark, Hegarty, Hansen,
Dalglish*, Hartford, Wallace (Jordan), Souness,
Graham.
Att: 20,371 Referee: Partridge (England)

May 22 v N Ireland (Hampden) 1-0
Graham
Wood; Burley, F.Gray, Wark (Narey), McQueen,
Souness, Dalglish*, Hartford, Jordan, Hegarty,
Graham (McGarvey).
Att: 28,524 Referee: Thomas (Wales)

May 26 v England (Wembley) 1-3
Wark
Wood; Burley, F.Gray, Wark, McQueen, Hegarty,
Dalglish*, Souness, Jordan, Hartford, Graham.
Att: 100,000 Referee: Garrido (Portugal)

Jun 2 v Argentina (Hampden) 1-3
Graham
Rough (Wood); Burley, Munro, Narey Hegarty,
Hansen, McGarvey, Wark, Dalglish*, Hartford
(F.Gray), Graham.
Att: 61,918 Referee: Partridge (England)

Jun 7 v Norway (Oslo) 4-0
Jordan, Dalglish, Robertson, McQueen
Rough; Burley (Hegarty) (Wark), Munro, Burns,
McQueen, Gemmill*, Graham, Dalglish, Jordan,
Hartford, Robertson.
Att: 17,269 Referee: Nielsen (Denmark)

Sep 12 v Peru (Hampden) 1-1
Olaechea (og)
Rough; Jardine*, Munro, Souness, McQueen, Burns,
Cooper (Aitken), Wark (Graham), Dalglish,
Hartford, Robertson.
Att: 41,035 Referee: Courtney (England)

Oct 17 v Austria (Hampden) 1-1
Gemmill
Rough; Jardine, Munro, Souness, McQueen, Burns,
Wark, Gemmill*, Dalglish, Graham (Cooper),
Robertson.
Att: 72,700 Referee: Palotai (Hungary)

Nov 21 v Belgium (Brussels) 0-2
Rough; Jardine*, Munro (F.Gray), Wark, Hansen,
Miller, Dalglish, Souness, Jordan (Provan), Hartford,
Robertson.
Att: 15,000 Referee: Zade (Russia)

Dec 19 v Belgium (Hampden) 1-3
Robertson
Rough; Jardine*, McGrain, Wark, McQueen, Burns,
Dalglish, Aitken, D.Johnstone, Bannon (Provan),
Robertson.
Att: 25,389 Referee: Aldinger (W Germany)

1980
Mar 26 v Portugal (Hampden) 4-1
Dalglish, Gray, Archibald, Gemmill (pen)
Rough; Burley, McGrain, Narey, McLeish, Hansen,
Dalglish (Archibald), Souness, A.Gray, Gemmill*,
Robertson (Provan).
Att: 20,233 Referee: Wurtz (France)

May 16 v N Ireland (Belfast Windsor Park) 0-1
Thomson; Burley, McGrain, Narey, McLeish,
Souness (Jordan), Strachan, Archibald, Dalglish,
Gemmill*, Weir (Provan).
Att: 20,000 Referee: Thomas (Wales)

May 21 v Wales (Hampden) 1-0
Miller
Rough; McGrain, Munro, Hegarty, McLeish,
Miller, Strachan, Gemmill*, Dalglish, Jordan,
Weir (Aitken).
Att: 31,359 Referee: Wilson (N Ireland)

May 24 v England (Hampden) 0-2
Rough; McGrain, Munro (Burley), Hegarty,
McLeish, Miller, Strachan, Aitken (A.Gray),
Dalglish, Jordan, Gemmill*.
Att: 85,000 Referee: Da Silva Garrido (Portugal)

May 28 v Poland (Poznan) 0-1
Rough; Burley (Dawson), McGrain*, Narey, McLeish,
Miller, Strachan, Aitken, Dalglish (Weir), Archibald,
Jordan (Brazil).
Att: 20,000 Referee: Carev (Bulgaria)

May 31 v Hungary (Budapest) 1-3
Archibald
Rough; McGrain, Dawson, Narey, McLeish, Miller,
Brazil (Strachan), Archibald, Dalglish, Gemmill*,
Weir.
Att: 6,600 Referee: Baumann (Switzerland)

Sep 10 v Sweden (Stockholm) 1-0
Strachan
Rough; McGrain, F.Gray, Miller, McLeish, Hansen,
Dalglish (Archibald), Strachan, A.Gray, Gemmill*,
Robertson.
Att: 39,831 Referee: Wohrer (Austria)

Oct 15 v Portugal (Hampden) 0-0
Rough; McGrain, F.Gray, Souness, Hansen, Miller,
Strachan, Dalglish, A.Gray, Gemmill*, Robertson.
Att: 60,765 Referee: Van Redelfs (W Germany)

1981
Feb 25 v Israel (Tel Aviv) 1-0
Dalglish
Rough; McGrain, F.Gray, Souness, McLeish,
K.Burns, Wark (Miller), Dalglish (A.Gray),
Archibald, Gemmill*, Robertson.
Att: 35,000 Referee: Andreco (Romania)

Mar 25 v N Ireland (Hampden) 1-1
Wark
Rough (Thomson); McGrain, F.Gray, K.Burns
(Hartford), McLeish, Miller, Wark, Archibald,
A.Gray, Gemmill*, Robertson.
Att: 78,444 Referee: Scheurell (W Germany)

Apr 28 v Israel (Hampden) 3-1
Robertson 2 (2 pens), Provan
Rough; McGrain*, F.Gray, Hansen, McLeish,
Souness, Provan, Archibald, Jordan, Hartford,
Robertson.
Att: 61,489 Referee: Haroldsson (Iceland)

May 16 v Wales (Swansea) 0-2
Rough; Burns, Stewart, F.Gray (McGrain), McQueen,
Miller, Hartford*, Narey, Jordan, Provan, Graham
(Sturrock).
Att: 18,935 Referee: Donnelly (N Ireland)

May 19 v N Ireland (Hampden) 2-0
Stewart, Archibald
Thomson; McGrain*, F.Gray, Stewart, McLeish,
Miller, Hartford, Sturrock, Archibald, T.Burns,
Robertson.
Att: 22,448 Referee: Partridge (England)

May 23 v England (Wembley) 1-0
Robertson (pen)
Rough; Stewart, F.Gray, McGrain*, McLeish,
Miller, Provan (Sturrock), Archibald, Jordan,
Hartford (Narey), Robertson.
Att: 90,000 Referee: Wurtz (France)

Sep 9 v Sweden (Hampden) 2-0
Jordan, Robertson (pen)
Rough; McGrain*, McLeish, Hansen, F.Gray, Wark,
Provan, Hartford, Dalglish (A.Gray), Jordan,
Robertson.
Att: 81,511 Referee: Daina (Switzerland)

Oct 14 v N Ireland (Belfast) 0-0
Rough; Stewart, Hansen, Miller, F.Gray, Strachan
(A.Gray), Souness, Hartford*, Dalglish, Archibald,
Robertson.
Att: 35,000 Referee: Butenko (USSR)

Nov 18 v Portugal (Lisbon) 1-2
Sturrock
Thomson; Stewart, Hansen, Miller, F.Gray
(Kennedy), Provan, Souness, Strachan, Hartford*,
Archibald (Dalglish), Sturrock.
Att: 25,000 Referee: Corver (Netherlands)

1982

Feb 24 v Spain (Valencia) 0-3
Rough; McGrain*, F.Gray, Strachan (Archibald), McLeish, Hansen, Brazil, Wark, Dalglish, Hartford, Souness.
Att: 30,000   Referee: Thomas (Netherlands)

Mar 23 v Netherlands (Hampden) 2-1
F.Gray 1(pen), Dalglish
Rough; McGrain*, F.Gray, Narey, Evans, Miller, Dalglish (Brazil), Archibald (T.Burns), Jordan (Strachan), Bett, Wark.
Att: 71,000   Referee: Courtney (England)

Apr 28 v N Ireland (Belfast) 1-1
Wark
Wood; McGrain*, Albiston, Wark, McLeish (Hansen), Evans, Provan, Brazil, Dalglish, Hartford, Robertson (Sturrock).
Att: 20,000   Referee: Hunting (England)

May 24 v Wales (Hampden) 1-0
Hartford
Rough; Stewart (Burley), F.Gray, Souness*, Hansen, Narey, Dalglish, Brazil, Jordan (Sturrock), T.Burns, Hartford.
Att: 25,284   Referee: McKnight (N Ireland)

May 29 v England (Hampden) 0-1
Rough; Burley, McGrain*, Hansen, Evans, Narey, Dalglish, Souness, Jordan (Sturrock), Hartford (Robertson), Brazil.
Att: 80,000   Referee: Van Redelfs (W Germany)

WORLD CUP FINALS

Jun 15 v New Zealand (Malaga) 5-2
Dalglish, Wark 2, Robertson, Archibald
Rough; McGrain*, F.Gray, Hansen, Evans, Souness, Strachan (Narey), Dalglish, Wark, Brazil (Archibald), Robertson.
Att: 20,000   Referee: Soucha (USA)

Jun 18 v Brazil (Seville) 1-4
Narey
Rough; Narey, F.Gray, Souness*, Hansen, Miller, Strachan (Dalglish), Hartford (McLeish), Archibald, Wark, Robertson.
Att:47,379   Referee: Calderon (Costa Rica)

Jun 22 v USSR (Malaga) 2-2
Jordan, Souness
Rough; Narey, F.Gray, Souness*, Hansen, Miller, Strachan (McGrain), Archibald, Jordan (Brazil), Wark, Robertson.
Att: 45,000   Referee: Rainea (Romania)

Oct 13 v E Germany (Hampden) 2-0
Wark, Sturrock
Leighton; Narey, Hansen, Miller, F.Gray, Strachan, Souness*, Wark, Archibald, Brazil (Sturrock), Robertson.
Att: 40,355   Referee: Konrath (France)

Nov 17 v Switzerland (Berne) 0-2
Leighton; Narey, F.Gray, Souness*, Hansen, Miller, Wark, Strachan, Sturrock (Archibald), Brazil, Robertson.
Att: 26,000   Referee: Christov (Czechoslavokia)

Dec 15 v Belgium (Brussels) 2-3
Dalglish 2
Leighton; Narey, F.Gray, Aitken, McLeish, Hansen, Strachan (Burns), Archibald, Dalglish, Bett (Sturrock), Souness*.
Att: 48,877   Referee: Garrido (Portugal)

1983

Mar 30 v Switzerland (Hampden) 2-2
Wark, Nicholas
Leighton; Gough, F.Gray, Souness*, Hansen (McLeish), Miller, Wark, Strachan, Dalglish, Nicholas, Weir.
Att: 36,923   Referee: Corver (Netherlands)

May 24 v N Ireland (Hampden) 0-0
Thomson; Dawson, Gough, Simpson (Strachan), Hegarty*, Narey, Wark, Bannon, A.Gray, Burns, Nicholas.
Att: 16,238   Referee: Hackett (England)

May 28 v Wales (Cardiff) 2-0
A.Gray, Brazil
Leighton; Gough, F.Gray, Narey, McLeish, Miller, Strachan, Bannon, A.Gray, Brazil, Souness*.
Att: 14,100   Referee: Moffatt (N Ireland)

Jun 1 v England (Wembley) 0-2
Leighton; Gough, F.Gray, Narey, McLeish, Miller, Strachan, Souness*, A.Gray, Nicholas (Wark), Bannon (Brazil).
Att: 84,000   Referee: Fredriksson (Sweden)

Jun 12 v Canada (Vancouver) 2-0
Strachan (pen), McGhee
Thomson; Gough, Dawson, Narey, McLeish, Miller*, Strachan (Souness), Sturrock, Nicholas (McGhee), Burns, Bannon.
Att: 15,000   Referee: Clarke (Canada)

Jun 16 v Canada (Edmonton) 3-0
Nicholas, Gough, Souness
Leighton; Gough, F.Gray, Narey, McLeish, Miller, Strachan (Aitken), Sturrock, Nicholas, McGhee (A.Gray), Souness*.
Att: 12,258   Referee: Fusco (Canada)

Jun 20 v Canada (Toronto) 2-0
A.Gray 2
Leighton; Gough, Dawson, Narey (Burns), McLeish, Miller, Aitken, Sturrock, Nicholas, A.Gray (Strachan), Souness*.
Att: 15,500   Referee: Evengelista (Canada)

Sep 21 v Uruguay (Hampden) 2-0
Robertson (pen), Dodds
Leighton; Gough, Albiston, Souness*, McLeish, Miller, Dalglish, McStay, McGarvey (Dodds), Wark, Robertson.
Att: 20,545   Referee: Richardson (England)

Oct 12 v Belgium (Hampden) 1-1
Nicholas
Leighton; Gough, Albiston, Wark (Aitken), McLeish, Miller*, Dalglish, McStay, Nicholas (McGarvey), Bett, Robertson.
Att: 23,475   Referee: Barbaresco (Italy)

Nov 16 v East Germany (Halle) 1-2
Bannon
Thomson; Gough, Albiston, Wark, McLeish, Miller*, Strachan, McStay (McGarvey), Dalglish, Archibald, Bannon.
Att: 18,000   Referee: Wohrer (Austria)

Dec 13 v N Ireland (Belfast) 0-2
Leighton; Gough, Rougvie, Souness*, McLeish, Aitken, Strachan, McStay, McGarvey (McGhee), Dodds, Weir.
Att: 10,000   Referee: Midgley (England)

1984

Feb 28 v Wales (Hampden) 2-1
Cooper (pen), Johnston
Leighton; Gough, Albiston, Souness*, McLeish, Miller, Sturrock, McStay (Aitken), McGarvey (Johnston), Bett, Cooper.
Att: 21,542   Referee: Poucher (N Ireland)

May 26 v England (Hampden) 1-1
McGhee
Leighton; Gough, Albiston, Wark, McLeish, Miller*, Strachan (McStay), Archibald, McGhee (Johnston), Bett, Cooper.
Att: 73,064   Referee: Casarin (Italy)

Jun 1 v France (Marseilles) 0-2
Leighton; Gough (Nicholas), Stewart, Miller*, McLeish, Malpas, Strachan (Simpson), Wark, Archibald, Bett, Johnston.
Att: 21,641   Referee: Agnolin (Italy)

Sep 12 v Yugoslavia (Hampden) 6-1
Cooper, Souness, Dalglish, Sturrock, Johnston, Nicholas
Leighton; Nicol, McLeish, Miller, Albiston, Wark, Souness*, Bett(Sturrock), Dalglish, Johnston, Cooper(Nicholas).
Att: 18,512   Referee: Hackett (England)

Oct 17 v Iceland (Hampden) 3-0
McStay 2, Nicholas
Leighton; Nicol, Albiston, Souness*, McLeish, Miller, Dalglish (Nicholas), McStay, Johnston, Bett, Cooper.
Att: 52,829   Referee: Mulder (Netherlands)

Nov 14 v Spain (Hampden) 3-1
Johnston 2, Dalglish
Leighton; Nicol, Albiston, Souness*, McLeish, Miller, Dalglish, McStay, Johnston, Bett, Cooper.
Att: 74,299   Referee: Prokop (E Germany)

1985

Feb 27 v Spain (Seville) 0-1
Leighton; Gough, Albiston, Souness*, McLeish, Miller, Archibald (Nicholas), McStay (Strachan), Johnston, Bett, Cooper.
Att: 70,000   Referee: Vautrot (France)

Mar 27 v Wales (Hampden) 0-1
Leighton; Nicol, Albiston (Hansen), Souness*, McLeish, Miller, Dalglish, McStay (Nicholas), Johnston, Bett, Cooper.
Att: 62,444   Referee: Ponnet (Belgium)

May 25 v England (Hampden) 1-0
Gough
Leighton; Gough, Malpas, Aitken, McLeish, Miller, Strachan (McLeod), Souness*, Archibald, Bett, Speedie.
Att: 66,489   Referee: Vautrot (France)

May 28 v Iceland (Reykjavik) 1-0
Bett
Leighton; Gough, Malpas, Aitken, McLeish, Miller, Strachan, Souness*, Gray (Archibald), Bett, Sharp.
Att: 15,000   Referee: Milchenko (USSR)

Sep 10 v Wales (Cardiff) 1-1
Cooper (pen)
Leighton (Rough); Gough, Malpas, Aitken, McLeish, Miller*, Nicol, Strachan (Cooper), Sharp, Bett, Speedie.
Att: 39,500   Referee: Keizer (Holland)

Oct 16 v E Germany (Hampden) 0-0
Leighton (Goram); Gough, Albiston, Souness*, McLeish, Miller, Dalglish, Nicol, Johnston (Speedie), Aitken (McStay), Cooper.
Att: 41,114   Referee: Worral (England)

Nov 20 v Australia (Hampden) 2-0
Cooper, McAvennie
Leighton; Nicol, Malpas, Souness*, McLeish, Miller, Dalglish (Sharp), Strachan (Bett), McAvennie, Aitken, Cooper.
Att: 63,500   Referee: Christov (Czechoslovakia)

Dec 4 v Australia (Melbourne) 0-0
Leighton; Gough, Malpas, Souness*, McLeish, Miller, Speedie (Sharp), McStay, McAvennie, Aitken, Cooper.
Att: 32,000   Referee: Wright (Brazil)

1986

Jan 28 v Israel (Tel Aviv) 1-0
McStay
Leighton; Gough, Narey, Miller*, Malpas, McStay, Aitken, Bett, Bannon, Sharp(Sturrock), Nicholas.
Att: 7,000   Referee: Thomas (Netherlands)

Mar 26 v Romania (Hampden) 3-0
Strachan, Gough, Aitken
Goram; Gough, Narey, Miller (Hansen), Malpas, Strachan(Nevin), Aitken, Souness, Bannon, Dalglish*, Sharp (Nicholas).
Att: 53,589   Referee: Roth (West Germany)

Apr 23 v England (Wembley) 1-2
Souness (pen)
Rough; Gough, McLeish, Miller, Malpas, Nicol, Souness*, Aitken, Bannon, Nicholas(Nevin), Speedie.
Att: 68,357   Referee: Vautrot (France)

Apr 29 v Netherlands (Eindhoven) 0-0
Goram; Narey, McLeish, Miller*, Albiston, Bett, Malpas, Connor, McCoist, Sturrock, Cooper.
Att: 14,500   Referee: Kohl (Austria)

WORLD CUP FINALS

Jun 4 v Denmark (Neza) 0-1
Leighton; Gough, Miller, McLeish, Malpas,
Strachan(Bannon), Souness*, Aitken, Nicol,
Nicholas, Sturrock(McAvennie).
Att: 18,000 Referee: Nameth (Hungary)

Jun 8 v West Germany (Queretaro)) 1-2
Strachan
Leighton; Gough, Miller, Narey, Malpas, Strachan,
Souness*, Aitken, Nicol(McAvennie), Archibald,
Bannon(Cooper).
Att: 35,000 Referee: Igna (Romania)

Jun 13 v Uruguay (Neza) 0-0
Leighton; Gough, Miller*, Narey, Albiston, Strachan,
McStay, Aitken, Nicol(Nicholas), Sharp, Sturrock
(Cooper).
Att: 15,000 Referee: Quiniou (France)

Gordon Strachan (centre) comes in for ▶
some rough treatment from Uruguay
skipper Barrios (left) and Santin during
the game at Neza in the Mexico World
Cup Finals.

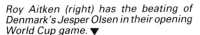

Roy Aitken (right) has the beating of
Denmark's Jesper Olsen in their opening
World Cup game. ▼

Sep 10 v Bulgaria (Hampden) 0-0
Leighton; Gough, Malpas, McStay, Narey, Miller*,
Cooper, Aitken, Johnston, Strachan, Nicholas
(Dalglish).
Att: 35,070 Referee: Fredriksson (Sweden)

Oct 15 v Rep of Ireland (Dublin) 0-0
Leighton; Stewart, Narey, Gough, Hansen, McStay,
Strachan, Sharp, Johnston, Aitken*, MacLeod.
Att: 48,000 Referee: Halle (Norway)

Nov 12 v Luxembourg (Hampden) 3-0
Cooper 2 (1 pen), Johnston
Leighton; Stewart, MacLeod(McCoist), Aitken*,
Gough, Hansen(McStay), Nevin, McClair, Johnston,
Dalglish, Cooper.
Att: 35,078 Referee: Gudmundsson (Iceland)

1987
Feb 18 v Rep of Ireland (Hampden) 0-1
Leighton; Stewart, Malpas(McCoist), Aitken*,
Gough, Hansen, Nevin, McClair, Johnston,
Strachan, Cooper(McStay).
Att: 45,081 Referee: Van Ettekoven (Holland)

Apr 1 v Belgium (Brussels) 1-4
McStay
Leighton; Gough, Malpas, McStay, McLeish,
Narey, Aitken*, McInally, Bett(Nevin), McCoist,
Sturrock.
Att: 26,650 Referee: Vautrot (France)

May 23 v England (Hampden) 0-0
Leighton; Gough, MacLeod, McStay, McLeish,
Miller, McCoist, Aitken*, McClair(Nicholas),
Simpson, Wilson.
Att: 64,713 Referee: Pauly (West Germany)

May 26 v Brazil (Hampden) 0-2
Goram; Gough, MacLeod, Aitken*, McLeish,
Miller, McStay, McInally(McClair), McCoist,
Wilson, Cooper.
Att: 41,384 Referee: Agnolin (Italy)

Scotland skipper Roy Aitken
bursts through the England
midfield to set up an attack in the
goalless Rous Cup game at
Hampden.

Unofficial Internationals

In simple terms an 'official' international is one deemed official by the SFA, but even this is not that simple to put into practice. For instance, the 1872 Scotland-England game is generally recognised to be the first official international yet astute observers will note that the SFA was not formed until the following year. And the converse can apply; a game may be played as an official international but later be considered unofficial. The players in the 1902 Scotland-England game at Ibrox took the field in the belief it was an official international. Only later, after the disaster, was it declared null and void.

The five games played before the 1872 Scotland-England game are considered unofficial because selection was unrepresentative, but then where does that leave some of the badly depleted Scottish sides of recent years? At the other extreme there is the distinction between the unofficial international and unofficial non-international. The later may include divisions of soldiers into Scots and the English for a wartime kickaround. An international, however, implies that the nation's best players will be included. But for all these reasons the following list of unofficial internationals must be considered subjective. It is, dare one say, an unofficial list of unofficial internationals.

1888
Sep 18 v Canada (Kelvingrove) 4-0
McLeod; Arnott, Smith, McQueen, McCreadie, Maley, Hamilton, Hector, Berry, McMahon, Bell.

1891
Oct 3 v Canada (Ibrox Park) 5-1

1902
Apr 5 v England (Ibrox Park) 1-1
(Ibrox Disaster Game)
Aug 9 v Ireland (Belfast) 3-0
Campbell 2, McDermott
Rennie; Drummond, Glen, Breslin, Buick, Robertson, Walker, McDermott, Campbell, Speedie, Smith.
(Ibrox Disaster Fund)

1916
May 13 v England Select (Goodison Park, Liverpool) 3-4
Campbell; Henry, Frew, Logan, Galt, Scott, J.C.Reid, Cunningham, W.Reid, Allan, Wilson.
(Mayor of Liverpool's War Fund)

> On 9 August 1902 Scotland fielded a team of Home-Scots to beat Ireland 3-0 in Belfast. The game was to benefit dependants of the Ibrox disaster, but the attendance was so small that the contribution to the fund was not much over £100. Campbell (2) and McDermott scored for the Scots whose team read: Rennie (Hibs), Drummond (Rangers), Glen (Hibs), Breslin (Hibs, capt), Buick (Hearts), Robertson (Rangers), Walker (Hearts), McDermott (Celtic), John Campbell (Celtic), Speedie (Rangers), Smith (Rangers).

1919 Victory Internationals

1919
Mar 22 v Ireland (Ibrox Park) 2-1
Wilson 2 (1 pen)
Brownlie; McNair, Orr, Gordon, Cringan, McMullan, Donaldson, Bowie, A.Wilson, Miller, Morton.
Att: 50,000

1919
Apr 19 v Ireland (Belfast) 0-0
Brownlie; Marshall, Blair, Gordon, McNames, McMullan, Donaldson, Crosbie, Richardson, Cairns, McPhail.
Att: Unknown

1919
Apr 26 v England (Goodison Park) 2-2
Wright, Bowie
Brownlie; McNair, Blair, Gordon, Wright, McMullan, Donaldson, Bowie, Richardson, McMenemy, Morton.
Att: 45,000

JOHN CAMPBELL

1919
May 3 v England (Hampden Park) 3-4
Wilson 2 (1 pen), Morton
Brownlie; McNair, Blair, Gordon, Wright, McMullan, Reid, Bowie, Wilson, McMenemy, Morton.
Att: 80,000

Wartime & Victory International Appearances 1919

Blair *Rangers & Sheff Wed* (3)
Bowie *Rangers* (3)
Brownlie *Morton* (4)
Cairns *Rangers* (1)
Cringan *Celtic* (1)
Crosbie *Ayr* (1)
Donaldson *Bolton* (3)
Gordon *Rangers* (4)
Marshall *St Mirren* (1)
McMenemy *Celtic* (2)
McMullan *Partick* (4)
McNair *Celtic* (3)
McNames *Hamilton* (1)
McPhail *Kilmarnock* (1)
Miller *Hearts* (1)
Morton *Queen's Park & Rangers* (3)
Orr *Third Lanark* (1)
Reid *Airdrie* (1)
Richardson *Ayr* (2)
Wilson *Hearts* (2)
Wright *Morton* (2)

1921
Jul 9 v Canada (Montreal) 1-0

1929
May 27 v Norwegian XI (Ulleval Stadium, Oslo) 4-0
Fleming, Rankin 2, Nisbet
McLaren; Gray, Crapnell, Morton, A.Craig, T.Craig, Nisbet, Cheyne, McCrae, Rankin, Fleming.
Att: 12,000

1935
May 19 v USA (New York) 5-1
Jun 8 v Canada (Toronto) 6-0
Aug 21 v England (Hampden) 4-2
(King George V Jubilee Fund)

1939-45 Wartime Internationals

1939
Dec 2 v England (Newcastle) 1-2
Dodds
Dawson; Carabine, Ancell, Pinkerton, Baxter, Brown, Finan, Walker, Dodds, Napier, Caskie.
Att: 15,000

1940
May 11 v England (Hampden Park) 1-1
Dougal
Dawson; Carabine, McClure, Shankly, Baxter, Brown, Caskie, Walker, McCulloch, Venters, Dougal.
Att: 75,000

1941
Feb 8 v England (Newcastle) 3-2
Wallace 2, Bacuzzi (og)
Dawson; Hogg, Beattie, McDonald, Dykes, Brown, Milne, Walker, J.Smith, Wallace, Caskie.
Att: 25,000

1941
May 3 v England (Hampden Park) 1-3
Venters
Dawson; Carabine, J.Shaw, Shankly, Dykes, Brown, Gillick, Walker, Smith, Venters, Caskie.
Att: 75,000

1941
Oct 4 v England (Wembley) 0-2
Dawson; Carabine, Beattie, Shankly, Dykes, McDonald, Caskie, Walker, Smith, Wallace, Williams.
Att: 60,000

1942
Jan 17 v England (Wembley) 0-3
Dawson; Carabine, Beattie, Shankly, Dykes, Busby, Caskie, Walker, Gillick, Black, Johnston.
Att: 65,000

1942
Apr 18 v England (Hampden Park) 5-4
Dodds 3, Liddell, Shankly
Dawson; Carabine, Beattie, Shankly, Smith, Busby, Waddell, Herd, Dodds, Bremner, Liddell.
Att: 91,000

1942
Oct 10 v England (Wembley) 0-0
Dawson; Carabine, Beattie, Shankly, Corbett, Busby, Waddell, Walker, Dodds, Bremner, Liddell.
Att: 75,000

1943
Apr 17 v England (Hampden Park) 0-4
Dawson; Carabine, J.Shaw, Shankly, Young, Kean, Waddell, Buchan, Wallace, Venters, Liddell.
Att: 100,000

1943
Oct 16 v England (Maine Road) 0-8
Crozier; Carabine, Miller, Little, Young, Campbell, Waddell, Gillick, Linwood, Walker, Deakin.
Att: 60,000

1944
Feb 19 v England (Wembley) 2-6
Dodds 2
Crozier; Kilmarnock, Stephen, Macaulay, Kirton, Busby, Flavell, Stenhouse, Dodds, Duncanson, Caskie.
Att: 80,000

1944
Apr 22 v England (Hampden Park) 2-3
Caskie, Cullis (og)
Crozier; McDonald, Stephen, Macaulay, Baxter, Busby, Delaney, Walker, Dodds, Duncanson, Caskie.
Att: 133,000

1945
Feb 3 v England (Villa Park) 2-3
Delaney, Dodds
R.Brown; Harley, Stephen, Busby, Thyne, Macaulay, Delaney, Fagan, Dodds, Black, Liddell.
Att: 61,000

1945
Apr 14 v England (Hampden Park) 1-6
Johnstone
R.Brown; Harley, Stephen, Busby, J.Harris (Wolves), Macaulay, Waddell, Bogan (Johnston), J.Harris (Queen's Park), Black, Kelly.
Att: 133,000

1945
Nov 12 v Wales (Hampden Park) 2-0
Waddell, Dodds
R.Brown; McPhee, J.Shaw, Campbell, Paton, Paterson, Waddell, Smith, Dodds, Deakin, Liddell.
Att: 97,000

1946
Jan 23 v Belgium (Hampden Park) 2-2
Delaney 2 (1 pen)
R.Brown; McGowan, J.Shaw, Campbell, Paton, Paterson, Smith, Baird, Delaney, Deakin, Walker.
Att: 46,000

1946
Feb 2 v Northern Ireland (Belfast) 3-2
Liddell 2, Hamilton
R.Brown; McGowan, J.Shaw, Campbell, Paton, Paterson, Waddell, Hamilton, Dodds, Chisholm, Liddell.
Att: 53,000

1946
Apr 13 v England (Hampden Park) 1-0
Delaney
R.Brown; D.Shaw, J.Shaw, Campbell, Brennan, Husband, Waddell, Dougal, Delaney, Hamilton, Liddell.
Att: 139,468

1946
May 15 v Switzerland (Hampden Park) 3-1
Liddell 2, Delaney
Brown; D.Shaw, J.Shaw, Campbell, Brennan, Husband, Waddell, Thornton, Delaney, Walker, Liddell.
Att: 113,000

Wartime & Victory International Appearances 1939-46

Ancell *Newcastle* (1)
Baird *Aberdeen* (1)
Baxter *Middlesbrough* (3)
Beattie *Preston* (5)
Black *Hearts* (3)
Bogan *Hibs* (1)
Bremner *Arsenal* (2)
Brennan *Airdrie* (2)
Brown *Hearts* (4)
Brown *Queen's Park* (7), *Rangers* (1)
Buchan *Blackpool* (1)
Busby *Liverpool* (7)
Campbell *Morton* (6)
Carabine *Third Lanark* (9)
Caskie *St Mirren* (8)
Chisholm *Queens Park* (1)
Corbett *Celtic* (1)
Crozier *Brentford* (3)
Dawson *Rangers* (9)
Deakin *St Mirren* (3)
Delaney *Celtic* (3), *Manchester United* (2)
Dodds *Blackpool* (8)
Dougal *Preston* (1)
Dougal *Birmingham* (1)
Duncanson *Rangers* (1)
Dykes *Hearts* (4)
Fagan *Liverpool* (1)
Finan *Blackpool* (1)
Flavell *Airdrie* (1)
Gillick *Everton* (3)
Hamilton *Aberdeen* (2)
Harley *Liverpool* (2)
Harris *Queen's Park* (1)
Harris *Wolves* (1)
Herd *Man City* (1)
Hogg *Celtic* (1)
Husband *Partick* (2)
Johnston *Clyde* (1 sub)
Johnston *Rangers* (1)
Kean *Hibs* (1)
Kelly *Morton* (1)
Kilmarnock *Motherwell* (1)
Kirton *Stoke* (1)
Liddell *Liverpool* (8)
Linwood *St Mirren* (1)
Little *Rangers* (1)
Macaulay *West Ham* (4)
McClure *Hearts* (1)
McCulloch *Derby* (1)
McDonald *Celtic* (3)
McGowan *Partick* (2)
McPhee *Falkirk* (1)
Miller *Hearts* (1)
Milne *Dumbarton* (1)
Napier *Sheff Wed* (1)
Paterson *Celtic* (3)
Paton *Motherwell* (3)
Pinkerton *Falkirk* (1)
Shankly *Preston* (7)
Shaw D. *Hibs* (2)
Shaw J. *Rangers* (6)
Smith *Rangers* (4)
Smith *Preston* (1)
Smith *Hibs* (2)
Stenhouse *St Mirren* (1)
Stephen *Bradford* (4)
Thyne *Darlington* (1)
Thornton *Rangers* (1)
Venters *Rangers* (3)
Waddell *Rangers* (9)
Wallace *Clyde* (3)
Walker *Hearts* (11)
Williams *Clyde* (1)
Young *Rangers* (2)

Goalkeeper Crozier punches the ball clear of Lawton in the wartime international against England at Hampden in April 1944.

1946
Aug v England (Maine Road, Manchester) 2-2
(Bolton Disaster Fund)

1949
v Canada (Regina) 6-0
v USA (New York) 4-0

1959
v Jutland XI (a) 3-3
Law, Kerr, Auld
Slater; MacKay, Baird, Smith, McGuigan, Stevenson, Scott, White, Kerr, Law, Auld.
Att: 6,000

Pre-1872 Unofficial International Matches Against England

1870
5 Mar (at The Oval) 1-1
Crawford
R.E.W.Crawford (Harrow School); W.H.Gladstone (Old Etonians), G.C.Gordon (Northern Nomads), C.R.B.Hamilton (Civil Servants), W.A.B.Hamilton, (Old Harrovians), A.F.Kinnaird (Crusaders), J.Kirkpatrick (Civil Service, captain), W.Lindsay (Old Wykehamists), J.W.Malcolm (London Scottish Rifles), A.Morten (Crystal Palace), K.Muir-Mackenzie (Old Carthusians).
W.Lindsay and A.Morten subsequently played for England when the official series started.

19 Nov (at The Oval) 0-1
G.F.Congreve (Old Rugbeians); R.E.Crawford (Harrow School), W.A.B.Hamilton (Old Harrovians), Quintin Hogg (Wanderers), G.G.Kennedy (Wanderers), A.F.Kinnaird (Old Etonians), J.Kirkpatrick (Civil Service, captain), W.Lindsay (Old Wykehamists), C.E.B.Nepean (Oxford University), H.W.Primrose (Civil Service), R.Smith (Queen's Park).

1871
25 Feb (at The Oval) 1-1
Nepean
J.Kirkpatrick (Civil Service); W.H.Gladstone (Old Etonians), Quintin Hogg (Wanderers), A.F.Kinnaird (Wanderers), F.B.Maddison (Oxford University), J.F.Inglis (Charterhouse School), W.Lindsay (Old Wykehamists), A.K.Smith (Oxford University), C.E.B.Nepean (Oxford University), R.Smith (Queen's Park), C.E.Primrose (Civil Service).
Formations were one goalkeeper, one back, one half-back and the rest forwards. F.B.Maddison and A.K.Smith, later became full England internationals.

18 Nov (at The Oval) 1-2
Renny-Taylour
R.Smith (Queen's Park); W.Lindsay (Old Wykehamists), C.E.B.Nepean (Oxford University), H.W.Renny-Taylour (Royal Engineers), H.E.Mitchell (Royal Engineers), R.E.W.Crawford (Old Harrovians), H.S.Ferguson (RMA, Woolwich), F.H.Crawford (Harrow Chequers), A.K.Smith (Oxford University), J.Kirkpatrick (Civil Service), E.H.M.Elliott (Harrow Chequers).

1872
24 Feb 1872 (at The Oval) 0-1
C.E.B.Nepean (Oxford University); E.H.M.Elliott (Harrow Chequers), W.Lindsay (Civil Service), M.Muir-Mackenzie (Old Carthusians, capt), R.E.W.Crawford (Harrow Chequers), H.S.Ferguson (Royal Artillery), H.E.Mitchell (Royal Engineers), F.H.Crawford (Harrow Chequers), E.V.Ravenshaw (Charterhouse School), H.H.Stewart (Wanderers), C.M.Thompson (Cambridge University).

In the last two games, as in the third match, the teams are as one goalkeeper, one back, one half-back and eight forwards. In the other games they are simply in alphabetical order.

Lord Kinnaird, who represented Scotland in the first three 'unofficial internationals' and who played for Scotland in the 1873 full international. Although born in London (in 1847), Kinnaird qualified as a Scottish landowner. He played for Eton College, Trinity College (Cambridge), the Wanderers and Old Etonians and won five English FA Cup-winners' medals. Later he became an English FA administrator. It was said that his position was unique for he was the only man who could enter the 'Upper Houses' both of Lords and Association Football.

World Tour 1967 (16 May to 13 June)

May 16 v Israel (Tel Aviv) 2-1
Morgan, Ferguson
Thomson; Callaghan, Colquhoun, Anderson, Ure, Fraser, Penman (Hood), Hope, McCalliog, Ferguson, Morgan.

May 25 v Hong Kong (Hong Kong) 4-1
Ferguson 2, Hood, Callaghan
Thomson; Callaghan, Tinney (Townsend), Colquhoun, Anderson, Fraser, Morgan, Hope (Harper), McCalliog, Ferguson, Hood.

May 28 v Australia (Sydney) 1-0
Ferguson
Thomson; Callaghan, Colquhoun, Townsend, Anderson, Fraser, Morgan, Hope, McCalliog, Ferguson, Hood.

May 31 v Australia (Adelaide) 2-1
Townsend, Morgan
Cruickshank; Callaghan, Townsend, Anderson, McGrory, Fraser, McLean, Hope, McCalliog, Ferguson, Morgan.

Jun 3 v Australia (Melbourne) 2-0
Ferguson 2
Cruickshank; Callaghan, Townsend, Anderson, McGrory, Fraser (Tinney), McLean (Penman), Hope, McCalliog, Ferguson, Morgan.

Jun 5 v New Zealand Under-23 (Wellington) 7-2
McLean (pen), Harper 3, McCalliog 2, Lake (og)
Cruickshank; Callaghan (McCalliog), Tinney, Townsend, McGrory, Woodward, McLean, Penman, Harper, Hope, Hood.

Jun 8 v Auckland Provincial XI (Auckland) 4-1
Ferguson 3, Penman
Thomson; Woodward, Tinney, Anderson, McGrory, Townsend, McLean, McCalliog, Penman, Ferguson, Morgan.

Jun 10 v Vancouver All-Stars (Vancouver) 4-1
McCalliog 2, Ferguson, McLean (pen)
Cruickshank; Woodward, Tinney, Townsend, McGrory, Fraser, McLean, Hope, McCalliog, Ferguson, Penman.

Jun 13 v Canada (Winnipeg) 7-2
Harper 5, Hope, Morgan
Cruickshank; Townsend, Tinney, Anderson, McGrory, Fraser (Penman), Morgan, Hope, Harper, Hood (McCalliog), McLean.

Appearances
Substitutes in brackets

A.Anderson (Hearts)	7
W.Callaghan (Dunfermline)	6
E.Colquhoun (West Brom)	3
J.Cruickshank (Hearts)	5
A.Ferguson (Dunfermline)	7
D.Fraser (West Brom)	7
J.Harper (Huddersfield T)	2(1)
H.Hood (Clyde)	4(1)
R.Hope (West Brom)	8
J.McCalliog (Sheffield W)	7(2)
J.McGrory (Kilmarnock)	6
T.McLean (Kilmarnock)	6
W.Morgan (Burnley)	7
A.Penman (Rangers)	4(2)
H.Thomson (Burnley)	4
H.Tinney (Bury)	5(1)
J.Townsend (Hearts)	7(1)
I.Ure (Arsenal)	1
J.Woodward (Arsenal)	3

'B' Internationals

Appearance Totals

Aird, J. (Burnley); 1953 v E; 1954 v E. (2)
Aitken, C. (Motherwell); 1957 v E. (1)
Anderson, J. (Leicester C); 1954 v E. (1)
Bonthrone, J. (East Fife); 1953 v E. (1)
Brown, W. (Dundee); 1956 v E. (1)
Buchanan, J. (Clyde); 1952 v F. (1)
Cowie, D. (Dundee); 1953 v E. (1)
Clarke, S. (Chelsea); 1987 v F. (1)
Cullen, M. (Luton T); 1956 v E. (1)
Cumming, J. (Hearts); 1954 v E; 1957 v E. (2)
Cunningham, W. (Preston NE); 1952 v F. (1)
Davidson, J. (Partick T); 1953 v F. (1)
Dick, J. (West Ham); 1954 v E. (1)
Docherty, T. (Preston NE); 1952 v F; 1953 v E. (2)
Dudley, J. (West Brom); 1954 v E. (1)
Ferguson, I. (St Mirren); 1987 v F(sub). (1)
Fernie, W. (Celtic); 1954 v E. (1)
Gardiner, I. (Motherwell); 1957 v E. (1)
Gardiner, W. (East Fife); 1952 v F. (1)
Gemmell, T. (St Mirren); 1952 v F. (1)
Glen, A. (Aberdeen); 1956 v E. (1)
Gunn, B. (Norwich C); 1987 v F. (1)
Haughney, M. (Celtic); 1954 v E. (1)
Henderson, J.(Portsmouth); 1953 v E; 1954 v E.(2)
Hewie, J. (Charlton A); 1953 v E. (1)
Kelly, B. (Raith R); 1957 v E. (1)
Kelly, H. (Blackpool); 1952 v F; 1953 v E. (2)
Kerr, A. (Partick T); 1956 v E. (1)
Kirk, R. (Hearts); 1957 v E. (1)
Ledgerwood, T. (Partick T); 1952 v F. (1)

McAllister, G. (Leicester C); 1987 v F. (1)
McAvennie, F. (West Ham); 1987 v F. (1)
McCann, J. (Barnsley); 1957 v E. (1)
McCulloch, W. (Airdrie); 1956 v E. (1)
McDonald, T. (Hibernian); 1954 v E. (1)
McKimmie, S. (Aberdeen); 1987 v F. (1)
McLeish, A. (Aberdeen); 1987 v F. (1)
McMillan, I. (Airdrie); 1953 v E. (1)
Malloy, D. (Cardiff C); 1956 v E; 1957 v E. (2)
Mochan, N. (Celtic); 1954 v E. (1)
Moir, W.(Bolton W); 1952 v F; 1953 v E. (2)
Morrison, A. (Preston NE); 1953 v E. (1)
Mulkerrin, J. (Hibernian); 1956 v E. (1)
Neilson, J. (St Mirren); 1956 v E. (1)
Nevin, P. (Chelsea); 1987 v F. (1)
Nicholas, C. (Arsenal); 1987 v F. (1)
Ormond, W. (Hibernian); 1952 v F. (1)
Parker, R. (Hearts); 1952 v F. (1)
Paterson, W. (Doncaster); 1954 v E. (1)
Rae, I. (Falkirk); 1956 v E. (1)
Robertson, D. (Aberdeen); 1987 v F. (1)
Scott, A. (Rangers); 1957 v E. (1)
Simpson, N. (Aberdeen); 1987 v F. (1)
Simpson, R. (Newcastle U); 1953 v E; 1957 v E. (2)
Turnbull, E. (Hibernian); 1956 v E. (1)
Wardhaugh, J. (Hearts); 1957 v E. (1)
Wilson, I. (Leicester C); 1987 v F. (1)
Winton, D. (Burnley); 1957 v E. (1)
Yorston, H. (Aberdeen); 1956 v E. (1)

1952
Nov 11 v France (Toulouse) 0-0
Ledgerwood; Parker, Cunningham, Docherty, Davidson, Kelly, Buchanan, Moir, Gardiner, Gemmell, Ormond.
Att: 19,649

1953
Mar 11 v England (Easter Road, Edinburgh) 2-2
McMillan, Morrison
Simpson; Aird, Hewie, Docherty, Cowie, Kelly, Henderson, Moir, Bonthrone, McMillan, Morrison.
Att: 25,000

1954
Mar 3 v England (Sunderland) 1-1
Cumming
Anderson; Haughney, Aird, Dudley, Paterson, Cumming, McDonald, Fernie, Henderson, Dick, Mochan.
Att: 21,048

1956
Feb 29 v England (Dens Park, Dundee) 2-2
McCulloch, Mulkerrin
Brown; Kerr, Rae, Neilson, Malloy, Glen, Cullen, Yorston, Mulkerrin, Turnbull, McCulloch.
Att: 11,500

1957
Feb 6 v England (Villa Park, Birmingham) 1-4
Gardiner
Simpson; Kirk, Winton, Aitken, Malloy, Cumming, Scott, Kelly, Gardiner, Wardhaugh, McCann.
Att: 39,376

1987
Apr 28 v France (Pittodrie, Aberdeen) 1-1
McAllister
Gunn; McKimmie, Robertson, Simpson, McLeish, Clarke, Nevin, McAllister(Ferguson), Nicholas, Wilson, McAvennie.
Att: 7,500

EDDIE TURNBULL

RONNIE SIMPSON

> Ronnie Simpson's full international debut (against England in 1967) came over 14 years after his first Scottish 'B' cap.

> Positive thinking might focus on the fact that Scotland lost only one of their first six 'B' internationals. Negativists might point out that there was not one win among them.

DOUG COWIE

Under-23 Matches

Asterisk denotes matches played in European Championship

THE most dramatic moment in the history of the Scotland Under-23 team was the last – a penalty kick taken by Kila of Holland.

After a thrilling extra-time period at Hampden, Scotland and Holland had finished their European Championship quarter-final match all-square at 2-2. The game went to penalties and when Joe Jordan and Tommy Craig missed for Scotland, it was 3-3 when Kila stepped up and scored to complete Scotland's Under-23 history.

It had begun 21 years earlier, in 1955, with a disastrous 6-0 defeat against England, for whom Duncan Edwards hit a ten-minute hat-trick in the second-half.

The first win over England was delayed until 1961, when the only goal of the game was fittingly scored by Denis Law, who had inspired the team the previous season. Law did not score in the 1960 game against England, but he schemed them into a 4-1 lead before Jimmy Greaves completed a hat-trick and England scrambled a draw.

In the early days, Under-23 matches attracted large crowds, but by the early 1970s, attendances had declined. Only 2,439 paid to see the game in Swansea in 1973, which was settled by Asa Hartford's last-kick winner.

The European Championship provided a much-needed fillip. Starting in Romania, Scotland won all four group games. Skipper Tommy Craig was the one over-age player allowed.

The first leg of the quarter-final tie against Holland erupted when Willie Miller was knocked down, the home team winning 2-0. In front of 23,593 at Hampden, the two goals were pulled back, and Joe Jordan twice hit the crossbar late in normal time. Then came the penalty finale.

The Under-23 era was over. A product of the 1950s, when players served longer apprenticeships, it gave way to Under-21 fixtures.

Scotland's team which met England at Hillsborough in the second Under-23 game. Back row (left to right): Parker, Rae, Morrison, Price, Nicol, McIntosh. Front: Hamilton, Young, Murray, Wishart, Baxter.

1955
Feb 8 v England (Shawfield Park, Glasgow) 0-6
Duff; Parker, Caldow, Mackay, Baillie, Holmes, Leggat, Walsh, Hill, Wishart, McParland.
Att: 17,000

1956
Feb 8 v England (Hillsborough, Sheffield) 1-3
Hamilton
Morrison; Parker, Rae, Price, Nicol, McIntosh, Hamilton, Young, Murray, Wishart, Baxter.
Att: 39,736

1957
Feb 26 v England (Ibrox Park, Glasgow) 1-1
Crawford (pen)
Forsyth; Parker, Caldow, Mackay, Plenderleith, Glen, Hamilton, Reilly, Murray, Young, Crawford.
Att: 14,000

1957
Oct 23 v Holland (Tynecastle, Edinburgh) 4-1
Currie, Herd, Young, Mackay (pen)
Beattie; Parker, McIntosh, Mackay, Plenderleith, Price, Herd, Currie, Young, Harrower, O'Hara.
Att: 25,000

1958
Jan 15 v England (Goodison Park, Liverpool) 1-3
Young
Beattie; Parker, McIntosh, Mackay, Plenderleith, Thomson, Scott, Currie, Young, Brand, O'Hara.
Att: 19,327

1958
Apr 30 v Holland (Amsterdam) 1-2
Cousin
Beattie; Parker, Holt, Nicol, Plenderleith, Kennedy, Herd, Currie, Cousin, Colrain, O'Hara.
Att: 13,500

1958
Dec 10 v Wales (Tynecastle, Edinburgh) 0-1
Slater; MacKay, Baird, Baxter (John), Baillie, Baxter (Jim), Ewen, Currie, Young, Sneddon, Wilson.
Att: 10,000

1959
Nov 25 v Wales (Wrexham) 1-1
Young
Blacklaw; MacKay, Milne, Gabriel, Plenderleith, Higgins, Hunter, White, Young, Law, Weir.
Att: 10,966

1960
Mar 2 v England (Ibrox Park, Glasgow) 4-4
St John 2, Cousin, MacKay (pen)
Blacklaw; MacKay, Riddell, Gabriel, Martis, Higgins, Hunter, Cousin, St John, Law, Weir.
Att: 25,000

1960
Apr 20 v Belgium (Ghent) 1-1
Cousin
Cruickshank; MacKay, Thomson, Gabriel, McNeill, Higgins, Penman, Hunter, St John, Cousin, Weir.
Att: 2,000

1961
Mar 1 v England (Middlesbrough) 1-0
Law
Ogston; Hogan, Riddell, Crerand, McNeill, Ure, Hilley, Law, Hughes, Gilzean, McLeod.
Att: 21,858

1961
Dec 6 v Wales (Wrexham) 0-0
Ogston; Fraser, Aitken, Gabriel, McNeill, R.Roberts, Henderson, Penman, Hughes, Gilzean, Robertson.
Att: 4,518

1962
Feb 28 v England (Aberdeen) 2-4
Hunter, Hughes
Ogston; McGillivray, Aitken, McLintock, McNeill, Higgins, Henderson, Hunter, Hughes, Gilzean, Robertson.
Att: 25,000

1962
Dec 5 v Wales (Aberdeen) 2-0
Smith, Jeffrey
Lawrence; Fraser, Aitken, Gabriel, McNeill, Smith, Brown, Allan, Lochhead, Cooke, Jeffrey.
Att: 20,000

1963
Dec 4 v Wales (Wrexham) 1-3
Smith
Cruickshank; King, Shevlane, Greig, Easton, Smith, Penman, Gibson, Forrest, Cooke, Robertson
Att: 12,000

1964
Feb 5 v England (Newcastle) 2-3
Provan (pen), Murdoch
Cruickshank; Provan, Shevlane, Greig, McGrory, Gabriel, Johnstone, Murdoch, Sharkey, Bremner, Hughes.
Att: 35,090

1964
May 24 v France (Nantes) 2-0
Martin, Robertson
Davie; King, Shevlane, Bremner, McGrory, Murray, Johnstone, Martin, Sharkey, Gibson, Robertson.
Att: 2,000

1964
Dec 2 v Wales (Kilmarnock) 3-0
Burton (og), Cormack, Bremner
Donaldson; King, Shevlane, Bremner, McGrory, Murray, Cormack, Graham, Hamilton, Cooke, Robertson.
Att: 6,000

1965
Feb 24 v England (Aberdeen) 0-0
Donaldson; Young, Hollywood, Bremner, D.Murray G.Murray, Penman, Graham, Forrest, Cooke, Cormack.
Att: 25,000

1966
Nov 30 v Wales (Wrexham) 6-0
McCalliog 2, Gray 2, Edwards, Mitchell
Clark; Whyte, Tinney, Stanton, McMillan, Gray, Edwards, Hope, McCalliog, Cormack, Mitchell.
Att: 5,000

1967
Mar 1 v England (Newcastle) 3-1
McCalliog, Cormack, Smith
Clark; Whyte, Tinney, Stanton, McMillan, Gray, Cormack, McLean, McCalliog, Smith, Mitchell.
Att: 19,750

1968
Feb 7 v England (Hampden Park, Glasgow) 1-2
Hood
Ferguson; Colquhoun, Burns, Stanton, Moncur, Murray, Morgan, Hood, Stein, Cormack, Robertson (Gibb).
Att: 14,497

1968
May 30 v Holland (Amsterdam) 0-0
Clark; Fraser, McCreadie, Moncur, McKinnon, D.Smith, Henderson, Hope (J.Smith), McLean, Greig, Cooke.
Att: 20,000

1969
Dec 3 v France (Hampden Park, Glasgow) 4-0
O'Hare 2, Lorimer 2 (1 pen)
Hughes; Malone, Hay, Blackley, Thomson, Munro, Lorimer, Carr, O'Hare, Robb (Marinello), Johnston.
Att: 5,004

1970
Jan 14 v Wales (Aberdeen) 1-1
O'Hare
Stewart; Clunie, Wilson, Blackley, Thomson, Campbell (Munro), Lorimer, Carr, O'Hare, Robb, Hartford (Harper).
Att: 14,500

1970
Mar 4 v England (Sunderland) 1-3
(abandoned 62 mins, snow)
Todd (og)
Hughes; Clunie, Dickson, Blackley, Thomson, Munro, McLean, Connelly (Marinello), O'Hare, Gemmill, Johnston.
Att: 12,885

1971
Jan 13 v Wales (Swansea) 0-1
MacRae; Hay (Jardine), Hermiston (Oliver), Kelly, Munro, Buchan, Hartford, Carr, Harper, Connolly, Hutchison.
Att: 9,000

1971
Feb 24 v England (Hampden Park, Glasgow) 2-2
Kelly, Robb
MacRae (Hunter); Jardine, Hay, Blackley, Connelly, Kelly, Young, Forsyth, Robb, Jarvie, Duncan.
Att: 13,839

1972
Jan 26 v Wales (Aberdeen) 2-0
Jardine, McQuade
Hunter; Brownlie, Donachie, Jardine, Young, Buchan, McGovern (McQuade), Macari, Bone, Dalglish, Cropley.
Att: 15,000

1972
Feb 16 v England (Derby) 2-2
Dalglish 2
Hunter; Brownlie, Donachie, Jardine, Connelly, Buchan, Carr, Hartford, Macari, Dalglish, Bone.
Att: 18,176

1973
Feb 13 v England (Kilmarnock) 1-2
Bone
Rough; Kennedy, McGrain, Phillip, Young, Hartford, Doyle, McCluskey, Alderson, Bone, Cropley (Parlane).
Att: 6,000

Charlie Cooke, who made five Under-23 appearances while with three different clubs, Aberdeen, Dundee and Chelsea.

1973
Mar 14 v Wales (Swansea) 2-1
Dalglish, Hartford
Stewart; S.Kennedy, McGrain, Anderson, Holton, Hartford, Doyle, McGovern (McCluskey), Parlane (McCulloch), Dalglish, Connolly.
Att: 2,439

1974
Feb 27 v Wales (Aberdeen) 3-0
Parlane (pen), Robinson, Pearson
Stewart (Brown); Forsyth, Wallace, Robinson, Johnstone, Burns, Parlane, Kelly, Pearson, Cropley, Prentice (Doyle).
Att: 5,900

1974
Mar 13 v England (Newcastle) 0-2
Stewart (Brown); Miller, Calderwood (Gow), Johnstone, McDonald, F.Gray, Souness, Bruce (Lamb), Pearson, T.Craig, Gillies.
Att: 4,511

1974
Dec 18 v England (Aberdeen) 0-3
Stewart (Brown); Bremner, Miller, McDonald, Burley, Sullivan (Purdie), Johnstone, McCluskey, Parlane, Gray, Graham.
Att: 14,141

1975
Feb 25 v Wales (Swansea) 0-2
Kennedy (Brown); Kennedy, McCluskey, McDougall (Sullivan), Young, Miller, Parlane, Bremner, Gray (Pearson), T.Craig, Smith.
Att: 3,383

1975
Apr 16 v Sweden (Gothenburg) 2-1
Craig 2 (1 pen)
Rough (Brown); Burley, Houston, Miller, Hansen, T.Craig, Bremner, Graham, Pearson, Pettigrew, G.Smith.
Att: 1,000

1975
May 31 v Romania* (Pitesti) 2-1
Young, Pettigrew
Rough; G.Smith(St Johnstone), Houston, McCluskey, Young, Narey, Conn(Graham), Pettigrew (G.Smith [Kilmarnock]), Pearson, A.Gray, T.Craig.
Att: 10,000

1975
Sep 2 v Denmark* (Frederikshavn) 1-0
Bremner
Rough; G.Smith (St Johnstone), F.Gray, Narey, Young, McCluskey, Pearson, Bremner, Pettigrew, J.Craig, T.Craig.
Att: 6,000

1975
Oct 28 v Denmark* (Easter Road, Edinburgh) 4-1
A.Gray 3, Prentice
Rough; G.Smith (St Johnstone), F.Gray, Narey (Prentice), McDonald, Miller, Conn, Bremner, Pettigrew, A.Gray, T.Craig.
Att: 16,500

1975
Dec 16 v Romania* (Falkirk) 4-0
Pettigrew 2, T.Craig (pen), Bremner
Rough; G.Smith (St Johnstone), F.Gray, Bremner, Hansen, Miller, Conn[G.Smith (Kilmarnock)], Pettigrew, J.Craig, T.Craig, Prentice.
Att: 8,000

1976
Feb 4 v Wales (Wrexham) 3-2
T.Craig, Pettigrew 2
Rough (Stewart); Brownlie, McLelland, Miller, McVie (Hansen), T.Craig, Johnstone, Bremner, Pettigrew, J.Craig, Prentice[G.Smith (Kilmarnock)].
Att: 2,222

1976
Feb 18 v Holland* (Breda) 0-2
Rough; Brownlie, McLelland, Miller, McVie (Narey), Souness, Burns, Bremner, J.Craig, Dalglish, Johnstone.
Att: 14,000

1976
Mar 24 v Holland* (Easter Road, Edinburgh) 2-0
(a.e.t. Holland won on penalties)
Johnstone, Jackson
Rough; Brownlie, F.Gray, Jackson, Miller, T.Craig, Bremner, Pettigrew, Jordan, Smith (Dickson), Johnstone.
Att: 32,593

Under-21 Matches

Asterisk denotes matches played in European Championship

1976
Oct 12 v Czechoslovakia* (Pilsen) 0-0
Clark; Burley, Albiston, Stanton, Aitken, Burns, Cooper, Wark, McNiven (Provan), Narey (Muir), Sturrock.
Att: 3,000

1977
Feb 9 v Wales (Easter Road, Edinburgh) 3-2
Sturrock, Wark, McNiven
Clark; Burley, Albiston, Ross (Fitzpatrick), Reid, Aitken, Cooper, Wark, Parlane, Burns, Sturrock (McNiven).
Att: 4,538
Mar 30 v Switzerland* (Wankdorf Stadium, Berne) 0-2
Clark; Reid(Fitzpatrick), Burley, Narey, Albiston, Wark, Hartford, Aitken, Cooper, Sturrock, Melrose (McNiven).
Att: 500
Apr 27 v England (Bramall Lane, Sheffield) 0-1
Ferguson(Thomson); Sinclair, Burns, Fitzpatrick, Reid, Stevens, McGarvey (Robertson), Watson, Sturrock, T.Craig, Cooper.
Att: 8,934
Sep 7 v Switzerland* (Ibrox, Glasgow) 3-1
Wallace 2, Cooper
Stewart; Burley, Albiston, Miller, Narey, Fitzpatrick Sturrock, Payne, Wallace, Burns(Watson), Cooper.
Att: 8,000
Sep 20 v Czechoslovakia* (Tynecastle, Edinburgh) 2-1
Burley, Sturrock
Stewart; Burley, Albiston, Miller, Narey, Fitzpatrick Sturrock, Payne, McGarvey, Aitken, Cooper.
Att: 14,115

1978
Feb 8 v Wales (Chester) 0-1
Thomson; Brazil, Casey (Orr), Wark, McLeish, Aitken, Payne, Russell, Dodds, Smith, McNab.
Att: 2,454
Sep 17 v USA (Pittodrie, Aberdeen) 3-1
Melrose, Orr, M.MacLeod
Thomson; Sneddon, Gillespie, Orr, McLeish, M.MacLeod, Melrose, Jardine, McCluskey, Bannon, Lindsay.
Att: 6,000
Oct 24 v Norway* (Easter Road, Edinburgh) 5-1
McCluskey 2, Stewart, Wark, MacLeod
Thomson; Narey, Stewart, Wark, McNichol, Orr, McCluskey, Bannon, A.MacLeod, Aitken, Melrose.
Att: 9,858
Nov 28 v Portugal* (Lisbon) 3-0
McCluskey, A.MacLeod 2(1 pen)
J.Stewart; R.Stewart, Dawson, Wark, McNichol, Orr, McCluskey, Bannon, A.MacLeod, Aitken, Melrose (M.MacLeod).
Att: 2,000

1979
Jun 7 v Norway* (Haugesund) 2-2
Bannon, A.MacLeod
Thomson; Stewart, Dawson, Aitken, Orr, McNichol, Bannon, A.MacLeod, Brazil, M.MacLeod, Melrose.
Att: 2,000
Nov 20 v Belgium* (Beveren) 1-0
McCluskey
Thomson; Stewart, Dawson, Orr, McNichol, Aitken Strachan, Bannon, McCluskey, Brazil, Ritchie.
Att: 3,000
Dec 18 v Belgium* (Tynecastle, Edinburgh) 2-2
Stewart(pen), Melrose
Thomson; Stewart, McNichol, Fulton, Dawson, Russell (Melrose), McLeish, MacLeod, McCluskey, Archibald, Brazil (Tolmie).
Att: 7,500

1980
Feb 12 v England* (Highfield Road, Coventry) 1-2
Archibald
Thomson; Stewart, Dawson, Orr, McLeish, Gillespie, Wark, Blair, Archibald, Aitken, Brazil.
Att: 15,382

Feb 26 v West Germany (Dortmund) 0-1
Thomson; Stewart, McNichol, Fulton, Dawson, Bannon (MacDonald), Wark, Richardson, Archibald, Brazil, Melrose.
Att: 10,000
Mar 4 v England (Pittodrie, Aberdeen) 0-0
Thomson; Dawson, Fulton, Stewart, McNichol, McLeish, Bannon(Richardson), Wark, Archibald, Brazil, Melrose.
Att: 24,000
Sep 9 v Sweden* (Degerfors) 0-2
McCulloch; Nicol, Connor, Blair, Paterson, Fulton, Nicholas, Watson, Brazil, Bett, MacDonald (Redford).
Att: 2,140
Nov 18 v Denmark* (Aberdeen) 2-1
Watson, Gillespie
Brough; Doyle, Stewart, Gillespie, McLaughlin, Bett, McGhee, Watson, Archibald, Bell (Fulton), McBride.
Att: 10,000

1981
Sep 8 v Sweden* (Easter Road, Edinburgh) 4-0
Blair, Brazil, MacDonald, Sturrock
Geddes; Nicol, Connor, Blair, McLaughlin, Gillespie, Sturrock, Bett, Nicholas (MacDonald), Brazil (Milne), Redford.
Att: 7,000
Oct 13 v Denmark* (Aarhus) 1-1
Blair
Geddes; Cooper, Nicol, Gillespie, McLaughlin, Watson (MacDonald), Blair, Bett, McGarvey, Redford, McCluskey.
Att: 2,000

1982
Quarter-final (1st leg)
Feb 23 v Italy* (Stadio Militaire, Catanzaro) 1-0
McAvennie
Leighton; Stewart, Nicol, Simpson, McLaughlin, Gillespie, Bett, McAvennie, McCluskey, Redford, MacDonald (Doyle).
Att: 20,000
Quarter-final (2nd leg)
Mar 24 v Italy* (Pittodrie, Aberdeen) 0-0 (agg 1-0)
Leighton; Stewart, Nicol, Blair (Watson), Paterson, Gillespie, MacDonald, Simpson, Sturrock, Redford, Hewitt.
Att: 15,000
Semi-final (1st leg)
Apr 19 v England* (Hampden Park, Glasgow) 0-1
Geddes; Stewart, Nicol, Cooper, McLaughlin, Gillespie, McCulloch, Bett, Sturrock, McAvennie, Redford (MacDonald).
Att: 16,130
Semi-final, (2nd leg)
Apr 28 v England* (Maine Road, Manchester) 1-1 (agg 1-2)
Sharp
Geddes; Nicol, Reid (MacDonald), Simpson, McLaughlin, Cooper, McCulloch, Bett, Sharp, T.Burns, McAvennie (McGarvey).
Att: 8,212

Oct 12 v East Germany* (Tynecastle, Edinburgh) 2-0
Walsh, Simpson
McAlpine; Gough, Nicol, Simpson, McLaughlin, Cooper, Black, McStay(Doyle), Nicholas(Ferguson), Walsh, Hewitt.
Att: 5,000
Nov 16 v Switzerland* (Aarau) 4-3
McStay, Nicholas, Hewitt, Gough
McAlpine; Gough, Nicol, McStay, McLaughlin, Cooper, Simpson, Nicholas, Walsh (Malpas), Hewitt (Crainie), Black.
Att: 1,900
Dec 14 v Belgium* (Ghent) 2-1
McGarvey, Nicholas
McAlpine; Malpas, Nicol, Cooper, McLaughlin, Gough, Black, Stephen, Walsh, Simpson, McGarvey (Nicholas).
Att: 1,500

1983
Mar 29 v Switzerland* (Dundee) 2-1
Black 2 (1 pen)
McAlpine; Nicol, Malpas, McStay, McLaughlin, Cooper, Black, Simpson, McGarvey, Walsh, Hewitt.
Att: 1,500
Oct 11 v Belgium* (Tannadice Park) 0-0
McAlpine; Nicol, Malpas, Cooper, McPherson, Clarke, Milne, Simpson, McGarvey (Ferguson), McCoist (McClair), Hewitt.
Att: 7,476
Nov 15 v East Germany* (Jena) 1-1
Aitken
Gunn; Clarke(McKinlay), Malpas, Simpson, Aitken, Cooper, Milne, McClair, Ferguson (Johnston), Nicol, Walsh.
Att: 500

1984
Quarter-final (1st leg)
Mar 14 v Yugoslavia* (Pittodrie, Aberdeen) 2-1
Johnston, McClair
Gunn; Nicol, Malpas, Aitken, Gough, Cooper, McStay, Simpson, McClair, Bell, Johnston.
Att: 11,300
Quarter-final (2nd leg)
Apr 4 v Yugoslavia* (Belgrade) 1-3 (a.e.t. agg 3-4)
Johnston
Gunn; Clarke, Reid, Gough, Hogg, Malpas, Russell (Hewitt), Aitken, Nicholas (McClair), McStay, Johnston.
Att: 6,000

Sep 11 v West Germany (Easter Road, Edinburgh 2-1
McClair, Nevin
Gunn; McKimmie, McKinlay, Aitken, Clarke (Beaumont), Hogg, Nevin, Grant, Robertson, Rice, McClair.
Att: 4,207
Oct 16 v Iceland* (Motherwell) 1-0
Aitken
Gunn; McKimmie, McKinlay, Aitken, Hogg (Robertson), Cooper, Nevin, Grant, Black, Clarke, McClair.
Att: 3,920
Nov 13 v Spain* (Dens Park, Dundee) 0-2
Gunn; McGinnis, McKinlay, Aitken, Clarke (Robertson), McPherson, Nevin, Grant, Black, Malpas, McClair.
Att: 5,004

1985
Feb 26 v Spain* (Cadiz) 0-0
Gunn; Burns, McKinlay, Cooper (Grant), Hogg, Clarke, Nevin(Robertson), Levein, Black, Simpson, Speedie.
Att: 18,000
May 27 v Iceland* (Reykjavik) 0-2
Gunn; McKimmie, McKinlay (Burns), Cooper, Clarke, Levein (Robertson), Stark, Beaumont, Black, McClair, Nevin.
Att: 200

1986
Sep 9 v West Germany (Ibrox, Glasgow) 1-0
Gallacher
Smith; Shannon, Tortolano, Ferguson, Hegarty, Boyd, Gray, Grant, Durie, Gallacher, Durrant.
Att: 2,872
Oct 14 v Rep of Ireland* (Dundalk) 2-1
Shannon, Gallacher
Goram; Shannon(Hunter), Whyte, Grant, Duffy, Boyd, I.Ferguson, D.Ferguson, Fleck, Gallacher, Tortolano.
Att: 2,682

1987
Feb 17 v Rep of Ireland* (Easter Road, Edinburgh) 4-1
Fleck 3, Ferguson
Money; Shannon, Whyte(Robertson), Grant, McLeish, Boyd, Gallacher(Miller), Durrant, Durie, Fleck, I.Ferguson.
Att: 4,136
Apr 1 v Belgium (Bruges)* 0-0
Smith; Shannon(Gallacher), Boyd, Grant, Hegarty, Whyte, I.Ferguson, D.Ferguson, Fleck(Wright), Durie, Durrant.
Att: 1,000

Davie Cooper, who played in Scotland's first-ever Under-21 international while with Clydebank.

Billy Bremner, pictured challenging his Leeds team-mate, England's Jackie Charlton, at Hampden in 1966.

International Appearances

Explanatory code for international matches: A represents Austria; Alb, Albania; Alg, Algeria; Arg, Argentina; Aus, Australia; Bel, Belgium; Br, Brazil; Bul, Bulgaria; Ca, Canada; Ch, Chile; Cy, Cyprus; Cz, Czechoslovakia; D, Denmark; E, England; Ei, Eire; EG, East Germany; F, France; Fi, Finland; G, Germany (pre-war); Gr, Greece; H, Hungary; Ho, Holland; I, Italy; Ic, Iceland; Ir, Iran; Is, Israel; L, Luxembourg; M, Mexico; Ma, Malta; N, Norway; Ni, Northern Ireland; Nz, New Zealand; P, Portugal; Par, Paraguay; Pe, Peru; Pol, Poland; R, Rumania; Se, Sweden; Sp, Spain; Sw, Switzerland; T, Turkey; U, Uruguay; USA, United States of America; USSR, Soviet Union; W, Wales; WG, West Germany; Y, Yugoslavia, Z, Zaire. The year indicated refers to the season; ie 1982 is the 1981-82 season.

Adams, J. (Hearts); 1889 v Ni; 1892 v W; 1893 v Ni. (3)

Agnew, W.B. (Kilmarnock); 1907 v Ni; 1908 v W, Ni. (3)

Aird, J. (Burnley); 1954 v N (2); A, U. (4)

Aitken, A. (Newcastle U); 1901 v E; 1902 v E; 1903 v E, W; 1904 v E; 1905 v E, W; 1906 v E; (Middlesbrough); 1907 v E, W; 1908 v E; (Leicester Fosse); 1910 v E; 1911 v E, Ni. (14)

Aitken, G.G. (East Fife); 1949 v E, F; 1950 v W, Ni, Sw; (Sunderland); 1953 v W, Ni; 1954 v E. (8)

Aitken, R. (Dumbarton); 1886 v E; 1888 v Ni. (2)

Aitken, R. (Celtic); 1980 v Pe(sub); Bel, W (sub); E, Pol; 1983 v Bel, Ca(1+1 sub); 1984 v Bel (sub); Ni, W (sub); 1985 v E, Ic; 1986 v W, EG, Aus (2); Is, R, E, D, WG, U; 1987 v Bul, Ei(2); Lux, Bel, E, Br. (30)

Aitkenhead, W.A.C. (Blackburn R); 1912 v Ni. (1)

Albiston, A. (Manchester U); 1982 v Ni; 1984 v U, Bel, EG, W, E; 1985 v Y, Ic, Sp (2); W; 1986 v EG, Ho, U. (14)

Alexander, D. (East Stirlingshire); 1894 v W, Ni. (2)

Allan, D.S. (Queen's Park); 1885 v E, W; 1886 v W. (3)

Allan, G. (Liverpool); 1897 v E. (1)

Allan, H. (Hearts); 1902 v W. (1)

Allan, J. (Queen's Park); 1887 v E, W. (2)

Allan, T. (Dundee); 1974 v W, G, N. (2)

Ancell, R.F.D. (Newcastle U); 1937 v W, Ni. (2)

Anderson, A. (Hearts); 1933 v E; 1934 v A, E, W, Ni; 1935 v E, W, Ni; 1936 v E, W, Ni; 1937 v G, E, W, Ni, A; 1938 v E, W, Ni, Cz, Ho; 1939 v W, H. (23)

Anderson, F. (Clydeside); 1874 v E. (1)

Anderson, G. (Kilmarnock); 1901 v Ni. (1)

Anderson, H.A. (Raith R); 1914 v W. (1)

Anderson, J. (Leicester C); 1954 v Fi. (1)

Anderson, K. (Queen's Park); 1896 v Ni; 1898 v E, Ni. (3)

Anderson, W. (Queen's Park); 1882 v E; 1883 v E, W; 1884 v E; 1885 v E, W. (6)

Andrews, P. (Eastern); 1875 v E. (1)

Archibald, A. (Rangers); 1921 v W; 1922 v W, E; 1923 v Ni; 1924 v E, W; 1931 v E; 1932 v E. (8)

Archibald, S. (Aberdeen); 1980 v P(sub); (Tottenham H); Ni, Pol, H; 1981 v Se(sub); Is, Ni, Is, Ni, E; 1982 v Ni, P, Sp(sub); Ho, Nz(sub); Br, USSR; 1983 v EG, Sw(sub); Bel; 1984 v EG, E, F; (Barcelona); 1985 v Sp, E, Ic(sub); 1986 v WG. (27)

Armstrong, M.W. (Aberdeen); , 1936 v W, Ni; 1937 v G. (3)

Arnott, W. (Queen's Park); 1883 v W; 1884 v E, Ni; 1985 v E, W; 1886 v E; 1887 v E, W; 1888 v E; 1889 v E; 1890 v E; 1891 v E; 1892 v E; 1893 v E. (14)

Auld, J.R. (Third Lanark); 1887 v E, W; 1889 v W. (3)

Auld, R. (Celtic); 1959 v H, P; 1960 v W. (3)

Baird, A. (Queen's Park); 1892 v Ni; 1894 v W. (2)

Baird, D. (Hearts); 1890 v Ni; 1891 v E; 1892 v W. (3)

Baird, H. (Airdrie); 1956 v A. (1)

Baird, J.C. (Vale of Leven); 1876 v E; 1878 v W, 1880 v E. (3)

Baird, S. (Rangers); 1957 v Y, Sp (2); Sw, WG; 1958 v F, Ni. (7)

Baird, W.U. (St Bernard); 1897 v Ni. (1)

Bannon, E. (Dundee Utd); 1980 v Bel; 1983 v Ni, W, E, Ca; 1984 v EG; 1986 v Is, R, E, D(sub); WG. (11)

Barbour, A. (Renton);1885 v Ni (1)

Barker, J.B. (Rangers); 1893 v W; 1894 v W. (2)

Barrett, F. (Dundee); 1894 v Ni; 1895 v W. (2)

Battles, B. (Celtic); 1901 v E, W, Ni. (3)

Battles, B.jun (Hearts); 1931 v W. (1)

Bauld, W. (Hearts); 1950 v E, Sw, P. (3)

Baxter, J.C. (Rangers); 1961 v Ni, Ei(2); Cz; 1962 v Ni, W, E, Cz(2); U; 1963 v W, Ni, E, A, N, Ei, Sp; 1964 v W, E, N, WG; 1965 v W, Ni, Fi; (Sunderland); 1966 v P, Br, Ni, W, E, I; 1967 v W, E, USSR; 1968 v W. (34)

Baxter, R.D. (Middlesbrough); 1939 v E, W, H. (3)

WILLIE BAULD

ANDY BEATTIE

Beattie, A. (Preston NE); 1937 v E, A, Cz; 1938 v E; 1939 v W, Ni, H. (7)

Beattie, R. (Preston NE); 1939 v W. (1)

Begbie, I. (Hearts); 1890 v Ni; 1891 v E; 1892 v W; 1894 v E. (4)

Bell, A. (Manchester U); 1912 v Ni. (1)

Bell, J. (Dumbarton); 1890 v Ni; 1892 v E; (Everton); 1896 v E; 1897 v E; 1898 v E; (Celtic); 1899 v E, W, Ni; 1900 v E, W. (10)

Bell, M. (Hearts); 1901 v W. (1)

Bell, W.J. (Leeds U); 1966 v P, Br. (2)

Bennett, A. (Celtic); 1904 v W; 1907 v Ni; 1908 v W, (Rangers); 1909 v W, Ni, E; 1910 v E, W; 1911 v E, W; 1913 v Ni. (11)

Bennie, R. (Airdrieonians); 1925 v W, Ni; 1926 v Ni. (3)

Berry, D. (Queen's Park); 1894 v W; 1899 v W, Ni. (3)

Berry, W.H. (Queen's Park); 1888 v E; 1889 v E; 1890 v E; 1891 v E. (4)

Bett, J. (Rangers); 1982 v Ho; 1983 v Bel; (Lokeren); 1984 v Bel,W, E, F; 1985 v Y, Ic, Sp(2); W, E, Ic; (Aberdeen); 1986 v W, Is, Ho; 1987 v Bel. (17)

Beveridge, W.W. (Glasgow University); 1879v E, W; 1880 v W. (3)

Black, A. (Hearts); 1938 v Cz, Ho; 1939 v H. (3)

Black, D. (Hurlford); 1889 v Ni. (1)

Black, I.H. (Southampton); 1948 v E. (1)

Blackburn, J.E. (Royal Engineers); 1873 v E. (1)

Blacklaw, A.S. (Burnley); 1963 v N, Sp; 1966 v I. (3)

Blackley, J. (Hibernian); 1974 v Cz, E, Bel, Z; 1976 v Sw; 1977 v W, Se. (7)

Blair, D. (Clyde); 1929 v W, Ni; 1931 v E, A, I; 1932 v W, Ni; (Aston Villa); 1933 v W. (8)

Blair, J. (Sheffield W); 1920 v E, Ni; (Cardiff); 1921 v E; 1922 v E; 1923 v E, W, Ni; 1924 v W. (8)

Blair, J. (Motherwell); 1934 v W. (1)

Blair, J.A. (Blackpool); 1947 v W. (1)

Blair, W. (Third Lanark); 1896 v W. (1)

Blessington, J. (Celtic); 1894 v E, Ni; 1896 v E, Ni. (4)

Blyth, J.A. (Coventry C); 1978 v Bul, W. (2)

Bone, J. (Norwich C); 1972 v Y(sub); 1973 v D. (2)

Bowie, J. (Rangers); 1920 v E, Ni. (2)

Bowie, W. (Linthouse); 1891 v Ni. (1)

Bowman, G.A. (Montrose); 1892 v Ni. (1)

Boyd, J.M. (Newcastle U); 1934 v Ni. (1)

Boyd, R. (Mossend Swifts); 1889 v Ni; 1891 v W. (2)

Boyd, W.G. (Clyde); 1931 v I, Sw. (2)

Brackenbridge, T. (Hearts); 1888 v Ni. (1)

Bradshaw, T. (Bury); 1928 v E. (1)

Brand, R. (Rangers); 1961 v Ni, Cz, Ei(2); 1962 v Ni, W, Cz, U. (8)

Branden, T. (Blackburn R); 1896 v E. (1)

Brazil, A. (Ipswich T); 1980 v Pol(sub); H; 1982 v Sp, Ho(sub); Ni, W, E, Nz, USSR(sub); 1983 v EG, Sw, W, E(sub). (13)

Bremner, D. (Hibernian); 1976 v Sw(sub). (1)

Bremner, W.J. (Leeds U); 1965 v Sp; 1966 v E, Pol, P, Br, I(2); 1967 v W, Ni, E; 1968 v W, E; 1969 v W, E, Ni, D, A, WG, Cy(2); 1970 v Ei, WG, A; 1971 v W, E; 1972 v P, Bel, Ho, Ni, W, E, Y, Cz, Br; 1973 v D(2); E(2); Ni(sub); Sw, Br; 1974 v Cz, WG, Ni, W, E, Bel, N, Z, Br, Y; 1975 v Sp(2); 1976 v D. (54)

Brennan, F. (Newcastle U); 1947 v W, Ni; 1953 v W, Ni, E; 1954 v Ni, E. (7)

Breslin, B. (Hibernian); 1897 v W. (1)

Brewster, G. (Everton); 1921 v E. (1)

Brogan, J. (Celtic); 1971 v W, Ni, P, E. (4)

Brown, A. (Middlesbrough); 1904 v E. (1)

Brown, A. (St Mirren); 1890 v W; 1891 v W. (2)

Brown, A.D. (East Fife); 1950 v Sw, P, F; (Blackpool); 1952 v USA, D, Se; 1953 v W; 1954 v W, E, N(2); Fi, A, U. (14)

Brown, G.C.P. (Rangers); 1931 v W; 1932 v E, W, Ni; 1933 v E; 1935 v A, E, W; 1936 v E, W; 1937 v G, E, W, Ni, Cz; 1938 v E, W, Cz, Ho. (19)

Brown, H. (Partick T); 1947 v W, Bel, L. (3)

Brown, J. (Cambuslang); 1890 v W. (1)

Brown, J.B. (Clyde); 1939 v W. (1)

Brown, J.G. (Sheffield U); 1975 v R. (1)
Brown, R. (Dumbarton); 1884 v W, Ni. (2)
Brown, R. (Rangers); 1947 v Ni; 1949 v Ni; 1952 v E. (3)
Brown, R.jun (Dumbarton); 1885 v W. (1)
Brown, W.D.F. (Dundee); 1958 v F; 1959 v E, W, Ni; (Tottenham H); 1960 v W, Ni, Pol, A, H, T; 1962 v W, E, Cz; 1963 v W, Ni, E, A; 1964 v Ni, W, N; 1965 v E, Fi, Pol, Sp; 1966 v Ni, Pol, I. (28)
Browning, J. (Celtic); 1914 v W. (1)
Brownlie, J. (Hibernian); 1971 v USSR; 1972 v Pe, Ni, E; 1973 v D(2); 1976 v R. (7)
Brownlie, J. (Third Lanark); 1909 v E, Ni; 1910 v E, W, Ni; 1911 v W, Ni; 1912 v W, Ni, E; 1913 v W, Ni, E; 1914 v W, Ni, E. (16)
Bruce, D. (Vale of Leven); 1890 v W. (1)
Bruce, R.F. (Middlesbrough); 1934 v A. (1)
Buchan, M.M. (Aberdeen); 1972 v P(sub); Bel; (Manchester U); W, Y, Cz, Br; 1973 v D(2); E; 1974 v WG, Ni, W, N, Br, Y; 1975 v EG, Sp, P; 1976 v D, R; 1977 v Fi, Cz, Ch, Arg, Br; 1978 v EG, W(sub); Ni, Pe, Ir, Ho; 1979 v A, N, P. (34)
Buchanan, J. (Cambuslang); 1889 v Ni. (1)
Buchanan, J. (Rangers); 1929 v E; 1930 v E. (2)
Buchanan, P.S. (Chelsea); 1938 v Cz. (1)
Buchanan, R. (Abercorn); 1891 v W. (1)
Buckley, P. (Aberdeen); 1954 v N; 1955 v W, Ni. (3)
Buick, A. (Hearts); 1902 v W, Ni. (2)
Burley, G. (Ipswich T); 1979 v W, Ni, E, Arg, N; 1980 v P, Ni, E(sub); Pol; 1982 v W(sub); E. (11)
Burns, F. (Manchester U); 1970 v A. (1)
Burns, K. (Birmingham C); 1974 v WG; 1975 v EG(sub); Sp(2); 1977 v Cz(sub); W, Se, W(sub); (Nottingham F); 1978 v Ni(sub); W, E, Pe, Ir; 1979 v N; 1980 v Pe, A, Bel; 1981 v Is, Ni, W. (20)
Burns, T. (Celtic); 1981 v Ni; 1982 v Ho(sub); W; 1983 v Bel(sub); Ni, Ca(1+1 sub). (7)
Busby, M.W. (Manchester C); 1934 v W. (1)

Cairns, T. (Rangers); 1920 v W; 1922 v E; 1923 v E, W; 1924 v Ni; 1925 v W, E, Ni. (8)
Calderhead, D. (Queen of the South); 1889 v Ni. (1)
Calderwood, R. (Cartvale); 1885 v Ni, E, W. (3)
Caldow, E. (Rangers); 1957 v Sp, EG, E; 1958 v Ni, W, Sw, Par, H, Pol, Y, F; 1959 v E, Ni, WG, Ho, P; 1960 v E, W, Ni, A, H, T; 1961 v E, W, Ni, Ei(2); Cz; 1962 v Ni, W, E, Cz(2); U; 1963 v W, Ni, E. (40)
Callaghan, P. (Hibernian); 1900 v Ni. (1)
Callaghan, W. (Dunfermline Ath); 1970 v Ei(sub); W. (2)
Cameron, J. (St Mirren); 1904 v Ni; (Chelsea); 1909 v E; (2)
Cameron, J. (Queen's Park); 1896 v Ni. (1)
Cameron, J. (Rangers); 1886 v Ni. (1)
Campbell, C. (Queen's Park); 1874 v E;; 1876 v W; 1877 v E, W; 1878 v E; 1879 v E; 1880 v E; 1881 v E; 1882 v E, W; 1884 v E; 1885 v E; 1886 v E. (13)
Campbell, H. (Renton); 1889 v W. (1)
Campbell, Jas. (Sheffield W); 1913 v W. (1)
Campbell, J. (South Western); 1880 v W. (1)
Campbell, J. (Kilmarnock); 1891 v Ni; 1892 v W. (2)
Campbell, John (Celtic); 1893 v E, Ni; 1898 v E, Ni; 1900 v E, Ni; 1901 v E, W, Ni; 1902 v W, Ni; 1903 v W. (12)
Campbell, John (Rangers); 1899 v E, W, Ni; 1901 v Ni. (4)
Campbell, K. (Liverpool); 1920 v E, W, Ni; (Partick T); 1921 v W, Ni; 1922 v W, Ni, E. (8)
Campbell, P. (Rangers); 1878 v W; 1879 v W. (2)
Campbell, P. (Morton); 1898 v W. (1)
Campbell, R. (Falkirk); 1947 v Bel, L; (Chelsea); 1950 v Sw, P, F. (5)
Campbell, W. (Morton); 1947 v Ni; 1948 v E, Bel, Sw, F. (5)
Carabine, J.(Third Lanark); 1938 v Ho; 1939 v E, Ni. (3)
Carr, W.M. (Coventry C); 1970 v Ni, W, E; 1971 v D; 1972 v Pe; 1973 v D(sub). (6)
Cassidy, J. (Celtic); 1921 v W, Ni; 1923 v Ni; 1924 v W. (4)
Chalmers, S. (Celtic); 1965 v W, Fi; 1966 v P(sub); Br; 1967 v Ni. (5)
Chalmers, W. (Rangers); 1885 v Ni. (1)
Chalmers, W.S. (Queen's Park); 1929 v Ni. (1)
Chambers, T. (Hearts); 1894 v W. (1)
Chaplin, G.D. (Dundee); 1908 v W. (1)
Cheyne, A.G. (Aberdeen); 1929 v E, N, G, Ho; 1930 v F. (5)
Christie, A.J. (Queen's Park); 1898 v W; 1899 v E, Ni. (3)

Christie, R.M. (Queen's Park); 1884 v E. (1)
Clark, J. (Celtic); 1966 v r; 1967 v W, Ni, USSR. (4)
Clark, R.B. (Aberdeen); 1968 v W, Ho; 1970 v Ni; 1971 v W, Ni, E, D, P, USSR; 1972 v Bel, Ni, W, E, Cz, Br; 1973 v D, E. (17)
Cleland, J. (Royal Albert); 1891 v Ni. (1)
Clements, R. (Leith A); 1891 v Ni. (1)
Clunas, W.L. (Sunderland); 1924 v E; 1926 v W. (2)
Collier, W. (Raith R); 1922 v W. (1)
Collins, R.Y. (Celtic); 1951 v W, Ni, A; 1955 v Y, A, H; 1956 v Ni, W; 1957 v E, W, Sp(2); Sw, WG; 1958 v Ni, W, Sw, H, Pol, Y, F, Par; (Everton); 1959 v E, W, Ni, WG, Ho, P; (Leeds); 1965 v E, Pol, Sp. (31)
Collins, T.(Hearts); 1909 v W. (1)
Colman, D. (Aberdeen); 1911 v E, W, Ni; 1913 v Ni. (4)
Colquhoun, E.P. (Sheffield U); 1972 v P, Ho, Pe, Y, Cz, Br; 1973 v D(2); E. (9)
Combe, J.R. (Hibernian); 1948 v E, Bel, Sw. (3)
Conn, A. (Hearts); 1956 v A. (1)
Conn, A. (Tottenham H); 1975 v Ni(sub); E. (2)
Connachan, E.D.(Dunfermline A); 1962 v Cz, U. (2)
Connelly, G. (Celtic); 1974 v Cz, WG. (2)
Connolly, J. (Everton); 1973 v Sw. (1)
Connor, J. (Airdrieonians); 1886 v Ni. (1)
Connor, J. (Sunderland); 1930 v F; 1932 v Ni; 1934 v E; 1935 v Ni. (4)
Connor, R. (Dundee); 1986 v Ho. (1)
Cook, W.L. (Bolton W); 1934 v E; 1935 v W, Ni. (3)

BILLY COOK

Cooke, C. (Dundee); 1966 v W, I; (Chelsea); P, Br; 1968 v E, Ho; 1969 v W, Ni, A, WG(sub); Cy(2); 1970 v A; 1971 v Bel; 1975 v Sp, P. (16)
Cooper, D. (Rangers); 1980 v Pe, A(sub); 1984 v W, E; 1985 v Y, Ic, Sp(2); W; 1986 v W(sub); EG, Aus(2); Ho, WG(sub); U(sub); 1987 v Bul, Lux, Ei, Br. (20)
Cormack, P.B. (Hibernian); 1966 v Br; 1969 v D(sub); 1970 v Ei, WG; (Nottingham F); 1971 v D(sub); W, P, E; 1972 v Ho(sub). (9)
Cowan, J. (Aston Villa); 1896 v E; 1897 v E; 1898 v E. (3)
Cowan, J. (Morton); 1948 v Bel, Sw, F; 1949 v E, W, F; 1950 v E, W, Ni, Sw, P, F; 1951 v E, W, Ni, A(2); D, F, Bel; 1952 v Ni, W, USA, D, Se. (25)
Cowan, W.D. (Newcastle U); 1924 v E. (1)
Cowie, D. (Dundee); 1953 v E, Se; 1954 v Ni, W, Fi, N, A, U; 1955 v W, Ni, A, H; 1956 v W, A; 1957 v Ni, W; 1958 v H, Pol, Y, Par. (20)
Cox, C.J. (Hearts); 1948 v F. (1)

Cox, S.(Rangers); 1948 v F; 1949 v E, F; 1950 v E, F, W, Ni, Sw, P; 1951 v E, D, F, Bel, A; 1952 v Ni, W, USA, D, Se; 1953 v W, Ni, E; 1954 v W, Ni, E. (25)
Craig, A. (Motherwell); 1929 v N, Ho; 1932 v E. (3)
Craig, J. (Celtic); 1977 v Se(sub). (1)
Craig, J.P. (Celtic); 1968 v W. (1)
Craig, T. (Rangers); 1927 v Ni; 192 v Ni; 1929 v N, G, Ho; 1930 v Ni, E, W. (8)
Craig, T.B. (Newcastle U); 1976 v Sw. (1)
Crapnell, J. (Airdrieonians); 1929 v E, N, G; 1930 v F; 1931 v Ni, W; 1932 v E, F; 1933 v Ni. (9)
Crawford, D. (St Mirren); 1894 v W, Ni; 1900 v W. (3)
Crawford, J. (Queen's Park); 1932 v F, Ni; 1933 v E, W, Ni. (5)
Crerand, P.T. (Celtic); 1961 v Ei(2); Cz; 1962 v Ni, W, E, Cz(2); U; 1963 v W, Ni; (Manchester U); 1964 v Ni; 1965 v E, Pol, Fi; 1966 v Pol. (16)
Cringan, W. (Celtic); 1920 v W; 1922 v E, Ni, 1923 v W, E. (5)
Crosbie, J.A. (Ayr U); 1920 v W;. (Birmingham); 1922 v E. (2)
Croal, J.A. (Falkirk); 1913 v Ni; 1914 v E, W. (3)
Cropley, A.J. (Hibernian); 1972 v P, Bel. (2)
Cross, J.H. (Third Lanark); 1903 v Ni. (1)
Cruickshank, J. (Hearts); 1964 v WG; 1970 v W, E; 1971 v D, Bel; 1976 v R. (6)
Crum, J. (Celtic); 1936 v E; 1939 v Ni. (2)
Cullen, M.J. (Luton T); 1956 v A. (1)
Cumming, D.S. (Middlesbrough); 1938 v E. (1)
Cumming, J.(Hearts); 1955 v E, H, P, Y; 1960 v E, Pol, A, H, T. (9)
Cummings, G. (Partick T); 1935 v E; 1936 v W, Ni; (Aston Villa); E; 1937 v G; 1938 v W, Ni, Cz; 1939 v E. (9)
Cunningham, A.N. (Rangers); 1920 v Ni; 1921 v W, E; 1922 v Ni; 1923 v E, W; 1924 v E, Ni; 1926 v E, Ni; 1927 v E, W. (12)
Cunningham, W.C. (Preston NE); 1954 v N(2); U, Fi, A; 1955 v W, E, H. (8)
Curran, H.P. (Wolverhampton W); 1970 v A; 1971 v Ni, E, D, USSR(sub). (5)

Dalglish, K. (Celtic); 1972 v Bel(sub); Ho; 1973 v D(1+1 sub); E(2); W, Ni, Sw, Br; 1974 v Cz(2); WG(2); Ni, W, E, Bel, N(sub); Z, Br, Y; 1975 v EG, Sp(sub +1); Se, P, W, Ni, E, R; 1976 v D(2); R, Sw, Ni, E; 1977 v Fi, Cz, W(2); Se, Ni, E, Ch, Arg, Br; (Liverpool); 1978 v EG, Cz, W, Bul, Ni(sub); W, E, Pe, Ir, Ho; 1979 v A, N, P, W, Ni, E, Arg, N; 1980 v Pe, A, Bel(2); P, Ni, W, E, Pol, H; 1981 v Se, P, Is; 1982 v Se, Ni, P(sub); Sp, Ho, Ni, W, E, Nz, Br(sub); 1983 v Bel, Sw; 1984 v U, Bel, EG; 1985 v Y, Ic, Sp, W; 1986 v EG, Aus, R; 1987 v Bul(sub), Lux. (102)
Davidson, D. (Queen's Park); 1878 v W; 1879 v W; 1880 v W; 1881 v E. (5)
Davidson, J.A. (Partick T); 1954 v N(2); A, U; 1955 v W, Ni, E, H. (8)
Davidson, S. (Middlesbrough); 1921 v E. (1)
Dawson, A. (Rangers); 1980 v Pol(sub); H; 1983 v Ni, Ca(2). (5)
Dawson, J. (Rangers); 1935 v Ni; 1936 v E; 1937 v G, E, W, Ni, A, Cz; 1938 v W, Hol Ni; 1939 v E, Ni, H. (14)
Deans, J. (Celtic); 1975 v EG, Sp. (2)
Delaney, J. (Celtic); 1936 v W, Ni; 1937 v G, E, A, Cz; 1938 v Ni; 1939 v W, Ni; (Manchester U); 1947 v E; 1948 v E, W, Ni. (13)
Devine, A. (Falkirk); 1910 v W. (1)
Dewar, G. (Dumbarton); 1888 v Ni; 1889 v E. (2)
Dewar, N.(Third Lanark); 1932 v E, F; 1933 v W. (3)
Dick, J. (West Ham U); 1959 v E. (1)
Dickie, M. (Rangers); 1897 v Ni; 1899 v Ni; 1900 v W. (3)
Dickson, W. (Kilmarnock); 1970 v Ni, W, E; 1971 v D, USSR. (5)
Dickson, W. (Dumbarton); 1888 v Ni. (1)
Divers, J. (Celtic); 1895 v W. (1)
Divers, J. (Celtic); 1939 v Ni. (1)
Docherty, T.H. (Preston NE); 1952 v W; 1953 v E, Se; 1954 v N(2); A, U; 1955 v W, E, H(2); A; 1957 v E, Y, Sp(2); Sw, WG; 1958 v Ni, W, E, Sw; (Arsenal); 1959 v W, E, Ni. (25)
Dodds, D. (Dundee U); 1984 v U(sub); Ni. (2)
Dodds, J. (Celtic); 1914 v E, W, Ni. (3)
Doig, J.E. (Arbroath); 1887 v Ni; 1889 v Ni; (Sunderland); 1896 v E; 1899 v E; 1903 v E. (5)
Donachie, W. (Manchester C); 1972 v Pe, Ni, E, Y, Cz, Br; 1973 v D, E, W, Ni; 1974 v Ni; 1976 v R, Ni, W, E; 1977 v Fi, Cz, W(2); Se, Ni, E, Ch, Arg, Br, 1978 v EG, W, Bul, W, E, Ir, Ho; 1979 v A, N, P(sub). (35)

Donaldson, A. (Bolton W); 1914 v E, Ni, W; 1920 v E, Ni; 1922 v Ni. (6)
Donnachie, J. (Oldham A); 1913 v E; 1914 v E, Ni. (3)
Dougall, C. (Birmingham C); 1947 v W. (1)
Dougall, J. (Preston NE); 1939 v E. (1)
Dougan, R. (Hearts); 1950 v Sw. (1)
Douglas, A. (Chelsea); 1911 v Ni. (1)
Douglas, J. (Renfrew); 1880 v W. (1)
Dowds, P. (Celtic); 1892 v Ni. (1)
Downie, R. (Third Lanark); 1892 v W. (1)
Doyle, D. (Celtic); 1892 v E; 1893 v W; 1894 v E; 1895 v E, Ni; 1897 v E; 1898 v E, Ni. (8)
Doyle, J. (Ayr U); 1976 v R. (1)
Drummond, J. (Falkirk); 1892 v Ni; (Rangers); 1894 v Ni; 1895 v Ni, E, 1896 v E, Ni; 1897 v Ni; 1898 v E; 1900 v E; 1901 v E;; 1902 v E, W, Ni; 1903 v Ni. (14)
Dunbar, M. (Cartvale); 1886 v Ni. (1)
Duncan, A. (Hibernian); 1975 v P(sub); W, Ni, E, R; 1976 v D. (6)
Duncan, D. (Derby C); 1933 v E, W; 1934 v A, W; 1935 v E, W; 1936 v E, W, Ni; 1937 v G, E, W, Ni; 1938 v W. (14)
Duncan, D.M. (East Fife); 1948 v Bel, Sw, F. (3)
Duncan, J. (Alexandra A); 1878 v W; 1882 v W. (2)
Duncan, J. (Leicester C); 1926 v W. (1)
Duncanson, J. (Rangers); 1947 v Ni. (1)
Dunlop, J. (St Mirren); 1890 v W. (1)
Dunlop, W. (Liverpool); 1906 v E. (1)
Dunn, J. (Hibernian); 1925 v W, Ni; 1927 v Ni; 1928 v Ni, E; (Everton); 1929 v W. (6)
Dykes, J. (Hearts); 1938 v Ho; 1939 v Ni. (2)

Easson, J.F. (Portsmouth); 1931 v A, Sw; 1934 v W. (3)
Ellis, J. (Mossend Swifts); 1892 v Ni. (1)
Evans, A. (Aston Villa); 1982 v Ho, Ni, E, Nz. (4)
Evans, R. (Celtic); 1949 v E, W, Ni, F; 1950 v W, Ni, Sw, P; 1951 v E, A; 1952 v Ni; 1953 v Se; 1954 v Ni, W, E, N, Fi; 1955 v Ni, P, Y, A, H; ;1956 v E, Ni, W, A; 1957 v WG, Sp; 1958 v Ni, W, E, Sw, H, Pol, Y, Par, F; 1959 v E, WG, Ho, P; 1960 v E, Ni, W, Pol; (Chelsea); 1960 v A, H, T. (48)
Ewart, J. (Bradford C); 1921 v E. (1)
Ewing, T. (Partick T); 1958 v W, E. (2)

Farm, G.N. (Blackpool); 1953 v W, Ni, E, Se; 1954 v Ni, W, E; 1959 v WG, Ho, P. (10)
Ferguson, J. (Vale of Leven); 1874 v E; 1876 v E, W; 1877 v E, W; 1878 v W. (6)
Ferguson, R. (Kilmarnock); 1966 v W, E, Ho, P, Br; 1967 v W, Ni. (7)
Fernie, W. (Celtic); 1954 v Fi, A, U; 1955 v W, Ni, 1957 v E, Ni, W, Y; 1958 v W, Sw, Par. (12)
Findlay, R. (Kilmarnock); 1898 v W. (1)
Fitchie, T.T. (Woolwich Arsenal); 1905 v W; 1906 v W, Ni; (Queen's Park); 1907 v W. (4)
Flavell, R. (Airdrieonians); 1947 v Bel, L. (2)
Fleming, C. (East Fife); 1954 v Ni. (1)
Fleming, J.W. (Rangers); 1929 v G, Ho; 1930 v E. (3)
Fleming, R. (Morton); 1886 v Ni. (1)
Forbes, A.R. (Sheffield U); 1947 v Bel, L, E; 1948 v W, Ni; (Arsenal); 1950 v E, P, F; 1951 v W, Ni, A; 1952 v W, D, Se. (14)

Forbes, J. (Vale of Leven); 1884 v E, W, Ni; 1887 v W, E. (5)
Ford, D. (Hearts); 1974 v Cz(sub), WG(sub), W. (3)
Forrest, J. (Rangers); 1966 v W, I; (Aberdeen); 1971 v Bel(sub), D, USSR. (5)
Forrest, J. (Motherwell); 1958 v E. (1)
Forsyth, A. (Partick T); 1972 v Y, Cz, Br; 1973 v D, (Manchester U); E; 1975 v Sp, Ni(sub), R, EG; 1976 v D. (10)
Forsyth, C. (Kilmarnock); 1964 v E; 1965 v W, Ni, Fi. (4)
Forsyth, T. (Motherwell); 1971 v D; (Rangers); 1974 v Cz; 1976 v Sw, Ni, W, E; 1977 v Fi, Se, W, Ni, E, Ch, Arg, Br; 1978 v Cz, W, Ni, W(sub), E, Pe, Ir(sub), Ho. (22)
Foyers, R. (St Bernards); 1893 v W; 1894 v W. (2)
Fraser, D.M. (West Brom); 1968 v Ho; 1969 v Cy. (2)
Fraser, J. (Moffat); 1891 v Ni. (1)
Fraser, M.J.E. (Queen's Park); 1880 v W; 1882 v W, E; 1883 v W, E. (5)
Fraser, J. (Dundee); 1907 v Ni. (1)
Fraser, W. (Sunderland); 1955 v W, Ni. (2)
Fulton, W. (Abercorn); 1884 v Ni. (1)
Fyfe, J.H. (Third Lanark); 1895 v W. (1)

Gabriel, J. (Everton); 1961 v W; 1964 v N(sub). (2)
Gallacher, H.K. (Airdrieonians); 1924 v Ni; 1925 v E, W, Ni; 1926 v W; (Newcastle); 1926 v E, Ni; 1927 v E, W, Ni; 1928 v E, W; 1929 v E, W, Ni; 1930 v W, Ni, F; (Chelsea); 1934 v E; (Derby Co); 1935 v E. (20)

Photocall for the Scotland squad en route to their appointment with England at Wembley in April 1957. Left to right are: John Hewie, Dawson Walker (trainer), Ian McColl, Jackie Mudie, Tommy Younger, Eric Caldow, Willie McNaught, Tommy Docherty, Bobby Collins, George Young, Willie Fernie, Tommy Ring, Lawrie Reilly.

Gallacher, P. (Sunderland); 1935 v Ni. (1)
Galt, J.H. (Rangers); 1908 v W, Ni. (2)
Gardiner, I. (Motherwell); 1958 v W. (1)
Gardner, D.R. (Third Lanark); 1897 v W. (1)
Gardner, R. (Queen's Park); 1872 v E; 1873 v E; (Clydesdale); 1874 v E; 1875 v E; 1878 v E. (5)
Gemmell, T. (St Mirren); 1955 v P, Y. (2)
Gemmell, T. (Celtic); 1966 v E; 1967 v W, Ni, E, USSR; 1968 v Ni, E; 1969 v W, Ni, E, D, A, WG, Cy; 1970 v E, Ei, WG; 1971 v Bel. (18)
Gemmill, A. (Derby Co); 1971 v Bel; 1972 v P, Ho, Pe, Ni, W, E; 1976 v D, R, Ni, W, E; 1977 v Fi, Cz, W(2), Ni(sub), E(sub), Ch(sub), Arg, Br; 1978 v EG(sub); (Nottingham F); Bul, Ni, W, E(sub), Pe(sub), Ir, Ho; 1979 v A, N, P, N; (Birmingham C); 1980 v A, P, Ni, W, E, H; 1981 v Se, P, Is, Ni. (43)
Gibb, W. (Clydesdale); 1873 v E. (1)
Gibson, D.W. (Leicester C); 1963 v A, N, Ei, Sp; 1964 v Ni; 1965 v W, Fi. (7)
Gibson, J.D. (Partick T); 1926 v E; 1927 v E, W, Ni; (Aston Villa); 1928 v E, W; 1930 v W, Ni. (8)
Gibson, N. (Rangers); 1895 v E, Ni; 1896 v E, Ni; 1897 v E, Ni; 1898 v E; 1899 v E, W, Ni; 1900 v E, Ni; 1901 v W; (Partick T); 1905 v Ni. (14)
Gilchrist, J.E. (Celtic); 1922 v E. (1)
Gilhooley, M. (Hull C); 1922 v W. (1)
Gillespie, G. (Rangers); 1880 v W; 1881 v E, W; 1882 v E; (Queen's Park); 1886 v W; 1890 v W; 1891 v Ni. (7)
Gillespie, Jas. (Third Lanark); 1898 v W. (1)
Gillespie, John (Queen's Park); 1896 v W. (1)
Gillespie, R. (Queen's Park); 1927 v W; 1931 v W; 1932 v F; 1933 v E. (4)
Gillick, T. (Everton); 1937 v A, Cz; 1939 v W, Ni, H. (5)
Gilmour, J. (Dundee); 1931 v W. (1)
Gilzean, A.J. (Dundee); 1964 v W, E, N, WG; 1965 v Ni, (Tottenham H); Sp; 1966 v Ni, W, Pol, I; 1968 v W; 1969 v W, E, WG, Cy(2), A(sub); 1970 v Ni, E(sub), WG, A; 1971 v P. (22)
Glavin, R. (Celtic); 1977 v Se. (1)
Glen, A. (Aberdeen); 1956 v E, Ni. (2)
Glen, R. (Renton); 1895 v W; 1896 v W; (Hibernian); 1900 v Ni. (3)
Goram, A.L. (Oldham A); 1986 v EG(sub), R, Ho; 1987 v Br. (4)
Gordon, J.E. (Rangers); 1912 v E, Ni; 1913 v E, Ni, W; 1914 v E, Ni; 1920 v W, E, Ni. (10)
Gossland, J. (Rangers); 1884 v Ni. (1)
Goudie, J. (Aberdeen); 1884 v Ni. (1)
Gough, C.R. (Dundee U); 1983 v Sw, Ni, W, E, Ca(3); 1984 v U, Bel, EG, Ni, W, E, F; 1985 v Sp, E, Ic; 1986 v W, EG, Aus, Is, R, E, D, WG, U; (Tottenham H); 1987 v Bul, Ei(2), Lux, Bel, E, Br. (33)
Gourlay, J. (Cambuslang); 1886 v Ni; 1888 v W. (2)
Govan, J. (Hibernian); 1948 v E, W, Bel, Sw, F; 1949 v Ni. (6)
Gow, D.R. (Rangers); 1888 v E. (1)
Gow, J.J. (Queen's Park); 1885 v E. (1)
Gow, J.R. (Rangers); 1888 v Ni. (1)
Graham, A. (Leeds U); 1978 v EG(sub); 1979 v A(sub), N, W, Ni, E, Arg, N; 1980 v A; 1981 v W. (10)
Graham, G. (Arsenal); 1972 v P, Ho, Ni, Y, Cz, Br; 1973 v D(2); (Manchester U); E, W, Ni, Br(sub). (12)
Graham, J. (Annbank); 1884 v Ni. (1)
Graham, J.A. (Arsenal); 1921 v Ni. (1)
Grant, J. (Hibernian); 1959 v W, Ni. (2)
Gray, A. (Hibernian); 1903 v Ni. (1)
Gray, A.M. (Aston Villa); 1976 v R, Sw; 1977 v Fi, Cz; 1979 v N; (Wolverhampton W); 1980 v P, E(sub); 1981 v Se, P, Is(sub), Ni; 1982 v Se(sub), Ni(sub); 1983 v Ni, W, E, Ca(1+1 sub); (Everton); 1985 v Ic. (20)
Gray, D. (Rangers); 1929 v W, Ni, G, Ho; 1930 v W, E, Ni; 1931 v W; 1933 v W, Ni. (10)
Gray, E. (Leeds U); 1969 v E, Cy; 1970 v WG, A; 1971 v W, Ni; 1972 v Bel, Ho; 1976 v W, E; 1977 v Fi, W. (12)
Gray, F.T. (Leeds U); 1976 v Sw; 1979 v N, P, W, Ni, E, Arg(sub); (Nottingham F); 1980 v Bel(sub); 1981 v Se, P, Is, Ni, Is, W, (Leeds U); Ni, E; 1982 v Se, Ni, P, Sp, Ho, W, Nz, Br, USSR; 1983 v EG, Sw, Bel, Sw, W, E, Ca. (32)
Gray, W. (Pollokshields Ath); 1886 v E. (1)
Green, A. (Blackpool); 1971 v Bel(sub), P(sub), Ni, E; 1972 v W, E(sub). (6)
Greig, J. (Rangers); 1964 v E, WG; 1965 v W, Ni, E, Fi(2), Sp, Pol; 1966 v Ni, W, E, Pol, I(2), P, Ho, Br; 1967 v W, Ni, E; 1968 v Ni, W, E, Ho; 1969 v W, Ni, E, D, A, WG, Cy(2); 1970 v W, E, Ei, WG, A; 1971 v D, Bel, W(sub), Ni, E; 1976 v D. (44)

Groves, W. (Hibenian); 1888 v W; (Celtic); 1889 v Ni; 1890 v E. (3)
Guilliland, W. (Queen's Park); 1891 v W; 1892 v Ni; 1894 v E; 1895 v E. (4)

Haddock, H. (Clyde); 1955 v E, H(2), P, Y; 1958 v E. (6)
Haddow, D. (Rangers); 1894 v E. (1)
Haffey, F. (Celtic); 1960 v E; 1961 v E. (2)
Hamilton, A. (Queen's Park); 1885 v E, W; 1886 v E; 1888 v E. (4)
Hamilton, A.W. (Dundee); 1962 v Cz, U, W, E; 1963 v W, Ni, E, A, N, Ei; 1964 v Ni, W, E, N, WG; 1965 v Ni, W, E, Fi(2), Pol, Sp; 1966 v Pol, Ni. (24)
Hamilton, G. (Aberdeen); 1947 v Ni; 1951 v Bel, A; 1954 v N(2). (5)
Hamilton, G. (Port Glasgow Ath); 1906 v Ni. (1)
Hamilton, J. (Queen's Park); 1892 v W; 1893 v E, Ni. (3)
Hamilton, J. (St Mirren); 1924 v Ni. (1)
Hamilton, R.C. (Rangers); 1899 v E, W, Ni; 1900 v W; 1901 v E, Ni; 1902 v W, Ni; 1903 v E; 1904 v Ni; (Dundee); 1911 v W. (11)
Hamilton, T. (Hurlford); 1891 v Ni. (1)
Hamilton, T. (Rangers); 1932 v E. (1)
Hamilton, W.M. (Hibernian); 1965 v Fi. (1)
Hannah, A.B. (Renton); 1888 v W. (1)
Hannah, J. (Third Lanark); 1889 v W. (1)
Hansen, A.D. (Liverpool); 1979 v W, Arg; 1980 v Bel, P; 1981 v Se, P, Is; 1982 v Se, Ni, P, Sp, Ni(sub), W, E, Nz, Br, USSR; 1983 v EG, Sw, Bel, Sw; 1985 v W(sub); 1986 v R(sub); 1987 v Ei(2), Lux. (26)
Hansen, J. (Partick T); 1972 v Bel(sub), Y(sub). (2)
Harkness, J.D. (Queen's Park); 1927 v E, Ni; 1928 v E; (Hearts); 1929 v W, E, Ni; 1930 v E, W; 1932 v W, 1934 v Ni, W. (12)
Harper, J.M. (Aberdeen); 1973 v D(1+1 sub); (Hibernian); 1976 v D; (Aberdeen); 1978 v Ir(sub). (4)
Harper, W. (Hibernian); 1923 v E, Ni, W; 1924 v E, Ni, W; 1925 v E, Ni, W; (Arsenal); 1926 v E, Ni. (11)
Harris, J. (Partick T); 1921 v W, Ni. (2)
Harris, N. (Newcastle U); 1924 v E. (1)
Harrower, W. (Queen's Park); 1882 v E; 1884 v Ni; 1886 v E. (3)
Hartford, R.A. (West Brom), 1972 v Pe, W(sub), E, Y, Cz, Br; (Manchester C); 1976 v D, R, Ni(sub); 1977 v Cz(sub), W(sub), Se, W, Ni, E, Ch, Arg, Br; 1978 v EG, Cz, W, Bul, W, E, Pe, Ir, Ho; 1979 v A, N, P, W, Ni, E, Arg, N; (Everton); 1980 v Pe, Bel; 1981 v Ni(sub), Is, W, Ni, E; 1982 v Se; (Manchester C); Ni, P, Sp, Ni, W, E, Br. (50)
Harvey, D. (Leeds U); 1973 v D 1974 v Cz, Wg, Ni, W, E, Bel, Z, Dr, Y; 1975 v Eg, Sp (2); 1976 v D (2); 1977 v Fi (sub). (16)
Hasting, A.C. (Sunderland); 1936 v Ni; 1938 v Ni. (2)
Haughney, M. (Celtic); 1954 v E. (1)
Hay, D. (Celtic); 1970 v Ni, W, E; 1971 v D, Bel, W, P, Ni; 1972 v P, Bel, Ho; 1973 v W, Ni, E, Sw, Br; 1974 v Cz (2), Wg, Ni, W, E, Bel, N, Z, Br, Y. (27)
Hay, J. (Celtic); 1905 v Ni; 1909 v Ni; 1910 v W, Ni, E; 1911 v Ni, E; (Newcastle U); 1912 v E, W; 1914 v E, Ni. (11)
Hegarty, P. (Dundee U); 1979 v W, Ni, E, Arg, N(sub); 1980 v W, E; 1983 v Ni. (8)
Heggie, C. (Rangers); 1886 v Ni. (1)
Henderson, G.H. (Rangers); 1904 v Ni. (1)
Henderson, J.G. (Portsmouth); 1953 v Se; 1954 v Ni, E, N; 1956 v W; (Arsenal); 1959 v W, Ni. (7)
Henderson, W. (Rangers); 1963 v W, Ni, E, A, N, Ei, Sp; 1964 v W, Ni, E, N, WG; 1965 v Fi, Pol, E, Sp; 1966 v Ni, W, Pol, I, Ho; 1967 v W, Ni; 1968 v Ho; 1969 v Ni, E, Cy; 1970 v Ei; 1971 v P. (29)
Hepburn, J. (Alloa Ath); 1891 v W. (1)
Hepburn, R. (Ayr U); 1932 v Ni. (1)
Herd, A.C. (Hearts); 1935 v Ni. (1)
Herd, D.G. (Arsenal); 1959 v E, W, Ni; 1961 v E, Cz. (5)
Herd, G. (Clyde); 1958 v E; 1960 v H, T; 1961 v W, Ni. (5)
Herriot, J. (Birmingham C); 1969 v Ni, E, D, Cy(2), W(sub); 1970 v Ei(sub), WG. (8)
Hewie, J.D. (Charlton Ath); 1956 v E, A; 1957 v E, Ni, W, Y, Sp(2), Sw, WG; 1958 v H, Pol, Y, F; 1959 v Ho, P; 1960 v Ni, W, Pol. (19)
Higgins, A. (Kilmarnock); 1885 v Ni. (1)
Higgins, A. (Newcastle U); 1910 v E, Ni; 1911 v E, Ni. (4)
Highet, T.C. (Queen's Park); 1875 v E; 1876 v E, W; 1878 v E. (4)

Hill, D. (Rangers); 1881 v E, W; 1882 v W. (3)
Hill, D.A. (Third Lanark); 1906 v Ni. (1)
Hill, F.R. (Aberdeen); 1930 v F; 1931 v W, Ni. (3)
Hill, J. (Hearts); 1891 v E; 1892 v W. (2)
Hogg, G. (Hearts); 1896 v E, Ni. (2)
Hogg, J. (Ayr U); 1922 v Ni. (1)
Hogg, R.M. (Celtic); 1937 v Cz. (1)
Holm, A.H. (Queen's Park); 1882 v W; 1883 v E, W. (3)
Holt, D.D. (Hearts); 1963 v A, N, Ei, Sp; 1964 v WG(sub). (5)
Holton, J.A. (Manchester U); 1973 v W, Ni, E, Sw, Br; 1974 v Cz, WG, Ni, W, E, N, Z, Br, Y; 1975 v EG. (15)
Hope, R. (West Brom); 1968 v Ho; 1969 v D. (2)
Houliston, W. (Queen of the South); 1949 v E, Ni, F. (3)
Houston, S. (Manchester U); 1976 v D. (1)
Howden, W. (Partick T); 1905 v Ni. (1)
Howe, R. (Hamilton A); 1929 v N, Ho. (2)
Howie, J. (Newcastle U); 1905 v E; 1906 v E; 1908 v E. (3)
Howie, H. (Hibernian); 1949 v W. (1)
Howieson, J. (St Mirren); 1927 v Ni. (1)
Hughes, J. (Celtic); 1965 v Pol, Sp; 1966 v Ni, I(2); 1968 v E; 1969 v A; 1970 v Ei. (8)
Hughes, W. (Sunderland); 1975 v Se(sub). (1)
Humphries, W. (Motherwell); 1952 v Se. (1)
Hunter, A. (Kilmarnock); 1972 v Pe, Y; (Celtic); 1973 v E; 1974 v Cz. (4)
Hunter, J. (Dundee); 1909 v W. (1)
Hunter, J. (Third Lanark); 1874 v E; (Eastern); 1875 v E; (Third Lanark); 1876 v E; 1877 v W. (4)
Hunter, R. (St Mirren); 1890 v Ni. (1)
Hunter, W. (Motherwell); 1960 v H, T; 1961 v W. (3)
Husband, J. (Partick T); 1947 v W. (1)
Hutchison, T. (Coventry C); 1974 v Cz(2), WG(2), Ni, W, Bel(sub), N, Z(sub), Y(sub); 1975 v EG, Sp(2), P, E(sub), R(sub); 1976 v D. (17)
Hutton, J. (Aberdeen); 1923 v E, W, Ni; 1924 v Ni; 1926 v W, E, Ni; (Blackburn R); 1927 v Ni; 1928 v W, Ni. (10)
Hutton, J. (St Bernards); 1887 v Ni ()
Hyslop, T. (Stoke); 1896 v E; (Rangers); 1897 v E. (2)

Imlach, J.J.S. (Nottingham F); 1958 v H, Pol, Y, F. (4)
Imrie, W.N. (St Johnstone); 1929 v N, G. (2)
Inglis, J. (Kilmarnock Ath); 1884 v Ni. (1)
Inglis, J. (Rangers); 1883 v E, W. (2)
Irons, J.H. (Queen's Park); 1900 v W. (1)

Jackson, A. (Cambuslang); 1886 v W; 1888 v Ni. (2)
Jackson, A. (Aberdeen); 1925 v E, W, Ni; (Huddersfield T); 1926 v E, W, Ni; 1927 v W, Ni; 1928 v E, W; 1929 v E, W, Ni; 1930 v E, W, Ni, F. (17)
Jackson, C. (Rangers); 1975 v Se, P(sub), W; 1976 v D, R, Ni, W, E. (8)
Jackson, J. (Partick T); 1931 v A, I, Sw; 1933 v E; (Chelsea); 1934 v E; 1935 v E; 1936 v W, Ni. (8)

JOHN JACKSON

Jackson, T.A. (St Mirren); 1904 v W, E, Ni; 1905 v W; 1907 v W, Ni. (6)

James, A.W. (Preston NE); 1926 v W; 1928 v E; 1929 v E, Ni (Arsenal); 1930 v E, W, Ni; 1933 v W. (8)

Jardine, A. (Rangers); 1971 v D(sub); 1972 v P, Bel, Ho; 1973 v E, Sw, Br; 1974 v Cz(2), WG(2), Ni, W, E, Bel, N, Z, Br, Y; 1975 v EG, Sp(2), Se, P, W, Ni, E; 1977 v Se(sub), Ch(sub), Br(sub); 1978 v Cz, W, Ni, Ir; 1980v Pe, A, Bel(2). (38)

Jarvie, A. (Airdrieonians); 1971 v P(sub), Ni(sub), E(sub). (3)

Jenkinson, T. (Hearts); 1887 v Ni. (1)

Johnston, L.H. (Clyde); 1948 v Bel, Sw. (2)

Johnston, M. (Watford); 1984 v W(sub), E(sub), F; (Celtic); 1985 v Y, Ic, Sp(2), W; 1986 v EG; 1987 v Bul, Ei(2), Lux. (13)

Johnston, R. (Sunderland); 1938 v Cz. (1)

Johnston, W. (Rangers); 1966 v W, E, Pol, Ho; 1968 v W, E; 1969 v Ni(sub); 1970 v Ni; 1971 v D; (West Brom) 1974 v Se, W(sub), Ni, E, Ch, Arg, Br; 1978 v EG, Cz, W, W, E, Pe. (22)

Johnstone, D. (Rangers); 1973 v W, Ni, E, Sw, Br; 1975 v EG(sub), Se(sub); 1976 v Sw, Ni(sub), E(sub); 1978 v Bul(sub), Ni, W; 1980 v Bel. (14)

Johnstone, J. (Abercorn); 1888 v W. (1)

Johnstone, J. (Celtic); 1965 v W, Fi; 1966 v E; 1967 v W, USSR; 1968 v W; 1969 v A, WG; 1970 v E, WG; 1971 v D, E; 1972 v P, Bel, Ho, Ni, E(sub); 1974 v W, E, Bel, N; 1975 v EG, Sp. (23)

Johnstone, Jas. (Kilmarnock); 1894 v W. (1)

Johnstone, J.A. (Hearts); 1930 v W; 1933 v W, Ni. (3)

Johnstone, R. (Hibernian); 1951 v E, D, F; 1952 v Ni, E; 1953 v E, Se; 1954 v W, E, N, Fi; 1955 v Ni, H; (Manchester C); 1955 v E; 1956 v E, Ni, W. (17)

Johnstone, W. (Third Lanark); 1887 v Ni; 1889 v W; 1890 v E. (3)

Jordan, J. (Leeds U); 1973 v E(sub), Sw(sub), Br; 1974 v Cz(1 sub + 1), WG(sub), Ni(sub), W, E, Bel, N, Z, Br, Y; 1975 v EG, Sp(2); 1976 v Ni, W, E; 1977 v Cz, W, Ni, E; 1978 v EG, Cz, W; (Manchester U); Bul, Ni, E, Pe, Ir, Ho; 1979 v A, P, W(sub), Ni, E, N; 1980 v Bel, Ni(sub), W, E, Pol; 1981 v Is, W, E; (AC Milan); 1982 v Se, Ho, W, E, USSR. (52)

Kay, J.L. (Queen's Park); 1880 v E; 1882 v E, W; 1883 v E, W; 1884 v W. (6)

Keillor, A. (Montrose); 1891 v W; 1892 v Ni; (Dundee); 1894 v Ni; 1895 v W; 1896 v W; 1897 v W. (6)

Keir, L. (Dumbarton); 1885 v W; 1886 v Ni; 1887 v E, W; 1888 v E. (5)

Kelly, H.T. (Blackpool); 1952 v USA. (1)

Kelly, J. (Renton); 1888 v E; (Celtic); 1889 v E; 1890 v E; 1892 v E; 1893 v E, Ni; 1894 v W; 1896 v Ni. (8)

Kelly, J.C. (Barnsley); 1949 v W, Ni. (2)

Kelso, R. (Renton); 1885 v W, Ni; 1886 v W; 1887 v E, W; 1888 v E, Ni; (Dundee); 1898 v Ni. (8)

Kelso, T. (Dundee); 1914 v W. (1)

Kennaway, J. (Celtic); 1934 v A. (1)

Kennedy, A. (Eastern); 1875 v E; 1876 v E, W; (Third Lanark); 1878 v E; 1882 v W; 1884 v W. (6)

Kennedy, J. (Celtic); 1964 v W, E, WG; 1965 v W, Ni, Fi. (6)

Kennedy, J. (Hibernian); 1897 v W. (1)

Kennedy, S. (Aberdeen); 1978 v Bul, W, E, Pe, Ho; 1979 v A, P; 1982 v P(sub). (8)

Kennedy, S. (Partick T); 1905 v W. (1)

Kennedy, S. (Rangers); 1975 v Se, P, W, Ni, E. (5)

Ker, G. (Queen's Park); 1880 v E; 1881 v E, W; 1882 v E, W. (5)

Ker, W. (Granville); 1872 v E; (Queen's Park); 1873 v E. (2)

Kerr, A. (Partick T); 1955 v A, H. (2)

Kerr, P. (Hibernian); 1924 v Ni. (1)

Key, G. (Hearts); 1902 v Ni. (1)

Key, W. (Queen's Park); 1907 v Ni. (1)

King, A. (Hearts); 1896 v E, W; (Celtic); 1897 v Ni; 1898 v Ni; 1899 v Ni. (6)

King, J. (Hamilton A); 1933 v Ni; 1934 v Ni. (2)

King, W.S. (Queen's Park); 1929 v W. (1)

Kinloch, J.D. (Partick T); 1922 v Ni. (1)

Kinnaird, A.F. (Partick T); 1922 v Ni. (1)

Kinnear, D. (Rangers); 1938 v Cz. (1)

Lambie, J.A. (Queen's Park); 1886 v Ni; 1887 v Ni; 1888 v E. (3)

Lambie, W.A. (Queen's Park); 1892 v Ni; 1893 v W; 1894 v E; 1895 v E, Ni; 1896 v E, Ni; 1897 v E, Ni. (9)

Lamont, D. (Pilgrims); 1885 v Ni. (1)

Lang, A. (Dumbarton); 1880 v W. (1)

ALEX JAMES

Lang, J.J. (Clydesdale); 1876 v W; (Third Lanark); 1878 v W. (2)

Latta, A. (Dumbarton); 1888 v W; 1889 v E. (2)

Law, D. (Huddersfield T); 1959 v W, Ni, Ho, P; 1960 v Ni, W; (Manchester C); 1960 v E, Pol, A; 1961 v E, Ni; (Torino); 1962 v Cz(2), E; (Manchester U); 1963 v W, Ni, E, A, N, Ei, Sp; 1964 v W, E, N, WG; 1965 v W, Ni, E, Fi(2), Pol, Sp; 1966 v Ni, E, Pol; 1967 v W, E, USSR; 1968 v Ni; 1969 v Ni, A, WG; 1972 v Pe, Ni, W, E, Y, Cz, Br; (Manchester C); 1974 v Cz(2), WG(2), Ni, Z. (55)

Law, G. (Rangers); 1910 v E, Ni, W. (3)

Law, T. (Chelsea); 1928 v E; 1930 v E. (2)

Lawrence, J. (Newcastle U); 1911 v E. (1)

Lawrence, T. (Liverpool); 1963 v Ei; 1969 v W, WG. (3)

Lawson, D. (St Mirren); 1923 v E. (1)

Leckie, R. (Queen's Park); 1872 v E. (1)

Leggat, G. (Aberdeen); 1956 v E; 1957 v W; 1958 v Ni, H, Pol, Y, Par; (Fulham); 1959 v E, W, Ni, WG, Ho; 1960 v E, Ni, W, Pol, A, H. (18)

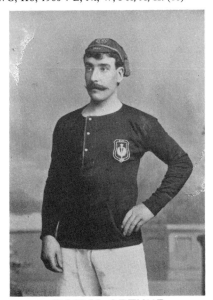

DAN McARTHUR

Leighton, J. (Aberdeen); 1983 v EG, Sw, Bel, Sw, W, E, Ca(2); 1984 v U, Bel, Ni, W, E, F; 1985 v Y, Ic, Sp(2), W, E, Ic; 1986 v W, EG, Aus(2), Is, D, WG, U; 1987 v Bul, Ei(2), Lux, Bel, E. (35)

Lennie, W. (Aberdeen); 1908 v W, Ni. (2)

Lennox, R. (Celtic); 1967 v Ni, E, USSR; 1968 v W, L; 1969 v D, A, WG, Cy(sub); 1970 v W(sub). (10)

Leslie, L.G. (Airdrieonians); 1961 v W, Ni, Ei(2), Cz. (5)

Liddell, W. (Liverpool); 1947 v W, Ni; 1948 v E, W, Ni; 1950 v E, W, P, F; 1951 v W, Ni, E, A; 1952 v W, Ni, E, USA, D, Se; 1953 v W, Ni, E; 1954 v W; 1955 v P, Y, A, H; 1965 v Ni. (28)

Liddle, D. (East Fife); 1931 v A, I, Sw. (3)

Lindsay, D. (St Mirren); 1903 v Ni. (1)

Lindsay, J. (Dumbarton); 1880 v W; 1881 v W, E; 1884 v W, E; 1885 v W, E; 1886 v E. (8)

Lindsay, J. (Renton); 1888 v E; 1893 v E, Ni. (3)

Linwood, A.B. (Clyde); 1950 v W. (1)

Little, R.J. (Rangers); 1953 v Se. (1)

Livingstone, G.T. (Manchester C); 1906 v E; (Rangers); 1907 v W. (2)

Lochhead, A. (Third Lanark); 1889 v W. (1)

Logan, J. (Ayr U); 1891 v W. (1)

Logan, T. (Falkirk); 1913 v Ni. (1)

Logie, J.T. (Arsenal); 1953 v Ni. (1)

Loney, W. (Celtic); 1910 v W, Ni. (2)

Long, H. (Clyde); 1947 v Ni. (1)

Longair, W. (Dundee); 1894 v Ni. (1)

Lorimer, P. (Leeds U); 1970 v A(sub); 1971 v W, Ni; 1972 v Ni(sub), W, E; 1973 v D(2), E(2); 1974 v WG(sub), E, Bel, N, Z, Br, Y; 1975 v Sp(sub); 1976 v D(2), R(sub). (21)

Love, A. (Aberdeen); 1931 v A, I, Sw. (3)

Low, A. (Falkirk); 1934 v Ni. (1)

Low, T.P. (Rangers); 1897 v Ni. (1)

Low, W.L. (Newcastle U); 1911 v E, W; 1912 v Ni; 1920 v E, Ni. (5)

Lowe, J. (Cambuslang); 1891 v Ni. (1)

Lowe, J. (St Bernards); 1887 v Ni. (1)

Lundie, J. (Hibernian); 1886 v W. (1)

Lyall, J. (Sheffield W); 1905 v E. (1)

McAdam, J. (Third Lanark); 1880 v W. (1)

McArthur, D. (Celtic); 1895 v E, Ni; 1899 v W. (3)

McAtee, A. (Celtic); 1913 v W. (1)

McAulay, J. (Dumbarton); 1882 v W; (Arthurlie); 1884 v Ni. (2)

McAulay, J. (Dumbarton); 1883 v E, W; 1884 v E; 1885 v E, W; 1886 v E; 1887 v E, W. (8)

McAuley, R. (Rangers); 1932 v Ni, W. (2)

McAvennie, F. (West Ham); 1986 v Aus(2), D(sub), WG(sub). (4)

McBain, E. (St Mirren); 1894 v W. (1)

McBain, N. (Manchester U); 1922 v E; (Everton); 1923 v Ni; 1924 v W. (3)

McBride, J. (Celtic); 1967 v W, Ni. (2)

McBride, P. (Preston NE); 1904 v E; 1906 v E; 1907 v E, W; 1908 v E; 1909 v W. (6)

McCall, J. (Renton); 1886 v W; 1887 v E, W; 1888 v E; 1890 v E. (5)

McCalliog, J. (Sheffield W); 1967 v E, USSR; 1968 v Ni; 1969 v D; (Wolverhampton W); 1971 v P. (5)

McCallum, N. (Renton); 1888 v Ni. (1)

McCann, R.J. (Motherwell); 1959 v WG; 1960 v E, Ni, W; 1961 v E. (5)

McCartney, W. (Hibernian); 1902 v Ni. (1)

McClair, B. (Celtic); 1987 v Lux, Ei, E, Br(sub). (4)

McClory, A. (Motherwell); 1927 v W; 1928 v Ni; 1935 v W. (3)

McCloy, P. (Ayr U); 1924 v E; 1925 v E. (2)

McCloy, P. (Rangers); 1973 v W, Ni, Sw, Br. (4)

McCoist, A. (Rangers); 1986 v Ho; 1987 v Lux(sub), Ei(sub), Bel, E, Br. (6)

McColl, A. (Renton); 1888 v Ni. (1)

McColl, I.M. (Rangers); 1950 v E, F; 1951 v W, Ni, Bel; 1957 v E, Ni, W, Y, Sp, Sw, WG; 1958 v Ni, E. (14)

McColl, R.S. (Queen's Park); 1896 v Ni; 1897 v Ni; 1898 v Ni; 1899 v Ni, E, W; 1900 v E, W; 1901 v E, W; (Newcastle U); 1902 v E; (Queen's Park); 1908 v Ni. (13)

McColl, W. (Renton); 1895 v W. (1)

McCombie, A. (Sunderland); 1903 v E, W; (Newcastle U); 1905 v E, W. (4)

McCorkindale, J. (Partick T); 1891 v W. (1)

McCormick, R. (Abercorn); 1886 v W. (1)

McCrae, D. (St Mirren); 1929 v N, G. (2)

McCreadie, A. (Rangers); 1893 v W; 1894 v E. (2)

McCreadie, E.G. (Chelsea); 1965 v E, Sp, Fi, Pol; 1966 v P, Ni, W, Pol, I; 1967 v E, USSR; 1968 v Ni, W, E, Ho; 1969 v W, Ni, E, D, A, WG, Cy(2). (23)
McCulloch, D. (Hearts); 1935 v W; (Brentford); 1936 v E; 1937 v W, Ni; 1938 v Cz; (Derby Co); 1939 v H, W. (7)
MacDonald, A. (Rangers); 1976 v Sw. (1)
McDonald, J. (Edinburgh University); 1886 v E. (1)
McDonald, J. (Sunderland); 1956 v W, Ni. (2)
MacDougall, E.J. (Norwich C); 1975 v Se, P, W, Ni, E; 1976 v D, R. (7)
McDougall, J. (Liverpool); 1931 v I, A. (2)
McDougall, J. (Airdrieonians); 1926 v Ni. (1)
McDougall, J. (Vale of Levan); 1877 v E, W; 1878 v E; 1879 v E, W. (5)
McFadyen, W. (Motherwell); 1934 v A, W. (2)
Mcfarlane, A. (Dundee); 1904 v W; 1906 v W; 1908 v W; 1909 v Ni; 1911 v W. (5)
McFarlane, R. (Greenock Morton); 1896 v W. (1)
Mcfarlane, W. (Hearts); 1947 v L. (1)
McGarr, E. (Aberdeen); 1970 v Ei, A. (2)
McGarvey, F.P. (Liverpool); 1979 v Ni(sub), Arg; (Celtic); 1984 v U, Bel(sub), EG(sub), Ni W. (7)
McGeoch, A. (Dumbreck); 1876 v E, W; 1877 v E, W. (4)
McGhee, J. (Hibernian); 1886 v W. (1)
McGhee, M. (Aberdeen); 1983 v Ca (1+1 sub); 1984 v Ni(sub), E. (4)
McGonagle, W. (Celtic); 1933 v E; 1934 v A, E, Ni; 1935 v Ni, W. (6)

W. 'PETER' McGONAGLE

McGrain, D. (Celtic); 1973 v W, Ni, E, Sw, Br; 1974 v Cz(2), WG, W(sub), E, Bel, N, Z, Br, Y; 1975 v Sp, Se, P, W, Ni, E, R; 1976 v D(2), Sw, Ni, W, E; 1977 v Fi, Cz, W(2), Se, Ni, E, Ch, Arg, Br; 1978 v EG, Cz; 1980 v Bel, P, Ni, W, E, Pol, H; 1981 v Se, P, Is, Ni, Is, W(sub), Ni, E; 1982 v Se, Sp, Ho, Ni, E, Nz, USSR(sub). (62)
McGregor, J.C. (Vale of Leven); 1877 v E, W; 1878 v E; 1880 v E. (4)
McGrory, J.E. (Kilmarnock); 1965 v Ni, Fi; 1966 v P. (3)
McGrory, J. (Celtic); 1928 v Ni; 1931 v E; 1932 v Ni, W; 1933 v E, Ni; 1934 v Ni. (7)
McGuire, W. (Celtic Beith), 1881 v E, W. (2)
McGurk, F. (Birmingham); 1934 v W. (1)
McHardy, H. (Rangers); 1885 v Ni. (1)
McInally, J. (Dundee U); 1987 v Bel, Br. (2)
McInally, T.B. (Celtic); 1926 v Ni; 1927 v W. (2)
McInnes, T. (Cowlairs); 1889 v Ni. (1)

McIntosh, W. (Third Lanark); 1905 v Ni. (1)
McIntyre, A. (Vale of Leven); 1878 v E; 1882 v E. (2)
McIntyre, H. (Rangers); 1880 v W. (1)
McIntyre, J. (Rangers); 1884 v W. (1)
McKay, D. (Celtic); 1959 v E, WG, Ho, P; 1960 v E, Pol, A, H, T; 1961 v W, Ni; 1962 v Ni, Cz, U(sub). (14)
Mackay, D.C. (Hearts); 1957 v Sp; 1958 v F; 1959 v W, Ni; (Tottenham H); 1959 v WG, E; 1960 v W, Ni, A, Pol, H, T; 1961 v W, Ni, E; 1963 v E, A, N; 1964 v Ni, W, N; 1966 v Ni. (22)
McKay, J. (Blackburn R); 1924 v W. (1)
McKay, R. (Newcastle U); 1928 v W. (1)
McKean, R. (Rangers); 1976 v Sw. (1)
McKenzie, D. (Brentford); 1938 v Ni. (1)
Mackenzie, J.A. (Partick T); 1954 v W, E, N, Fi, A, U; 1955 v E, H; 1956 v A. (9)
McKeown, M. (Celtic); 1889 v Ni; 1890 v E. (2)
McKie, J. (East Stirling); 1898 v W. (1)
McKillop, T.R. (Rangers); 1938 v Ho. (1)
McKinlay, D. (Liverpool); 1922 v W, Ni. (2)
McKinnon, A. (Queen's Park); 1874 v E. (1)
McKinnon, R. (Rangers); 1966 v W, E, I(2), Ho, Br; 1967 v W, Ni, E; 1968 v Ni, W, E, Ho; 1969 v D, A, WG, Cy; 1970 v Ni, W, E, Ei, WG, A; 1971 v D, Bel, P, USSR, D. (28)
MacKinnon, W. (Dumbarton); 1883 v E, W; 1884 v E, W. (4)
MacKinnon, W.W. (Queen's Park); 1872 v E; 1873 v E; 1874 v E; 1875 v E; 1876 v E, W; 1877 v E; 1878 v E; 1879 v E. (9)
McLaren, A. (St Johnstone); 1929 v N, G, Ho; 1933 v W, Ni. (5)
McLaren, A. (Preston NE); 1947 v E, Bel, L; 1948 v W. (4)
McLaren, J. (Hibernian); 1888 v W; (Celtic); 1889 v E; 1890 v E. (3)
McLean, A. (Celtic); 1926 v W, Ni; 1927 v W, E. (4)
McLean, D. (St Bernards); 1896 v W; 1897 v Ni. (2)
McLean, D. (Sheffield W); 1912 v E. (1)
McLean, G. (Dundee); 1968 v Ho. (1)
McLean, T. (Kilmarnock); 1969 v D, Cy, W; 1970 v Ni, W; 1971 v D. (6)
McLeish, A. (Aberdeen); 1980 v F, Ni, W, E, Pol, H; 1981 v Se, Is, Ni, Is, Ni, E; 1982 v Se, Sp, Ni, Br(sub); 1983 v Bel, Sw(sub), W, E, Ca(3); 1984 v U, Bel, EG, Ni, W, E, F; 1985 v Y, Ic, Sp(2), W, E, Ic; 1986 v W, EG, Aus(2), E, Ho, D; 1987 v Bel, E, Br. (47)
McLeod, D. (Celtic); 1905 v Ni; 1906 v E, W, Ni. (4)
McLeod, J. (Dumbarton); 1888 v Ni; 1889 v W; 1890 v Ni; 1892 v E; 1893 v W. (5)
MacLeod, J.M. (Hibernian); 1961 v E, Ei(2), Cz. (4)
MacLeod, M. (Celtic); 1985 v E(sub); 1987 v Ei, Lux, E, Br. (5)
McLeod, W. (Cowlairs); 1886 v Ni. (1)
McLintock, A. (Vale of Leven); 1875 v E; 1876 v E; 1880 v E. (3)
McLintock, F. (Leicester C); 1963 v N(sub), Ei, Sp; (Arsenal); 1965 v Ni; 1967 v USSR; 1970 v Ni; 1971 v W, Ni, E. (9)
McLuckie, J.S. (Manchester C); 1934 v W. (1)
McMahon, A. (Celtic); 1892 v E; 1893 v E, Ni; 1894 v E; 1901 v Ni; 1902 v W. (6)
McMenemy, J. (Celtic); 1905 v Ni; 1909 v Ni; 1910 v E, W; 1911 v Ni, W, E; 1912 v W; 1914 v W, Ni, E; 1920 v Ni. (12)
McMenemy, J. (Motherwell); 1934 v W. (1)
McMillan, J. (St Bernards); 1897 v W. (1)
McMillan, I.L. (Airdrieonians); 1952 v E, USA, D; 1955 v E; 1956 v E; (Rangers); 1961 v Cz. (6)
McMillan, T. (Dumbarton); 1887 v Ni. (1)
McMullan, J. (Partick T); 1920 v W; 1921 v W, Ni, E; 1924 v E, Ni; 1925 v E; 1926 v W; (Manchester C); 1926 v E; 1927 v E, W; 1928 v E, W; 1929 v W, E, Ni. (16)
McNab, A. (Morton); 1921 v E, Ni. (2)
McNab, A. (Sunderland); 1937 v A; (West Brom); 1939 v E. (2)
McNab, C.D. (Dundee); 1931 v E, W, A, I, Sw; 1932 v E. (6)
McNab, J.S. (Liverpool); 1923 v W. (1)
McNair, A. (Celtic); 1906 v W; 1907 v Ni; 1908 v E, W; 1909 v W; 1910 v W; 1912 v E, W, Ni; 1913 v E; 1914 v E, Ni; 1920 v E, W, Ni. (15)
McNaught, W. (Raith R); 1951 v A, W, Ni; 1952 v E; 1955 v Ni. (5)
McNeil, H. (Queen's Park); 1874 v E; 1875 v E; 1876 v E, W; 1877 v W; 1878 v E; 1879 v E, W; 1881 v E, W. (10)
McNeil, M. (Rangers); 1876 v W; 1880 v E. (2)

McNeill, W. (Celtic); 1961 v E, Ei(2), Cz; 1962 v Ni, E, Cz, U; 1963 v Ei, Sp; 1964 v W, E, WG; 1965 v E, Fi, Pol, Sp; 1966 v Ni, Pol; 1967 v USSR; 1968 v E; 1969 v Cy, W, E, Cy(sub); 1970 v WG; 1972 v Ni, W, E. (29)
McPhail, J. (Celtic); 1950 v W; 1951 v W, Ni, A; 1954 v Ni. (5)
McPhail, R. (Airdrieonians); 1927 v E; (Rangers); 1929 v W; 1931 v E, Ni; 1932 v W, Ni, F; 1933 v E, Ni; 1934 v A, Ni; 1935 v E; 1937 v G, E, Cz; 1938 v W, Ni. (17)
McPherson, D. (Kilmarnock); 1892 v Ni. (1)
McPherson, J. (Kilmarnock); 1888 v W; (Cowlairs); 1889 v E; 1890 v Ni, E; (Rangers); 1892 v W; 1894 v E; 1895 v E, Ni; 1897 v Ni. (9)
McPherson, J. (Clydesdale); 1875 v E. (1)
McPherson, J. (Vale of Leven); 1879 v E, W; 1880 v E; 1881 v W; 1883 v E, W; 184 v E; 1885 v N. (8)
McPherson, J. (Hearts); 1891 v E. (1)
McPherson, R. (Arthurlie); 1882 v E. (1)
McQueen, G. (Leeds U); 1974 v Bel; 1975 v Sp(2), P, W, Ni, E, R; 1976 v D; 1977 v Cz, W(2), Ni, E; 1978 v EG, Cz, W; (Manchester U); Bul, Ni, W; 1979 v A, N, P, Ni, E, N; 1980 v Pe, A, Bel; 1981 v W. (30)
McQueen, M. (Leith Ath); 1890 v W; 1891 v W. (2)
McRorie, D.M. (Morton); 1931 v W. (1)
McSpadyen, A. (Partick T); 1939 v E, H. (2)
McStay, P. (Celtic); 1984 v U, Bel, EG, Ni, W, E(sub); 1985 v Ic, Sp(2), W; 1986 v EG(sub), Aus, Is, U; 1987 v Bul, Ei(1+1 sub), Lux(sub), Bel, E, Br. (21)
McStay, W. (Celtic); 1921 v W, Ni; 1925 v E, Ni, W; 1926 v E, Ni, W; 1927 v E, Ni, W; 1928 v W, Ni. (13)
McTavish, J. (Falkirk); 1910 v Ni. (1)
McWhattie, G.C. (Queen's Park); 1901 v W, Ni. (2)
McWilliam, P. (Newcastle U); 1905 v E; 1906 v E; 1907 v E, W; 1909 v E, W; 1910 v E; 1911 v W (8)
Macari, L. (Celtic); 1972 v W(sub); E, Y, Cz, Br; 1973 v D; (Manchester U); E(2); W(sub); Ni(sub); 1975 v Se, P(sub); W, E(sub); R; 1977 v Ni(sub); E(sub); Ch, Arg; 1978 v EG, W, Bul, Pe(sub); Ir. (24)
Macauley, A.R. (Brentford); 1947 v E; (Arsenal); 1948 v E, W, Ni, Bel, Sw, F. (7)
Madden, J. (Celtic); 1893 v W; 1895 v W. (2)
Main, F.R. (Rangers); 1938 v W. (1)
Main, J. (Hibernian); 1909 v Ni. (1)
Maley, W. (Celtic); 1893 v E, Ni. (2)
Malpas, M. (Dundee U); 1984 v F; 1985 v E, Ic; 1986 v W, Aus(2); Is, R, E, Ho, D, WG; 1987 v Bul, Ei, Bel. (15)
Marshall, H. (Celtic); 1899 v W; 1900 v Ni. (2)
Marshall, J. (Rangers); 1932 v E; 1933 v E; 1934 v E. (3)
Marshall, J. (Middlesbrough); 1921 v E, W, Ni; 1922 v E, W, Ni; (Llanelli); 1924 v W. (7)
Marshall, J. (Third Lanark); 1885 v Ni; 1886 v W; 1887 v E, W. (4)
Marshall, R.W. (Rangers); 1892 v Ni; 1894 v Ni. (2)
Martin, F. (Aberdeen); 1954 v N(2); A, U; 1955 v E, H. (6)
Martin, N. (Hibernian); 1965 v Fi, Pol; (Sunderland); 1966 v I. (3)
Martis, J. (Motherwell); 1961 v W. (1)
Mason, J. (Third Lanark); 1949 v E, W, Ni; 1950 v Ni; 1951 v Ni, Bel, A. (7)
Massie, A. (Hearts); 1932 v Ni, W, F; 1933 v Ni; 1934 v E, Ni; 1935 v E, Ni, W; 1936 v W, Ni; (Aston Villa); 1936 v E; 1937 v G, E, W, Ni, A; 1938 v W. (18)
Masson, D.S. (Queen's Park R); 1976 v Ni, W, E; 1977 v F, Cz, W, Ni, E, Ch, Arg, Br; 1978 v EG, Cz, W; (Derby Co); Ni, E, Pe. (17)
Mathers, D. (Partick T); 1954 v Fi. (1)
Maxwell, W.S. (Stoke C); 1898 v E. (1)
May, J. (Rangers); 1906 v W, Ni; 1908 v E, Ni; 1909 v W. (5)
Meechan, P. (Celtic); 1896 v Ni. (1)
Meiklejohn, D.D. (Rangers); 1922 v W; 1924 v W; 1925 v W, N, E; 1928 v W, Ni; 1929 v E, Ni; 1930 v E, Ni; 1931 v E; 1932 v W, Ni; 1934 v A. (15)
Menzies, A. (Hearts); 1906 v E. (1)
Mercer, R. (Hearts); 1912 v W; 1913 v Ni. (2)
Middleton, R. (Cowdenbeath); 1930 v Ni. (1)
Millar, J. (Rangers); 1897 v E; 1898 v E, W. (3)
Millar, J. (Rangers); 1963 v A, Ei. (2)
Millar, A. (Hearts); 1939 v W. (1)
Miller, J. (St Mirren); 1931 v E, I, Sw; 1932 v F; 1934 v E. (5)
Miller, P. (Dumbarton); 1882 v E; 1883 v E, W. (3)
Miller, T. (Liverpool); 1920 v E; (Manchester U); 1921 v E, Ni. (3)

Miller, W. (Third Lanark); 1876 v E. (1)
Miller, W. (Celtic); 1947 v E, W, Bel, L; 1948 v W, Ni. (6)
Miller, W. (Aberdeen); 1975 v R; 1978 v Bul; 1980 v Bel, W, E, Pol, H; 1981 v Se, P, Is(sub); Ni, W, Ni, E; 1982 v Ni, P, Ho, Br, USSR; 1983 v EG, Sw, Sw, W, E, Ca(3); 1984 v U, Bel, EG, W, E, F; 1985 v Y, Ic, Sp(2); W, E, Ic; 1986 v W, EG, Aus(2); Is, R, E, Ho, D, WG, U; 1987 v Bul, E, Br. (54)
Mills, W. (Aberdeen); 1936 v W, Ni; 1937 v W. (3)
Milne, J.V. (Middlesbrough); 1938 v E; 1939 v E. (2)
Mitchell, D. (Rangers); 1890 v Ni; 1892 v E; 1893 v E, Ni; 1894 v E. (5)
Mitchell, J. (Kilmarnock); 1908 v Ni; 1910 v Ni, W. (3)
Mitchell, R.C. (Newcastle U); 1951 v D, F. (2)
Mochan, N. (Celtic); 1954 v N, A, U. (3)
Moir, W. (Bolton W); 1950 v E. (1)
Moncur, R. (Newcastle U); 1968 v Ho; 1970 v Ni, W, E, Ei; 1971 v D, Bel, W, P, Ni, E, D; 1972 v Pe, Ni, W, E. (16)
Morgan, H. (St Mirren); 1898 v W; (Liverpool); 1899 v E. (2)
Morgan, W. (Burnley); 1968 v Ni; (Manchester U); 1972 v Pe, Y, Cz, Br; 1973 v D(2); E(2); W, Ni, Sw, Br; 1974 v Cz(2); WG(2); Ni, Bel(sub); Br, Y. (21)
Morris, D. (Raith R); 1923 v Ni; 1924 v E, Ni; 1925 v E, W, Ni. (6)
Morris, H. (East Fife); 1950 v Ni. (1)
Morrison, T. (St Mirren); 1927 v E. (1)
Morton, A.L. (Queen's Park); 1920 v W, Ni; (Rangers); 1921 v E; 1922 v E, W; 1923 v E, W, Ni; 1924 v E, W, Ni; 1925 v E, W, Ni; 1927 v E, Ni; 1928 v E, W, Ni; 1929 v E, W, Ni; 1930 v E, W, Ni; 1931 v E, W, Ni; 1932 v E, W, F. (31)
Morton, H.A. (Kilmarnock); 1929 v G, Ho. (2)
Mudie, J.K. (Blackpool); 1957 v W, Ni, E, Y, Sw, Sp(2); WG; 1958 v Ni, E, W, Sw, H, Pol, Y, Par, F. (17)
Muir, W. (Dundee); 1907 v Ni. (1)
Muirhead, T.A. (Rangers); 1922 v Ni; 1923 v E; 1924 v W; 1927 v Ni; 1928 v Ni; 1929 v W, Ni; 1930 v W. (8)
Mulhall, G. (Aberdeen); 1960 v Ni; (Sunderland); 1963 v Ni; 1964 v Ni. (3)
Munro, A.D. (Hearts); 1937 v W, Ni;. (Blackpool); 1938 v Ho. (3)
Munro, F.M. (Wolverhampton W); 1971 v Ni(sub); E(sub); D, USSR; 1975 v Se, W(sub); Ni, E, R. (9)
Munro, I. (St Mirren); 1979 v Arg, N; 1980 v Pe, A, Bel, W, E. (7)
Munro, N. (Abercorn); 1888 v W; 1889 v E. (2)
Murdoch, J. (Motherwell); 1931 v Ni. (1)
Murdoch, R. (Celtic); 1966 v W, E, I(2); 1967 v Ni; 1968 v Ni; 1969 v W, Ni, E, WG, Cy; 1970 v A. (12)
Murphy, F. (Celtic); 1938 v Ho. (1)
Murray, J. (Renton); 1895 v W. (1)
Murray, J. (Hearts); 1958 v E, H, Pol, Y, F. (5)
Murray, J.W. (Vale of Leven); 1890 v W. (1)
Murray, P. (Hibernian); 1896 v Ni; 1897 v W. (2)
Murray, S. (Aberdeen); 1972 v Bel. (1)
Mutch, G. (Preston NE); 1938 v E. (1)

Napier, C.E. (Celtic); 1932 v E; 1935 v E, W; (Derby Co); 1937 v Ni, A. (5)
Narey, D. (Dundee U); 1977 v Se(sub); 1979 v P, Ni(sub); Arg; 1980 v P, Ni, Pol, H; 1981 v W, E(sub); 1982 v Ho, W, E, Nz(sub); Br, USSR; 1983 v EG, Sw, Bel, Ni, W, E, Ca(3); 1986 v Is, R, Ho, WG, U; 1987 v Bul, Ei, Bel. (33)
Neil, R.G. (Hibernian); 1896 v W; (Rangers); 1900 v W. (2)
Neill, R. (Queen's Park); 1876 v W; 1877 v E, W; 1878 v W; 1880 v E. (5)
Neilles, P. (Hearts); 1914 v W, Ni. (2)
Nelson, J. (Cardiff C); 1925 v W, Ni; 1928 v E; 1930 v F. (4)
Nevin, P.K.F. (Chelsea); 1986 v R(sub); E(sub); 1987 v Lux, Ei, Bel(sub). (5)
Niblo, T.D. (Aston Villa); 1904 v E. (1)
Nibloe, J. (Kilmarnock); 1929 v E, Ni, Ho; 1930 v W; 1931 v E, Ni, A, I, Sw; 1932 v E, F. (11)
Nicholas, C. (Celtic); 1983 v Sw, Ni, E, Ca(3);. (with Arsenal); 1984 v Bel, F(sub); 1985 v Y(sub); Ic(sub); Sp(sub); W(sub); 1986 v Is, R(sub); E, D, U(sub); 1987 v Bul, E(sub). (19)
Nicol, S. (Liverpool); 1985 v Y, Ic, Sp, W; 1986 v W, EG, Aus, E, D, WG, U. (11)
Nisbet, J. (Ayr U); 1929 v N, G, Ho. (3)
Niven, J.B. (Moffatt); 1885 v Ni. (1)

O'Donnell, F. (Preston NE); 1937 v E, A, Cz; 1938 v E, W; (Blackpool); Ho. (6)

FRANK O'DONNELL

ALEX PARKER

Ogilvie, D.H. (Motherwell); 1934 v A. (1)
O'Hare, J. (Derby Co); 1970 v W, Ni, E; 1971 v D, Bel, W, Ni; 1972 v P, Bel, Ho(sub); Pe, Ni, W. (13)
Ormond, W.E. (Hibernian); 1954 v E, N, Fi, A, U; 1959 v E. (6)
O'Rourke, F. (Airdrieonians); 1907 v Ni. (1)
Orr, J. (Kilmarnock); 1892 v W. (1)
Orr, R. (Newcastle U); 1902 v E; 1904 v E. (2)
Orr, T. (Morton); 1952 v Ni, W. (2)
Orr, W. (Celtic); 1900 v Ni; 1903 v Ni; 1904 v W. (3)
Orrock, R. (Falkirk); 1913 v W. (1)
Oswald, J. (Third Lanark); 1889 v E; (St Bernards); 1895 v E; (Rangers); 1897 v W. (3)

Parker, A.H. (Falkirk); 1955 v P, Y, A; 1956 v E, Ni, W, A; 1957 v Ni, W, Y; 1958 v Ni, W, E, Sw; (Everton); Par. (15)
Parlane, D. (Rangers); 1973 v W, Sw, Br; 1975 v Sp(sub); Se, P, W, Ni, E, R; 1976 v D(sub); 1977 v W. (12)
Parlane, R. (Vale of Leven); 1878 v W; 1879 v E, W. (3)
Paterson, G.D. (Celtic); 1939 v Ni. (1)
Paterson, J. (Leicester C); 1920 v E. (1)
Paterson, J. (Cowdenbeath); 1931 v A, I, Sw. (3)
Paton, A. (Motherwell); 1952 v D, Se. (2)
Paton, D. (St Bernards); 1896 v W. (1)
Paton, M. (Dumbarton); 1883 v E; 1884 v W; 1885 v W, E; 1886 v E. (5)
Paton, R. (Vale of Leven); 1879 v E, W. (2)
Patrick, J. (St Mirren); 1897 v E, W. (2)
Paul, H.McD. (Queen's Park); 1909 v E, W, Ni. (3)
Paul, W. (Partick T); 1888 v W; 1889 v W; 1890 v W. (3)
Paul, W. (Dykebar); 1891 v Ni. (1)
Pearson, T. (Newcastle U); 1947 v E, Bel. (2)
Penman, A. (Dundee); 1966 v Ho. (1)
Pettigrew, W. (Motherwell); 1976 v Sw, Ni, W; 1977 v W(sub); Se. (5)
Phillips, J. (Queen's Park); 1877 v E, W; 1878 v W. (3)
Plenderleith, J.B. (Manchester C); 1961 v Ni. (1)
Porteous, W. (Hearts); 1903 v Ni. (1)
Pringle, C. (St Mirren); 1921 v W. (1)
Provan, D. (Rangers); 1964 v Ni, N; 1966 v I(2); Ho. (5)
Provan, D. (Celtic); 1980 v Bel(2 sub); P(sub); Ni(sub); 1981 v Is, W, E; 1982 v Se, P, Ni. (10)
Pursell, P. (Queen's Park); 1914 v W. (1)

Quinn, J. (Celtic); 1905 v Ni; 1906 v Ni, W; 1908 v Ni, E; 1909 v E; 1910 v E, Ni, W; 1912 v E, W. (11)
Quinn, P. (Motherwell); 1961 v E, Ei(2); 1962 v U. (4)

Rae, J. (Third Lanark); 1889 v W; 1890 v Ni. (2)
Raeside, J.S. (Third Lanark); 1906 v W. (1)
Raisbeck, A.G. (Liverpool); 1900 v E; 1901 v E; 1902 v E; 1903 v E, W; 1904 v E; 1906 v E; 1907 v E. (8)
Rankin, G. (Vale of Leven); 1890 v Ni; 1891 v E. (2)
Rankin, R. (St Mirren); 1929 v N, G, Ho. (3)
Redpath, W. (Motherwell); 1949 v W, Ni; 1951 v E, D, F, Bel, A; 1952 v Ni, E. (9)
Reid, J.G. (Airdrieonians); 1914 v W; 1920 v W; 1924 v N (3)
Reid, R. (Brentford); 1938 v E, Ni. (2)
Reid, W. (Rangers); 1911 v E, W, Ni; 1912 v Ni; 1913 v E, W, Ni; 1914 v E, Ni. (9)
Reilly, L. (Hibernian); 1949 v W, E, F; 1950 v W, Ni, Sw, F; 1951 v W, E, D, F, Bel, A; 1952 v Ni, W, E, USA, D, Se; 1953 v Ni, W, E, Se; 1954 v W; 1955 v H(2); P, Y, A, E; 1956 v E, W, Ni, A; 1957 v E, Ni, W, Y. (38)
Rennie, H.G. (Hearts); 1900 v E, Ni; (Hibernian); 1901 v E; 1902 v E, Ni, W; 1903 v Ni, W; 1904 v Ni; 1905 v W; 1906 v Ni; 1908 v Ni, W. (13)
Renny-Tailyour, H.W. (Royal Engineers); 1873 v E. (1)
Rhind, A. (Queen's Park); 1872 v E. (1)
Richmond, A. (Queen's Park); 1906 v W. (1)
Richmond, J.T. (Clydesdale); 1877 v E; (Queen's Park); 1878 v E; 1882 v W. (3)
Ring, T. (Clyde); 1953 v Se; 1955 v W, Ni, E, H; 1957 v E, Sp(2); Sw, WG; 1958 v Ni, Sw. (12)
Rioch, B.D. (Derby Co); 1975 v P, W, Ni, E, R; 1976 v D(2); R, Ni, W, E; 1977 v Fi, Cz, W; (Everton); W, Ni, E, Ch, Br; 1978 v Cz; (Derby Co); Ni, E, Pe, Ho. (24)
Ritchie, A. (East Stirlingshire); 1891 v W. (1)
Ritchie, H. (Hibernian); 1923 v W; 1928 v Ni. (2)
Ritchie, J. (Queen's Park); 1897 v W. (1)
Ritchie, W. (Rangers); 1962 v U(sub). (1)

Robb, D.T. (Aberdeen); 1971 v W, E, P, D(sub); USSR. (5)
Robb, W. (Rangers); 1926 v W; (Hibernian); 1928 v W. (2)
Robertson, A. (Clyde); 1955 v P, A, H; 1958 v Sw, Par. (5)
Robertson, G. (Motherwell); 1910 v W; (Sheffield W); 1912 v W; 1913 v E, Ni. (4)
Robertson, G. (Kilmarnock); 1938 v Cz. (1)
Robertson, H. (Dundee); 1962 v Cz. (1)
Robertson, J. (Dundee); 1931 v A, I. (2)
Robertson, J. (Nottingham F); 1978 v Ni, W(sub); Ir; 1979 v P, N; 1980 v Pe, A, Bel(2); P; 1981 v Se, P, Is, Ni, Is, Ni, E; 1982 v Se, Ni(2); E(sub); Nz, Br, USSR; 1983 v EG, Sw; (Derby Co); 1984 v U, Bel. (28)
Robertson, J.G. (Tottenham H); 1965 v W. (1)
Robertson, J.T. (Everton); 1898 v E; (Southampton); 1899 v E; (Rangers); 1900 v E, W; 1901 v W, Ni, E; 1902 v W, Ni, E; 1903 v E, W; 1904 v E, W, Ni; 1905 v W. (16)
Robertson, P. (Dundee); 1903 v Ni. (1)
Robertson, T. (Queen's Park); 1889 v Ni; 1890 v E; 1891 v W; 1892 v Ni. (4)
Robertson, T. (Hearts); 1898 v Ni. (1)
Robertson, W. (Dumbarton); 1887 v E, W. (2)
Robinson, R. (Dundee); 1974 v WG(sub); 1975 v Se, Ni, R(sub). (4)
Rough, A. (Partick T); 1976 v Sw, Ni, W, E; 1977 v Fi, Cz, W(2); Se, Ni, E, Ch, Arg, Br; 1978 v Cz, W, Ni, E, Pe, Ir, Ho; 1979 v A, P, W, Arg, N; 1980 v Pe, A, Bel(2); P, W, E, Pol, H; 1981 v Se, P, Is, Ni, Is, W, E; 1982 v Se, Ni, Sp, Ho, W, E, Nz, Br, USSR; (Hibernian); 1986 v W(sub); E. (53)
Rougvie, D. (Aberdeen); 1984 v Ni. (1)
Rowan, A. (Caledonian); 1880 v E; (Queen's Park); 1882 v W. (2)
Russell, D. (Hearts); 1895 v E, Ni; (Celtic); 1897 v W; 1898 v Ni; 1901 v W, Ni. (6)
Russell, J. (Cambuslang); 1890 v Ni. (1)
Russell, W.F. (Airdrieonians); 1924 v W; 1925 v E. (2)
Rutherford, E. (Rangers); 1948 v F. (1)

St John, I. (Motherwell); 1959 v WG; 1960 v E, Ni, W, Pol, A; 1961 v E; (Liverpool); 1962 v Ni, W, E, Cz(2); U; 1963 v W, Ni, E, N, Ei(sub); Sp; 1964 v Ni; 1965 v E. (21)
Sawers, W. (Dundee); 1895 v W. (1)
Scarff, P. (Celtic); 1931 v Ni. (1)
Schaedler, E. (Hibernian); 1974 v WG. (1)
Scott, A.S. (Rangers); 1957 v Ni, Y, WG; 1958 v W, Sw; 1959 v P; 1962 v Ni, W, E, Cz, U; (Everton); 1964 v W, N; 1965 v Fi; 1966 v P, Br. (16)
Scott, J. (Hibernian); 1966 v Ho. (1)
Scott, J. (Dundee); 1971 v D(sub); USSR. (2)
Scott, M. (Airdrieonians); 1898 v W. (1)
Scott, R. (Airdrieonians); 1894 v Ni. (1)
Scoular, J. (Portsmouth); 1951 v D, F, A; 1952 v E, USA, D, Se; 1953 v W, Ni. (9)
Sellar, W. (Battlefield); 1885 v E; 1886 v E; 1887 v E; 1888 v E; (Queen's Park); 1891 v E; 1892 v E; 1893 v E, Ni. (9)
Semple, W. (Cambuslang); 1886 v W. (1)
Shankly, W. (Preston NE); 1938 v E; 1939 v E, W, Ni, H. (5)
Sharp, G.M. (Everton); 1985 v Ic; 1986 v W, Aus(2 subs); Is, R, U; 1987 v Ei. (8)
Sharp, J. (Dundee); 1904 v W; (Woolwich Arsenal); 1907 v W, E; 1908 v E; (Fulham); 1909 v W. (5)
Shaw, D. (Hibernian); 1947 v W, Ni; 1948 v E, Bel, Sw, F; 1949 v W, Ni. (8)
Shaw, F.W. (Pollokshields Ath); 1884 v E, W. (2)
Shaw, J. (Rangers); 1947 v E, Bel, L; 1948 v Ni. (4)
Shearer, R. (Rangers); 1961 v E, Ei(2); Cz. (4)
Sillars, D.C. (Queen's Park); 1891 v Ni; 1892 v E; 1893 v W; 1894 v E; 1895 v W. (5)
Simpson, J. (Third Lanark); 1895 v E, W, Ni. (3)
Simpson, J. (Rangers); 1935 v E, W, Ni; 1936 v E, W, Ni; 1937 v G, E, W, Ni, A, Cz; 1938 v Ni. (14)
Simpson, N. (Aberdeen); 1983 v Ni; 1984 v F(sub); 1987 v E. (3)
Simpson, R.C. (Celtic); 1967 v E, USSR; 1968 v Ni, E; 1969 v A. (5)
Sinclair, G.L. (Hearts); 1910 v Ni; 1912 v W, Ni. (3)
Sinclair, J.W.E. (Leicester C); 1966 v P. (1)
Skene, L.H. (Queen's Park); 1904 v W. (1)
Sloan, T. (Third Lanark); 1904 v W. (1)
Smellie, R. (Queen's Park); 1887 v Ni; 1888 v W; 1889 v E; 1891 v E; 1893 v E, Ni. (6)
Smith, A. (Rangers); 1898 v E; 1900 v E, Ni, W; 1901 v E, Ni, W; 1902 v E, Ni, W; 1903 v E, Ni, W;

1904 v Ni; 1905 v W; 1906 v E, Ni; 1907 v W; 1911 v E, Ni. (20)
Smith, D. (Aberdeen); 1966 v Ho; (Rangers); 1968 v Ho. (2)
Smith, G. (Hibernian); 1947 v E, Ni; 1948 v W, Bel, Sw, F; 1952 v E, USA; 1955 v P, Y, A, H; 1956 v E, Ni, W; 1957 v Sp(2); Sw. (18)
Smith, J. (Rangers); 1935 v Ni; 1938 v Ni. (2)
Smith, J. (Ayr U); 1924 v E. (1)

JIMMY SIMPSON
(Third Lanark)

JOHN THOMSON

Smith, J. (Aberdeen); 1968 v Ho(sub); (Newcastle U); 1974 v WG, Ni(sub); W(sub). (4)
Smith, J.E. (Celtic); 1959 v H, P. (2)
Smith, Jas. (Queen's Park); 1872 v E. (1)
Smith, John (Mauchline); 1877 v E, W; 1879 v E, W; (Edinburgh Univ); 1880 v E; (Queen's Park); 1881 v W, E; 1883 v E, W; 1884 v E. (10)
Smith, N. (Rangers); 1897 v E; 1898 v W; 1899 v E, W, Ni; 1900 v E, W, Ni; 1901 v Ni, W; 1902 v E, Ni. (12)

Smith, R. (Queen's Park); 1872 v E; 1873 v E. (2)
Smith, T.M. (Kilmarnock); 1934 v E; (Preston NE); 1938 v E. (2)
Somers, P. (Celtic); 1905 v E, Ni; 1907 v Ni; 1909 v W. (4)
Somers, W.S. (Third Lanark); 1879 v E, W; (Queen's Park); 1880 v W. (3)
Somerville, G. (Queen's Park); 1886 v E. (1)
Souness, G. (Middlesbrough); 1975 v EG, Sp, Se; (Liverpool); 1978 v Bul, W, E(sub); Ho; 1979 v A, N, W, Ni, E; 1980 v Pe, A, Bel, P, Ni; 1981 v P, Is(2); 1982 v Ni, P, Sp, W, E, Nz, Br, USSR; 1983 v EG, Sw, Bel, Sw, W, E, Ca(2+1 sub); 1984 v U, Ni, W; (Sampdoria); 1985 v Y, Ic, Sp(2); W, E, Ic; 1986 v EG, Aus(2); R, E, D, WG. (54)
Speedie, D.R. (Chelsea); 1985 v E; 1986 v W, EG(sub); Aus, E. (5)
Speedie, F. (Rangers); 1903 v E, W, Ni. (3)
Speirs, J.H. (Rangers); 1908 v W. (1)
Stanton, P. (Hibernian); 1966 v Ho; 1969 v Ni; 1970 v Ei, A; 1971 v D, Bel, P, USSR, D; 1972 v P, Bel, Ho, W; 1973 v W, Ni; 1974 v WG. (16)
Stark, J. (Rangers); 1909 v E, Ni. (2)
Steel, W. (Greenock Morton); 1947 v E, Bel, L; (Derby Co); 1948 v F, E, W, Ni; 1949 v E, W, Ni, F; 1950 v E, W, Ni, Sw, P, F; (Dundee); 1951 v W, Ni, E, A(2); D, F, Bel; 1952 v W; 1953 v W, E, Ni, Se. (30)
Steele, D.M. (Huddersfield T); 1923 v E, W, Ni. (3)
Stein, C. (Rangers); 1969 v W, Ni, D, E, Cy(2); 1970 v A(sub); Ni(sub); W, E, Ei, WG; 1971 v D, USSR, Bel, D; 1972 v Cz(sub); (Coventry C); 1973 v E(2 subs); W(sub); Ni. (21)
Stephen, J.F. (Bradford); 1947 v W; 1948 v W. (2)
Stevenson, G. (Motherwell); 1928 v W, Ni; 1930 v Ni, E, F; 1931 v E, W; 1932 v W, Ni; 1933 v Ni; 1934 v E; 1935 v Ni. (12)
Stewart, A. (Queen's Park); 1888 v Ni; 1889 v W. (2)
Stewart, A. (Third Lanark); 1894 v W. (1)
Stewart, D. (Dumbarton); 1888 v Ni. (1)
Stewart, D. (Queen's Park); 1893 v W; 1894 v Ni; 1897 v Ni. (3)
Stewart, D.S. (Leeds U); 1978 v EG. (1)
Stewart, G. (Hibernian); 1906 v W, E; (Manchester C); 1907 v E, W. (4)
Stewart, J. (Kilmarnock); 1977 v Ch(sub); (Middlesbrough); 1979 v N. (2)
Stewart, R. (West Ham); 1981 v W, Ni, E; 1982 v Ni, P, W; 1984 v F; 1987 v Ei(2), Lux. (10)
Stewart, W.E. (Queen's Park); 1898 v Ni; 1900 v Ni. (2)
Storrier, D. (Celtic); 1899 v E, W, Ni. (3)
Strachan, G. (Aberdeen); 1980 v Ni, W, E, Pol, H(sub); 1981 v Se, P; 1982 v Ni, P, Sp, Ho(sub); Nz, Br, USSR; 1983 v EG, Sw, Bel, Sw, Ni(sub); W, E, Ca(2+1 sub); 1984 v EG, Ni, E, F; (Manchester U); 1985 v Sp(sub); E, Ic; 1986 v W, Aus, R, D, WG, U; 1987 v Bul, Ei(2). (40)
Sturrock, P. (Dundee U); 1981 v W(sub); Ni, E(sub); 1982 v P, Ni(sub); W(sub); E(sub); 1983 v EG(sub); Sw, Bel(sub); Ca(3); 1984 v W; 1985 v Y(sub); 1986 v Is(sub); Ho, D, U; 1987 v Bel. (20)
Summers, W. (St Mirren); 1926 v E. (1)
Symon, J.S. (Rangers); 1939 v H. (1)

Tait, T.S. (Sunderland); 1911 v W. (1)
Taylor, J. (Queen's Park); 1872 v E; 1873 v E; 1874 v E; 1875 v E; 1876 v E, W. (6)
Taylor, J.D. (Dumbarton); 1892 v W; 1893 v W; 1894 v Ni; (St Mirren); 1895 v Ni. (4)
Taylor, W. (Hearts); 1892 v E. (1)
Telfer, W. (Motherwell); 1933 v Ni; 1934 v Ni. (2)
Telfer, W.D. (St Mirren); 1954 v W. (1)
Templeton, R. (Aston Villa); 1902 v E; (Newcastle U); 1903 v E, W; 1904 v E; (Woolwich Arsenal); 1905 v W; (Kilmarnock); 1908 v Ni; 1910 v E, Ni; 1912 v E, Ni; 1913 v W. (11)
Thomson, A. (Arthurlie); 1886 v Ni. (1)
Thomson, A. (Airdrieonians); 1909 v Ni. (1)
Thomson, A. (Celtic); 1926 v E; 1932 v F; 1933 v W. (3)
Thomson, A. (Third Lanark); 1889 v W. (1)
Thomson, C. (Hearts); 1904 v Ni; 1905 v E, W, Ni; 1906 v W, Ni; 1907 v E, W, Ni; 1908 v E, W, Ni; (Sunderland); 1909 v W; 1910 v E; 1911 v Ni; 1912 v E, W; 1913 v E, W; 1914 v E, Ni. (21)
Thomson, C. (Sunderland); 1937 v Cz. (1)
Thomson, D. (Dundee); 1920 v W. (1)
Thomson, J. (Celtic); 1930 v F; 1931 v E, W, Ni. (4)
Thomson, J.J. (Queen's Park); 1872 v E; 1873 v E; 1874 v E. (3)

ALEC TROUP

Thomson, J.R. (Everton); 1933 v W. (1)
Thomson, R. (Celtic); 1932 v W. (1)
Thomson, R.W. (Falkirk); 1927 v E. (1)
Thomson, S. (Rangers); 1884 v W, Ni. (2)
Thomson, W. (Dumbarton); 1892 v W; 1893 v W; 1898 v Ni, W. (4)
Thomson, W. (Dundee); 1896 v W. (1)
Thornton, W. (Rangers); 1947 v W, Ni; 1948 v E, Ni; 1949 v F; 1952 v D, Se. (7)
Thomson, W. (St Mirren); 1980 v Ni; 1981 v Ni(sub); Ni; 1982 v P; 1983 v Ni, Ca; 1984 v EG. (7)
Toner, W. (Kilmarnock); 1959 v W, Ni. (2)
Townsley, T. (Falkirk); 1926 v W. (1)
Troup, A. (Dundee); 1920 v E; 1921 v W, Ni; 1922 v Ni; (Everton); 1926 v E. (5)
Turnbull, E. (Hibernian); 1948 v Bel, Sw; 1951 v A; 1958 v H, Pol, Y, Par, F. (8)
Turner, T. (Arthurlie); 1884 v W. (1)
Turner, W. (Pollokshields); 1885 v Ni; 1886 v Ni. (2)

Ure, J.I. (Dundee); 1962 v W, Cz; 1963 v W, Ni, E, A, N, Sp; (Arsenal); 1964 v Ni, N; 1968 v Ni. (11)
Urquhart, D. (Hibernian); 1934 v W. (1)

Vallance, T. (Rangers); 1877 v E, W; 1878 v E; 1879 v E, W; 1881 v E, W. (7)
Venters, A. (Cowdenbeath); 1934 v Ni; (Rangers); 1936 v E; 1939 v E. (3)

IAN URE

Waddell, T.S. (Queen's Park); 1891 v Ni; 1892 v E; 1893 v E, Ni; 1895 v E, Ni. (6)
Waddell, W. (Rangers); 1947 v W; 1949 v E, W, Ni, F; 1950 v E, Ni; 1951 v E, D, F, Bel, A; 1952 v Ni, W; 1954 v Ni; 1955 v W, Ni. (17)
Wales, H.M. (Motherwell); 1933 v W. (1)
Walker, F. (Third Lanark); 1922 v W. (1)
Walker, G. (St Mirren); 1930 v F; 1931 v Ni, A, Sw. (4)
Walker, J. (Hearts); 1895 v Ni; 1897 v W; 1898 v Ni; (Rangers); 1904 v W, Ni. (5)
Walker, J. (Swindon T); 1911 v E, W, Ni; 1912 v E, W, Ni; 1913 v E, W, Ni. (9)
Walker, R. (Hearts); 1900 v E, Ni; 1901 v E, W; 1902 v E, W, Ni; 1903 v E, W, Ni; 1904 v E, W, Ni; 1905 v E, W, Ni; 1906 v Ni; 1907 v E, Ni; 1908 v E, W, Ni; 1909 v E, W; 1912 v E, W, Ni; 1913 v E, W. (29)
Walker, T. (Hearts); 1935 v E, W; 1936 v E, W, Ni; 1937 v G, E, W, Ni, A, Cz; 1938 v E, W, Ni, Cz, Ho; 1939 v E, W, Ni, H. (20)
Walker, W. (Clyde); 1909 v Ni; 1910 v Ni. (2)
Wallace, I.A. (Coventry C); 1978 v Bul(sub); 1979 v P(sub); W. (3)
Wallace, W.S.B. (Hearts); 1965 v Ni; 1966 v E, Ho; (Celtic); 1967 v E, USSR(sub); 1968 v Ni; 1969 v E(sub). (7)
Wardhaugh, J. (Hearts); 1955 v H; 1957 v Ni. (2)
Wark, J. (Ipswich T); 1979 v W, Ni, E, Arg, N(sub); 1980 v Pe, A, Bel(2); 1981 v Is, Ni; 1982 v Se, Sp, Ho, Ni, Nz, Br, USSR; 1983 v EG, Sw, Sw, Ni, E(sub); 1984 v U, Bel, EG; (Liverpool); E, F; 1985 v Y. (29)
Watson, A. (Queen's Park); 1881 v E, W; 1882 v E. (3)
Watson, J. (Sunderland); 1903 v E, W; 1904 v E; 1905 v E; (Middlesbrough); 1909 v E, Ni. (6)
Watson, J. (Motherwell); 1948 v Ni; (Huddersfield T); 1954 v Ni. (2)
Watson, J.A.K. (Rangers); 1878 v W. (1)
Watson, P.R. (Blackpool); 1934 v A. (1)
Watson, R. (Motherwell); 1971 v USSR. (1)
Watson, W. (Falkirk); 1898 v W. (1)
Watt, F. (Kilbirnie); 1889 v W, Ni; 1890 v W; 1891 v E. (4)
Watt, W.W. (Queen's Park); 1887 v Ni. (1)
Waugh, W. (Hearts); 1938 v Cz. (1)
Weir, A. (Motherwell); 1959 v WG; 1960 v E, P, A, H, T. (6)
Weir, J. (Third Lanark); 1887 v Ni. (1)
Weir, J.B. (Queen's Park); 1872 v E; 1874 v E; 1875 v E; 1878 v W. (4)
Weir, P. (St Mirren); 1980 v N(sub); W, Pol(sub); H; (Aberdeen); 1983 v Sw; 1984 v Ni. (6)
White, J. (Albion R); 1922 v W; (Hearts); 1923 v Ni. (2)
White, J.A. (Falkirk); 1959 v WG, Ho, P; 1960 v Ni (Tottenham H); W, Pol, A, T; 1961 v W; 1962 v Ni, W, E, Cz(2); 1963 v W, Ni, E; 1964 v Ni, W, E, N, WG. (22)
White, W. (Bolton W); 1907 v E; 1908 v E. (2)
Whitelaw, A. (Vale of Leven); 1887 v Ni; 1890 v W. (2)
Wilson, A. (Sheffield W); 1907 v E; 1908 v E; 1912 v E; 1913 v E, W; 1914 v Ni. (6)
Wilson, A. (Portsmouth); 1954 v Fi. (1)
Wilson, A.N. (Dunfermline); 1920 v E, W, Ni; 1921 v E, W, Ni; (Middlesbrough); 1922 v E, W, Ni; 1923 v E, W, Ni. (12)
Wilson, D. (Queen's Park); 1900 v W. (1)
Wilson, D. (Oldham A); 1913 v E. (1)
Wilson, D. (Rangers); 1961 v E, W, Ni, Ei(2); Cz; 1962 v Ni, W, E, Cz, U; 1963 v W, E, A, N, Ei, Sp; 1964 v E, WG; 1965 v Ni, E, Fi. (22)
Wilson, G.W. (Hearts); 1904 v W; 1905 v E, Ni; 1906 v W; (Everton); 1907 v E; (Newcastle U); 1909 v E. (6)
Wilson, H. (Newmilns); 1890 v W; (Sunderland); 1897 v E; (Third Lanark); 1902 v W; 1904 v Ni. (4)
Wilson, I. (Leicester C); 1987 v E, Br. (2)
Wilson, J. (Vale of Leven); 1888 v W; 1889 v E; 1890 v E; 1891 v E. (4)
Wilson, P. (Celtic); 1926 v Ni; 1930 v F; 1931 v Ni; 1933 v E. (4)
Wilson, P. (Celtic); 1975 v Sp(sub). (1)
Wilson, R.P. (Arsenal); 1972 v P, Ho. (2)
Wiseman, W. (Queen's Park); 1927 v W; 1930 v Ni. (2)
Wood, G. (Everton); 1979 v Ni, E, Arg(sub); (Arsenal); 1982 v Ni. (4)

JOHN WALKER

Woodburn, W.A. (Rangers); 1947 v E, Bel, L; 1948 v W, Ni; 1949 v E, F; 1950 v E, W, Ni, P, F; 1951 v E, W, Ni, A(2); D, F, Bel; 1952 v E, W, Ni, USA. (24)
Wotherspoon, D.N. (Queen's Park); 1872 v E; 1873 v E. (2)
Wright, T. (Sunderland); 1953 v W, Ni, E. (3)
Wylie, T.G. (Rangers); 1890 v Ni. (1)

Yeats, R. (Liverpool); 1965 v W; 1966 v I. (2)
Yorston, B.C. (Aberdeen); 1931 v Ni. (1)
Yorston, H. (Aberdeen); 1955 v W. (1)
Young, A. (Hearts); 1960 v E, A(sub); H, T; 1961 v W, Ni (Everton); Ei; 1966 v P. (8)
Young, A. (Everton); 1905 v E; 1907 v W. (2)
Young, G.L. (Rangers); 1947 v E, Ni, Bel, L; 1948 v E, Ni, Bel, Sw, F; 1949 v E, W, Ni, F; 1950 v E, W, Ni, Sw, P,F; 1951 v E, W, Ni, A(2); D, F, Bel; 1952 v E, W, Ni, USA, D, Se; 1953 v W, E, Ni, Se; 1954 v Ni, W; 1955 v W, Ni, P, Y; 1956 v Ni, W, E, A; 1957 v E, Ni, W, Y, Sp, Sw. (53)
Young, J. (Celtic); 1906 v Ni. (1)
Younger, T. (Hibernian); 1955 v P, Y, A, H; 1956 v E, Ni, W, A; (Liverpool); 1957 v E, Ni, W, Y, Sp(2); Sw, WG; 1958 v Ni, W, E, Sw, H, Pol, Y, Par. (24)

ALEX YOUNG

Under-23 Appearances

Aitken, C. (Aston Villa); 1962 v E, W; 1963 v W. (3)
Alderson, B. (Coventry C); 1973 v E. (1)
Allan, W. (Aberdeen); 1963 v W. (1)
Anderson, G. (Morton); 1973 v W. (1)
Baillie, D. (Airdrieonians); 1955 v E; 1959 v W. (2)
Baird, D. (Partick T); 1959 v W. (1)
Baxter, James (Raith R); 1959 v W. (1)
Baxter, John (Hibernian); 1959 v W. (1)
Baxter, T. (Queen of the South); 1956 v E. (1)
Beattie, R. (Celtic); 1958 v Ho (2), E. (3)
Blacklaw, A. (Burnley); 1960 v E, W. (2)
Blackley, J. (Hibernian); 1970 v F, E, W; 1971 v E. (4)
Bone, J. (Partick T); 1972 v E, W; (Norwich C); 1973 v E. (3)
Brand, R. (Rangers); 1958 v E. (1)
Bremner, D. (Hibernian); 1975 v E, W, Se; 1976 v D (2), R, W, Ho (2). (9)
Bremner, W. (Leeds U); 1964 v E, F; 1965 v W, E. (4)
Brown, H. (Kilmarnock); 1963 v W. (1)
Brown, J. (Chesterfield); 1974 v W(sub), E(sub) (Sheffield U); 1975 v E(sub), Se(sub), W(sub). (5)
Brownlie, J. (Hibernian); 1972 v E, W; 1976 v W, Ho (2). (5)
Bruce A. (Newcastle U); 1974 v E. (1)
Buchan, M. (Aberdeen); 1971 v W; 1972 v W, E. (3)
Burley, G. (Ipswich T); 1975 v E, Se. (2)
Burns, F. (Manchester U); 1968 v E. (1)
Burns, K. (Birmingham C); 1974 v W; 1976 v Ho. (2)
Calderwood, R. (Birmingham C); 1974 v E. (1)
Caldow, E. (Rangers); 1955 v E; 1957 v E. (2)
Campbell, A. (Charlton A); 1970 v W. (1)
Carr, W. (Coventry C); 1970 v F, W; 1971 v W; 1972 v E. (4)
Clark, R. (Aberdeen); 1967 v W, E; 1968 v Ho. (3)
Clunie, D. (Hearts); 1970 v E, W. (2)
Colquhoun, E. (West Brom A); 1968 v E. (1)
Colrain, J. (Celtic); 1958 v Ho. (1)
Conn, A. (Tottenham H); 1975 v R; 1976 v D, R. (3)
Connelly, G. (Celtic); 1970 v E; 1971 v E; 1972 v E. (3)
Connolly, J. (Everton); 1971 v W; 1973 v W. (2)
Cooke, C. (Aberdeen); 1963 v W; 1964 v W; 1965 v W; (Dundee) 1965 v E; (Chelsea) 1968 v Ho. (5)
Cormack, P. (Hibernian); 1965 v W, E; 1967 v W, E; 1968 v E. (5)
Cousin, A. (Dundee); 1958 v Ho; 1960 v E, Bel. (3)
Craig, J. (Partick T); 1976 v D, R, W, Ho. (4)
Craig, T. (Sheffield W); 1974 v E; (Newcastle U); 1975 v W, Se, R; 1976 v D(2), R, W, Ho. (9)
Crawford, J. (Hearts); 1957 v E. (1)
Crerand, P. (Celtic); 1961 v E. (1)
Cropley, A. (Hibernian); 1972 v W; 1973 v E; 1974 v W (3)
Cruickshank, J. (Queen's Park); 1960 v Bel; (Hearts); 1964 v W, E. (3)
Currie, D. (Clyde); 1958 v Ho(2), E; 1959 v W. (4)
Dalglish, K. (Celtic); 1972 v W, E; 1973 v W; 1976 v Ho. (4)
Davie, A. (Dundee U); 1964 v F. (1)
Dickson, P. (Queen of the South); 1976 v Ho(sub). (1)
Dickson, W. (Kilmarnock); 1970 v E. (1)
Donachie, W. (Manchester C); 1972 v W, E. (2)
Donaldson, A. (Dundee); 1965 v W, E.(2)
Doyle, J. (Ayr U); 1973 v E, W; 1974 v W(sub). (3)
Duff, W. (Hearts); 1955 v E. (1)
Duncan, A. (Hibernian); 1971 v E. (1)
Easton, J. (Hibernian); 1964 v W. (1)
Edwards, A. (Dunfermline Ath); 1967 v W. (1)
Ewen, A. (Aberdeen); 1959 v W. (1)
Ferguson, R. (West Ham U); 1968 v E. (1)
Forrest, J. (Rangers); 1964 v W; 1965 v E. (2)
Forsyth, A. (Manchester U); 1974 v W. (1)
Forsyth, C. (St Mirren); 1957 v E. (1)
Forsyth, T. (Motherwell); 1971 v E. (1)
Fraser, C. (Dunfermline Ath); 1962 v W; (Aston Villa) 1963 v W. (2)
Fraser, D. (West Brom); 1968 v Ho. (1)
Gabriel, J. (Dundee); 1960 v W (Everton); E, Bel; 1962 v W; 1963 v W; 1964 v E. (6)
Gemmill, A. (Preston NE); 1970 v E. (1)
Gibb, T. (Partick T); 1968 v E(sub). (1)
Gibson, I. (Middlesbrough); 1964 v W, F. (2)
Gillies, D. (Bristol C); 1974 v E (1)
Gilzean, A. (Dundee); 1961 v E; 1962 v W, E. (3)
Glen, A. (Queen's Park); 1957 v E. (1)
Gow, G. (Bristol C); 1974 v E(sub). (1)
Graham, A. (Aberdeen); 1975 v E, Se, R(sub). (3)
Graham, G. (Chelsea); 1965 v W, E. (2)
Gray, A. (Dundee U); 1975 v E, W, R; (Aston Villa), 1976 v D. (4)

Gray, E. (Leeds U); 1967 v W, E. (2)
Gray, F. (Leeds U); 1974 v E; 1976 v D(2), R, Ho. (5)
Greig, J. (Rangers); 1964 v W, E; 1968 v Ho. (3)
Hamilton, J. (Hearts); 1956 v E; 1957 v E. (2)
Hamilton, R. (Kilmarnock); 1965 v W. (1)
Hansen, A. (Partick T); 1975 v Se; 1976 v R, W(sub). (3)
Harper, J. (Aberdeen); 1970 v W(sub); 1971 v W. (2)
Harrower, J. (Hibernian); 1958 v Ho. (1)
Hartford, A. (West Brom); 1970 v W; 1971 v W; 1972 v E; 1973 v E, W. (5)
Hay, D. (Celtic); 1970 v F; 1971 v E, W. (3)
Henderson, W. (Rangers); 1962 v W, E; 1968 v Ho. (3)
Herd, G. (Clyde); 1958 v Ho(2). (2)
Hermiston, J. (Aberdeen); 1971 v W. (1)
Higgins, W. (Hearts); 1960 v E, W, Bel; 1962 v E. (4)
Hill, A. (Clyde); 1955 v E. (1)
Hilley, D. (Third Lanark); 1961 v E. (1)
Hogan, J. (Partick T); 1961 v E (1)
Hollywood, D. (Southampton); 1965 v E. (1)
Holmes, R. (St Mirren); 1955 v E. (1)
Holt, D. (Queen's Park); 1958 v Ho. (1)
Holton, J. (Manchester U); 1973 v W (1)
Hood, H. (Clyde); 1968 v E. (1)
Hope, R. (West Brom); 1967 v W; 1968 v Ho. (2)
Houston, S. (Manchester U); 1975 v Se, R. (2)
Hughes, J. (Celtic); 1961 v E; 1962 v W, E; 1964 v E. (4)
Hughes, T. (Chelsea); 1970 v F, E. (2)
Hunter, A. (Kilmarnock); 1971 v E(sub); 1972 v W, E. (3)
Hunter, W. (Motherwell); 1960 v W, E, Bel; 1962 v E. (4)
Hutchison, T. (Blackpool); 1971 v W. (1)
Jackson, C. (Rangers); 1976 v Ho. (1)
Jardine, S. (Rangers); 1971 v E, W(sub); 1972 v W, E. (4)
Jarvie, A. (Airdrieonians); 1971 v E. (1)
Jeffrey, R. (Celtic); 1963 v W. (1)
Johnston, W. (Rangers); 1970 v F, E. (2)
Johnstone, D. (Rangers); 1974 v W, E; 1975 v E; 1976 v W, Ho(2). (6)
Johnstone, J. (Celtic); 1964 v F, E. (2)
Jordan, J. (Leeds U); 1976 v Ho. (1)
Kelly, E. (Arsenal); 1971 v E, W; 1974 v W. (3)
Kennedy, J. (Kilmarnock); 1958 v Ho. (1)
Kennedy, S. (Falkirk); 1973 v E, W; 1975 v W. (3)
Kennedy, S. (Rangers); 1975 v W. (1)
King, A. (Kilmarnock); 1964 v W, F; 1965 v W. (3)
Lamb, A. (Preston NE); 1974 v E(sub). (1)
Law, D. (Huddersfield T); 1960 v W, E; (Manchester C) 1961 v E. (3)
Lawrence, T. (Liverpool); 1963 v W. (1)
Leggat, G. (Aberdeen); 1955 v E. (1)
Lochhead, A. (Burnley); 1963 v W. (1)
Lorimer, P. (Leeds U); 1970 v W, F. (2)
Macari, L. (Celtic); 1972 v W, E. (2)
Mackay, D. (Hearts); 1955 v E; 1957 v E; 1958 v Ho, E. (4)
MacKay, D. (Celtic); 1959 v W; 1960 v E, W, Bel. (4)
McCalliog, J. (Sheffield W); 1967 v W, E. (2);
McCluskey, P. (Celtic); 1973 v E, W(sub); 1975 v E, W, R; 1976 v D. (6)
McCreadie, E. (Chelsea); 1968 v Ho. (1)
McCulloch, W. (Cardiff C); 1973 v W(sub). (1)
McDonald, I. (St Johnstone); 1974 v E; 1975 v E. (2)
MacDonald, A. (Rangers); 1975 v E. (1)
McDonald, R. (Celtic); 1976 v D. (1)
McDougall, I. (Rangers); 1975 v W. (1)
McGillivray, A. (Third Lanark); 1962 v E. (1)
McGovern, J. (Derby Co); 1972 v W; 1973 v W. (2)
McGrain, D. (Celtic); 1973 v W, E. (2)
McGrory, J. (Kilmarnock); 1964 v F, E; 1965 v W. (3)
McIntosh, J. (Falkirk); 1956 v E; 1958 v E, Ho. (3)
McKinnon, R. (Rangers); 1968 v Ho. (1)
McLean, G. (Dundee); 1968 v Ho. (1)
McLean, T. (Kilmarnock); 1967 v E; 1970 v E. (2)
McLelland, D. (Aberdeen); 1976 v W, Ho. (2)
McLeod, J.M. (Hibernian); 1961 v E. (1)
McLintock, F. (Leicester C); 1962 v E. (1)
McMillan, T. (Aberdeen); 1967 v W, E. (2)
McNeill, W. (Celtic); 1960 v Bel; 1961 v E; 1962 v W, E; 1963 v W. (5)
McParland, D. (Partick T); 1955 v E. (1)
McQuade, D. (Partick T); 1972 v W(sub). (1)
MacRae, K. (Motherwell); 1971 v E, W. (2)
McVie, W. (Motherwell); 1976 v W, Ho. (2)
Malone, D. (Ayr U); 1970 v F. (1)
Martin, N. (Hibernian); 1964 v F. (1)
Martis, J. (Motherwell); 1960 v E. (1)

Marinello, P. (Hibernian); 1970 v F(sub), (Arsenal) v E(sub). (2)
Miller, W. (Aberdeen); 1974 v E; 1975 v E, W, Se; 1976 v D, R, W, Ho(2). (9)
Milne, A. (Cardiff C); 1960 v W. (1)
Mitchell, I. (Dundee U); 1967 v W, E. (2)
Moncur, R. (Newcastle U); 1968 v E, Ho. (2)
Morgan, W. (Burnley); 1968 v E. (1)
Morrison, R. (Aberdeen); 1956 v E. (1)
Munro, F. (Wolverhampton W); 1970 v F, E, W(sub); 1971 v W. (4)
Murdoch, R. (Celtic); 1964 v E. (1)
Murray, D. (Cardiff C); 1965 v E. (1)
Murray, G. (Motherwell); 1964 v F; 1965 v W, E. (3)
Murray, M. (Rangers); 1956 v E; 1957 v E. (2)
Murray, S. (Dundee); 1968 v E. (1)
Narey, D. (Dundee U); 1975 v R; 1976 v D(2), Ho(sub).(4)
Nicol, R. (Hibernian); 1956 v E; 1958 v Ho. (2)
Ogston, J. (Aberdeen); 1961 v E; 1962 v W, E. (3)
O'Hara, E. (Falkirk); 1958 v Ho (2), E. (3)
O'Hare, J. (Derby C); 1970 v F, E, W. (3)
Oliver, J. (Hearts); 1971 v W(sub). (1)
Parker, A. (Falkirk); 1955 v E; 1956 v E; 1957 v E; 1958 v Ho (2), E. (6)
Parlane, D. (Rangers); 1973 v E(sub), W; 1974 v W; 1975 v E, W. (5)
Pearson, J. (St Johnstone); 1974 v W, E; 1975 (Everton) v W(sub), Se, R; 1976 v D. (6)
Penman, A. (Dundee); 1960 v Bel; 1962 v W; 1964 v W; 1965 v E. (4)
Pettigrew, W. (Motherwell); 1975 v Se, R; 1976 v D (2), R, W, Ho. (7)
Phillip, I. (Crystal Palace); 1973 v E. (1)
Plenderleith, J. (Hibernian); 1957 v E; 1958 v Ho (2), E; 1960 v W. (5)
Prentice, R. (Hearts); 1974 v W; 1976 v D(sub), R, W. (4)
Price, W. (Airdrieonians); 1956 v E; 1958 v Ho. (2)
Provan, D. (Rangers); 1964 v E. (1)
Purdie, I. (Aberdeen); 1975 v E(sub). (1)
Rae, I. (Falkirk); 1956 v E. (1)
Reilly, F. (Dunfermline Ath); 1957 v E. (1)
Riddell, I. (St Mirren); 1960 v E; 1961 v E. (2)
Robb, D. (Aberdeen); 1970 v F, W; 1971 v E. (3)
Roberts, R. (Motherwell); 1962 v W. (1)
Robertson, H. (Dundee); 1962 v W, E. (2)
Robertson, J. (St Mirren); 1964 v W; (Tottenham H) 1964 v F; 1965 v W; 1968 v E. (4)
Robinson, R. (Dundee); 1974 v W. (1)
Rough, A. (Partick T); 1973 v E; 1975 v Se, R; 1976 v D(2), R, W, Ho(2). (9)
St John, I (Motherwell); 1960 v E, Bel. (2)
Scott, A. (Rangers); 1958 v E. (1)
Sharkey, D. (Sunderland); 1964 v F, E. (2)
Shevlane, C. (Hearts); 1964 v W, F, E; 1965 v W. (4)
Slater, R. (Falkirk); 1959 v W. (1)
Smith, D. (Aberdeen); 1963 v W; 1964 v W. (2)
Smith, D. (Rangers); 1968 v Ho. (1)
Smith, G. (Kilmarnock); 1975 v W, Se, R(sub); 1976 v W(sub), R(sub), Ho. (6)
Smith, G. (St Johnstone); 1975 v R; 1976 v D(2), R. (4)
Smith, J. (Aberdeen); 1967 v E; 1968 v Ho. (2)
Smith, J. (Aberdeen); 1976 v Ho. (1)
Sneddon, D. (Dundee); 1959 v W. (1)
Souness, G. (Middlesbrough); 1974 v E; 1976 v Ho. (2)
Stanton, P. (Hibernian); 1967 v W, E; 1968 v E. (3)
Stein, C. (Hibernian); 1968 v E. (1)
Stewart, D. (Ayr U); 1970 v W. (1)
Stewart, J. (Kilmarnock); 1973 v W; 1974 v W, E; 1975 v E; 1976 v W(sub). (5)
Sullivan, D. (Clyde); 1975 v E, W(sub), (2)
Thomson, A. (Hearts); 1970 v F, E, W. (3)
Thomson, J. (Hearts); 1958 v E; 1960 v Bel. (2)
Tinney, H. (Partick T); 1967 v W, E. (2)
Ure, I. (Dundee); 1961 v E. (1)
Wallace, J. (Dunfermline Ath); 1974 v W (1)
Walsh, J. (Celtic); 1955 v E. (1)
Weir, A. (Motherwell); 1960 v E, Bel, W. (3)
White, J. (Tottenham H); 1960 v W. (1)
Whyte, J. (Aberdeen); ;1967 v W, E. (2)
Wilson, D. (Rangers); 1959 v W. (1)
Wilson, R. (West Brom); 1970 v W. (1)
Wishart, R. (Aberdeen); 1955 v E; 1956 v E. (2)
Young, A. (Hearts); 1956 v E; 1957 v E; 1958 v E, Ho; 1959 v W; 1960 v W. (6)
Young, I. (Celtic); 1965 v E. (1)
Young, Q. (Ayr U); 1971 v E. (1)
Young, W. (Aberdeen); 1972 v W; 1973 v E; 1975 v W, R; 1976 v D. (5)

Under-21 Appearances

Abercromby, W. (St Mirren); 1979 v N. (1)
Aitken, R. (Celtic); 1977 v Cz, W, Sw; 1978 v Cz, W; 1979 v P, N(2); 1980 v B, E; 1984 v EG, Y(2); 1985 v WG, Ic, Sp. (16)
Albiston, A.(Manchester U); 1977 v Cz, W, Sw; 1978 v Sw, Cz. (5)
Archibald, S. (Aberdeen); 1980 v B, E(2), WG; (Tottenham H); 1981 v D. (5)
Bannon, E.J.P.(Hearts); 1979 v US, N, P (Chelsea); N (2); (Dundee U); 1980 v B, WG, E. (7)
Beaumont, D. (Dundee U); 1985 v Ic, WG(sub). (2)
Bell, D. (Aberdeen); 1981 v D; 1984 v Y. (2)
Bett, J. (Rangers); 1981 v Se, D; 1982 v Se, D,I, E(2). (7)
Black, E. (Aberdeen); 1983 v EG, Sw(2), Bel; 1985 v Ic(2), Sp(2). (8)
Blair, A. (Coventry C); 1980 v E; 1981 v Se. (Aston Villa); 1982 v Se, D, I. (5)
Boyd, T. (Motherwell); 1986 v Ei; 1987 v Ei, Bel, WG. (4)
Bowman, D. (Hearts); 1985 v WG(sub). (1)
Brazil, A. (Hibernian); 1978 v W. (1)
Brazil, A. (Ipswich T); 1979 v N; 1980 v B(2), E(2), WG; 1981 v Se; 1982 v Se. (8)
Brough, J. (Hearts); 1981 v D. (1)
Burley, G.E. (Ipswich T); 1977 v Cz, W, S; 1978 v Sw, Cz. (5)
Burns, H. (Rangers); 1985 v Sp, Ic(sub). (2)
Burns, T. (Celtic); 1977 v Cz, W, E; 1978 v Sw; 1982 v E. (5)
Casey, J. (Celtic); 1978 v W. (1)
Clark, R. (Aberdeen); 1977 v Cz, W, Sw. (3)
Clarke, S. (St Mirren); 1984 v Bel, EG, Y; 1985 v WG, Sp(2), Ic(2). (8)
Connor, R. (Ayr U); 1981 v Se; 1982 v Se. (2)
Cooper, D. (Clydebank); 1977 v Cz, W, Sw, E; (Rangers); 1978 v Sw, Cz. (6)
Cooper, N.(Aberdeen); 1982 v D, E(2); 1983 v Bel, EG, Sw(2); 1984 v Bel, EG, Y; 1985 v Sp, Ic(2). (13)
Craig, T. (Newcastle U); 1977 v E. (1)
Crainie, D. (Celtic); 1983 v Sw(sub). (1)
Dawson, A. (Rangers); 1979 v P, N; 1980 v B(2), E(2), WG. (7)
Dodds, D. (Dundee U); 1978 v W. (1)
Doyle, J. (Partick T); 1981 v D, I(sub); 1983 v EG(sub). (3)
Duffy, J. (Dundee); 1986 v Ei. (1)
Durie, G. (Chelsea); 1987 v Ei, Bel, WG. (3)
Durrant, I. (Rangers); 1987 v Ei, Bel, WG. (3)
Ferguson, D. (Rangers); 1986 v Ei; 1987 v Bel, WG. (3)
Ferguson, I. (Dundee); 1983 v EG(sub), Sw(sub); 1984 v Bel(sub), EG. (4)
Ferguson, I.(St Mirren); 1986 v Ei; 1987 v Ei, Bel. (3)
Ferguson, R. (Hamilton A); 1977 v E (1)
Fitzpatrick, A. (St Mirren); 1977 v W(sub), Sw(sub), E; 1978 v Sw, Cz. (5)
Fleck, R. (Rangers); 1986 v Ei; 1987 v Ei, Bel. (3)
Fulton, M. (St Mirren); 1980 v B, WG, E; 1981 v Se, D(sub). (5)
Gallacher, K. (Dundee U); 1986 v Ei; 1987 v Ei, Bel, WG. (4)
Geddes, R. (Dundee); 1982 v Se, D, E(2). (4)
Gillespie, G. (Coventry C); 1979 v US; 1980 v E; 1981 v D; 1982 v Se, D, I(2), E. (8)
Goram, A. (Oldham A); 1986 v Ei. (1)
Gough, C.R. (Dundee U); 1983 v EG, Sw, Bel; 1984 v Y(2). (5)
Grant, P. (Celtic); 1985 v WG, Ic, Sp(sub); 1986 v Ei; 1987 v Ei, Bel, WG. (8)
Gray, S. (Aberdeen); 1987 v WG. (1)
Gunn, B. (Aberdeen); 1984 v EG, Y(2); 1985 v WG, Ic(2), Sp(2). (8)
Hartford, R.A. (Manchester C); 1977 v Sw. (1)
Hegarty, P. (Dundee U); 1987 v Bel, WG. (2)
Hewitt, J. (Aberdeen); 1982 v I; 1983 v EG, Sw(2); 1984 v Bel, Y(sub). (6)
Hogg, G. (Manchester U); 1984 v Y; 1985 v WG, Ic, Sp. (4)
Hunter, G. (Hibernian); 1986 v Ei(sub). (1)
Jardine, I. (Kilmarnock); 1979 v US. (1)
Johnston, M. (Partick T); 1984 v EG(sub); (Watford); v Y(2). (3)
Leighton, J. (Aberdeen); 1982 v I(2). (2)
Levein, C. (Hearts); 1985 v Sp, Ic. (2)
Lindsay, J. (Motherwell); 1979 v US. (1)
McAlpine, H. (Dundee U); 1983 v EG, Sw(2), Bel; 1984 v Bel. (5)

McAvennie, F. (St Mirren); 1982 v I, E(2); 1985 v Is, Ei, R. (6)

FRANK McAVENNIE

McBride, J. (Everton); 1981 v D. (1)
McClair, B. (Celtic); 1984 v Bel(sub), EG, Y(1+sub); 1985 v WG, Sp, Ic(2). (8)
McCluskey, G. (Celtic); 1979 v US, N, P; 1980 v B(2); 1982 v D, I. (7)
McCoist, A. (Rangers); 1984 v Bel. (1)
McCulloch, A. (Kilmarnock); 1981 v Se. (1)
McCulloch, I. (Notts Co); 1982 v E(2). (2)
MacDonald, J. (Rangers); 1980 v WG(sub); 1981 v Se; 1982 v Se(sub), D(sub), I(2), E(2 sub). (8)
McGarvey, F. (St Mirren); 1977 v E; 1978 v Cz; (Celtic); 1982 v D. (3)
McGarvey, S. (Manchester U); 1982 v E(sub); 1983 v Bel, Sw; 1984 v Bel. (4)
McGhee, M. (Aberdeen); 1981 v D. (1)
McGinnis, G. (Dundee U); 1985 v Sp. (1)
McKimmie, S. (Aberdeen); 1985 v WG, Ic(2). (3)
McKinlay, T. (Dundee); 1984 v EG(sub); 1985 v WG, Sp(2), Ic(2). (6)
McLaughlin, J.(Morton); 1981 v D; 1982 v Se, D, I, E(2); 1983 v EG, Sw(2), Bel. (10)
McLeish, A. (Aberdeen); 1978 v W; 1979 v US; 1980 v B, E(2); 1987 v Ei. (6)
MacLeod, A. (Hibernian); 1979 v P, N(2). (3)
MacLeod, M. (Dumbarton); 1979 v US; (Celtic); P(sub), N(2); 1980 v B. (5)
McNab, N. (Tottenham H); 1978 v W. (1)
McNichol, J. (Brentford); 1979 v P, N(2); 1980 v B(2), WG, E. (7)

CHARLIE NICHOLAS

McNiven, D. (Leeds U); 1977 v Cz, W(sub), Sw(sub). (3)
McPherson, D. (Rangers); 1984 v Bel; 1985 v Sp. (2)
McStay, P. (Celtic); 1983 v EG, Sw(2); 1984 v Y(2). (5)
Malpas, M. (Dundee U); 1983 v Bel, Sw(1+sub); 1984 v Bel, EG, Y(2); 1985 v Sp. (8)
Melrose, J. (Partick T); 1977 v Sw; 1979 v US, P, N(2); 1980 v B(sub), WG, E. (8)
Miller, J. (Aberdeen); 1987 v Ei(sub). (1)
Miller, W. (Aberdeen); 1978 v Sw, Cz. (2)
Milne, R. (Dundee U); 1982 v Se(sub); 1984 v Bel, EG. (3)
Mitchell, I. (Queen of the South); 1979 v US(sub). (1)
Money, C. (St Mirren); 1987 v Ei. (1)
Muir, L. (Hibernian); 1977 v Cz(sub). (1)
Narey, D. (Dundee U); 1977 v Cz, Sw; 1978 v Sw, Cz; 1979 v N. (5)
Nevin, P. (Chelsea); 1985 v WG, Ic(2), Sp(2). (5)
Nicholas, C. (Celtic); 1981 v Se; 1982 v Se; 1983 v EG, Sw, Bel(sub); (Arsenal); 1984 v Y. (6)
Nicol, S. (Ayr U); 1981 v Se; 1982 v Se, D; (Liverpool); 1982 v I(2), E(2); 1983 v EG, Sw(2), Bel; 1984 v Bel, EG, Y. (14)
Orr, N. (Morton); 1978 v W(sub); 1979 v US, P, N(2); 1980 v B, E. (7)
Parlane, D. (Rangers); 1977 v W. (1)
Paterson, C. (Hibernian); 1981 v Se; 1982 v I. (2)
Payne, G. (Dundee U); 1978 v Sw, Cz, W. (3)
Provan, D. (Kilmarnock); 1977 v Cz(sub). (1)
Redford, I. (Rangers); 1981 v Se(sub); 1982 v Se, D, I(2), E. (6)
Reid, M. (Celtic); 1982 v E; 1984 v Y. (2)
Reid, R. (St Mirren); 1977 v W, Sw, E. (3)
Rice, B. (Hibernian); 1985 v WG. (1)
Richardson, L. (St Mirren); 1980 v WG, E(sub). (2)
Ritchie, A. (Morton); 1980 v B. (1)
Robertson, C. (Rangers); 1977 v E (sub). (1)
Robertson, D. (Aberdeen); 1987 v Ei(sub). (1)
Robertson, J.(Hearts); 1985 v WG, Ic(sub) v Sp(2 sub). (4)
Ross, T.W. (Arsenal); 1977 v W. (1)
Russell, R. (Rangers); 1978 v W; 1980 v B; 1984 v Y. (3)
Shannon, R. (Dundee); 1986 v Ei; 1987 v Ei, Bel, WG. (4)
Sharp, G. (Everton); 1982 v E. (1)
Simpson, N. (Aberdeen); 1982 v I(2), E; 1983 v EG, Sw(2), Bel; 1984 v Bel, EG, Y; 1985 v Sp. (11)
Sinclair, G. (Dumbarton); 1977 v E. (1)
Smith, G. (Rangers); 1978 v W. (1)
Smith, H. (Hearts); 1987 v Bel, WG. (2)
Sneddon, A. (Celtic); 1979 v US. (1)
Speedie, D. (Chelsea); 1985 v Sp. (1)
Stanton, P. (Hibernian); 1977 v Cz. (1)
Stark, W. (Aberdeen); 1985 v Ic. (1)
Stephen, R. (Dundee); 1983 v Bel. (1)
Stevens, G. (Motherwell); 1977 v E. (1)
Stewart, J. (Kilmarnock); 1978 v Sw, Cz; (Middlesbrough); 1979 v P. (3)
Stewart, R. (Dundee U); 1979 v P, N(2); (West Ham); 1980 v B(2), E(2), WG; 1981 v D; 1982 v I(2), E. (12)
Strachan, G. (Aberdeen); 1980 v B. (1)
Sturrock, P (Dundee U); 1977 v Cz, W, Sw, E; 1978 v Sw, Cz; 1982 v Se, I, E. (9)
Thomson, W. (Partick T); 1977 v E(sub); 1978 v W: (St Mirren); 1979 v US, N(2); 1980 v B(2), E(2), WG. (10)
Tolmie, J. (Morton); 1980 v B(sub). (1)
Tortolano, J. (Hibernian); 1986 v Ei, WG. (2)
Wallace, I. (Coventry C); 1978 v Sw. (1)
Walsh, N.(Nottingham F); 1983 v EG, Sw(2), Bel; 1984 v EG. (5)
Wark, J. (Ipswich T); 1977 v Cz, W, Sw; 1978 v W; 1979 v N, P; 1980 v E(2), WG. (9)
Watson, A. (Aberdeen); 1981 v Se, D; 1982 v D, I(sub). (4)
Watson, K. (Rangers); 1977 v E; 1978 v Sw(sub). (2)
Whyte, D. (Celtic); 1986 v Ei; 1987 v Ei, Bel. (3)
Wilson, T. (St Mirren); 1983 v Sw(sub). (1)
Wright, T. (Oldham A); 1987 v Bel. (1)